Building Distributed Systems with Go and NATS

A Comprehensive Guide

Delio D'Anna

Apress®

Building Distributed Systems with Go and NATS: A Comprehensive Guide

Delio D'Anna
Athens, Greece

ISBN-13 (pbk): 979-8-8688-2088-5   ISBN-13 (electronic): 979-8-8688-2089-2
https://doi.org/10.1007/979-8-8688-2089-2

Copyright © 2025 by Delio D'Anna

This work is subject to copyright. All rights are reserved by the Publisher, whether the whole or part of the material is concerned, specifically the rights of translation, reprinting, reuse of illustrations, recitation, broadcasting, reproduction on microfilms or in any other physical way, and transmission or information storage and retrieval, electronic adaptation, computer software, or by similar or dissimilar methodology now known or hereafter developed.

Trademarked names, logos, and images may appear in this book. Rather than use a trademark symbol with every occurrence of a trademarked name, logo, or image we use the names, logos, and images only in an editorial fashion and to the benefit of the trademark owner, with no intention of infringement of the trademark.

The use in this publication of trade names, trademarks, service marks, and similar terms, even if they are not identified as such, is not to be taken as an expression of opinion as to whether or not they are subject to proprietary rights.

While the advice and information in this book are believed to be true and accurate at the date of publication, neither the authors nor the editors nor the publisher can accept any legal responsibility for any errors or omissions that may be made. The publisher makes no warranty, express or implied, with respect to the material contained herein.

Managing Director, Apress Media LLC: Welmoed Spahr
Acquisitions Editor: Melissa Duffy
Editorial Assistant: Gryffin Winkler

Cover designed by eStudioCalamar

Distributed to the book trade worldwide by Springer Science+Business Media New York, 1 New York Plaza, New York, NY 10004. Phone 1-800-SPRINGER, fax (201) 348-4505, e-mail orders-ny@springer-sbm.com, or visit www.springeronline.com. Apress Media, LLC is a Delaware LLC and the sole member (owner) is Springer Science + Business Media Finance Inc (SSBM Finance Inc). SSBM Finance Inc is a **Delaware** corporation.

For information on translations, please e-mail booktranslations@springernature.com; for reprint, paperback, or audio rights, please e-mail bookpermissions@springernature.com.

Apress titles may be purchased in bulk for academic, corporate, or promotional use. eBook versions and licenses are also available for most titles. For more information, reference our Print and eBook Bulk Sales web page at http://www.apress.com/bulk-sales.

Any source code or other supplementary material referenced by the author in this book is available to readers on GitHub. For more detailed information, please visit https://www.apress.com/gp/services/source-code.

If disposing of this product, please recycle the paper

*To all who are amazed by complexity and strive to
bring order to chaos.*

Table of Contents

About the Author xiii

About the Technical Reviewer xv

Part I: The Fundamentals: Low-Level Building Blocks and Communication 1

Chapter 1: Overview of Distributed Systems 3

   1.1 About This Book 3

   1.2 Building Blocks of a Distributed System 6

   1.3 Software Systems Architectures 8

      1.3.1 Introduction 8

      1.3.2 Monolith 9

      1.3.3 Kernel-Based 11

      1.3.4 Service-Oriented 13

      1.3.5 Microservices 15

      1.3.6 Space-Based Architecture 16

      1.3.7 Reactive Systems 18

   1.4 Distributed Systems 19

      1.4.1 Distributed System vs. Distributed Computing 19

      1.4.2 Synchronous Communication 20

      1.4.3 Asynchronous Communication 21

   1.5 Summary 22

   1.6 Questions 24

Chapter 2: Distributed Communication Basics 27

   2.1 Introduction 27

   2.2 Communication Items 29

      2.2.1 Socket 29

TABLE OF CONTENTS

    2.2.2 Protocol 30

    2.2.3 Transports 32

  2.3 Topologies 34

    2.3.1 Mangos Library 35

    2.3.2 Req/Rep 36

    2.3.3 Push/Pull 45

    2.3.4 Pub/Sub 53

    2.3.5 Composed Topologies 64

  2.4 Multitransport 66

    2.4.1 TCP 66

    2.4.2 IPC 71

    2.4.3 Memory 72

    2.4.4 Memory Transport for Concurrency 78

  2.5 Summary 79

  2.6 Questions 81

Chapter 3: NATS Fundamentals 83

  3.1 Introduction 83

    3.1.1 What Is NATS 83

    3.1.2 Alternatives 85

    3.1.3 Why NATS 86

  3.2 Brokered vs. Unbrokered 86

  3.3 Running NATS 87

    3.3.1 NATS-Server 87

    3.3.2 Docker 88

    3.3.3 Kubernetes 90

    3.3.4 NATS CLI 92

  3.4 NATS Core 93

    3.4.1 Command Line 93

    3.4.2 Go SDK 97

3.5 Core Topologies 103

3.5.1 Pub/Sub 103

3.5.2 Queue Groups (Push/Pull) 103

3.5.3 Req/Rep (Base for Services) 107

3.5.4 More Complex Topologies 116

3.6 Summary 117

3.7 Questions 118

Chapter 4: Working System 121

4.1 Introduction 121

4.2 NATS 122

4.3 Restaurant Gateway 123

4.4 Order Processor 128

4.5 Delivery Tracker 133

4.6 Customer 137

4.7 Summary 148

4.8 Full Example with Minikube 149

Part II: Inside a Service: Core Architecture 161

Chapter 5: Anatomy of a Service 163

5.1 Foreword to Part 2 163

5.2 From Low-Level Building Blocks to Services 164

5.3 Service or Microservice 165

5.4 Developer vs. Engineer 167

5.5 Summary 169

Chapter 6: Domain-Driven Design (DDD) 171

6.1 Business First 171

6.1.1 A New Approach 171

6.1.2 Cohesion Across Crafts 173

6.1.3 The Importance of Language 174

6.1.4 Product Focus 176

TABLE OF CONTENTS

6.2 The Domain 178
- 6.2.1 Introduction 178
- 6.2.2 Data Structures 182
- 6.2.3 Services 189

6.3 App Layer 195

6.4 Infrastructure Layer 198
- 6.4.1 Introduction 198
- 6.4.2 Database 199
- 6.4.3 External Services 208

6.5 Presentation Layer 211

6.6 Summary 213

6.7 Questions 214

Chapter 7: Hexagonal Architecture 217

7.1 Layered Systems 217

7.2 Layered Communication Styles 220

7.3 Hexagonality 222

7.4 Communication in Hexagonal Systems 226

7.5 Summary 230

7.6 Questions 232

Chapter 8: Sample Service 235

8.1 Introduction 235

8.2 Domain Layer 237

8.3 Application Layer 243

8.4 Database Layer 249

8.5 Presentation Layer 253

8.6 Infrastructure 258

8.7 Running Everything 261

8.8 Summary 271

Part III: Macroscopic View: Designing Distributed Systems 273

Chapter 9: A Whole System vs. a Bunch of Services 275

9.1 Foreword to Part 3 275

9.2 One Level Up 276

9.3 Is This the End? 278

9.4 Service-Oriented and Other Experiments 281

9.5 Like Russian Dolls 284

9.6 Infrastructure 289

    9.6.1 Distributed Data Management 290

    9.6.2 Message Brokers 291

    9.6.3 Comprehensive Observability 292

    9.6.4 Security Infrastructure 292

    9.6.5 Configuration Management 294

9.7 Orchestration 295

9.8 Summary 303

9.9 Questions 305

Chapter 10: DDD for Systems 307

10.1 DDD Refresher 307

10.2 At a System Level 309

    10.2.1 Business 310

    10.2.2 Layers vs. Components 311

    10.2.3 Do We Always Need It? 313

10.3 Bounded Context and Segregation 314

10.4 Different Levels of Depth 318

10.5 What About REST 319

10.6 Infrastructure and Orchestration 320

10.7 Summary 336

10.8 Questions 337

TABLE OF CONTENTS

Chapter 11: Fully Synchronous Systems 341

11.1 Introduction 341
11.2 REST and Direct Service Access 343
11.2.1 A Dummy Example 345
11.2.2 Managing Traffic with Nginx 346
11.2.3 Service Mesh 350
11.3 NATS Services 352
11.3.1 Direct Access 352
11.3.2 REST Proxy 354
11.3.3 NATS Microservices Package 356
11.4 Authorization 365
11.5 The API Gateway 372
11.5.1 The Pattern 372
11.5.2 Authentication 383
11.5.3 Authorization 384
11.5.4 First-Level Communication 390
11.5.5 Deeper Level Communication 391
11.6 Space-Based Architecture 395
11.6.1 Refresher 395
11.6.2 Tools 396
11.6.3 Implementation Example 397
11.7 Summary 399
11.8 Questions 400

Chapter 12: Asynchronous Systems 403

12.1 Introduction 403
12.2 Fully Asynchronous 404
12.2.1 Introduction 404
12.2.2 An Example 405
12.3 Internally Asynchronous 410
12.3.1 Introduction 410
12.3.2 API Gateway 410

  12.3.3 Actor Model 420

  12.3.4 Asynchronous Services 426

 12.4 Long-Running Processes 432

  12.4.1 Introduction 432

  12.4.2 REST 433

  12.4.3 Scaling Up 433

  12.4.4 Piling Up 434

 12.5 JetStream 434

  12.5.1 Persistence 434

  12.5.2 Retention 439

  12.5.3 Consumers 442

  12.5.4 Asynchronous Services (JetStream) 452

 12.6 NATS KV Store 458

 12.7 NATS Object Store 464

 12.8 Summary 470

 12.9 Questions 471

Chapter 13: Reactive Systems 475

 13.1 Reactivity 475

  13.1.1 Introduction 475

  13.1.2 The Reactive Manifesto 476

  13.1.3 Reactive Systems vs. Reactive Programming 478

  13.1.4 The Other Reactive Principles 479

 13.2 Relation with DDD 480

  13.2.1 Introduction 480

  13.2.2 Bounded Contexts as Autonomous Units 481

  13.2.3 Domain Events and the Ubiquitous Language 482

  13.2.4 Aggregates and Consistency Boundaries 483

 13.3 Relation with Hexagonality 484

  13.3.1 Introduction 484

  13.3.2 The Inner Core and the Reactive System 484

  13.3.3 Ports and Adapters as Communication Boundaries 485

TABLE OF CONTENTS

13.4 Checking the Tools We Have 486

13.5 In-Depth Examples 488

13.6 Summary 499

13.7 Questions 500

Chapter 14: A Working System 503

14.1 Introduction 503

14.2 Minikube Skeleton 506

14.3 GitHub Actions 507

14.4 Dockerfile 509

14.5 NATS Deployment and Initialization 510

14.6 Menu Service: NATS KV and Object Store for Menu Data 512

14.7 Order Processor 522

14.8 Full System Overview and Remaining Services 526

14.9 Database 531

14.10 Conclusion 535

Conclusion 537

Answers to the Questions 539

Index 547

About the Author

Delio D'Anna brings a wealth of knowledge in building scalable and resilient web applications with over 15 years of experience in software engineering and architecture. Throughout his career, he's been passionate about exploring different programming languages, including PHP, JavaScript, Python, Java, and Go. As a strong advocate for Go, he co-authored a book on the subject and created a live project series for Manning, focused on deploying machine learning models in production. With a keen focus on microservices, scalability, and domain-driven design (DDD), he's recently delved into machine learning engineering, leveraging Python extensively. As a Chief Technology Officer (CTO), he has spearheaded efforts to ensure the scalability of the microservices AI system, predominantly based on Go and Python technologies. His decision to write this book stems from a desire to share his expertise and practical insights, offering developers a comprehensive guide to building distributed systems with Go and NATS, drawing from his extensive experience in software engineering and architecture.

LinkedIn: https://www.linkedin.com/in/delio-d-anna-b55989a/

About the Technical Reviewer

Giancarlo Zaccone holds a degree in Physics and a master's in Scientific Computing. He has over 20 years of experience in research and industry, working on system engineering, cybersecurity, artificial intelligence, and high-performance computing. He began his career at the Italian National Research Council (CNR) and later contributed to industrial projects in defense, environmental monitoring, and secure communications. He currently supports the European Space Agency in the Galileo program as a Security Verification Engineer and also serves as Technical Lead in the IRIDE Earth Observation program, focusing on cryptography and key management systems for satellite communications. He is the author of several publications on deep learning, applied AI, and parallel computational methods.

LinkedIn: `https://www.linkedin.com/in/giancarlozaccone/`

PART I

The Fundamentals: Low-Level Building Blocks and Communication

CHAPTER 1

Overview of Distributed Systems

1.1 About This Book

In the constantly evolving field of software engineering, complexity is a constant characteristic, which leads to larger systems and increased resource demands, particularly with the surge in AI technologies. Despite the ubiquity of distributed systems as the base of modern software engineering, many organizations find themselves caught in the complexities of outdated codebases, desperately seeking modernization. Banking and healthcare are examples of this, where highly complex and outdated code is still used today. As the demand for scalable and reliable systems grows, distributed systems emerge as the model of resilience and efficiency, which today's software engineering landscape suggests as the solution.

However, transitioning to a distributed architecture is no easy feat. Even projects conceived with scalability in mind can quickly succumb to the complexities of distributed systems.

Recognizing the imperative of robust system design, this book serves as a guide for academics and practitioners alike. Through a comprehensive exploration of distributed systems' principles and practices, readers will gain the essential knowledge and skills necessary to navigate the intricacies of modern system architectures. Our aim is to empower readers to design resilient, scalable systems that meet the exacting standards of contemporary software engineering.

Throughout this book, we will guide you through the concepts and practices required to design a complete, working distributed system, and we will use examples from the Go programming language, and we will use the NATS messaging system to manage the communication between the different parts of this system.

CHAPTER 1   OVERVIEW OF DISTRIBUTED SYSTEMS

Part 1 of this book aims to give an overview of distributed systems at a lower level, starting with the ideas of what distributed computing and distributed systems are and what architectural styles are used in distributed systems, and then provides the basic communication paradigms between very small and simple components. It will teach about the building blocks of a distributed system and will first use the scalability protocols implementation in Go, known as the **mangos** library, to create highly performant distributed systems. The book will finally progress with diving into the usage of the NATS server, revisiting the same low-level protocols and paradigms from the perspective of this higher-level tool.

This will conclude the first part of the book, where all the basics of distributed systems, the building blocks of such systems, will have been explored, and we will be ready for the next level, where the book will explore the internals of more complex components that make up a distributed system.

Part 2 will start with explaining what a service is and how the software engineer will have to approach the building of a service inside a bigger project/system and in cooperation with other people, not necessarily engineers.

We will then progress with showing what a service looks like, with a complete example, and then we will explore what DDD is, from a holistic perspective, and why it is good for distributed systems. The book will then progress with explaining the hexagonal architecture style and why it fits with what was previously shown.

The hexagonal architecture will end the second part of the book, and the third and last part will start, which will focus on exploring more complex systems built on top of what has been seen in the previous two parts.

Part 3 of this book delves into the macroscopic view of designing distributed systems, transitioning from foundational principles to practical, real-world applications. This part is tailored for readers who have grasped the basics and are ready to tackle more complex and integrated systems, exploring how individual services coalesce into a cohesive whole.

In Part 3, we elevate our perspective to examine distributed systems as a cohesive whole rather than merely collections of individual services. This part is tailored for readers who have grasped the foundational principles of distributed systems and are now ready to delve into the intricacies of designing, orchestrating, and managing complex, integrated systems.

We begin with an exploration of what it means to view a distributed system as a unified entity vs. a collection of discrete services. This chapter lays the groundwork for understanding the systemic approach essential for effective distributed systems design, which we define here as focusing on the interactions and coherence of the whole system rather than just its parts, and that we will explore further in Parts 2 and 3 of this book. We discuss infrastructure, orchestration, and the challenges of maintaining coherence and efficiency in large-scale systems.

Next, we offer a hands-on tutorial that guides readers through constructing a fully functional distributed system. This practical approach, although challenging, provides a tangible framework for understanding how various components interact. Using Minikube to establish a skeleton, we explore the deployment and initialization of the NATS messaging system, database setup, API gateway implementation, and the critical aspects of authentication, authorization, and logging. This chapter aims to provide a solid foundation, even if all concepts are not immediately clear, fostering a deeper understanding through practical application.

Moving forward, we delve into the application of Domain-Driven Design (DDD) at a system level. We revisit core DDD concepts and apply them to the broader architecture of distributed systems, aligning technical design with business objectives. This chapter explores bounded contexts, segregation, and the nuanced layers of abstraction necessary for a holistic approach to system design. We also discuss the integration of RESTful services within a DDD framework and how infrastructure and orchestration principles align with DDD.

We then turn our attention to fully synchronous systems, examining the design and implementation of such systems using REST and direct service access. This chapter covers the intricacies of synchronous communication, including the use of Nginx for request routing, the role of service mesh architectures, and the integration of NATS for synchronous service interactions. We also explore the space-based architecture model, providing practical tools and examples to illustrate its implementation.

In the following chapter, we focus on asynchronous communication, detailing the benefits and challenges of designing systems with asynchronous components. We explore fully asynchronous systems, internally asynchronous systems, and the management of long-running processes. The advanced features of NATS Jetstream, including persistence, retention, and consumer management, are discussed in depth. We also cover the use of NATS for key-value and object storage, highlighting its versatility in handling asynchronous tasks.

Finally, we explore reactive systems, emphasizing the principles of responsiveness, resilience, and elasticity. This chapter examines the integration of reactive paradigms with DDD and hexagonal architecture, evaluating the tools and techniques necessary for building robust, reactive systems. Through detailed examples, we illustrate how to design systems that can dynamically respond to varying workloads and maintain high levels of performance and reliability.

Part 3 aims to provide readers with a comprehensive understanding of the macroscopic aspects of distributed systems design. By exploring theoretical concepts and practical applications, we equip readers with the knowledge and tools necessary to design, implement, and manage complex distributed systems that meet the demanding standards of modern software engineering.

1.2 Building Blocks of a Distributed System

At the core of any distributed system are the fundamental building blocks that ensure seamless communication, coordination, and functionality across diverse components. These low-level components include nodes, which represent the individual computing units; communication protocols, which facilitate data exchange between nodes; and data storage mechanisms, which ensure consistent and reliable data management. Additionally, message queues and brokers play a crucial role in managing asynchronous communication, while load balancers distribute workloads efficiently to prevent bottlenecks. Together, these elements form the backbone of distributed systems, enabling them to achieve scalability, fault tolerance, and high availability.

As you can see, a distributed system must be composed of several key components, as it is designed to operate across multiple physical or virtual machines. However, it is entirely feasible to construct a distributed system that runs on a single machine. The critical aspect is that each part of the system operates independently, making the physical location of these components irrelevant.

The essence of building a distributed system lies in the abstraction level that allows all system components to function without relying on the computational power or internal communication mechanisms of a single machine. For instance, relying on threads for communication can lead to tightly coupled components, which is not ideal for a distributed architecture. On the other hand, message passing is an excellent solution because it promotes loose coupling and independence among components.

Even if a specific implementation uses threads internally, this is acceptable as long as the system is designed with an abstraction that allows it to switch to different mechanisms without changing the interfaces. This design principle ensures that the system remains flexible and scalable, maintaining the core benefits of a distributed system regardless of the underlying implementation details.

As we discussed in the introduction to this book, any system, including a distributed system, can be viewed from various levels of abstraction. At each level, the components of the system take on different roles and forms. However, at its core, a distributed system must have fundamental low-level building blocks that facilitate communication between different components at any level. These core elements include mechanisms for transporting information, adherence to specific communication protocols, and sockets capable of utilizing these transports and protocols.

Understanding these concepts is crucial, and the first part of this book will delve into building a system at this foundational level. While most systems are not constructed directly at such a low level due to the availability of libraries and tools that abstract these details for us, there are scenarios where a deep understanding of these low-level operations is beneficial. Whether you aim to develop such a library or need to leverage the flexibility and control that comes with low-level programming, it is essential to grasp how these building blocks work.

Even if you primarily use higher-level tools to build your system, having knowledge of the underlying low-level details and theoretical principles can significantly enhance your understanding and troubleshooting capabilities. In this book, we will focus on using NATS as a primary tool, but it is important to recognize that many developers use alternatives such as Kafka, Pulsar, or frameworks based on reactive or actor models. Ultimately, all these tools are built upon the same fundamental concepts of low-level distributed system components.

By understanding these core principles, you will be better equipped to utilize any of these tools effectively and appreciate the intricate workings of distributed systems. This foundational knowledge will enable you to design and maintain robust, scalable, and efficient distributed systems, regardless of the specific technologies you choose to employ.

1.3 Software Systems Architectures

1.3.1 Introduction

Software architecture is the bedrock upon which robust software systems are built and maintained. It involves the high-level structuring of a system, outlining its components, their interactions, and the guiding principles that influence its design and evolution. A well-defined architecture is vital, as it affects key aspects of software development, including scalability, performance, maintainability, and adaptability.

Grasping software architecture is crucial for managing the complexity inherent in modern software systems. Architecture breaks down a system into modular components, helping developers and architects manage dependencies and interactions effectively. It acts as a blueprint to ensure that the components work in harmony to achieve the desired functionality.

The choice of architecture profoundly impacts both the technical and business facets of a system. It dictates how easily the system can adapt to changing requirements, integrate with other systems, and scale to handle increased loads. Various architectural styles offer unique benefits and address specific challenges, making the selection of the right architecture contingent upon comprehending the system's requirements and constraints.

This section introduces a variety of software system architectures, shedding light on their core principles and design philosophies. Each architectural style presents different strategies for organizing system components and managing their interactions. By understanding these strategies, you will be better equipped to design systems that meet specific needs, whether that involves rapid development, high scalability, fault tolerance, or ease of maintenance.

Throughout this chapter, we will explore fundamental concepts that underpin different architectural styles. These include modularity, which promotes separation of concerns and easier maintenance; scalability, which ensures that the system can grow effectively; and fault tolerance, which allows the system to remain operational despite failures. By delving into these foundational ideas, you will gain a deeper appreciation of how various architectures address common software engineering challenges.

Moreover, a comprehensive understanding of software architectures enhances your ability to make informed design decisions. It enables you to evaluate trade-offs and select the most suitable architecture for your project's specific goals and constraints. Whether you are building a new system from scratch or evolving an existing one, knowledge of architectural principles will guide you in creating robust, efficient, and adaptable software solutions.

In the forthcoming sections, we will examine various architectural styles, highlighting their unique characteristics, advantages, and challenges. This exploration offers a broad perspective on how different architectures can be applied to solve real-world problems effectively. Understanding these styles, whether distributed or not, clarifies the circumstances under which a distributed system becomes necessary as systems grow in size and complexity. Such scenarios often demand benefits like scalability, fault tolerance, and high availability.

By understanding and comparing these architectural styles, you will be better positioned to identify the most fitting approach for your specific requirements. Whether the focus is on creating a distributed system to handle significant growth or crafting a tightly coupled module for rapid prototyping, this knowledge allows you to make strategic decisions that lead to sustainable and high-performing software solutions.

1.3.2 Monolith

We will start with the most traditional form of architectural style, which is the monolith. The monolithic architectural style represents a traditional approach where a single, unified software application is designed as one indivisible unit. This encompasses the entire codebase and is typically managed and deployed as a single unit, often backed by a single database. One of the primary advantages of a monolithic architecture is its simplicity: development, testing, and deployment processes are straightforward, as everything is contained within one large codebase. This can be particularly appealing for smaller applications or startups with limited resources, where the overhead of more complex architectures may not be justified.

CHAPTER 1 OVERVIEW OF DISTRIBUTED SYSTEMS

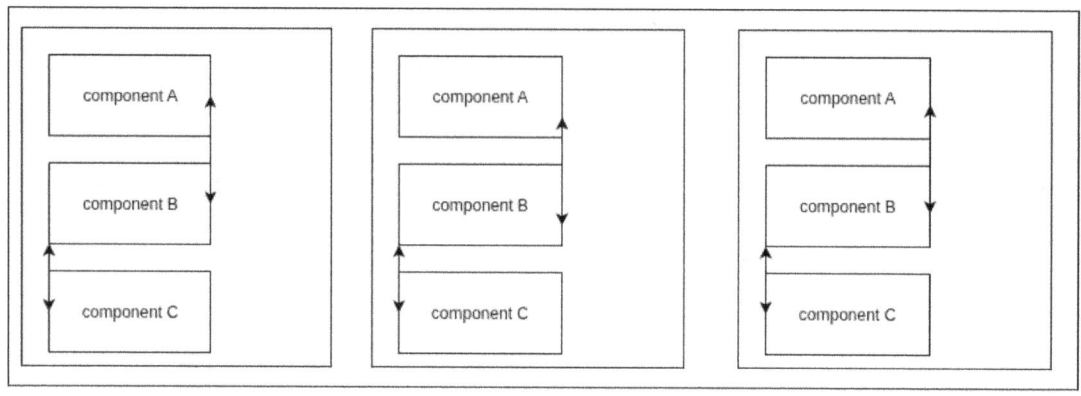

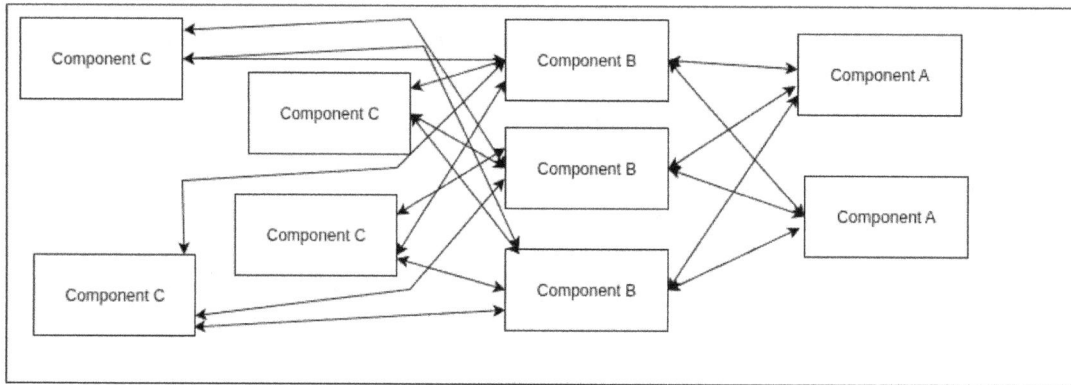

Figure 1-1. Monolithic vs. distributed system

A monolithic architecture, however, does have significant drawbacks as applications grow in size and complexity. Since the entire software system is deployed as a single entity, even small changes require the entire system to be redeployed. This is clearly visible in Figure 1-1, where a monolithic system made of three components is replicated as a whole three times in order to scale it, while the equivalent monolith has a different replication for each one of the services. This can lead to longer testing cycles and increased risk, as bugs in one part of the system can impact the entire application. Furthermore, the lack of modularity can hinder scalability and maintainability. As monolithic applications grow, they often devolve into what is known as a "big ball of mud," wherein the system becomes a tangled web of interdependencies, making it difficult to manage and extend.Another intrinsic problem of a monolithic architecture is the tight coupling of its parts. Monolithic architectures are typically tightly coupled since they are designed as a single, indivisible unit. This means that all of an application's components, including the user interface, business logic, and data access layers, are bound together and deployed as one. As a result, components within a monolith often have numerous dependencies on each other. For instance, changes to one part of the system, such as a database schema or a business logic module, may necessitate changes to other parts of the system due to these interdependencies. However, efforts can be made to reduce the coupling within a monolithic architecture. By adhering to principles such as well-defined interfaces and high cohesion, developers can organize the monolith into more manageable modules. These modules can encapsulate functionality within specific boundaries, attempting to minimize the interactions and dependencies between different parts of the system. Despite these efforts, the monolithic nature of the architecture inherently imposes a level of coupling that typically cannot be completely eliminated.

Thus, although it is possible to achieve some level of decoupling within a monolithic architecture through careful design and modularization, the architecture as a whole remains more tightly coupled compared to distributed architectures, which we will see soon.

It is always possible to build a monolithic application that is ready to be broken down into distributed parts, but this still takes almost the same effort as building a distributed system from the very start. Such a system will actually be a distributed system, deployed as a single unit.

1.3.3 Kernel-Based

The kernel-based architectural style, commonly referred to as the microkernel architecture, is fundamentally characterized by a minimalistic core system (kernel) that provides essential services and a collection of plug-in components that extend the functionality of the core. The structure of this architecture can be seen in Figure 1-2 with its core and plug-ins. This style is notably advantageous for applications requiring high customizability and extensibility. The core system is responsible for managing system resources, executing fundamental services, and acting as a mediator between the plug-ins. You can think generally about your favorite IDE or text editor, and the chance is it will be based on this architecture. A core part of the system will provide the main functionalities but will provide an API to extend it with several plugins.

CHAPTER 1   OVERVIEW OF DISTRIBUTED SYSTEMS

One of the defining attributes of the microkernel architecture is its modularity. The plug-in components are designed to be self-contained and independent, reducing interdependencies and facilitating the dynamic addition or removal of functionalities without necessitating changes to the core system. This allows for high adaptability, as new features can be introduced or outdated ones retired with minimal disruption.

Furthermore, the microkernel style often demonstrates enhanced testability and maintainability. These characteristics arise from the encapsulation of complex application logic within independently deployable plug-ins, which can be evolved or tested in isolation. This compartmentalization lowers the risk associated with system updates, as changes to a plug-in can be validated independently of the entire system.

One important thing to consider is that although extensible, the core, or kernel, of the system might be quite complex by itself, and growing this core will not be much different from growing a monolith into a big ball of mud. Having a very small core and an API, which is versatile but succinct, will ensure a kernel-based system will not grow its complexity out of hand, but this is the base for more suitable distributed architectures, which we will see soon.

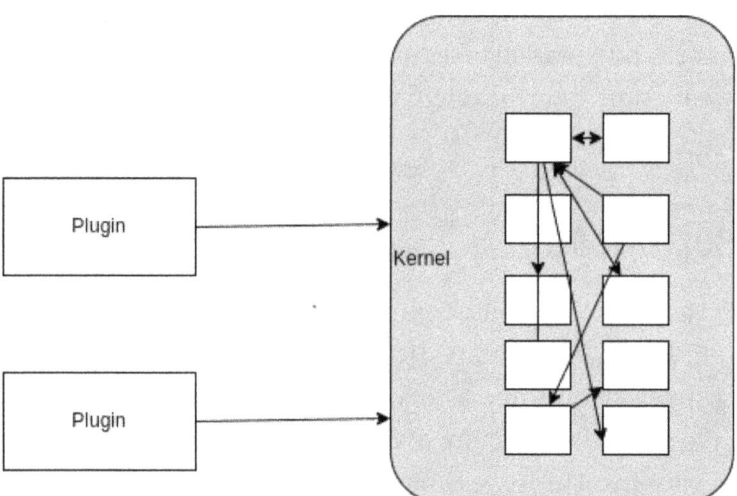

Figure 1-2. *Kernel-based architecture*

1.3.4 Service-Oriented

Service-oriented architecture (SOA) is a design approach in which software components provide services to other components via a communication protocol, typically over a network. This architectural style is characterized by the distribution of discrete services that perform specific business functions. In a typical SOA, an orchestration engine or service bus coordinates the integration of services and handles tasks such as routing, security, and monitoring.

The architecture, as clearly visible in Figure 1-3, comprises multiple complex layers, with each layer being responsible for specific aspects of service interaction and execution. Services within SOA are designed to be reusable, modular units that can be independently developed, deployed, and maintained. These services communicate through well-defined interfaces, typically using messaging protocols such as SOAP, REST, or RPC. The orchestration engine acts as the central point of communication, not only mediating and executing service transactions but also managing tasks such as transaction coordination and message transformation.

One important consideration to make is that even the communication between two services is handled by a different layer, a communication layer, where the communication between these two services is held and centralized in the communication layer.

This brings up a lot of coupling, because the communication layer needs to be aware of all the communicating services so that it can provide the correct communication between them. This tight coupling can lead to challenges in scaling and maintaining the system, as changes in one service often influence the health of the others, necessitating coordinated deployments and extensive testing. As a result, an SOA can inherit the complications of both monolithic and distributed architectures, highlighting the importance of managing dependencies and service interactions carefully to avoid substantial complexity.

CHAPTER 1   OVERVIEW OF DISTRIBUTED SYSTEMS

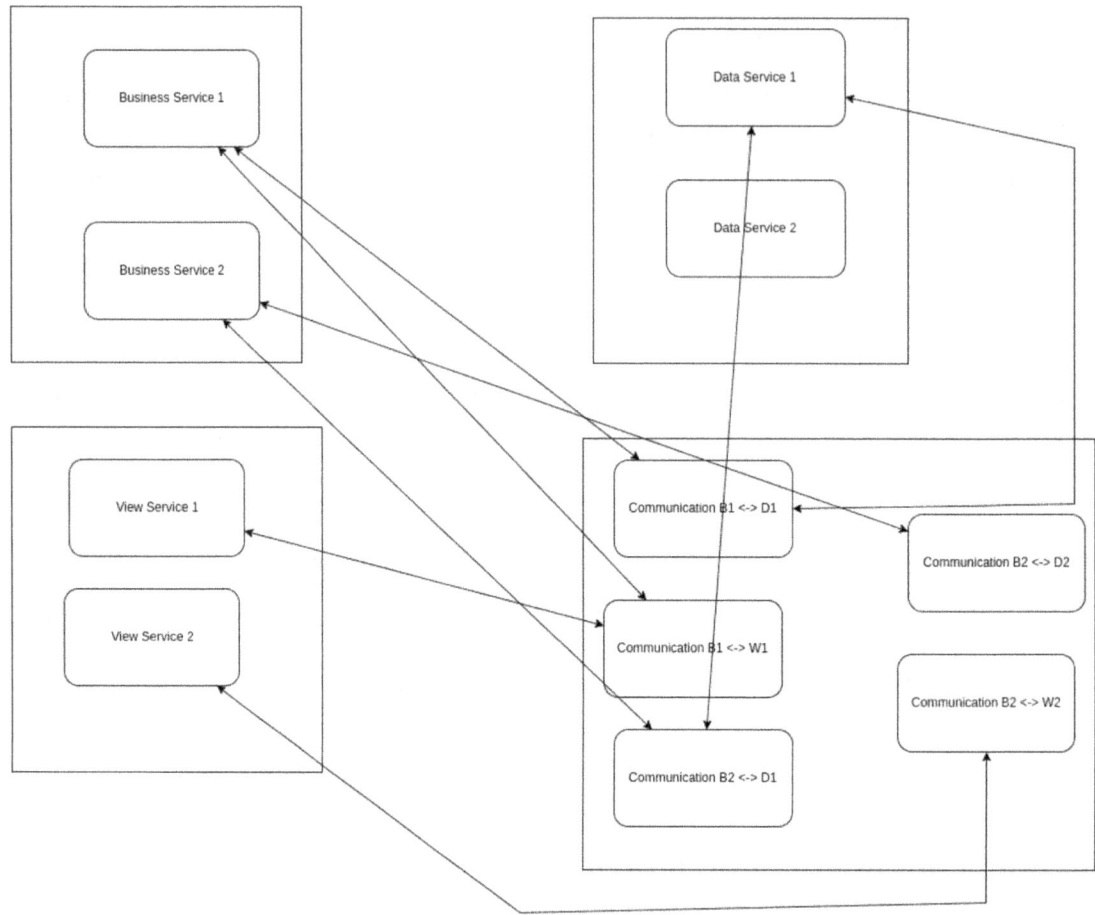

Figure 1-3. *Service-oriented architecture*

The SOA was an initial experiment on how to build scalable systems, and we need to give it credit for having opened the research for better ways of handling complexity in software systems. We can say that although SOA is essentially dead nowadays, it has paved the way to microservices and can be used to show the shortcomings of just reusing the same ideas from part of the monolithic architecture to a distributed system. An SOA, oftentimes, is not much different from a distributed monolith, which means a system that, although is effectively distributed, still mimics a monolith in the way components are tightly coupled and their scalability is effectively reduced from the optimal possible.

1.3.5 Microservices

We now analyze the most talked about architectural styles, which are often misimplemented. Microservices architecture is a highly modular approach to building software applications. In this architectural style, an application is divided into a set of small, independent services, each running in its own process and communicating through lightweight mechanisms, often HTTP-based, but not only, APIs. Each microservice focuses on a specific business domain and can be developed, deployed, and scaled independently, favoring a decoupled and distributed system structure. We will see in more detail how the microservices architecture is implemented; we will dive into it in the second and third parts of this book, but we will give here only some general, language-independent information.

The key difference between SOA and microservices, as seen in Figure 1-4, is that each microservice has a specific context to which it is bound and does not rely on other centralized layers to communicate. Each microservice will expose an API and will be as independent as possible from other microservices. In practice microservices will communicate with each other but will not rely on each other for functioning. It is inevitable that some trade-offs will have to be accepted, but in an ideal scenario microservices will only exchange notifications with other services and will only reply actively to the user requests.

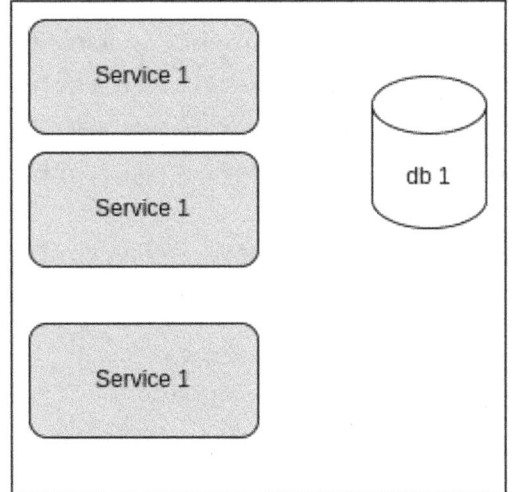
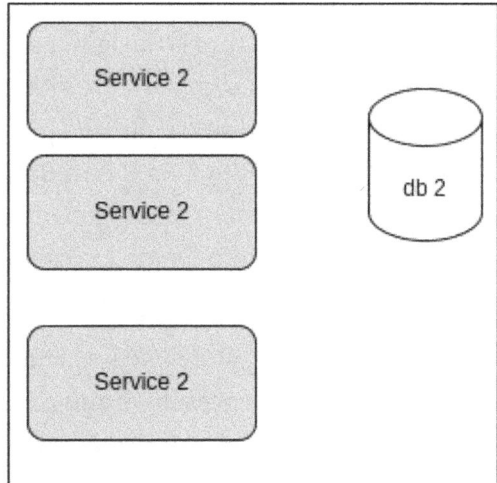

Figure 1-4. *Microservices architecture*

CHAPTER 1   OVERVIEW OF DISTRIBUTED SYSTEMS

The key advantage of microservices lies in their ability to enhance agility and scalability. By allowing teams to work on different services simultaneously and independently, organizations can iterate rapidly and deploy updates without impacting the entire system. Each microservice typically encapsulates its own data store, which aligns with the principle of data isolation and independence, though this can lead to complexities in maintaining consistency across the system.

Microservices too, however, come with their own set of challenges. The interaction between multiple microservices introduces complexity in terms of communication, data consistency, and overall system integration. These services often require robust methods for discovering each other, load balancing, and handling failures to maintain system stability. The communication overhead can also impact performance, particularly when services make synchronous calls, creating potential bottlenecks.

The essence of this book is to offer you a way to create a system that leverages pretty solid techniques to reduce the shortcomings of a badly designed microservices architecture and modern tools that can help with the complexity of managing such a complex system. We will see how domain-driven design helps with designing robust and scalable microservices-based systems and how tools like NATS will help with service discovery and load balancing.

1.3.6 Space-Based Architecture

Space-based architecture is designed to handle scalability and concurrency, making it ideal for applications with variable and unpredictable user loads. Instead of relying on a central database, it uses replicated in-memory data grids to store and sync data across all processing units. When data is updated in one unit, it is asynchronously sent to the database using persistent messaging queues.

To go a bit more into detail, a space-based architecture is made of several types of components, which you can see in Figure 1-5 and that are

> **Processing Units (PUs):** These are the individual instances that handle business logic and processing. Each PU is independent and stateless, which allows for easy scaling.

> **In-Memory Data Grid (IMDG):** This is a distributed data store that holds the shared data in memory. It ensures low-latency access and high availability.

Messaging Grid: This component facilitates communication between PUs and other parts of the system.

Synchronization and Replication: Ensures data consistency and availability across multiple nodes.

Load Balancer: Distributes incoming requests evenly across the PUs.

Clients: The user interfaces or services that interact with the architecture.

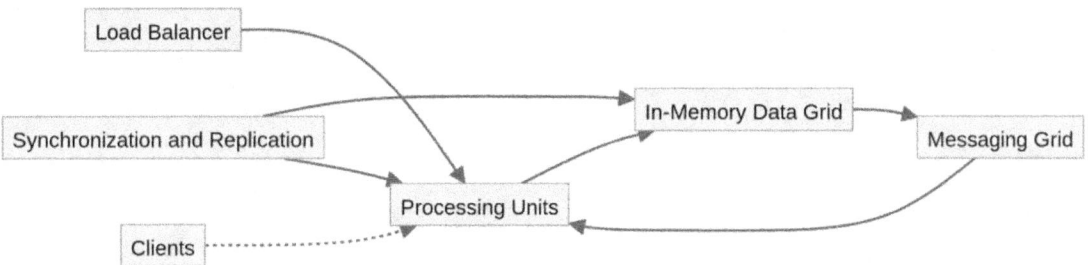

Figure 1-5. *Space-based architecture components*

In reality, you could simplify this architecture in your mind, thinking that a service (micro or not) will use a specific tool to store and retrieve data instead of a database, and this tool will then store the data in the database when possible. The external tool is the in-memory data grid, which will generally replicate its data for each instance of the service. Let's call for a moment one instance of this service with its external tool a "unit," and you can see how this simplified version looks like in Figure 1-6.

CHAPTER 1   OVERVIEW OF DISTRIBUTED SYSTEMS

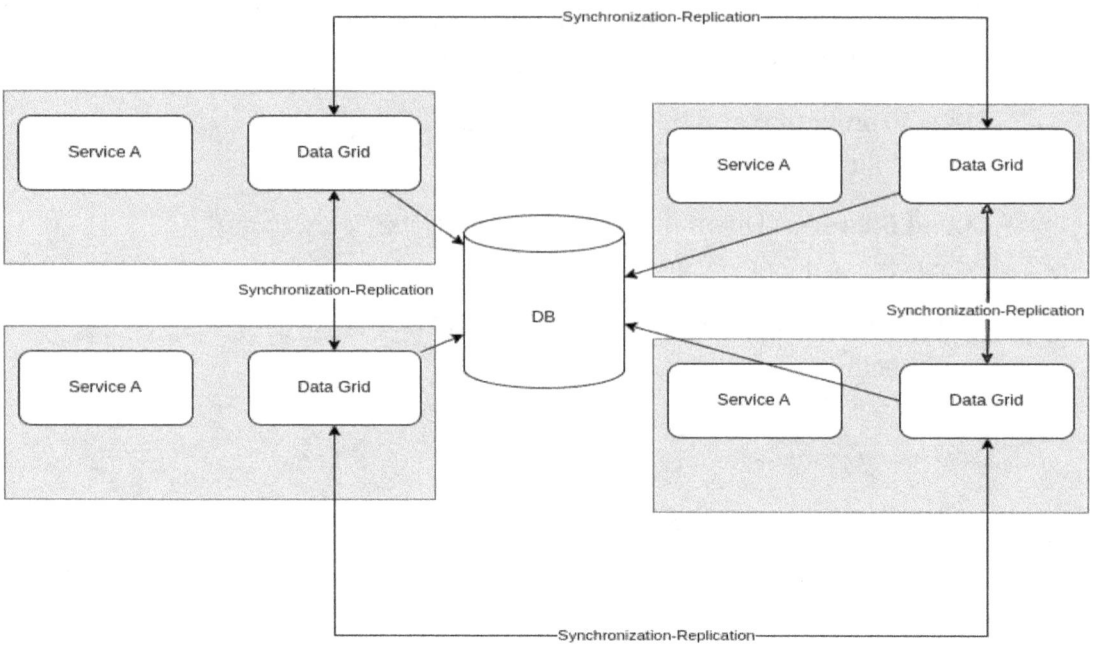

Figure 1-6. Simplified space-based architecture diagram

1.3.7 Reactive Systems

Reactive systems represent a paradigm focused on building responsive, resilient, elastic, and message-driven applications. These systems aim to provide consistent, prompt responses to user requests by handling errors gracefully and ensuring that individual component failures do not result in system-wide failures. Four key traits define reactive systems: responsivity ensures the system stays interactive under all conditions; resiliency makes certain the system remains responsive even in the face of failure; elasticity involves the system's ability to adjust to varying loads, maintaining responsivity; and being message-driven implies that the system relies on asynchronous message-passing to establish boundaries between components, reducing coupling and complexity. Together, these characteristics form a robust approach to designing modern applications that are prepared for the uncertain and dynamic nature of distributed environments.

We will actually delve into how to build a reactive system towards the end of this book, but we want to finish this high-level introduction to architectural styles to give you an idea of how complex this area of software development is.

In a reactive system, different components need to be able to operate independently from each other and with asynchronous messaging so that if one part of the system fails, the rest of the system will still work. It is here that a tool like a messaging queue or a pub/sub server will be very important, and we will focus during this book on NATS.

You might have noticed the similarities with microservices, and actually, the two styles can be mixed and used together. The same can happen with space-based architecture, which means that not all architectural styles are mutually exclusive. You might even think to build a microservices-based system, where a single service might be developed as a monolith. There are no limits except what is best to solve a specific problem.

1.4 Distributed Systems

1.4.1 Distributed System vs. Distributed Computing

Distributed systems and distributed computing are two fundamental concepts in computer science, often used interchangeably but distinctly different in their definitions and applications. A distributed system refers to a network of independent computers that appears to its users as a single coherent system. These systems are designed to share the execution of tasks, data storage, and other computing resources across multiple machines, which can be geographically dispersed. The primary objective of distributed systems is to enhance efficiency, reliability, fault tolerance, and scalability. Examples include cloud computing platforms, distributed databases, and large-scale web applications where the failure of a single node does not bring down the entire system.

On the other hand, distributed computing deals more specifically with the methodologies and algorithms used to achieve cooperative execution of tasks by a set of distributed processes. This involves designing algorithms that enable processes to work together to achieve a common goal, despite the challenges posed by asynchrony and potential failures. Distributed computing is fundamentally about ensuring that multiple independent entities can coordinate their actions in a consistent manner, even under conditions of partial failure or unreliable communication. For example, distributed computing tackles issues like consensus algorithms, fault tolerance protocols, and distributed transaction management.

The critical difference lies in scope and application: distributed systems encompass the overall architecture and infrastructure facilitating the distribution of resources and processes, whereas distributed computing focuses on algorithmic techniques that enable process synchronization and robustness in a distributed setup. This separation is vital to comprehend the layered structure of how distributed services are architected and implemented.

To see it from a different perspective, a distributed system is made of components that are built as pieces that must run on a specific machine and cannot span over several machines, components that are big enough to need their architecture, and which generally are coded by the developers. Distributed computing is generally handled by a specific compiler/language, which allows for execution of tasks across several distributed machines. Some distributed languages or libraries allow the programmer to write code that seems non-distributed but which can run across several machines. To simplify it again, distributed computing happens when the components of a distributed system are so tiny that they can be part of the language the engineer writes in.

1.4.2 Synchronous Communication

Synchronous communication is a mode of interaction where the participating entities (e.g., processes, services, or systems) engage in a communication session that requires both parties to be available and actively exchanging messages concurrently. This mechanism mandates that the sender of the message wait until a response is received from the receiver before proceeding with further tasks. The synchronous approach ensures immediate feedback and is akin to a real-time conversation where both parties must be present and ready to communicate simultaneously.

In the context of distributed systems, synchronous communication involves fundamental timing assumptions about the processes and the communication links. Specifically, there are known upper bounds on processing delays and message transmission delays. This means that the time taken by any process to execute a step and the time period between sending and receiving a message are both predictable and limited to certain maximum values. These constraints help implement various critical services like timed failure detection, coordination based on time, and ensuring worst-case performance metrics, which are crucial for maintaining the robustness and reliability of distributed systems operations.

However, the assumption of synchronous communication is often difficult to uphold in large-scale or unpredictable environments like the Internet due to the variability in message transmission times and processing delays. Despite these challenges, synchronous models can be quite effective in controlled network environments, such as Local Area Networks (LANs), where timing assumptions are more likely to hold true. The synchronous model provides a straightforward approach to designing distributed systems by simplifying many aspects of timing and coordination.

Most distributed systems that use this communication method use REST, which is built on top of HTTP with its strengths and weaknesses. We have already hinted that the best distributed systems tend to be communicating asynchronously, but sometimes that is not possible (rarely) or the developers are not confident with other patterns. We hope you will lose any fear of asynchronous communication after reading this book, but still, there is space for some synchronous communication in distributed systems, and we will touch on this also using again the messaging broker of our choice: NATS.

1.4.3 Asynchronous Communication

Asynchronous communication is characterized by a non-blocking exchange of messages between interacting entities, allowing the sender to continue processing without waiting for the receiver's response. In this model, after sending a message, the sender can proceed with its tasks, while the receiver processes the message at its convenience and responds when ready. This mode of communication is typically implemented using mechanisms such as message queues or middleware that decouples the sender and receiver, leading to increased flexibility and efficiency.

In distributed systems, asynchronous communication offers significant benefits in terms of scalability and robustness. Processes communicate without the need for immediate coordination, making the system less vulnerable to delays and failures that might occur in synchronous communication. For example, asynchronous messaging allows for tasks like database updates or web service calls to proceed without waiting for an immediate response, thus improving system responsiveness and throughput.

However, asynchronous communication brings its own set of challenges, particularly around maintaining consistency and handling errors. Since messages are processed independently and possibly out of order, systems must incorporate mechanisms to manage message sequencing, deduplication, and error handling. Middleware solutions and message-oriented middleware (MOM) frameworks are often used to address these issues by providing reliable message delivery, transaction support, and message queuing.

CHAPTER 1   OVERVIEW OF DISTRIBUTED SYSTEMS

In this book we will focus mainly on how to use NATS for exchanging asynchronous messages, but we will also see a more low-level tool, **mangos**, which will help you understand the internals of asynchronous communication.

As we mentioned earlier, a lot of systems out there still rely on synchronous communication, and this is due to the fact that asynchronous communication is challenging, but if you build a system that is scalable, based on DDD principles and reactive principles, you'll have way fewer problems in implementing asynchronous communication, because these styles strive to make decoupled, independent components.

1.5 Summary

This chapter effectively introduces the foundational concepts of distributed systems. It balances theoretical clarity with practical motivation, and it establishes a logical flow from system complexity to architectural styles. It begins by addressing the evolving complexity in software engineering and the increasing resource demands due to advancements in AI technologies. This complexity underscores the necessity for scalable, reliable systems, which distributed architectures provide.

Goals of the Book

> The book aims to guide readers through designing and implementing a fully functional, scalable distributed system using Go and NATS.
>
> It plans to cover foundational theories and practical implementations, breaking down complex systems into manageable parts.

Distributed Systems A distributed system is defined as a network of independent computers appearing to users as a single coherent system, aimed at enhancing efficiency, reliability, fault tolerance, and scalability.

Distributed Computing In contrast, distributed computing focuses on the algorithms and methodologies that enable cooperative task execution by a set of distributed processes. It addresses issues like consensus algorithms, fault tolerance protocols, and distributed transaction management.

Architectural Styles Discussed:

Monolith

A single unified software application managed and deployed as one unit.

Simplifies initial development but poses maintainability and scalability issues as the system grows.

Kernel-Based Architecture (Microkernel)

Minimalistic core system with a collection of plug-in components.

Enhances modularity, customizability, and extensibility, providing independent deployment of functionalities while maintaining a slim core.

Service-Oriented Architecture (SOA)

Components provide services to other components via network communication.

An orchestration engine coordinates services, but tight coupling between services and the communication layer can complicate scalability.

Microservices

Highly modular approach where applications are divided into independent services, each with its own process.

Focuses on domain-specific functionalities that can be independently developed, deployed, and scaled.

Space-Based Architecture

Designed for scalability and concurrency using replicated in-memory data grids instead of a central database.

Ensures asynchronous data updates with persistent messaging queues to handle variable loads efficiently.

Reactive Systems

Emphasizes responsiveness, resilience, elasticity, and message-driven communication.

Intended to dynamically respond to varying workloads while maintaining performance and reliability in a distributed environment.

Communication Paradigms

Synchronous Communication: Immediate feedback during data exchange is required but can be challenging due to timing assumptions and variability in large-scale systems.

Asynchronous Communication: Non-blocking message exchange that decouples sender and receiver, improving flexibility and efficiency but requiring mechanisms to handle message sequencing and error management.

1.6 Questions

1. **What is the primary objective of a distributed system?**
   a) To enhance complexity
   b) To focus on centralized processing
   c) To improve efficiency, reliability, fault tolerance, and scalability
   d) To simplify single-machine operations

2. **What differentiates distributed computing from distributed systems?**
   a) Distributed computing focuses on the overall architecture, while distributed systems focus on algorithms.
   b) Distributed systems encompass the infrastructure and resources, while distributed computing focuses on methodology and algorithms.

c) Distributed computing involves only single-node operations, unlike distributed systems.

d) There is no difference between the two.

3. **Which architectural style is best for applications requiring high customizability and extensibility through plug-ins?**

   a) Monolithic architecture

   b) Microservices architecture

   c) Kernel-based (Microkernel) architecture

   d) Space-based architecture

4. **Why is asynchronous communication preferred in large-scale distributed systems?**

   a) It ensures immediate feedback.

   b) It relies on synchronous messaging protocols.

   c) It decouples sender and receiver, improving scalability and robustness.

   d) It simplifies real-time conversation-like interactions.

5. **What is one major drawback of the monolithic architectural style?**

   a) It is highly scalable.

   b) It enables independent deployment of services.

   c) It poses significant maintainability and scalability issues as the system grows.

   d) It eliminates the need for communication protocols.

6. **Define reactive systems in the context of distributed systems.**

   a) Systems that rely on synchronous communication.

   b) Systems designed to be responsive, resilient, and message-driven.

   c) Systems built using monolithic architecture.

   d) Systems that use only in-memory data grids for storage.

CHAPTER 1   OVERVIEW OF DISTRIBUTED SYSTEMS

7. **Which component in a distributed system is critical for managing asynchronous communication?**

    a) Nodes

    b) Communication protocols

    c) Message queues and brokers

    d) Load balancers

CHAPTER 2

Distributed Communication Basics

2.1 Introduction

We can analyze a distributed system, or any system, at many levels. In this section, we will delve into the most low-level approach and play with the basic components of a distributed system so that you will know how each element relates to the others. In most of your career, you most likely won't use this approach or program at such a low level, but you will use higher-level tools that will simplify your work. However, it might be that you will work on one of such tools; hence, you will need to know how to use them. Even if you never work on such a product, it is essential to know where all the terminology in these tools comes from. This knowledge helps you understand how things work under the hood. This will help you design your system for speed, resilience, or any other characteristic and will put you in a position to make the right architectural choice for your needs and navigate the trade-offs you will make. Although this section works at a very low level, we will still use a library called Mangos to facilitate our job.

Let's start with some history now. In 2007, a project called ZeroMQ came out. This was essentially a library allowing C++ developers to build distributed systems where each component could communicate with other components via synchronous messages. This library provides a queuing system with different communication protocols without the need for a broker. Many tools available today rely on a broker, where all messages arrive and depart.

CHAPTER 2 DISTRIBUTED COMMUNICATION BASICS

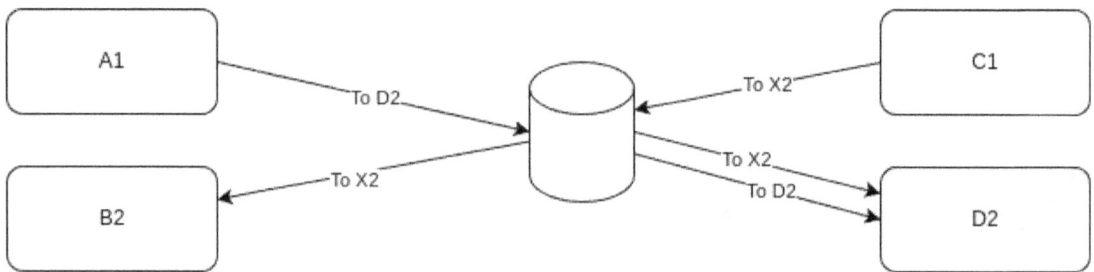

Figure 2-1. *Brokered messaging*

As shown in Figure 2-1, a broker is like a post office; a message gets sent to one or more recipients, and the post office will manage to deliver the message to the correct recipients. This messaging pattern is very simple because the senders need to know only where the broker is, and everything is loosely coupled. The significant disadvantage of this communication method is that the broker is a single point of failure. If the broker fails, crashes, or is unavailable, the whole system will stop working. Look again at Figure 2-1; if the broker is unavailable, A1 won't be able to send its message to D2, but also C1 won't be able to send a message to either B2 or D2, and this is even if all the components are up and running.

ZeroMQ solved this problem by allowing the system to manage the communication between the components manually, meaning without the help of a broker, and avoiding the single point of failure problem. This pattern enhances reliability, but as you can imagine, it comes at the cost of loose coupling and higher complexity.

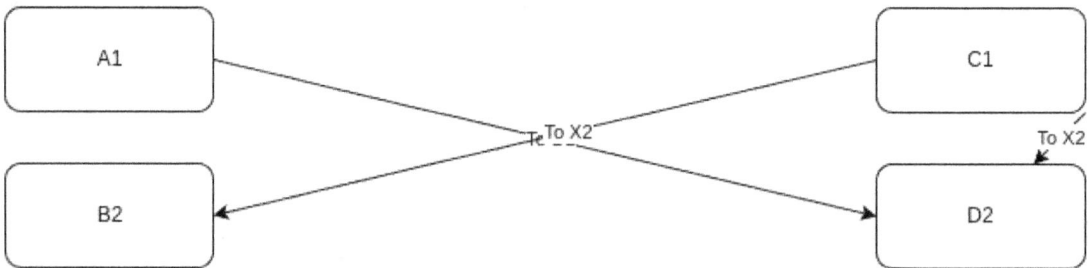

Figure 2-2. *Unbrokered system*

As you can see in Figure 2-2, if one component fails, some other components can still communicate with each other. Why is there a need for a tool like ZeroMQ if we do everything ourselves? In reality, this is a messaging tool that allows the definition of some types of connection and communication patterns between components so that once the connection is made, the sender will need just to send a message with some characteristics. The correct receiver(s) will receive it. We will see these different types of connections in detail later; this is enough for you to understand where we are going.

As mentioned earlier, ZeroMQ is a C++ library, but several bindings exist for many languages. Go, the language used in this book is one of them. Apart from the complexity of this approach, however, some design decisions made when creating ZeroMQ were contested, specifically the non-POSIX compliance and the fact that the API was not open for extension, so it was not easy to create new "protocols" or communication patterns for this library. One project trying to overcome those limitations was called **scalability protocols**, a specification for a new tool allowing for whatever ZeroMQ was allowing, plus the characteristics mentioned above. One more idea was that writing this "scalability protocols" library in C rather than C++ would help with binding to other languages. This is how the library **nanomsg** came out. As the specification for the scalability protocols is freely available, a specific implementation for them in Go is called Mangos, which is the library we will focus on throughout this part. We believe that using this library, whose code is open source and freely available, will allow the reader of this book to dig into the specifics of this kind of programming, enhance their appetite for such tools, and maybe push them to start contributing to the next distributed computing tool/framework.

2.2 Communication Items

2.2.1 Socket

We spoke in the previous paragraph about components and that they must communicate somehow by exchanging some sort of message. As a software engineer, you must understand that a component inside a distributed system will have some parts and characteristics that are not different from the components of any other system. Several parts of this component can grab data from a data source, perform some computation, or do anything else that a component of a software system should do. You will also understand that many parts of any system, hence of any component, will have some sort of trigger. The system reacts upon receiving a stimulus. While you might be used to thinking of a stimulus as a request, such as "Retrieve the user's data" or "Log in the user," it is important to recognize the architectural implications. Designing around triggers encourages decoupling because components respond independently and promotes reactivity by allowing the system to handle events dynamically and efficiently. From now on, you should start to think of these stimuli as events and not requests. Indeed, there will be some requests at some point, but let's see how you can handle a log-in situation in this fashion.

The user is presented with a web form and submits the "request," which will trigger a message stating "The user with these credentials requested to log in." Upon receiving this message, a component will fetch the data of the user and check if the credentials are correct; if they are not, an error message will come back, but if they are, it will send another message: "The user with ID 123 needs to log in." At this point, another component will receive this message and possibly create a new record in a store where the user is set as logged in with a specific token. This component might send another message stating "User with ID 123 has just logged in." Some other components will acknowledge that this event happened and act upon it. What is essential here is that the components will not obey a request; they will just act upon the fact that something happened. Thinking this way will help you write better programs that are less coupled and help you understand the following parts of this book.

We must understand how this component will accept or receive a notification now. We will see different layers of a component later on, but for now, know that a component will need some sort of "open door" to receive or send notifications. The common name comes from electrical components; this access point to the other components is called a socket. A socket can be in two states: open and closed. A basic socket can receive or send messages, but you might decide that that specific socket will always only send messages.

In contrast, another socket will only receive messages. You can decide that one socket will be opened to send a message and closed straightaway. This last situation is precisely what happens when making HTTP requests: a socket gets opened, a message is sent, a message is received, and then the socket is closed. This process might be slow in some cases, so we can create a configuration where the sockets are always open, and the components keep sending and receiving messages through this channel between the two sockets.

2.2.2 Protocol

Every field has its jargon, but you might be puzzled that when we talk about a protocol in this context, we do not mean what you think. We saw in the previous paragraph that components can send messages to multiple other components, sometimes the

CHAPTER 2 DISTRIBUTED COMMUNICATION BASICS

same message to numerous components. Some components will want to just receive messages, but from whom? Let's look at Figure 2-3, where different components exchange messages.

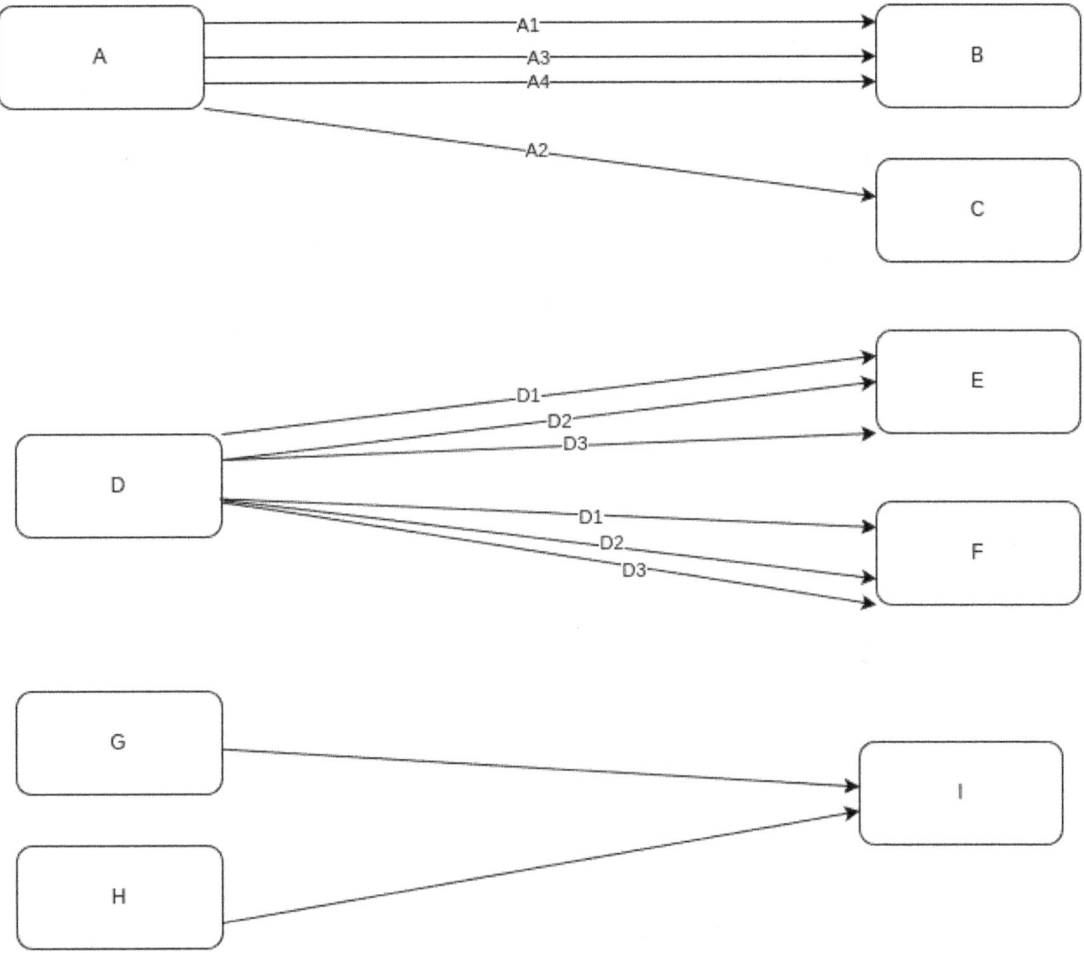

Figure 2-3. *Different protocols*

Notice that components **B** and **C** receive messages from **A**, but they do not receive the same messages. The messages are distributed across the two components, and the distribution is not equal in number. In contrast, components **E** and **F** receive exactly the same messages, all of which come from **D**. Finally, component **I** receives every message sent by both **G** and H. Looking at it from the sender's perspective, component **A** distributes its messages unevenly between **B** and **C**, while **D** sends all of its messages to both **E** and **F**. We leave the behavior of component I for you to consider.

31

In the following paragraphs, we will explore these specific patterns practically using **Mangos**. Still, you need to understand that the way each component decides whether to send one copy of the same message to only one component, to multiple components, or to receive messages from one or more components is what we will call a protocol.

To be more precise, it will not be a component to use a protocol, but the protocol is a characteristic of a socket, and each component can have multiple sockets; each socket will only use one protocol.

A protocol defines how a socket will act. A socket can send a message to all the other connected sockets or load balance between them. Some sockets can send a message and then wait for a reply, while others won't expect any reply. The next thing that might come to your mind is that if a socket sends messages following a specific protocol, the receiving protocols should match, specularly, the sender's protocol. This is true, and it means that to create a system where communication makes sense, the sockets used by the components must follow some guidelines, and different protocols can be bound into couples to create different topologies.

Everything we have said so far is quite theoretical, but we will soon see how all this builds up with examples in Go.

2.2.3 Transports

We've seen that a socket is what receives and sends messages, and we saw that the way these messages are shared is the protocol. Now, we need to talk about the actual means of transportation. If you think of a whole distributed system as an irrigation system, the water will be the transport. If you let oil flow through the pipes, oil would be the transport, although all the transports would effectively be some sort of liquid. In our case, we use electricity to share messages, but the different "liquids" are things like HTTP, UDP, WebSocket, IPC, and Memory.

Several reasons will drive the choice of transport. Some transports might be equivalent and used to join an existing wider ecosystem. Other transports, though, have specific reasons to be chosen, which we will analyze in a later paragraph.

An interesting characteristic of sockets is that although they can only have one protocol, they might actually use several transports. This means building a distributed system where messages can be delivered via different transports to components performing the same duties is possible.

CHAPTER 2   DISTRIBUTED COMMUNICATION BASICS

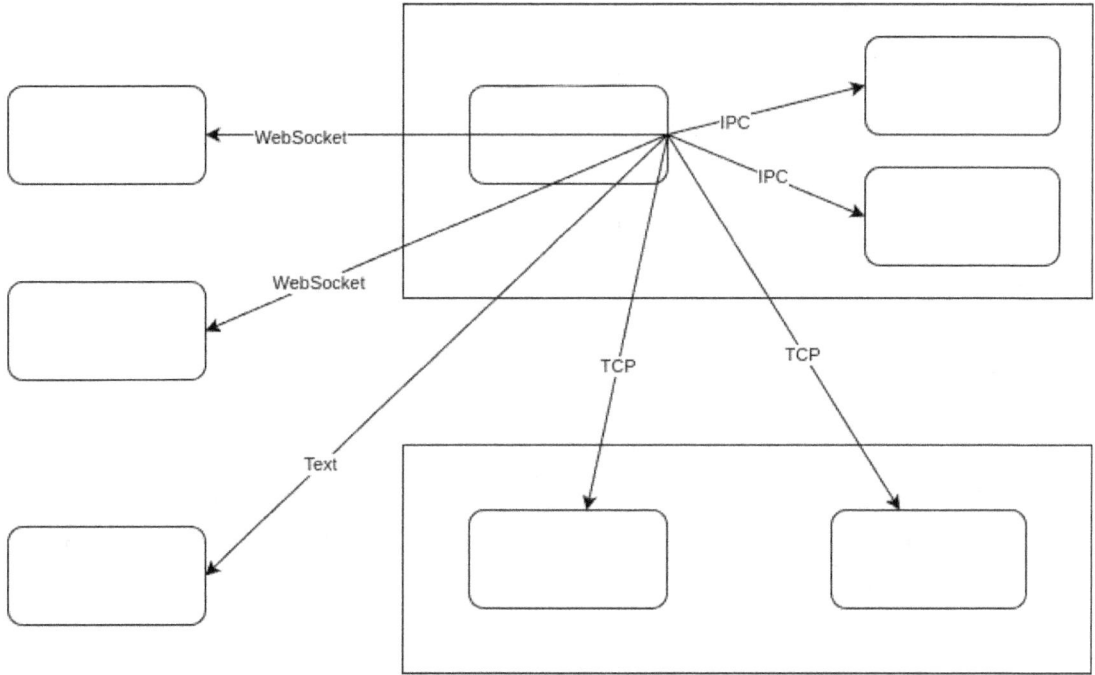

Figure 2-4. *Multitransport system*

Consider Figure 2-4. It represents a possible diagram for a browser game. On the left, browsers communicate with a server component via WebSockets; the same socket is used to exchange messages with other clients and internal components. The internal components on the server side communicate via IPC if they are inside the same machine or TCP if they are inside different machines. This diagram assumes that all these components are connected with one specific component via the same socket.

Another interesting case is shown in Figure 2-5, where each square represents an instance of the same app, made of the same components but running on different machines.

Component A needs to communicate with component B, and it would be preferable to contact the one in the same application instance. If component B instance 1 is overloaded, however, it could be a good choice to try contacting component B in a different instance. Every component can expose a TCP port with its socket. Still, a transport specific to in-process communication could be preferred for components communicating inside the same application. In the diagram, component B will expose a TCP port only to communicate with an external component, but an in-process transport for communicating with its same instance.

33

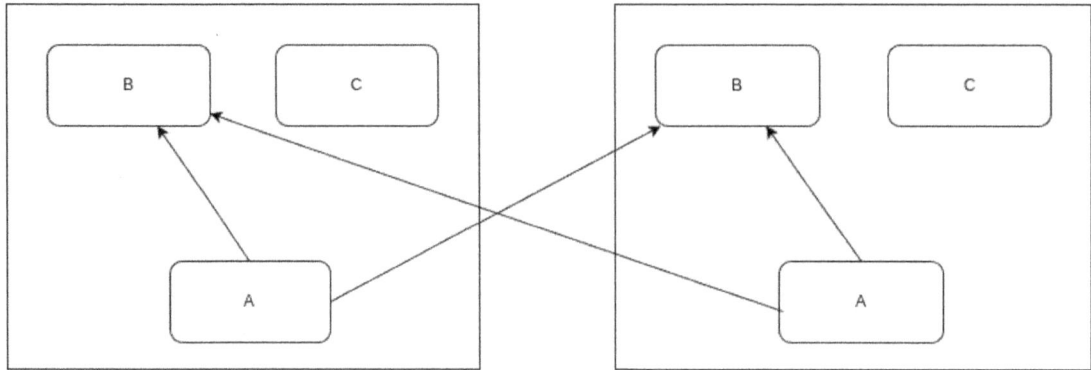

Figure 2-5. *Multitransport*

Generally, if an application or component is under heavy load, we tend to scale up that component or add another instance of the whole application. This is a good way to scale the system, but often, internal components do not communicate with components inside another instance of the application; using the technique above, we make sure that adding a new instance of the application distributes the load equally across instances. Creating an application this way is thought to be complicated, but people have tried to make that simple by building several tools. One is a whole framework, AKKA, for the JVM, and another is an entire language, Scala, built around these principles. The Mangos library and NATS are tools that allow for the same thing but are not tied to a specific ecosystem, the JVM, nor force you to learn a different language. You can use any language with Mangos bindings or a client library for NATS. We will use Go.

2.3 Topologies

We've seen that different protocols are available to us, but we haven't seen what each protocol does, why we would use more of them, or in what combination. In reality, each protocol and combination has a specific reason, and we might need these different combinations of protocols to achieve various goals. Combining sockets with different protocols into different configurations generates what we call a **topology**. Using two sockets with matching protocols makes one topology, so we can talk about req/rep topology, pub/sub topology, etc. Combining different topologies makes a new topology. In this paragraph, we will see how and why this is done, but let's start by finally introducing the Mangos library.

2.3.1 Mangos Library

The Mangos library can be found at https://github.com/nanomsg/mangos. We will assume that you already have the Go interpreter installed on your machine; the current version at the time of writing this book is 1.23. We will then see how to use this library.

We will assume you already have a Go project created and that you are using Go modules; if you still need one, just create one. At this point, just type in your terminal

> go get go.nanomsg.org/mangos/v3
>
> go get go.nanomsg.org/mangos/v3/protocol/rep
>
> go get go.nanomsg.org/mangos/v3/transport/all

This will add the dependency to your module file. We suggest you run also:

> go mod download
>
> go mod vendor

This will make the library available in your project folder. Now that you are ready to start using it and see how sockets, protocols, and transports work, we will create a basic socket. For simplicity, we will begin by making this in the **main.go** file.

```go
package main
import (
    "go.nanomsg.org/mangos/v3/protocol/rep"
    "log"
    _ "go.nanomsg.org/mangos/v3/transport/tcp"
)
func main() {
    url := "tcp://127.0.0.1:40899"
    sock, err := rep.NewSocket()
    if err != nil {
        log.Fatal("can't get new rep socket: %s", err.Error())
    }
    if err = sock.Listen(url); err != nil {
        log.Fatal("can't listen on rep socket: %s", err.Error())
    }
}
```

CHAPTER 2   DISTRIBUTED COMMUNICATION BASICS

Apart from importing a specific protocol:

"go.nanomsg.org/mangos/v3/protocol/rep"

And a specific transport:

_ "go.nanomsg.org/mangos/v3/transport/tcp"

We simply use that protocol to create a new socket:

sock, err := rep.NewSocket()

And then we listen to a URL:

```
if err = sock.Listen(url); err != nil {
    log.Fatal("can't listen on rep socket: %s", err.Error())
}
```

In this case, the URL is set to **tcp://127.0.0.1:40899** via a registered variable. Bear in mind that

_ "go.nanomsg.org/mangos/v3/transport/tcp"

will make the **TCP** transport available, so you just need to set the socket to listen to a TCP port, and it will work. Importing other transports requires you just to use a URL with the proper format, and the library will know how to manage the messages.

This program does not do much but gives you a glimpse of how things work. For instance, it is clear that you need to choose a protocol first, create a socket with that protocol, and then somehow bind it to a URL. We will now see the protocols in depth and how they make topologies.

2.3.2 Req/Rep

We will now see the first topology in our list, the one that you might be most familiar with: the req/rep. The name req/rep stands for **requester/replier** and is made of at minimum two sockets, one following the req(uester)protocol, the other the rep(lier) protocol.

A requester is a socket that sends a message and waits for a response before sending new messages. As you can see, this happens whenever you open a browser and type a URL. The browser will wait for the page data to return and display it. You might be familiar with REST APIs; in case you are, these all follow the req/rep protocol; when a request is made, the requester will stop and wait until the response comes back or enough time has passed, and it decides to time out.

In the previous paragraph, you saw how to create a rep socket that listens to a specific port. We will now see how to create a req socket and send a message.

Let's assume you created a new project and installed the transport and the rep protocol. As you might imagine, here is how you will install the req protocol:

```
go get go.nanomsg.org/mangos/v3/protocol/req
```

Now, let's make sure your project has this structure:

```
|root/
|------req/
|------rep/
```

You can put whatever you've seen in the previous paragraph under the rep folder, and here we have a main.go file for the req folder:

```go
package main

import (
    "go.nanomsg.org/mangos/v3/protocol/req"
    "log"
    _ "go.nanomsg.org/mangos/v3/transport/tcp"
)
func main() {
    url := "tcp://127.0.0.1:40899"
    sock, err := req.NewSocket()
    if err != nil {
        log.Fatal("can't get new rep socket: %s", err.Error())
    }
    if err = sock.Dial(url); err != nil {
        log.Fatal("can't listen on rep socket: %s", err.Error())
    }
}
```

CHAPTER 2   DISTRIBUTED COMMUNICATION BASICS

The idea is that the rep socket will listen to a port, and the req socket will dial to it and then send messages. If you now run these two modules, you might see that the rep runs and stops, and the req module just throws an error. This is because the replier will have already been terminated by the time we run the requester app. We can add a simple loop in the replier so that it will listen forever.

```
........................
if err = sock.Listen(url); err != nil {
    log.Fatal("can't listen on rep socket: %s", err.Error())
}
for {
  }
}
```

What we want to do now is for the replier to be able to read a message and the requester actually to send messages.

Let's change our empty loop inside the replier with the following:

```
for {
    msg, err := sock.Recv()
    if err != nil {
        log.Fatal("cannot receive on rep socket: %s", err.Error())
    }
    log.Println(string(msg))
    sock.Send([]byte("Received: " + string(msg)))
}
```

Here, we wait until a message arrives and print it out. Then, we send a response back saying "Received:" and the original message.

Now let's modify the requester so that we send a message and wait for the reply:

```
............................
if err = sock.Dial(url); err != nil {
    log.Fatal("can't listen on rep socket: %s", err.Error())
}
err = sock.Send([]byte("Message 1"))
if err != nil {
```

```
        log.Fatal("can't send message to rep socket: %s", err.Error())
}
msg, err := sock.Recv()
log.Println(string(msg), err)
```

If you now run the replier first and then the requester, you will see that the replier receives a message with the content **Message 1** and sends back a message **Received: Message 1** to the requester.

Here is an example console printout.

Figure 2-6 shows how the replier receives a message, and Figure 2-7 shows how the requester receives a reply after sending a message.

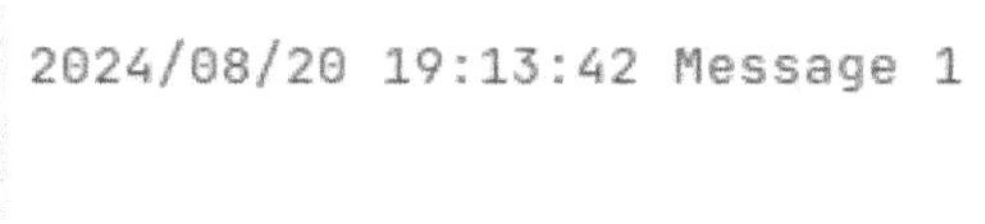

```
2024/08/20 19:13:42 Message 1
```

Figure 2-6. *Replier printout*

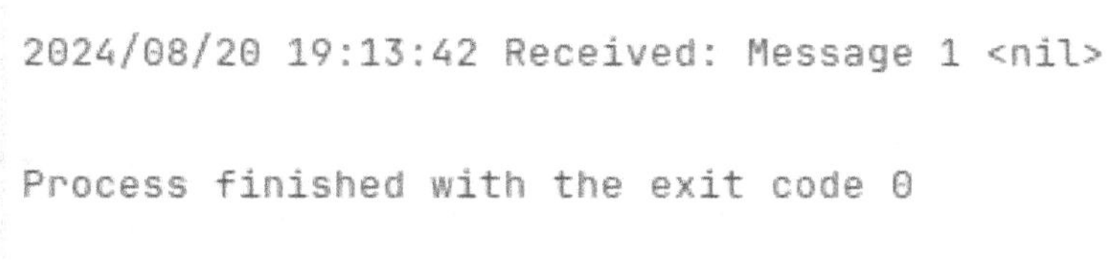

```
2024/08/20 19:13:42 Received: Message 1 <nil>

Process finished with the exit code 0
```

Figure 2-7. *Requester printout*

Be careful that the **req** protocol has state management. Trying to receive two messages after sending only one will return an error.

You can try this by modifying your req main function to:

```
err = sock.Send([]byte("Message 1"))
if err != nil {
    log.Fatal("can't send message to rep socket: %s", err.Error())
}
msg, err := sock.Recv()
log.Println(string(msg), err)
msg, err = sock.Recv()
log.Println(string(msg), err)
```

The result will look like Figure 2-8.

```
2024/08/21 18:03:47 Received: Message 1 <nil>
2024/08/21 18:03:47  incorrect protocol state

Process finished with the exit code 0
```

Figure 2-8. *Incorrect req state*

You might wonder how useful this protocol is, implemented this way, if we can always only send one message at a time and wait for the response to get back. Furthermore, we are using Go as our programming language, which is famous for its simple approach to concurrency. For all we know at this point, if we want to handle multiple message requests, we need to create numerous sockets dialling to the same URL, and from the **rep** side, we might have to create various sockets listening to multiple URLs. This is quite impractical and can lead to an enormous number of ports open, which, using TCP, is heavy on the component we are building.

Fortunately, there is a solution: the context. Mangos offers a context API that allows us to handle multiple requests with one single socket. Not all protocols allow it, but both req and rep do. We will see later why other protocols might not benefit from the context API and might not implement it, but let's now focus on a practical example with a req/rep topology.

We want to send two messages and receive the responses; let's see how we can modify our req program to do so. We will rewrite the main function:

```
func main() {
    url := "tcp://127.0.0.1:40899"
    sock, err := req.NewSocket()
    if err != nil {
        log.Fatal("can't get new rep socket: %s", err.Error())
    }
    if err = sock.Dial(url); err != nil {
        log.Fatal("can't listen on rep socket: %s", err.Error())
    }
```

```go
    ctx1, err := sock.OpenContext()
    if err != nil {
        log.Fatal("can't create context: %s", err.Error())
    }
    ctx2, err := sock.OpenContext()
    if err != nil {
        log.Fatal("can't create context: %s", err.Error())
    }
    err = ctx1.Send([]byte("Message 1"))
    if err != nil {
        log.Fatal("can't send message to rep socket: %s", err.Error())
    }
    err = ctx2.Send([]byte("Message 2"))
    if err != nil {
        log.Fatal("can't send message to rep socket: %s", err.Error())
    }
    msg, err := ctx1.Recv()
    log.Println(string(msg), err)
    msg, err = ctx2.Recv()
    log.Println(string(msg), err)
}
```

The main change is that we open two different contexts after creating a socket and dialling to a rep socket. We send a message from each of these contexts and then receive the response from each context again.

```go
ctx1, err := sock.OpenContext()
```

Opens the context, and we can use the context like we would use the socket.

```go
err = ctx1.Send([]byte("Message 1"))
..................................................
msg, err := ctx1.Recv()
```

This version shows how to use contexts, and the more expert Go programmer can already understand how to take advantage of this feature effectively. However, for the less experienced, this might seem a waste of time, as we are still doing things

CHAPTER 2   DISTRIBUTED COMMUNICATION BASICS

sequentially. The same result could be achieved by just sending one message, receiving the response, and iterating the process again without using contexts but just the regular socket.

We will now see an example where the context API's power is more evident.

```go
package main

import (
    "go.nanomsg.org/mangos/v3"
    "go.nanomsg.org/mangos/v3/protocol/req"
    "log"

    _ "go.nanomsg.org/mangos/v3/transport/tcp"
)

func sendMessage(sk mangos.Socket, msg string, ch chan bool) {
    ctx, err := sk.OpenContext()
    defer sk.Close()
    if err != nil {
        ch <- false
        return
    }
    err = ctx.Send([]byte(msg))
    if err != nil {
        ch <- false
        log.Fatal("can't send message to rep socket: %s", err.Error())
    }
    rsp, err := ctx.Recv()
    if err != nil {
        ch <- false
        log.Fatal("can't receive message from rep socket: %s", err.Error())
    }
    log.Println(string(rsp), err)
    ch <- true
}
```

```go
func main() {
    url := "tcp://127.0.0.1:40899"
    sock, err := req.NewSocket()
    if err != nil {
        log.Fatal("can't get new rep socket: %s", err.Error())
    }
    if err = sock.Dial(url); err != nil {
        log.Fatal("can't listen on rep socket: %s", err.Error())
    }

    ch := make(chan bool, 3)

    go sendMessage(sock, "Message 1", ch)
    go sendMessage(sock, "Message 2", ch)
    go sendMessage(sock, "Message 3", ch)

    c := 0
    for rsp := range ch {
        log.Println(rsp)
        c += 1
        if c >= 3 {
            break
        }
    }
}
```

The main change is the function **sendMessage**, which receives the socket, the message, and a channel and sends the message to the rep socket.

```go
ctx, err := sk.OpenContext()
..............................................
err = ctx.Send([]byte(msg))
```

The channel function is to make sure all messages have been received. We notify via the channel that a message has been sent and received, and then we gather all the notifications in the main function:

```go
c := 0
for rsp := range ch {
    log.Println(rsp)
```

```
        c += 1
        if c >= 3 {
            break
        }
    }
}
```

Each message is handled via a goroutine

```
go sendMessage(sock, "Message 1", ch)
go sendMessage(sock, "Message 2", ch)
go sendMessage(sock, "Message 3", ch)
```

The same benefits of using the context in the req program apply to the rep program. A real-world program will handle messages, performing some actions, and won't simply reply with the same message without taking action, so being able to accept several messages and handle them concurrently is highly important.

One possibility is that we open a new context after receiving any message in the rep program, which is something like

```
func main() {
    url := "tcp://127.0.0.1:40899"
    sock, err := rep.NewSocket()
    if err != nil {
        log.Fatal("can't get new rep socket: %s", err.Error())
    }
    if err = sock.Listen(url); err != nil {
        log.Fatal("can't listen on rep socket: %s", err.Error())
    }
    for {
        ctx, err := sock.OpenContext()
        if err != nil {
            log.Fatal("cannot open context: %s", err.Error())
        }
        msg, err := ctx.Recv()
        if err != nil {
            log.Fatal("cannot receive on rep socket: %s", err.Error())
        }
```

```
        log.Println(string(msg))
        go func(ctx mangos.Context) {
            ctx.Send([]byte("Received: " + string(msg)))
        }(ctx)

    }
}
```

We create a context, get a message via it, and then use a goroutine to handle the action, which, in this case, is trivial. What we've just done might be the right choice. However, you might want to limit the number of contexts the application handles at the same time, so you could create a pool of contexts and make goroutines for each context.

2.3.3 Push/Pull

We will now analyze a different topology, which is relatively simpler than req/rep but more complex to integrate properly in a bog system. This topology is made of two protocols: push and pull.

The push protocol simply sends messages to whoever can receive them, but it does not wait for a reply. This is essentially a req that does not hold two states and hence cannot be in the wrong state. This topology might seem useless if we have req/rep, but that's because most programs still use synchronous communication, which is what req/rep provides us. Let's start by seeing how we can create this topology, and then we will see how useful it is.

We assume you have a new empty Go project and a push and a pull folder. You will need to install the push and pull protocols with the following:

```
go get go.nanomsg.org/mangos/v3/protocol/push
go get go.nanomsg.org/mangos/v3/protocol/pull
```

This is the content of the **push/main.go** file:

```
package main

import (
    "go.nanomsg.org/mangos/v3/protocol/push"
    _ "go.nanomsg.org/mangos/v3/transport/tcp"
```

```go
    "log"
    "time"
)

func main() {
    url := "tcp://127.0.0.1:40899"
    sock, err := push.NewSocket()
    if err != nil {
        log.Fatal("can't get new rep socket: %s", err.Error())
    }
    if err = sock.Dial(url); err != nil {
        log.Fatal("can't listen on rep socket: %s", err.Error())
    }

    err = sock.Send([]byte("Message 1"))
    if err != nil {
        log.Fatal("can't send message to rep socket: %s", err.Error())
    }
    time.Sleep(time.Second * 5)
    sock.Close()
}
```

This looks very similar to the original req in the previous paragraph, which uses the sock directly rather than the context. Unsurprisingly, the main difference is that we do not wait for any message to return. You might ask why we would want to send a message without expecting a response, and that might have two answers.

In the first scenario, the simplest one, we may want to notify a component that something happened or that we need an action to be performed, but we do not need a response—think about a logging system, for example. We tell the logging component: The user logged in, the user requested his profile details, the user requested to change his personal info, etc. You can think of many other possibilities, but if you ask why we wouldn't want to use req/rep for this scenario, the answer is both "theoretical"—you do not need to request; you are just pushing a message, so you use the correct verb (protocol). The answer is also practical, as the push protocol is lighter, uses less memory, and takes less time, as we do not care to receive a response, so we do not waste time by circling messages when not needed. Notice also that we use a sleep command to ensure the message is delivered. This might seem unnecessary in this example, but in

CHAPTER 2 DISTRIBUTED COMMUNICATION BASICS

real deployments a component will always be running, so this sleep will not be needed. Internally, the Mangos library uses a goroutine to send messages. Without waiting an appropriate time, the command-line tool we created might terminate before the message gets sent concurrently.

In the second scenario, we care about a response but do not want to wait for it. We do not want an ever-growing queue of goroutines waiting for a message back and filling up the memory for no reason.

We can do this by completely separating the sending and receiving of the response as two different actions performed by two different sockets.

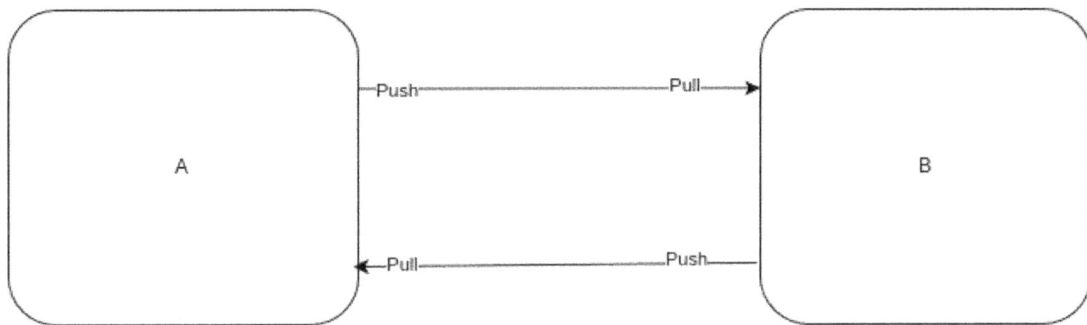

Figure 2-9. *Push/Pull both ways*

This scenario is shown in Figure 2-9, where both components have a push and a pull socket. Component A will push a message, and component B will pull it. Then, after working on the task, component B will push a message, and component A will pull it. We will now see a possible implementation and discuss it.

Component B is implemented as

```
package main

import (
    "go.nanomsg.org/mangos/v3"
    "go.nanomsg.org/mangos/v3/protocol/pull"
    "go.nanomsg.org/mangos/v3/protocol/push"
    _ "go.nanomsg.org/mangos/v3/transport/tcp"
    "log"
)
```

CHAPTER 2   DISTRIBUTED COMMUNICATION BASICS

```go
func handleMessage(ch chan []byte, sk mangos.Socket, id int) {
    for {
        msg := <-ch
        log.Println("worker ", id, " Working on message ", string(msg))
        sk.Send([]byte("Sending back: " + string(msg)))
    }

}

func main() {

    ch := make(chan []byte)
    plhurl := "tcp://127.0.0.1:40898"
    plsock, err := pull.NewSocket()
    if err != nil {
        log.Fatal("can't get new rep socket: %s", err.Error())
    }
    if err = plsock.Listen(plhurl); err != nil {
        log.Fatal("can't listen on rep socket: %s", err.Error())
    }

    psurl := "tcp://127.0.0.1:40899"
    pssock, err := push.NewSocket()
    if err != nil {
        log.Fatal("can't get new rep socket: %s", err.Error())
    }
    if err = pssock.Listen(psurl); err != nil {
        log.Fatal("can't listen on rep socket: %s", err.Error())
    }
    go handleMessage(ch, pssock, 1)
    go handleMessage(ch, pssock, 2)
    for {
        msg, err := plsock.Recv()
        if err != nil {
            log.Fatal("cannot receive on pull socket: %s", err.Error())
        }
```

```
            log.Println(string(msg))
            ch <- msg
    }
}
```

This component needs to wait for messages and then handle a message and send a response.

We create two sockets, a pull and a push socket:

```
plhurl := "tcp://127.0.0.1:40898"
plsock, err := pull.NewSocket()
if err != nil {
    log.Fatal("can't get new rep socket: %s", err.Error())
}
if err = plsock.Listen(plhurl); err != nil {
    log.Fatal("can't listen on rep socket: %s", err.Error())
}
.................................................
psurl := "tcp://127.0.0.1:40899"
pssock, err := push.NewSocket()
if err != nil {
    log.Fatal("can't get new rep socket: %s", err.Error())
}
if err = pssock.Listen(psurl); err != nil {
    log.Fatal("can't listen on rep socket: %s", err.Error())
}
```

As you can see, we listen here in both cases. Before, in this book, the pull socket listened to a TCP port while the push dialed. In reality, every socket can either listen to a port or dial; we used the previous configuration as, by instinct, people would make a server receiving messages, like an HTTP server, listen to a port, while a client would dial to that socket. With Mangos, we create sockets for every protocol, and every socket can either listen to a port and expect connections or connect to another socket. In the earlier examples, a pull socket would listen to a port and expect interested sockets to connect to it to push messages. In this case, we have a push socket listening to a port, and every pull socket interested in receiving messages will dial into this push socket. You can create your sockets as you wish, but there are two reasons that should drive your decision:

1) The logical "storytelling" interest of sockets to join another socket or act as servers.

2) The order in which the components using the sockets will get deployed.

In the specific case we implemented above, component B will first receive messages and then send responses; hence, it will run first. If component B was trying to dial to a push socket expected to be present in component A, and such a component was not running yet, component B would crash. We then listen to a port for both sockets in component B and, as you might expect, will dial to these sockets from component A.

Carrying on analyzing the code, the component has a main for loop where the pull socket receives messages:

```
msg, err := plsock.Recv()
if err != nil {
    log.Fatal("cannot receive on pull socket: %s", err.Error())
}
log.Println(string(msg))
ch <- msg
```

We print the message, and then we send the message to a channel. This channel is used by two goroutines:

```
go handleMessage(ch, pssock, 1)
go handleMessage(ch, pssock, 2)
```

The function **handleMessage** is the one that does the job, which in this case is trivial, being that this is an example. At the end, **handleMessage** sends the message via the push socket.

The channel is used here to have two separate goroutines, allowing us to handle two messages concurrently. We could have as many goroutines as we please.

Let's now see how component A looks:

```go
package main

import (
    "fmt"
    "go.nanomsg.org/mangos/v3/protocol/pull"
    "go.nanomsg.org/mangos/v3/protocol/push"
    _ "go.nanomsg.org/mangos/v3/transport/tcp"
    "log"
)

func receiver(ch chan bool) {
    plurl := "tcp://127.0.0.1:40899"
    plsock, err := pull.NewSocket()
    if err != nil {
        log.Fatal("can't get new rep socket: %s", err.Error())
    }
    if err = plsock.Dial(plurl); err != nil {
        log.Fatalf("can't listen on push socket: %s URL: %s", err.
        Error(), plurl)
    }

    for {
        msg, err := plsock.Recv()
        if err != nil {
            log.Fatal("cannot send to pull socket: %s", err.Error())
        }
        log.Println(string(msg))

        ch <- true
    }

}
func main() {

    ch := make(chan bool)

    psurl := "tcp://127.0.0.1:40898"
    pssock, err := push.NewSocket()
```

```go
    if err != nil {
        log.Fatal("can't get new rep socket: %s", err.Error())
    }
    if err = pssock.Dial(psurl); err != nil {
        log.Fatalf("can't listen on pull socket: %s URL: %s", err.
        Error(), psurl)
    }

    go receiver(ch)
    i := 0
    for {
        i += 1
        err := pssock.Send([]byte(fmt.Sprintf("message %d", i)))
        if err != nil {
            log.Fatal("cannot send to pull socket: %s", err.Error())
        }

        if i == 10 {
            break
        }
    }

    for i := 0; i < 10; i++ {
        <-ch
    }
    log.Println("Finished")
}
```

This component looks similar to component B. The difference is that the main loop sends ten messages, while a goroutine runs a secondary function, which receives messages via a pull socket. A channel is used here to ensure we terminate the script when ten messages have been received. As you can see, we can send ten messages quickly; while we send them, the goroutine might already receive them. To see if messages are received in between, you could try adding a printout when sending a message via the push socket. If you do not see this happening, try changing the number 10 to 100 in the main loop of component A.

2.3.4 Pub/Sub

We will now see a very popular topology widely used by many modern tools to solve any case. We would argue that this is a stretch. Using the right protocol for the right case would be better, but using one single protocol seems easier to remember and implement. Kafka and Pulsar use this topology, which is Pub/Sub. Pub stands for punisher, while Sub stands for subscriber. The idea is that the publisher publishes a message to all the interested components while the subscribers only subscribe to what they want. You might be puzzled after having studied push/pull, as this seems exactly the same; however, there is one thing we haven't touched with our examples yet, and that is running multiple instances of a component.

Let's rewrite our simple push/pull example using this new topology:

```go
func main() {
    url := "tcp://127.0.0.1:40899"
    sock, err := pub.NewSocket()
    if err != nil {
        log.Fatal("can't get new pub socket: %s", err.Error())
    }
    if err = sock.Listen(url); err != nil {
        log.Fatal("can't listen on pub socket: %s", err.Error())
    }

    i := 0
    for {
        i += 1
        err = sock.Send([]byte(fmt.Sprintf("Message %d", i)))
        if err != nil {
            log.Fatal("can't send message to sub socket: %s", err.Error())
        }
        log.Println("Sent message")
        time.Sleep(time.Second * 5)
    }
}
```

This program is a simple publishing server that sends a message every 5 seconds forever. We want now to get a subscriber who reads the messages coming from this publisher:

```go
package main

import (
    "go.nanomsg.org/mangos/v3"
    "go.nanomsg.org/mangos/v3/protocol/sub"
    _ "go.nanomsg.org/mangos/v3/transport/tcp"
    "log"
)

func main() {
    //TIP Press <shortcut actionId="ShowIntentionActions"/> when your caret is at the underlined or highlighted text
    // to see how GoLand suggests fixing it.
    url := "tcp://127.0.0.1:40899"
    sock, err := sub.NewSocket()
    if err != nil {
        log.Fatal("can't get new rep socket: %s", err.Error())
    }
    if err = sock.Dial(url); err != nil {
        log.Fatal("can't listen on pull socket: %s", err.Error())
    }
    err = sock.SetOption(mangos.OptionSubscribe, []byte(""))
    if err != nil {
        log.Fatal("cannot subscribe: %s", err.Error())
    }
    for {
        log.Println("Waiting")
        msg, err := sock.Recv()
        if err != nil {
            log.Fatal("cannot receive on pull socket: %s", err.Error())
        }
        log.Println(string(msg))
    }
}
```

CHAPTER 2   DISTRIBUTED COMMUNICATION BASICS

This code creates a subscriber (sub) socket and dials into the publisher, then waits for every incoming message and prints it out.

Now, you might wonder about the difference between push and pub and between pull and sub. One first thing you might notice is:

err = sock.SetOption(mangos.OptionSubscribe, []byte(""))

A sub socket subscribes to incoming messages but only from some specific topics. We will see this soon. For now, understand that the code above allows the subscriber to accept every incoming message; without it, it wouldn't subscribe to any topic, and hence, no message would be received.

The second thing to note here is what happens if we run two instances of the subscriber. We will show here a printout:

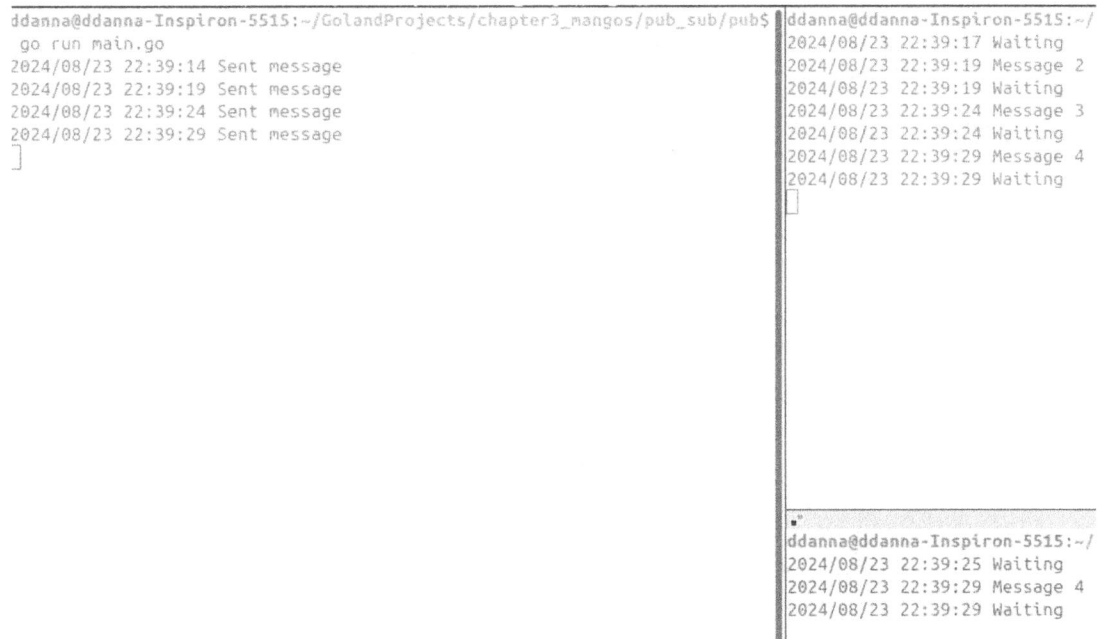

Figure 2-10. *Two subscribers and one publisher*

As you can see in Figure 2-10, the publisher has started, and then one subscriber starts at the top right, and another subscriber starts at the bottom right. The publisher sends four messages, and the first subscriber gets only three because it starts after the first message gets sent. The second subscriber starts even later and receives only one message. From then on, both subscribers get the same messages, as seen in Figure 2-11.

55

```
024/08/23 22:42:59 Message 46
024/08/23 22:42:59 Waiting
024/08/23 22:43:04 Message 47
024/08/23 22:43:04 Waiting
024/08/23 22:43:09 Message 48
024/08/23 22:43:09 Waiting
024/08/23 22:43:14 Message 49
024/08/23 22:43:14 Waiting
024/08/23 22:43:19 Message 50
024/08/23 22:43:19 Waiting
024/08/23 22:43:24 Message 51
024/08/23 22:43:24 Waiting
024/08/23 22:43:29 Message 52
024/08/23 22:43:29 Waiting
024/08/23 22:43:34 Message 53
024/08/23 22:43:34 Waiting
024/08/23 22:43:39 Message 54
024/08/23 22:43:39 Waiting
024/08/23 22:43:44 Message 55
024/08/23 22:43:44 Waiting
```

```
                                             ddanna@ddann
024/08/23 22:42:54 Waiting
024/08/23 22:42:59 Message 46
024/08/23 22:42:59 Waiting
024/08/23 22:43:04 Message 47
024/08/23 22:43:04 Waiting
024/08/23 22:43:09 Message 48
024/08/23 22:43:09 Waiting
024/08/23 22:43:14 Message 49
024/08/23 22:43:14 Waiting
024/08/23 22:43:19 Message 50
024/08/23 22:43:19 Waiting
024/08/23 22:43:24 Message 51
024/08/23 22:43:24 Waiting
024/08/23 22:43:29 Message 52
024/08/23 22:43:29 Waiting
024/08/23 22:43:34 Message 53
024/08/23 22:43:34 Waiting
024/08/23 22:43:39 Message 54
024/08/23 22:43:39 Waiting
024/08/23 22:43:44 Message 55
024/08/23 22:43:44 Waiting
```

Figure 2-11. *Pub/Sub printout*

CHAPTER 2   DISTRIBUTED COMMUNICATION BASICS

To recap what's happening, the messages get published by a pub socket; whenever a sub socket subscribes to them, it starts receiving them. If multiple subscribers subscribe to the messages from one publisher, they all receive the same messages from the moment they join.

Let's see the difference with a push/pull topology. You can get the same code from the pub/sub example; substitute the Pub socket with a Push socket and a Sub socket with a Pull socket. Also, remove the MangoSubscribe options, which are not available to a pull socket. We leave the exercise to you and show just the results.

```
ddanna@ddanna-Inspiron-5515:~/GolandProjects/chapter3_mangos/push_pull_mu
lti/push$ go run main.go
2024/08/23 23:04:07 Sent message
2024/08/23 23:04:12 Sent message
2024/08/23 23:04:17 Sent message
2024/08/23 23:04:22 Sent message
2024/08/23 23:04:27 Sent message
2024/08/23 23:04:32 Sent message
2024/08/23 23:04:37 Sent message
2024/08/23 23:04:42 Sent message
2024/08/23 23:04:47 Sent message
]
```

```
ddanna@ddanna-Inspiron-5515:~/Gol
2024/08/23 23:04:21 Waiting
2024/08/23 23:04:21 Message 1
2024/08/23 23:04:21 Waiting
2024/08/23 23:04:21 Message 2
2024/08/23 23:04:21 Waiting
2024/08/23 23:04:21 Message 3
2024/08/23 23:04:21 Waiting
2024/08/23 23:04:22 Message 4
2024/08/23 23:04:22 Waiting
2024/08/23 23:04:27 Message 5
2024/08/23 23:04:27 Waiting
2024/08/23 23:04:32 Message 6
2024/08/23 23:04:32 Waiting
2024/08/23 23:04:42 Message 8
2024/08/23 23:04:42 Waiting
```

```
ddanna@ddanna-Inspiron-5515:~/Gol
2024/08/23 23:04:27 Waiting
2024/08/23 23:04:37 Message 7
2024/08/23 23:04:37 Waiting
2024/08/23 23:04:47 Message 9
2024/08/23 23:04:47 Waiting
```

Figure 2-12. *Push/Pull with multiple pullers*

Let's consider a run in which the push server sends five messages before a pull client decides to join it, and then a second pull client joins after five more seconds. The results are shown in Figure 2-12; the first pull socket is at the top right and receives all the past messages, unlike the sub socket, but then, when the second pull socket joins, the messages are load balanced between the two sockets, so two pull sockets won't receive the same messages, but the messages will be distributed across the two pull instances.

57

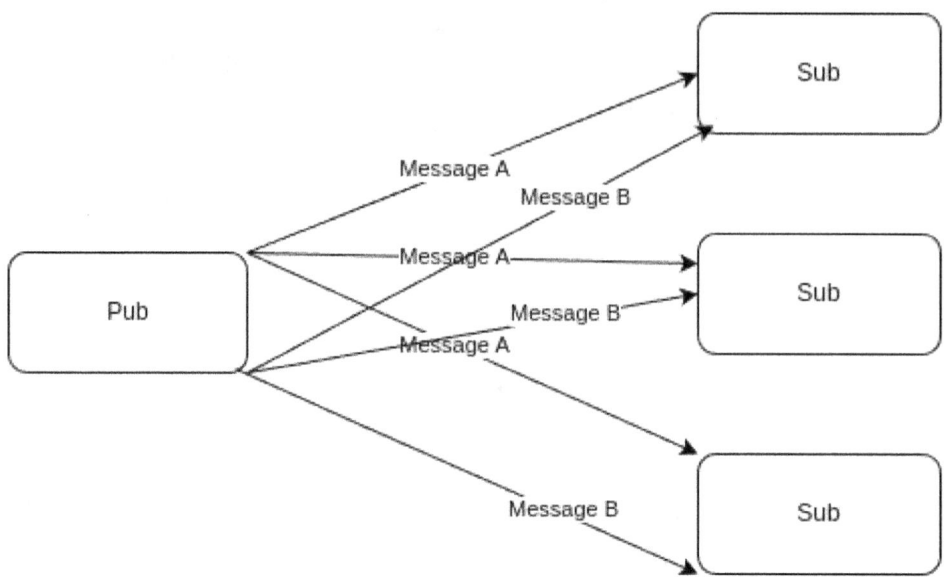

Figure 2-13. *Pub/Sub topology in action*

The main difference between the Push protocol and the Pub protocol is that Push will load balance (distribute) the message across all the connected pull sockets, while a Pub socket will send messages to everybody interested (connected).

The difference between a pull socket and a sub socket is that a pull socket will just receive every message, while a sub socket needs topics to be defined. In substance, a sub socket receiving from every topic will act much like a pull socket. This is all shown in Figures 2-13 and 2-14.

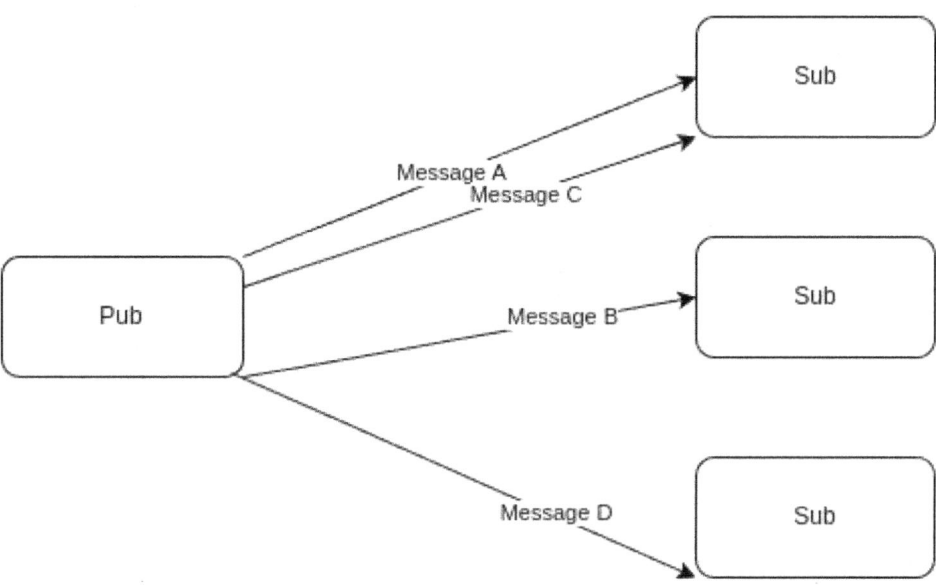

Figure 2-14. *Push/Pull topology in action*

As you might have guessed, rep/req works exactly like push/pull, load-balancing the messages but with a state machine for the synchronous message wait.

Let's now go back to the topic option for the sub socket. Imagine you are distributing music magazines, the publisher of several magazines focusing on Jazz, Classical music, Blues, and other styles, one magazine per style. You must bring the magazines to all the subscribers, as you are the publisher (and distributor). Still, not all your subscribers will be interested in all the music genres you offer. One subscriber will only care about jazz, another will only care about blues, and another will care about jazz and classical music. You will do it by passing at every subscriber's doorstep, and they will take just the magazines they subscribed to, but you will still pass by everybody's door.

Now that we understand how the pub/sub topology and its protocols work, let's see how to implement it with Mangos. We will start by writing the publisher:

```
package main

import (
    "fmt"
    "go.nanomsg.org/mangos/v3/protocol/pub"
    _ "go.nanomsg.org/mangos/v3/transport/tcp"
```

CHAPTER 2   DISTRIBUTED COMMUNICATION BASICS

```
    "log"
    "time"
)

func main() {
    tt := []string{"Blue - ", "Red - ", "Yellow - "}
    url := "tcp://127.0.0.1:40899"
    sock, err := pub.NewSocket()
    if err != nil {
        log.Fatal("can't get new push socket: %s", err.Error())
    }
    if err = sock.Listen(url); err != nil {
        log.Fatal("can't listen on push socket: %s", err.Error())
    }

    i := 0
    for {
        msg := fmt.Sprintf("%s Message %d", tt[i%3], i)
        i += 1
        err = sock.Send([]byte(msg))
        if err != nil {
            log.Fatal("can't send message to pull socket: %s", err.Error())
        }
        log.Println("Sent message", msg)
        time.Sleep(time.Second * 5)
    }

}
```

We are just making the same publisher as in earlier examples, but we have a set of prefixes:

```
tt := []string{"Blue - ", "Red - ", "Yellow - "}
```

And we send each message with a different prefix:

```
msg := fmt.Sprintf("%s Message %d", tt[i%3], i)
```

The prefix from the slice **tt** is taken with the index equal to the remainder of the division between the current message number and the number of possible prefixes.

Let's now see the subscriber:

```go
package main

import (
    "go.nanomsg.org/mangos/v3"
    "go.nanomsg.org/mangos/v3/protocol/sub"
    _ "go.nanomsg.org/mangos/v3/transport/tcp"
    "log"
    "os"
    "strings"
)

func main() {
    ts := os.Getenv("TOPICS")
    tt := strings.Split(ts, ",")
    url := "tcp://127.0.0.1:40899"
    sock, err := sub.NewSocket()
    if err != nil {
        log.Fatal("can't get new rep socket: %s", err.Error())
    }
    if err = sock.Dial(url); err != nil {
        log.Fatal("can't listen on pull socket: %s", err.Error())
    }
    for _, t := range tt {
        err = sock.SetOption(mangos.OptionSubscribe, []byte(t))
        if err != nil {
            log.Fatal("cannot subscribe: %s", err.Error())
        }
    }
    for {
        log.Println("Waiting")
        msg, err := sock.Recv()
```

```
        if err != nil {
            log.Fatal("cannot receive on pull socket: %s", err.Error())
        }
        log.Println(string(msg))
    }
}
```

This program starts by taking an environment variable:

```
ts := os.Getenv("TOPICS")
```

The variable is supposed to have a comma-separated list of topics, so the code splits the string into a slice, using the comma character as the separator:

```
tt := strings.Split(ts, ",")
```

This slice is then used to subscribe to each topic in the list:

```
for _, t := range tt {
    err = sock.SetOption(mangos.OptionSubscribe, []byte(t))
    if err != nil {
        log.Fatal("cannot subscribe: %s", err.Error())
    }
}
```

The rest of the code is not different from what we've seen in the previous subscribers. We have added a few more logs to know what the publisher is sending:

```
log.Println("Sent message", msg)
```

We can run the publisher and two subscribers, setting the topics as we wish; we will now show a printout where one subscriber only subscribes to "Blue - " and the other to "Yellow - ".

```
:/pub$ go run main.go
2024/08/24 18:18:32 Sent message Blue -   Message 0
2024/08/24 18:18:37 Sent message Red -    Message 1
2024/08/24 18:18:42 Sent message Yellow - Message 2
2024/08/24 18:18:47 Sent message Blue -   Message 3
2024/08/24 18:18:52 Sent message Red -    Message 4
2024/08/24 18:18:57 Sent message Yellow - Message 5
2024/08/24 18:19:02 Sent message Blue -   Message 6
2024/08/24 18:19:07 Sent message Red -    Message 7
]
```

```
2024/08/24 18:18:34 Waiting
2024/08/24 18:18:47 Blue -   Message 3
2024/08/24 18:18:47 Waiting
2024/08/24 18:19:02 Blue -   Message 6
2024/08/24 18:19:02 Waiting
```

```
                                                    ddanna@ddanna-In
ddanna@ddanna-Inspiron-5515:~/GolandProje
2024/08/24 18:18:36 Waiting
2024/08/24 18:18:42 Yellow -  Message 2
2024/08/24 18:18:42 Waiting
2024/08/24 18:18:57 Yellow -  Message 5
2024/08/24 18:18:57 Waiting
```

Figure 2-15. *Subscriber topics*

We can see that the subscriber at the top right only receives messages starting with "Blue - " while the subscriber at the bottom right only receives messages starting with "Yellow - ".

We can now set the subscriber at the bottom right to accept both "Yellow - " and "Red - " and see the result, as shown in Figures 2-15 and 2-16.

If we do not pass any topics, the string will be empty; hence, the subscriber will accept everything. You might be wondering why these protocols work this way and seem inconsistent; some accept topics, some do not, some use contexts, and others do not. We mentioned that a pull socket will need to get messages from a push socket, and their reason for existence is to handle messages from a source; if a push socket sends messages, it is because we expect that some other socket will receive them. We might have never received messages if a pull socket was using topics. With subscribers, we saw, with the magazine publisher example, that some messages might get lost. This is what we expect; not everybody cares about all magazines, and possibly nobody will care about some magazines.

CHAPTER 2   DISTRIBUTED COMMUNICATION BASICS

```
:/pub$ go run main.go
2024/08/24 18:25:29 Sent message Blue - Message 0
2024/08/24 18:25:34 Sent message Red - Message 1
2024/08/24 18:25:39 Sent message Yellow - Message 2
2024/08/24 18:25:44 Sent message Blue - Message 3
2024/08/24 18:25:49 Sent message Red - Message 4
2024/08/24 18:25:54 Sent message Yellow - Message 5
2024/08/24 18:25:59 Sent message Blue - Message 6
]
```

```
2024/08/24 18:25:33 Waiting
2024/08/24 18:25:44 Blue - Message 3
2024/08/24 18:25:44 Waiting
2024/08/24 18:25:59 Blue - Message 6
2024/08/24 18:25:59 Waiting
```

```
                                        ddanna@ddanna-in
ddanna@ddanna-Inspiron-5515:~/GolandProje
n.go
2024/08/24 18:25:35 Waiting
2024/08/24 18:25:39 Yellow - Message 2
2024/08/24 18:25:39 Waiting
2024/08/24 18:25:49 Red - Message 4
2024/08/24 18:25:49 Waiting
2024/08/24 18:25:54 Yellow - Message 5
2024/08/24 18:25:54 Waiting
```

Figure 2-16. *Subscriber with multiple topics*

With push/pull, the idea is to send messages only to whoever must receive them and load-balance the results across all the pull sockets.

After all this, you might still be thinking about why these protocols have been implemented this way, and the answer is that somebody has thought about these protocols and has implemented them; there are more protocols than the ones we've seen, and some are implemented by Mangos, and some others are not. You might want to think of a new protocol or several protocols to make a topology you deem interesting, and you can implement it. All you need is to abide by the interface Mangos provides, and you will be able to use these protocols.

2.3.5 Composed Topologies

All the topologies we've touched so far are made by pairs of protocols that have been thought to be complementary from the beginning. Mixing different protocols, like push/sub, is possible, but this won't make much sense, although you might want to try it for reasons arising from the structure of your system.

What is more interesting, though, is combining several topologies to create a new compound topology.

If you look again at Figure 2-13, you will notice that each subscriber will receive all the messages; now, we can expect that the publisher is sending a notification, like something that happened inside the system, and several components will have to act upon it. Think about a bank; somebody opens an account, and several checks have to be made, and several actions have to be performed, all belonging to different logical domains. Every component must do its job, but we do not know how difficult these actions are. It would be naive to expect that all a component, a real scenario component, has to do is send a message back. Handling a message might be a long-running task, consuming many resources. We know that Go can perform many actions concurrently; still, too many messages to handle might mean that we need to scale up the resources, which means scaling up the number of instances of a running component.

Looking again at Figure 2-13, each subscriber might need to be made into multiple instances.

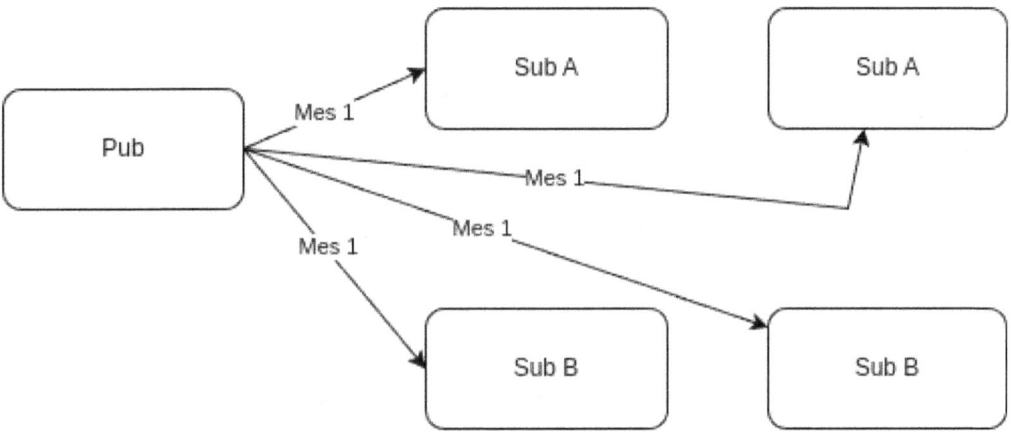

Figure 2-17. *Multiple instances of the same subscriber*

This would look like Figure 2-17, where both Sub A and Sub B instances will receive all the messages. It makes sense that two components receive the same messages, as they might perform different actions after being notified of an event via "message 1." However, two instances of the same component should not receive the same messages, or they will perform the same action twice.

Imagine somebody requesting to withdraw money from their account. A message with the request gets sent, and two instances of the same components deduct the amount from the bank account. The user will see that when he withdraws 100£, he will get 200£ less in his account. If our system was built like this and would autoscale, the more people withdraw money, the more instances would be created of a specific component to cope with the huge amount of requests, but the users will see their accounts depleted of X times the amount they decide to withdraw.

65

CHAPTER 2   DISTRIBUTED COMMUNICATION BASICS

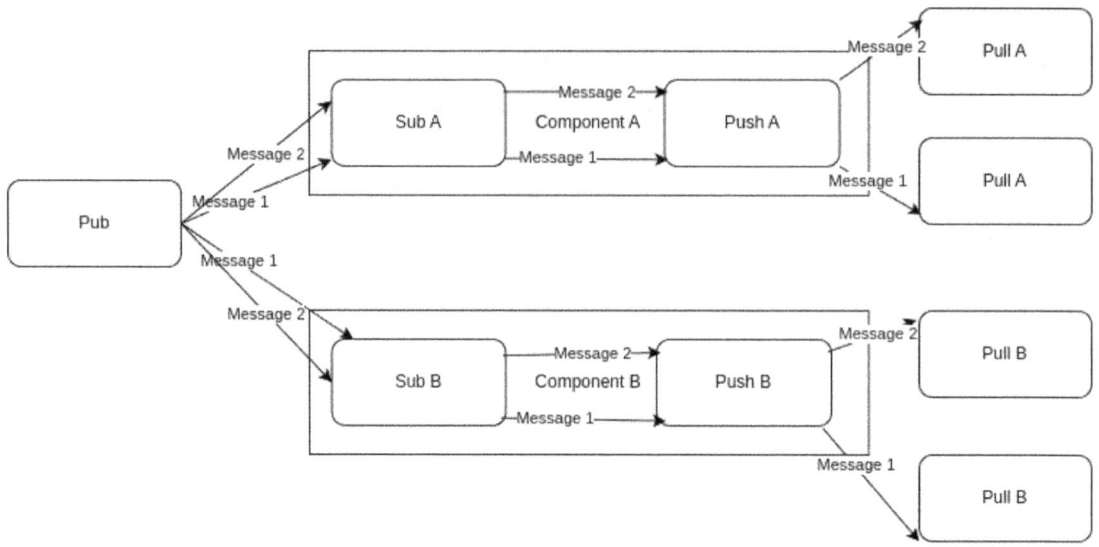

Figure 2-18. Compound topology

Figure 2-18 shows a solution where a component holds both a subscriber and a pusher so that both components get all the messages. Still, each component will load balance the request to another component via a pull socket.

We will leave the implementation of such a topology to you, and we hope this will fire up your creativity so that you can think of many other useful topologies made with the combination of the protocols you already know.

2.4 Multitransport
2.4.1 TCP

In the previous examples, we've used the TCP transport. Let's have a quick but deeper look at it now.

As we've seen, the way we create a socket is:

```
sock, err := sub.NewSocket()
```

Wherever we start from any protocol, in this case we use the **subprotocol,** and we call the **NewSocket** function.

CHAPTER 2   DISTRIBUTED COMMUNICATION BASICS

After this, we decide if we want to listen or dial a URL:

```
if err = sock.Dial(url); err != nil {
    log.Fatal("can't listen on pull socket: %s", err.Error())
}
if err = sock.Listen(url); err != nil {
    log.Fatal("can't listen on pull socket: %s", err.Error())
}
```

At this point, we need to see how we decide that we are using the TCP protocol, and we do that by simply using a URL that is like this:

```
url := "tcp://127.0.0.1:40899"
```

So, we rely on the URL format to inform the program that we are using a specific protocol. That is pretty simple, and you might think now that you could put a URL like "http://…" or "ws://…" or "tls+tcp://" or something with UDP or any transport you might think of. This is what, in theory, you could do, but there is still one missing bit of code, as you might have noticed in the earlier examples:

```
_ "go.nanomsg.org/mangos/v3/transport/tcp"
```

This simply loads the definitions of how to handle a TCP URL. Mangos provides a few transports: TCP, TLSTCP, WS, WSS, inproc, and IPC. We will see the last two in detail later; for the others, we can all put them under the similar umbrella of TCP. TLSTCP is a secure TCP, like HTTPS. WS is the WebSocket transport, and WSS is its secure version. What they have in common is that we define a URL with a port, and this allows clients or servers from any other machine anywhere in the world to communicate with the socket we are creating. You could run a pub server on your laptop and a pull socket on the cloud. All these transports allow you to do this. If you want to use the TLSTCP transport, you will have to include this line instead of the one above:

```
_ "go.nanomsg.org/mangos/v3/transport/tlstcp"
```

And, as you might guess, we will also have:

```
_ "go.nanomsg.org/mangos/v3/transport/ws"
_ "go.nanomsg.org/mangos/v3/transport/wss"
```

CHAPTER 2   DISTRIBUTED COMMUNICATION BASICS

Of course, you could implement another transport and load it instead.

Let's now go back to an earlier example to see another important characteristic of the sockets and the URLs they listen to or dial; here is an abstract of an earlier pub/sub example:

```
url := "tcp://127.0.0.1:40899"
sock, err := sub.NewSocket()
if err != nil {
    log.Fatal("can't get new rep socket: %s", err.Error())
}
if err = sock.Dial(url); err != nil {
    log.Fatal("can't listen on pull socket: %s", err.Error())
}
```

The sample above defines a subscriber and expects a publisher to listen to port 40899 on IP 127.0.0.1 (your machine's localhost). We could, however, have subscribers listening to their own ports:

Sub1

```
url := "tcp://127.0.0.1:40898"
if err = sock.Listen(url); err != nil {
    log.Fatal("can't listen on pull socket: %s", err.Error())
}
```

Sub2

```
url := "tcp://127.0.0.1:40899"
if err = sock.Listen(url); err != nil {
    log.Fatal("can't listen on pull socket: %s", err.Error())
}
```

In this case, we would have two subscriber servers listening on different URLs, and the publisher must now have a way to contact them to publish its messages to both of them. Here we can see how:

```
sock, err := pub.NewSocket()
if err != nil {
    log.Fatal("can't get new pub socket: %s", err.Error())
}
```

```
if err = sock.Dial("tcp://127.0.0.1:40898"); err != nil {
    log.Fatal("can't listen on pub socket: %s", err.Error())
}
if err = sock.Dial("tcp://127.0.0.1:40899"); err != nil {
    log.Fatal("can't listen on pub socket: %s", err.Error())
}
```

We can dial and listen to as many URLs as we want, as well as listen to one URL and dial another. This is quite important in a distributed system, as shown in Figure 2-19, where a new publisher is added when scaling up the system and needs to join the existing subscribers.

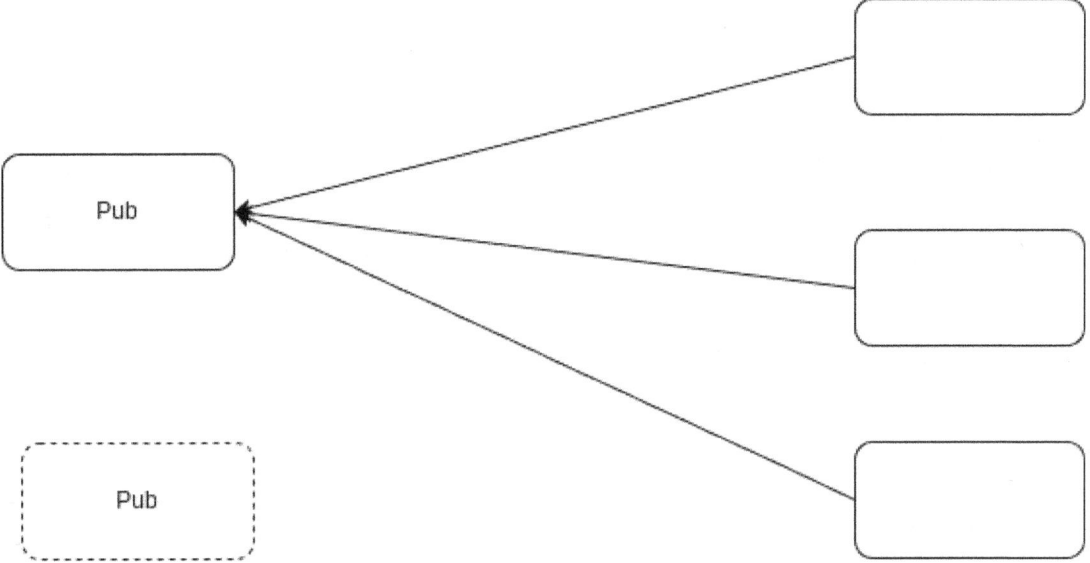

Figure 2-19. *Scaling up publisher*

We have two options in this case: either the new publisher needs to know somehow all the existing subscribers and dial them in, or each subscriber needs now to dial in the new publisher's URL. These scenarios are shown in Figures 2-20 and 2-21.

CHAPTER 2   DISTRIBUTED COMMUNICATION BASICS

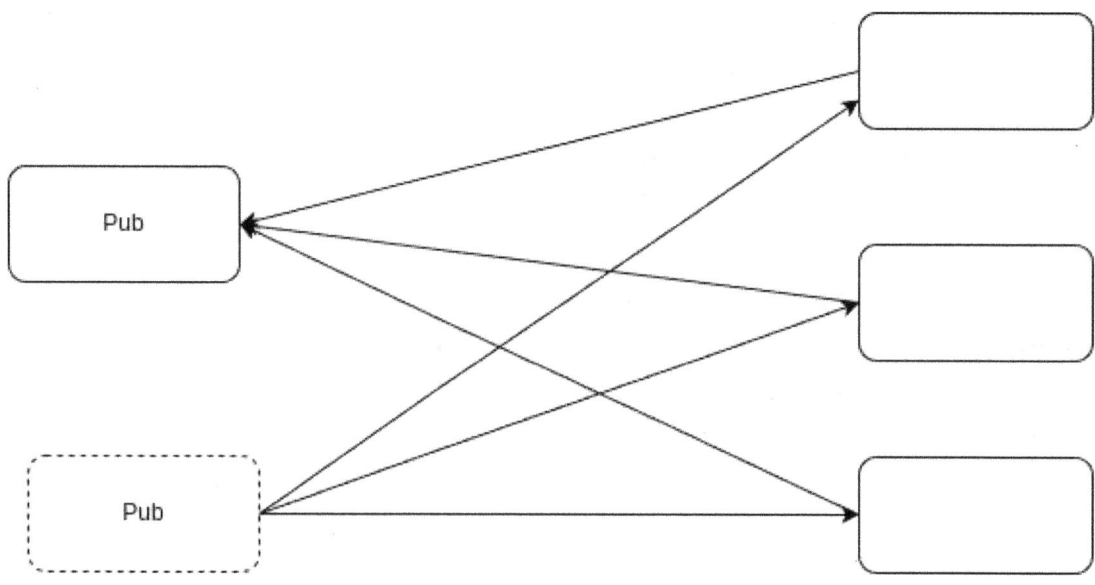

Figure 2-20. *New publisher dialling*

We can choose either option, but we need to decide how the existing components will be made aware of the new instance, that is, the new URL they need to connect to.

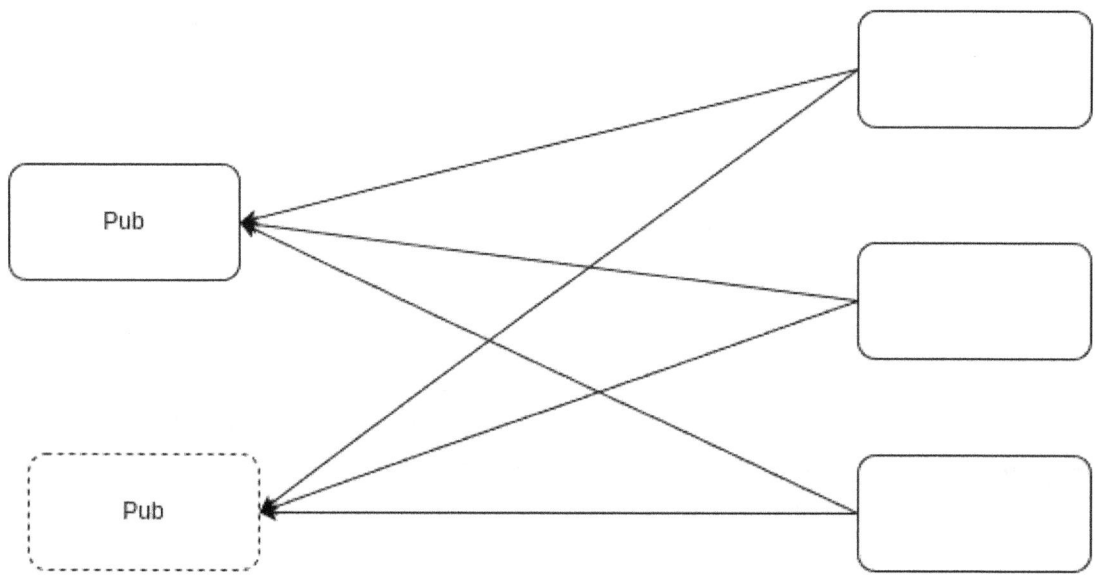

Figure 2-21. *Subscribers dialling to the new publisher*

There are many ways to solve this issue, the most notable one being to use a discovery service like Consul. We will not explore this option, as we will focus on NATS in the rest of the book, but we'd suggest to whoever is interested in pursuing this type of lower-level system design to check Consul and maybe see how it is used in a framework, again for Go, called go-micro (https://github.com/micro/go-micro) or its newer and more featureful child micro (https://micro.dev/).

2.4.2 IPC

The TCP protocol and similar ones can be used everywhere, but if you know you are working with components running as separate processes on the same machine, you might want to use a protocol that saves you some resources. This protocol is available in Mangos and is called IPC (Interprocess Communication). You can use it with

```
_ "go.nanomsg.org/mangos/v3/transport/ipc"
```

In the import section, after installing it, you can then do something like:

```
if err = sock.Listen("ipc://my_awesome_url"); err != nil {
    log.Fatal("can't listen on pub socket: %s", err.Error())
}
```

or

```
if err = sock.Dial("ipc://my_awesome_url"); err != nil {
    log.Fatal("can't listen on pub socket: %s", err.Error())
}
```

The only thing to be careful with here is where you run your applications. Let's imagine we have two programs in the same folder doing what you see above, and everything will work without troubles, but if you have a file structure like this:

```
|example
        \pub
            - main.go
        \sub
            - main.go
```

Things will not work if you try to run each program from its folder. You could go into either of the two folders (pub, sub), let's say sub, and do

```
if err = sock.Dial("ipc://my_awesome_url"); err != nil {

go run main.go
go run ../pub/main.go
```

So that you run both applications from the same folder, or you need to change the pub code to:

```
if err = sock.Dial("ipc://../sub/my_awesome_url"); err != nil {
    log.Fatal("can't listen on pub socket: %s", err.Error())
}
```

We assume the subscriber listens to the awesome URL while the publisher dials in. With this change, we can run with

```
go run main.go
```

both of the programs from their folders.

A better option would be to use command-line parameters or environment variables, but this is not a Go course, and we leave this to the reader.

2.4.3 Memory

Much like the IPC transport, we also have the inproc (In process), which allows us to create URLs to exchange messages between parts of the same component. We install and use it with

```
_ "go.nanomsg.org/mangos/v3/transport/inproc"
```

and then we use URLs like

```
if err = sock.Listen("inproc://my_awesome_url"); err != nil {
    log.Fatal("can't listen on pub socket: %s", err.Error())
}
```

The difference with IPC is that you cannot use this with processes running as different programs, but only inside one program. We can see an example here:

```go
package main

import (
    "fmt"
    "go.nanomsg.org/mangos/v3"
    "go.nanomsg.org/mangos/v3/protocol/pub"
    "go.nanomsg.org/mangos/v3/protocol/sub"
    _ "go.nanomsg.org/mangos/v3/transport/inproc"
    "log"
    "time"
)

func publisher() {
    url := "inproc://publisher"
    sock, err := pub.NewSocket()
    if err != nil {
        log.Fatal("can't get new push socket: %s", err.Error())
    }
    if err = sock.Listen(url); err != nil {
        log.Fatal("can't listen on push socket: %s", err.Error())
    }

    time.Sleep(time.Second * 5)
    i := 0
    for {
        i += 1
        err = sock.Send([]byte(fmt.Sprintf("Message %d", i)))
        if err != nil {
            log.Fatal("can't send message to pull socket: %s", err.Error())
        }
        log.Println("Sent message")
        time.Sleep(time.Second)
    }
}
```

```go
func subscriber(name string) {
    url := "inproc://publisher"
    sock, err := sub.NewSocket()
    if err != nil {
        log.Fatal("can't get new sub socket: %s", err.Error())
    }
    if err = sock.Dial(url); err != nil {
        log.Fatal("can't listen on pub socket: %s", err.Error())
    }
    err = sock.SetOption(mangos.OptionSubscribe, []byte(""))
    if err != nil {
        log.Fatal("cannot subscribe: %s", err.Error())
    }
    for {
        log.Println(name, " Waiting")
        msg, err := sock.Recv()
        if err != nil {
            log.Fatal("cannot receive on sub socket: %s", err.Error())
        }
        log.Println(name, " ", string(msg))
    }
}

func main() {

    go publisher()
    time.Sleep(time.Second * 1)
    go subscriber("First")
    go subscriber("Second")

    for {
        time.Sleep(time.Minute)
    }
}
```

This code has a very simple main function:

```go
func main() {

    go publisher()
    time.Sleep(time.Second * 1)
    go subscriber("First")
    go subscriber("Second")

    for {
        time.Sleep(time.Minute)
    }
}
```

In this function, we simply call as a goroutine a function called **publisher** and twice a function called **subscriber**. As the names imply, the first will create and run a pub socket, while the other will run a sub socket. We also have an infinite loop to have the program run forever and a small sleep between the publisher and subscriber calls. The reason for the sleep is that we want to make sure the publisher is up and running before we can dial in.

Very much as expected, the two functions are just a copy-paste from the earlier pub/sub examples' main functions:

```go
func publisher() {
    url := "inproc://publisher"
    sock, err := pub.NewSocket()
    if err != nil {
        log.Fatal("can't get new push socket: %s", err.Error())
    }
    if err = sock.Listen(url); err != nil {
        log.Fatal("can't listen on push socket: %s", err.Error())
    }
    time.Sleep(time.Second * 5)
    i := 0
    for {
        i += 1
        err = sock.Send([]byte(fmt.Sprintf("Message %d", i)))
```

```
        if err != nil {
            log.Fatal("can't send message to pull socket: %s", err.Error())
        }
        log.Println("Sent message")
        time.Sleep(time.Second)
    }
}
```

We create a socket, listen to a URL using the **inproc** transport, wait five seconds to ensure the possible subscriber does not lose messages, and then start sending messages every second. The subscriber is, as expected, as follows:

```
func subscriber(name string) {
    url := "inproc://publisher"
    sock, err := sub.NewSocket()
    if err != nil {
        log.Fatal("can't get new sub socket: %s", err.Error())
    }
    if err = sock.Dial(url); err != nil {
        log.Fatal("can't listen on pub socket: %s", err.Error())
    }
    err = sock.SetOption(mangos.OptionSubscribe, []byte(""))
    if err != nil {
        log.Fatal("cannot subscribe: %s", err.Error())
    }
    for {
        log.Println(name, " Waiting")
        msg, err := sock.Recv()
        if err != nil {
            log.Fatal("cannot receive on sub socket: %s", err.Error())
        }
        log.Println(name, " ", string(msg))
    }
}
```

We create the socket, dial the publisher URL, and start receiving messages.

We also added a **name** parameter to the subscriber function to log who receives the messages.

```
/home/ddanna/.cache/JetBrains/GoLand2024.2/tmp/GoLand/___go_build_chapter3_mangos_inproc
2024/08/26 11:06:44 Second    Waiting
2024/08/26 11:06:44 First     Waiting
2024/08/26 11:06:48 Sent message
2024/08/26 11:06:48 First     Message 1
2024/08/26 11:06:48 First     Waiting
2024/08/26 11:06:48 Second    Message 1
2024/08/26 11:06:48 Second    Waiting
2024/08/26 11:06:49 Sent message
2024/08/26 11:06:49 Second    Message 2
2024/08/26 11:06:49 Second    Waiting
2024/08/26 11:06:49 First     Message 2
2024/08/26 11:06:49 First     Waiting
2024/08/26 11:06:50 Sent message
2024/08/26 11:06:50 First     Message 3
2024/08/26 11:06:50 First     Waiting
2024/08/26 11:06:50 Second    Message 3
2024/08/26 11:06:50 Second    Waiting
2024/08/26 11:06:51 Sent message
2024/08/26 11:06:51 First     Message 4
2024/08/26 11:06:51 First     Waiting
```

Figure 2-22. *Inproc transport*

We can see a printout with the publisher sending messages and the two subscribers receiving messages in Figure 2-22.

You might wonder why we need this transport, as Go already has a system of channels with goroutines, and it is one of the actual selling points of the language. We must step back here and think that libraries like Mangos and ZeroMQ have not been built just for one language. Mangos implements the **scalability protocols**, as mentioned at the beginning of this chapter, and these protocols can be used by any language offering drivers or pure implementations of these protocols. Some languages might not have such a nice concurrency as part of the language as Go has. Still, Mangos' inproc transport can also be helpful for the Go programmer.

Imagine that you are writing a simple program, and you just use Go concurrency features without Mangos. At some point, the program becomes more complex, and you need to turn it into a distributed system. You might think of using Mangos for ease, and you need to take the goroutines in your code, make them standalone programs, and then use Mangos to exchange messages in place of channels.

What if you had been using Mangos from the beginning? You could have just used Mangos inproc, and when the right moment came, you could turn the goroutines into standalone applications. You would just have to change the URLs from proc URLs into IPC or TCP ones.

One more thing to notice is that you can include this in your program in the import section:

_ "go.nanomsg.org/mangos/v3/transport/all"

And load all the transports available. Then you can use an environment variable for your URLs, and your code won't change at all when moving from inproc to IPC.

2.4.4 Memory Transport for Concurrency

We did see how to use all the available transports, and we've seen how to use memory transport as a good strategy to make an evolutionary architecture, which means designing a system with in mind the fact we will expand it. This is not the only possible use of the memory transport. We mentioned a different way to scale up an application. If you look at Figure 2-5 again, you will understand better how that works.

We can create an application where different parts of one component use the inproc transport for concurrency. When we scale up one component, we can have these different parts adding an extra transport and dialing into the sockets inside a different instance of the same component. At this point, one socket will communicate either with other sockets in the same instance or with the ones in another without caring about where the other sockets are. This helps with concurrency in a way where we can do computation concurrently using processes inside the same machine (same CPUs) or another machine.

This requires, however, that the program be built so that every socket needs to work independently and not rely on some application state. We will see this in the next parts of the book; we will not go into it now, but keep this in mind.

2.5 Summary

In this chapter, we discussed the development of distributed systems using the Mangos library in Go, and we employed various communication patterns, focusing on the Req/Rep, Push/Pull, Pub/Sub, and other composed topologies.

Key concepts touched:

Sockets and Protocols:

Sockets are the primary components for sending and receiving messages.

Protocols define how these messages are managed.

Transports:

Different transports like TCP, IPC, and Inproc manage the message flow.

Flexibility in using different transports is essential for building scalable systems.

Detailed Breakdown

Req/Rep Topology:

The Req/Rep pattern stands for Requester/Replier, similar to HTTP requests and responses.

Code snippets show setting up Req and Rep sockets to send and receive messages.

It allows using contexts to manage multiple requests concurrently and load-balance requests across multiple instances.

Push/Pull Topology:

Push sockets send messages without expecting a response, which is helpful for logging systems.

Pull sockets receive messages without the necessity for topic subscriptions.

This pattern is asynchronous and suitable for load-balancing tasks between multiple workers.

CHAPTER 2   DISTRIBUTED COMMUNICATION BASICS

> **Pub/Sub Topology:**
>
> > Pub sockets publish messages that all subscribed (Sub) sockets receive.
> >
> > Messages can be filtered by topics, making it suitable for scenarios needing specific message handling by different components.
> >
> > A practical example highlights how multiple subscribers can filter messages by defined topics.
>
> **Composed Topologies:**
>
> > Combining multiple topologies leads to more complex but highly scalable and manageable architectures.
> >
> > An example combines Pub/Sub for broadcasting and Push/Pull for balancing load between instances of the same service.
>
> **Multitransport Utilization:**
>
> > Using different transports, such as TCP for remote communication and IPC or Inproc for local inter-process communication, enhances performance and scalability.
> >
> > The chapter discusses scenarios where different transports could be beneficial depending on requirements.

Practical Examples

We've seen several code snippets that demonstrate real-world applications of these topologies:

> Creating and managing contexts in Req/Rep patterns to handle multiple simultaneous requests.
>
> Using channels and goroutines to execute received tasks in the Push/Pull pattern.
>
> Load balancing using multiple instances of subscribers while ensuring each message is processed only once.

2.6 Questions

1. **What is the primary purpose of the Req/Rep topology?**

    a) To broadcast messages to multiple subscribers.

    b) To load balance messages across multiple receivers.

    c) To send a message and wait for a response before sending another.

    d) To send and receive messages asynchronously.

2. **Which transport protocol is recommended for components running as separate processes on the same machine?**

    a) HTTP

    b) Inproc

    c) TCP

    d) IPC

3. **In a Pub/Sub topology, what feature allows subscribers to receive only certain messages?**

    a) Transport layer

    b) Push protocol

    c) Topic subscription

    d) Context API

4. **Why might one use the Push/Pull pattern instead of Req/Rep?**

    a) For lightweight, asynchronous message sending without expecting a response

    b) For sending messages to all interested subscribers

    c) For synchronous communication

    d) For managing contexts in high-concurrency situations

5. **What benefit does combining multiple topologies (composed topologies) offer?**

    a) Increases scalability and adaptability of system architecture

    b) Simplifies implementation

    c) Reduces the need for transports

    d) Eliminates the need for Req/Rep patterns

CHAPTER 3

NATS Fundamentals

3.1 Introduction

3.1.1 What Is NATS

NATS is an open-source tool that was born as a messaging system and expanded into much more. Besides the messaging functionalities, it offers a way to communicate between clients via messaging, a shared key/value store, and an object store for sharing bigger files/objects between clients. It also includes a tiny yet powerful framework for building microservices. NATS can be used in most of the same situations where you would use mangos, but it removes a lot of burdens related to service discovery and DevOps in general. You might recall that when using mangos, we had to specify the address of every socket we wanted to connect to, one way or another. Whatever protocol we were following, we had to dial to an address unless we were listening to a specific address, and everybody else connecting to us had to dial to our address. This might get very cumbersome when we want to scale up or down the instances of our services on the fly. Every time a new service instance would go up, it would have to dial into the same addresses its peers dialled to, or every client connected to its peers would have to start dialling to it too.

NATS solves this problem by being a centralized messaging hub through which every message has to pass. You can see it as a post office; if you want to send a message, it will first go there and then reach the destination. The main difference between how NATS works and a post office is that you will not have to know the address of the destination; you will just send a message with a subject, and the post office will deliver the message to the right client.

We need to understand how NATS knows every destination. Essentially, every NATS client knows the NATS address and either sends messages with a specific subject or expresses interest in receiving messages about a specific subject. At this point, every client (or service) will still need to know the NATS address, but it is just one and always the same. You might ask what happens if we build a NATS cluster with several "post offices." In this case, the NATS servers belonging to the cluster will form a mesh. Essentially, when a new server joins the cluster, it will notify only one other server already belonging to the cluster, and this will start gossiping (sharing information gradually with other servers in a decentralized way) about the existence of the new server to all the remaining servers.

We can see how this works in Figure 3-1, where a new server is added to the cluster. It notifies the closest server of its existence, and gossip does the rest. In the picture, it is also used straightaway to deliver a message.

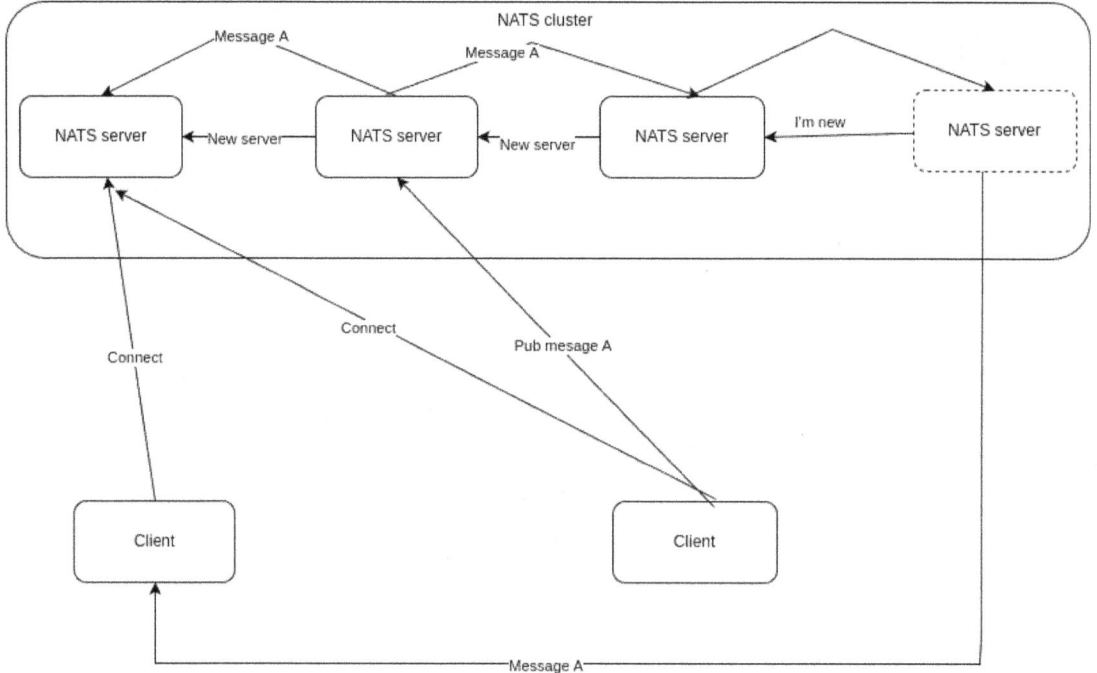

Figure 3-1. *NATS cluster*

From the perspective of the NATS clients, they will also need to know the address of only one NATS server, which will notify the client of all the other possible servers. From the developer's perspective, this is much simpler than using something like mangos, where maintaining all the whole structure details is left to him. It surely is possible to build something around mangos to do something similar, but then, from one perspective, building something similar on top of mangos will look similar to building something like NATS. We are not claiming that NATS is built on mangos; rather, we mean that NATS goes beyond a basic messaging library by offering many additional features, such as clustering, key/value and object stores, and easier out-of-the-box deployment.

The next question is whether NATS provides all the same protocols and topologies as mangoes. The short answer is no, but the long answer is more subtle. NATS is essentially a pub/sub streaming service, which technically allows only this topology but also provides users with a req/rep topology, reusing its core functionalities. Only req/rep and pub/sub are available for the user, but using features like queue groups and subjects makes it possible to mimic the way other topologies work. We will see these functionalities later, but a queue group tells NATS to load-balance some messages across some clients rather than delivering to all of them. As you might guess, this is similar to a compound pub/sub plus push/pull topology.

3.1.2 Alternatives

There are several alternatives to NATS, each with its benefits and drawbacks. We've seen mangos earlier and mentioned ZeroMQ. Leaving aside such low-level libraries, similar tools to NATS are the very famous Kafka, Pulsar, AxonIQ, and AKKA, to cite some.

Most of these tools are open-source or free to use; AxonIQ is a paid tool. Apart from that, they all blend different functionalities and present their approach to the problem of building scalable systems. Some focus on messaging only, some are frameworks, and some are software applications. Although they might all be different, they all try to help developers build resilient, reliable, distributed architectures, each providing its unique set of features and approaches.

Different reasons can drive the choice of your favorite tool; some might be a matter of preference. You might prefer a whole framework that abstracts everything for you and reduces your infrastructure management to the minimum, or you might prefer a low-level library that gives you all the freedom. Some other choices are dictated by the language you are using, so if you use Java or Scala, AKKA might be your favorite choice. Even if Kafka has clients for many languages, most of its users will come from the Java world. This same thing might apply to ZeroMQ, where C++ programmers are amongst the ones who will use it the most, although they are still very few.

In addition, after having managed to get a low-level idea of all the concepts you need via mangos and after having learned how to use one of the tools above, switching to another one will be pretty easy. You will know most of what you need; you will just have to focus on the peculiarity of your tool of choice and quickly and easily understand how to use it.

3.1.3 Why NATS

It remains to answer now why we chose to use NATS in this book. The reasons are many. First of all, NATS is written in Go. All the examples in this book use Go, and having NATS written in Go brings many helpful characteristics.

Testing code that needs NATS is as simple as importing the NATS server as a library and using it as if it were an external server. There is no need to do integration tests with complex CI.

Many new functionalities are developed first in Go, so the Go client is the first to have them available. Also, the microservices framework built on top of NATS was developed in Go first. There is a Node.js version, but other languages might not have it implemented. This does not mean that other languages cannot be used to build microservices using NATS, but simply that the developer needs to handle quite a few things by himself.

All these characteristics make NATS the perfect choice to learn distributed systems with Go. Plus, its popularity is constantly growing, and new features are shipped.

To cite one of the latest examples of the adoption of NATS at the time this book is being written, the Bacalhau project, a tool for distributed data-intensive loads for ML, recently started using NATS as its core messaging tool.

Another great characteristic of NATS is that it is very easy to use and set up and does not require difficult orchestrators for service discovery, like Bookkeeper for Kafka (although this has recently been simplified).

We will dig into how to run NATS and use it on your local machine soon, so it will be clear how easy this is.

3.2 Brokered vs. Unbrokered

Now, let's discuss the main argument between supporters of libraries like Mangos and ZeroMQ and those of tools like NATS or Kafka: Should we have a broker or not?

A broker is a central point where all messages go. We've seen that NATS provides that, and we associated it with a post office. This setup helps simplify many things, like service discovery and handling new clients or servers. From what we've seen, a tool like this is way better than a low-level library, so what is the argument against it? It turns out that a broker through which to pass all messages is a single point of failure. Imagine what would happen if you relied on traditional mail for your communication, that you had only one post office in your country, and suddenly, it collapsed. The result would be that you would not be able to send nor receive any letter. Still, the situation would be quite different if you were manually sending your letters to the destination via a private transport service. You could have issues with your provider, but somebody else might use a different courier and still be able to send and receive letters. This is a no-brainer in real life, as a centralized service is way cheaper than a private personal service. We also know that we have several post offices that are part of the same national post service. When writing software, however, things change, and if we want to take upon us the burden of such complexity for the sake of resilience, we can surely do it.

This is a trade-off, indeed, but brokered systems and tools have tried to deal with this issue in several ways. As mentioned before, it is possible to create a cluster of NATS servers, and they will all try to share the same messages to replicate them via some form of gossiping with each other. If one server goes down, it is improbable that the others will go down, too, so the system will still be reliable. We cannot think of this system as a hundred percent fail-proof, but it is strong enough for us to rely on it.

Considering everything stated in this paragraph, we do not want to assert any superiority of one approach over the other; we simply want to put things in the right perspective so that the developer can choose wisely. In the rest of this book, we will use NATS over tools like Mangos because NATS is simpler to use and to design systems with. Brokered systems are also way more popular than unbrokered ones. Anybody will hardly find a job posting citing mangos, but NATS is way more present.

3.3 Running NATS

3.3.1 NATS-Server

We will now consider the simplest way to run NATS: installing the NATS server for your platform. This is how you should do it locally for all your tests, as it is very simple and does not require anything else. We will see other options for a production installation, but for quick tests and development, the NATS-server CLI is the best option.

You can go to https://github.com/nats-io/nats-server and see various releases; if you click on the releases page, you can choose the one that suits you best. Let's say we chose release v2.10.21. Then, we will find a series of assets at https://github.com/nats-io/nats-server/releases/tag/v2.10.21, and you could use, for example, nats-server-v2.10.21-amd64.deb. If you use Windows or a different Linux system, you can choose the binary that works for your system and architecture. Installing the binary will depend on your platform. You will likely double-click on the downloaded file or use a package manager.

Let's imagine you are using an Ubuntu-based system, and you can do like in Figure 3-2.

```
~$ nats-server
```

Figure 3-2. Calling the NATS server

which will lead to

```
[250734] 2024/10/03 13:14:52.857008 [INF] Starting nats-server
[250734] 2024/10/03 13:14:52.857080 [INF]   Version:  2.10.21
[250734] 2024/10/03 13:14:52.857083 [INF]   Git:      [d3a8868]
[250734] 2024/10/03 13:14:52.857086 [INF]   Name:     NDSOHXTFROHOCNBKA55SZ4UWX6
EEFYZRNW7ZOA3JSCYZ5OY7CTQELUZE
[250734] 2024/10/03 13:14:52.857088 [INF]   ID:       NDSOHXTFROHOCNBKA55SZ4UWX6
EEFYZRNW7ZOA3JSCYZ5OY7CTQELUZE
[250734] 2024/10/03 13:14:52.857510 [INF] Listening for client connections on 0.
0.0.0:4222
[250734] 2024/10/03 13:14:52.857744 [INF] Server is ready
```

Figure 3-3. NATS server running

If everything has been installed correctly, you will see something similar to Figure 3-3.

You are now ready to use your NATS server, but before seeing how to send a message to it, we will need to see some other options to run the server.

3.3.2 Docker

Running a NATS server inside Docker is very easy; if you don't know what Docker is, it is a platform that allows developers to package applications and their dependencies into lightweight, portable containers. These containers can run consistently across different computing environments, ensuring that software behaves the same regardless of where it's deployed—on a developer's machine, a testing server, or in production. Docker

CHAPTER 3 NATS FUNDAMENTALS

simplifies the deployment process by using containers and making it easier to scale applications. This ensures better collaboration between teams and reduces the "it works on my machine" problem commonly faced in software development, as no matter what OS or hardware your machine is running, Docker will provide a reliable, specific way of running software.

You can learn more about Docker at its official home page: https://www.docker.com/.

We will assume now that you are confident with Docker, at least enough to run a simple command like

```
sudo docker run -p 4444:4444 nats -p 4444
```

Which will pull, if you still need to pull it, the NATS server Docker image and then run the server. You will see something like in Figure 3-4 if everything is done correctly.

```
Unable to find image 'nats:latest' locally
latest: Pulling from library/nats
f61b3ff756de: Pull complete
5b7a1bc5b621: Pull complete
Digest: sha256:a0ba454c4751168a975396a4bb3d846506ca574658d9cbddbbf2d3ca7d2a0b2a
Status: Downloaded newer image for nats:latest
[1] 2024/10/03 10:20:00.721614 [INF] Starting nats-server
[1] 2024/10/03 10:20:00.721729 [INF]   Version:  2.10.21
[1] 2024/10/03 10:20:00.721731 [INF]   Git:      [d3a8868]
[1] 2024/10/03 10:20:00.721733 [INF]   Name:     NCUA375LFFKIRE72FXJ3E5FGPW2Q6ONOKTIHJ3TWYNZWGPZQKVWQ7MIR
[1] 2024/10/03 10:20:00.721739 [INF]   ID:       NCUA375LFFKIRE72FXJ3E5FGPW2Q6ONOKTIHJ3TWYNZWGPZQKVWQ7MIR
[1] 2024/10/03 10:20:00.722344 [INF] Listening for client connections on 0.0.0.0:4444
[1] 2024/10/03 10:20:00.722510 [INF] Server is ready
```

Figure 3-4. *NATS server running*

This is a good option if you are confident with Docker or want to become confident. If you are working with other people or you need to run a complex software architecture, it can be good not just to run a NATS-server installation but to use Docker. If you are working alone, the NATS-server installation is still the most straightforward option. If you are working on a big project, though, we will now see the most reliable solution.

3.3.3 Kubernetes

If Docker provides a way to run software in an expected environment, when a project is very complex, we need a way to manage all the different applications that are part of the system. An orchestrator is usually used, which allows us to define what applications compose a system, what versions of each application to use, how they communicate, and much more. Docker provides us with its orchestrator, Docker Swarm, but the industry standard and most used software is Kubernetes. We will not dig into how Kubernetes works in this paragraph or chapter, but we suggest looking at `https://kubernetes.io/`, which is the official page for the project. There are many possible ways to install Kubernetes on your machine; we recommend, as the most developer-friendly option, Minikube, which we will use in the following parts of this book when orchestration becomes more critical. You can find all the information about Minikube at `https://minikube.sigs.k8s.io/docs/`.

If you already know how Kubernetes works, here is a partial YAML file that shows you how to deploy NATS inside a Kubernetes cluster. If you are not confident with Kubernetes yet, we will see later how to use it in more detail, plus you will be able to download a fully working version of the NATS template from the linked GitHub profile.

```yaml
apiVersion: apps/v1
kind: Deployment
metadata:
  labels:
    app: nats
    name: nats
  name: nats
spec:
  replicas: 1
  revisionHistoryLimit: 4
  selector:
    matchLabels:
      name: nats
  strategy:
    rollingUpdate:
      maxSurge: 25%
      maxUnavailable: 25%
    type: RollingUpdate
```

```yaml
template:
  metadata:
    labels:
      name: nats
  spec:
    containers:
      - name: nats
        image: nats:2.8.4-alpine
        ports:
          - containerPort: 4222
            name: client
            hostPort: 4222
          - containerPort: 7422
            name: leafnodes
            hostPort: 7422
          - containerPort: 6222
            name: cluster
          - containerPort: 8222
            name: monitor
          - containerPort: 7777
            name: metrics
        command:
          - "nats-server"
        env:
          - name: CLUSTER_ADVERTISE
            value: nats.default.svc.cluster.local
        resources:
          limits:
            cpu: "0.5"
            memory: "200M"
          requests:
            cpu: "0.2"
            memory: "100M"

    dnsPolicy: ClusterFirst

    restartPolicy: Always
```

With this YAML file, we run a simple NATS server inside a Kubernetes cluster.

If you have installed Minikube, you can run:

```
minikube start --cpus='2' --memory='2g' --kubernetes-version='1.25.3' -p nats-test
```

and this will create a minimal Kubernetes cluster using a profile called NATS-test. Profiles are available in Minikube, which allows us to create as many clusters as we want so we can work on several projects on the same machine.

If you then save the YAML file above as **nats-deployment.yml** and you run:

```
kubectl apply -f nats-deployment.yml
```

You will be able to see the NATS server running. We leave it to you to experiment with Kubernetes, but as said earlier, we will expand on orchestration and Minikube when needed. For now, the easiest way to carry on with this chapter is to use the native installers and run the NATS server like this.

3.3.4 NATS CLI

We will use NATS to build our applications, but before that, we will experiment in a different, more immediate way. The NATS project provides a command-line tool for sending and receiving messages via the NATS server. The command-line tool is called NATS-CLI, and it can be downloaded from

https://github.com/nats-io/natscli/releases/tag/v0.1.5

Again, you can choose the package that most suits your environment, for example:

```
nats-0.1.5-amd64.deb
```

which is the 64-bit application for Debian-based systems based on a common Intel/AMD architecture.

Once installed, the application can be used to send and receive messages if you have the NATS server running. By default, the NATS-CLI application will expect the NATS server to run on port 4222, so if you are running the server via the native app and you do not provide any specific configuration, everything will work out of the box.

If you open two terminals on your machine, you can write in one:

```
nats sub test1
```

and in the other, you can type

`nats pub test1 "hello"`

The result should be like Figure 3-5, which means you sent a message from one terminal and received it in the other.

```
ddanna@ddanna-Inspiron-5515:~$ nats sub test1      ddanna@ddanna-Inspiron-5515:~$ nats pub test1 "hello"
16:15:23 Subscribing on test1                      16:15:25 Published 5 bytes to "test1"
[#1] Received on "test1"                           ddanna@ddanna-Inspiron-5515:~$
hello
```

Figure 3-5. *Interacting with NATS*

You can guess what's happening by reading these simple commands, but in the next few paragraphs, we will explore all the topologies further so that we can make a parallel with what we've seen using mangos.

Bear in mind that NATS is a very complete tool that allows you to change many configurations. You can add passwords, change ports, and much more. We will not touch this here, so we advise you to read the official documentation if you are interested in administering a NATS cluster. In these examples, we will assume a very simple setup, running with default options for the server and CLI in a private machine.

You are now all set to learn how to use NATS and create all the topologies you need.

3.4 NATS Core
3.4.1 Command Line

NATS is software that includes many functionalities, but everything is built around a set of core functionalities, which are the subject of this chapter. The key concept in NATS is one of the **subjects**. From what we've learned using mangos, the concept of topic is exactly the same thing that NATS calls a subject. NATS is, first of all, a pub/sub streaming server, which means its core functionality is to receive messages and distribute them to whoever is interested in them. To register an interest in receiving specific messages, we use subjects. You've seen this in the previous paragraph, but let's see it again:

`nats sub test1`

CHAPTER 3   NATS FUNDAMENTALS

This command tells the NATS server that the client, which in this case is the NATS CLI, is interested in receiving all the messages belonging to the **test1** category. The category **test1** is the actual subject. We do not need to define subjects in advance; expressing an interest in something called **test1** is enough for NATS to create the subject and make it available.

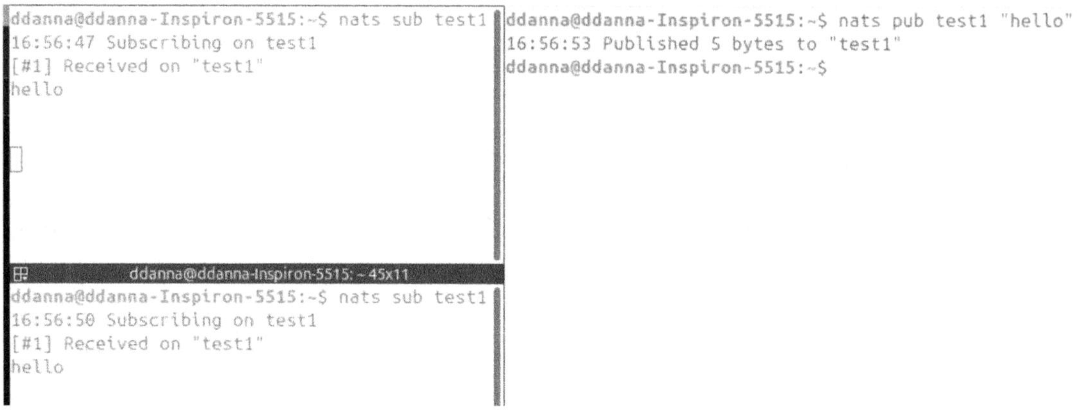

```
ddanna@ddanna-Inspiron-5515:~$ nats sub test1      ddanna@ddanna-Inspiron-5515:~$ nats pub test1 "hello"
16:56:47 Subscribing on test1                      16:56:53 Published 5 bytes to "test1"
[#1] Received on "test1"                           ddanna@ddanna-Inspiron-5515:~$
hello




              ddanna@ddanna-Inspiron-5515: ~ 45x11
ddanna@ddanna-Inspiron-5515:~$ nats sub test1
16:56:50 Subscribing on test1
[#1] Received on "test1"
hello
```

Figure 3-6. *Two subscribers*

Registering an interest in a subject defines the client that registers that interest as a subscriber, and this is what the **sub** part of the command line command means: we are subscribing to the subject called **test1**. In Figure 3-6, we have two subscribers to the same subject, and whenever we send a message that belongs to that subject, all the subscribers will receive it.

If two clients subscribe to different subjects, they will only receive messages belonging to the subject they subscribe to.

```
ddanna@ddanna-Inspiron-5515:~$ nats sub test1      ddanna@ddanna-Inspiron-5515:~$ nats pub test1 "hello"
17:01:52 Subscribing on test1                      17:02:00 Published 5 bytes to "test1"
[#1] Received on "test1"                           ddanna@ddanna-Inspiron-5515:~$ nats pub test2 "hello"
hello                                              17:02:03 Published 5 bytes to "test2"
                                                   ddanna@ddanna-Inspiron-5515:~$




              ddanna@ddanna-Inspiron-5515: ~ 45x11
ddanna@ddanna-Inspiron-5515:~$ nats sub test2
17:01:55 Subscribing on test2
[#1] Received on "test2"
hello
```

Figure 3-7. *Subscribers on different subjects*

CHAPTER 3 NATS FUNDAMENTALS

This is clearly visible in Figure 3-7, where the subscribers subscribe to the two different subjects, **test1** and **test2**.

Subscribing to multiple subjects is impossible, but there is a way to achieve something similar with wildcards. Let's consider the subject **test1.a**; it is a subject made of two parts, which create a hierarchy where **test1** comes on top of **a**. We can capture every subject like **test.1**, **test.2**, **test.a**, and **test.b** using the wildcard *.

Figure 3-8. *Wildcard* *

We can see from Figure 3-8 that the subscriber captured all the subjects of form **test1.X,** where there is only one dot and one character, but not the subject with two dots. This is how the * wildcard works; if we want to capture more than one level in the hierarchy, we need to use the wildcard >.

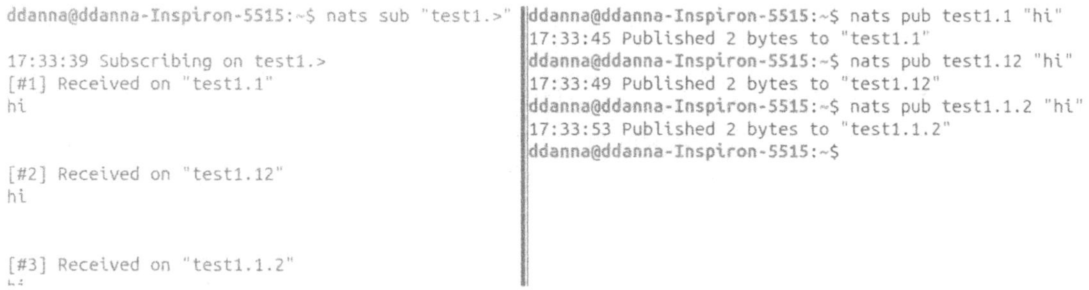

Figure 3-9. *Wildcard >*

95

CHAPTER 3 NATS FUNDAMENTALS

As seen in Figure 3-9, we can now capture more than one level after the first dot. However, test1.12 can be captured by the simple wildcard *, and there is no need to use > because there is no dot separation between 1 and 2.

If the messages are categorized into subjects and the subscribers are those who express an interest in a subject, we still need to discuss who sends these messages.

In the previous images, the messages are sent via a command:

```
nats pub test1 "hello"
```

The NATS command-line app includes the **pub** command, which sends a message. The format of this command is **nats pub subject message**, as it's pretty clear from the previous examples.

With all we have learned so far, we can send messages and register an interest in receiving them; we can play with subjects to organize our subscribers better. What we need to realize, however, is that this messaging is all in a fire-and-forget fashion. If you see the previous images, like Figure 3-9 or 3-8, we did not specify the order in which we ran the commands, but following along the conversation, it was clear that we first subscribed to a subject and then published a message. Let's see what would happen if we were doing the opposite. Let's try to send a few messages and then subscribe to the subject.

```
ddanna@ddanna-Inspiron-5515:~$ nats sub "test1"      ddanna@ddanna-Inspiron-5515:~$ nats pub test1 "hi"
12:52:55 Subscribing on test1                        12:52:38 Published 2 bytes to "test1"
                                                     ddanna@ddanna-Inspiron-5515:~$ nats pub test1 "there"
                                                     12:52:43 Published 5 bytes to "test1"
                                                     ddanna@ddanna-Inspiron-5515:~$ nats pub test1 "hello"
                                                     12:52:48 Published 5 bytes to "test1"
                                                     ddanna@ddanna-Inspiron-5515:~$
```

Figure 3-10. *Publishing before subscribing*

As you can see in Figure 3-10, if we start publishing messages and then subscribe to a subject, we won't receive these messages because no subscriber registered any interest in the subject at the time they were sent. However, this does not mean we will never receive any message from that subject.

```
ddanna@ddanna-Inspiron-5515:~$ nats sub "test1"      ddanna@ddanna-Inspiron-5515:~$ nats pub test1 "hi"
12:52:55 Subscribing on test1                        12:52:38 Published 2 bytes to "test1"
[#1] Received on "test1"                             ddanna@ddanna-Inspiron-5515:~$ nats pub test1 "there"
how are you?                                         12:52:43 Published 5 bytes to "test1"
                                                     ddanna@ddanna-Inspiron-5515:~$ nats pub test1 "hello"
                                                     12:52:48 Published 5 bytes to "test1"
                                                     ddanna@ddanna-Inspiron-5515:~$ nats pub test1 "how are you?"
                                                     12:56:00 Published 12 bytes to "test1"
                                                     ddanna@ddanna-Inspiron-5515:~$
```

Figure 3-11. *Receiving new messages*

As you can see in Figure 3-11, this is what happens after we subscribe to the **test1** subject in the previous scenario (Figure 3-10): the message "How are you?" sent after the subscriber was started gets received.

The behavior just explained might seem awkward because we think of a message as something that will be delivered, much like what happens when we use WhatsApp or similar tools. The perspective changes if we think of an HTTP request instead: We would never expect an HTTP request to an unavailable server to be received when the server goes up again. We just cope with the fact that we received a 500 error and try again later.

We need to understand that this messaging system acts like sending a letter; if the receiver is not at home, the letter will be discarded. You can think of whatever application of this approach. One that comes to mind easily is a logging system; we need to gather a lot of inputs quickly, and missing a few is not a big problem; we send messages, and only when the logger is down might we lose some logs. We will see better applications of this approach later in this book when talking about reactivity and reactive systems, and we will also see how to persist messages and not lose them. What we care for now, however, is mastering the core functionalities of NATS so that we can put them into use for our systems.

3.4.2 Go SDK

The NATS CLI is a quick way to experiment with NATS and test its functionality. We will most likely build apps that need to receive messages, and the CLI is a great way to send these messages manually. However, we will not build a whole system using the CLI; we will program in our favorite language, so we will need an SDK to interact with the NATS server. We will explore the Go SDK, which is also the language in which NATS is written, and we will build a few applications to receive and send messages.

The Go SDK for NTAS can be found at https://github.com/nats-io/nats.go, and to install it, we will need to do the following:

```
go get github.com/nats-io/nats.go/
```

We highly suggest doing this in a new folder after initiating a new go module:

```
go mod init test1
```

CHAPTER 3   NATS FUNDAMENTALS

The SDK will be added to the module, making it available for use. Let's have a look now at a simple program that prints out the received message:

```go
package main

import (
    "fmt"
    "github.com/nats-io/nats.go"
    "log"
    "time"
)

func main() {
    // Connect to a server
    nc, err := nats.Connect(nats.DefaultURL)
    if err != nil {
        log.Fatal(err)
    }

    // Simple Async Subscriber
    nc.Subscribe("test1", func(m *nats.Msg) {
        fmt.Printf("Received a message: %s\n", string(m.Data))
    })

    for {
        time.Sleep(time.Second)
    }
}
```

You can save this file as **main.go** in the project's folder and then build and run it.

The code above expects you to have an instance of the NATS server running on the default port. If you are running it on a different port, you should change the line:

```go
nc, err := nats.Connect(nats.DefaultURL)
```

With the URL of the NATS server, you are running or connecting to.

In order to subscribe to a subject, we can use an async subscriber function:

```go
// Simple Async Subscriber
nc.Subscribe("test1", func(m *nats.Msg) {
    fmt.Printf("Received a message: %s\n", string(m.Data))
})
```

Which needs a subject as the first parameter and a callback function as the second parameter.

At the end of the program, we run an infinite loop so that the execution continues indefinitely and the program is always active and listening to messages.

We might prefer to use a synchronous approach, so we can use the function **SubscribeSync** to achieve that. Here is the code for this option:

```go
package main

import (
    "fmt"
    "github.com/nats-io/nats.go"
    "log"
    "time"
)

func main() {
    // Connect to a server
    nc, err := nats.Connect(nats.DefaultURL)
    if err != nil {
        log.Fatal(err)
    }

    for {
        sub, err := nc.SubscribeSync("test1")
        if err != nil {
            log.Println(err)
        }
        m, err := sub.NextMsg(time.Second)
```

```
        if err != nil {
            if !errors.Is(err, nats.ErrTimeout) {
                log.Println(err)
            }
            continue
        }
        fmt.Printf("Received a message: %s\n", string(m.Data))
    }
}
```

In this case, the **SybscribeSync** function returns a subscriber struct, which we can use to get each message iteratively:

```
sub, err := nc.SubscribeSync("test1")
```

And then:

```
m, err := sub.NextMsg(time.Second)
```

Finally, we can use the retrieved message and display it:

```
fmt.Printf("Received a message: %s\n", string(m.Data))
```

The rest of the code has some error handling, and the message retrieval is inside a loop, which pauses the execution while the function tries to retrieve a message. Notice that:

```
m, err := sub.NextMsg(time.Second)
```

Includes a timeout value, here set to one second, which is used to retry to get a message. If a message does not arrive in one second, an error is thrown; hence, we would have the screen full of messages if we were not sending one message per second. This is why inside the error handling, there is this code block:

```
if !errors.Is(err, nats.ErrTimeout) {
    log.Println(err)
}
```

We exclude the timeout from the errors that get printed. We still run the **continue** instruction; otherwise, we would go to the next line, where the message would be nil, throwing a panic.

```
c.iUci/u0yiic/muin.yu nyuoctup
/home/ddanna/.cache/JetBrains/GoLand2024.3/tmp/GoLand/___go_build_main_go
Received a message: how are you?
⊓
```

Figure 3-12. Running a subscriber

The two functions used in the previous examples, **Subscribe** and **SubscribeSync**, are the most commonly used. There is another one, **SubscribeChan**, which uses channels to cast messages. We leave it to you to try it out.

In the snippets above, we avoided adding something that is very important to add to your programs when using NATS.

```
// Unsubscribe
defer sub.Unsubscribe()
// Drain
defer sub.Drain()
```

or

```
// Unsubscribe
defer nc.Unsubscribe()

// Drain
defer nc.Drain()
```

These make sure that there is a graceful shutdown when the program is terminated.

Unsubscribe ensures there is no hanging subscriber in the NTAS server (which tracks all the existing subscribers), while **Drain** ensures nobody will try to send messages to an application that no longer exists.

In Figure 3-12, we can see a running application that exposes a subscriber and receives a message. This will work for both async and sync versions, and to test it we can simply publish a message with the following:

```
nats pub test1 "hello"
```

Using the NATS CLI.

If we need to build an application, we will mainly use subscribers, as we need to act upon messages. When we are building it as a distributed system, however, there is a chance a component will send messages that have to be captured by other components (see Figure 3-13).

CHAPTER 3 NATS FUNDAMENTALS

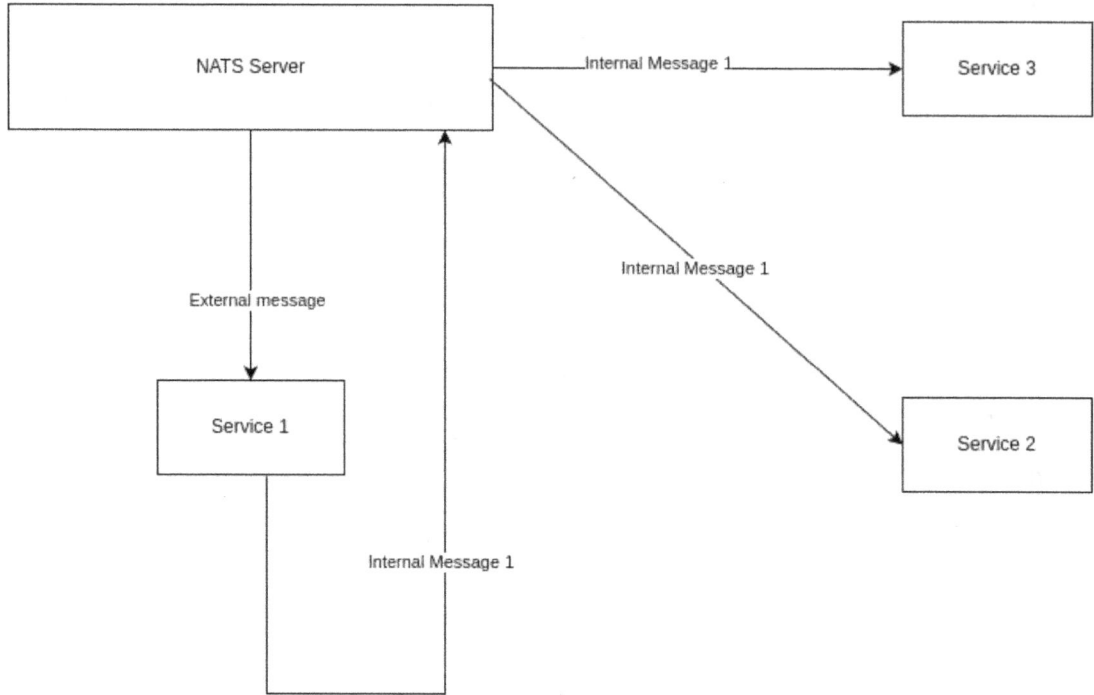

Figure 3-13. *Internal communication*

This situation can happen in multiple cases: a bank transaction needs to result in several parts of the system creating records. Each part of the system is a different application that works when receiving a message. An example of this scenario is shown in Figure 3-13, where a message comes from an external source, the user. After **Service 1** has done its job, it publishes a new message, which gets captured by both the remaining services.

To send a message via the Go SDK, all you need is:

```
nc.Publish("foo", []byte("Hello World"))
```

where **nc** is the variable representing the NATS connection. The function **Publish** expects two parameters: the subject and the message.

With this, we have covered everything we need to start being productive with NATS and can already start building meaningful applications.

3.5 Core Topologies
3.5.1 Pub/Sub

We've seen what a Pub/Sub topology is already in Chapter 2, "Distributed Communication Basics," and even if we haven't mentioned it explicitly, the whole chapter, till now, has used this topology.

When we used:

```
nats pub test1 "hello"
```

or the equivalent code, we were publishing a message, and when we used **nats sub test1,** we were subscribing to a subject, so the mix of **pub** and **sub** instructions effectively defined a pub/sub topology.

This scenario is the original scope for which NATS was created and how it was built from the beginning. It would be silly to think that the project had stopped at this, but the core functioning way of NATS is that it is able to publish messages and to subscribe to subjects; every other feature has been built on top of this.

The project has, in fact, expanded into many very interesting features, but everything is built on top of this original configuration: a pub/sub streaming server.

One important consideration is that this core functionality has some limitations, one of which is the size of the message. There is not much to worry about unless you plan to send a whole video as a message. Still, if you keep your messages to the point and only share what you need between publishers and subscribers, in most cases, you will find that the few megabytes limit is way more than what you need. In most cases, you will find yourself sending small JSON objects with notifications and information that your services need to share with each other.

3.5.2 Queue Groups (Push/Pull)

From what we've seen so far, a push/pull topology cannot be achieved unless we use only one publisher and one subscriber. Fortunately, we can achieve exactly this topology by using another core functionality provided by NATS: queue groups. A queue group is a way to group several subscribers so that instead of all the subscribers receiving a message, only one will. The subscriber receiving a message is taken at random, but this happens for each message a publisher will send. This means that if a publisher sends ten messages to a specific subject, all the subscribers who registered interest in that subject

CHAPTER 3   NATS FUNDAMENTALS

are potential receivers. Still, each delivery of the ten messages will only happen to one of the random subscribers in the same group. Effectively, a queue group is a way to load-balance the messages across the subscribers in the group.

If we are using the CLI, here is how we can define a queue group.

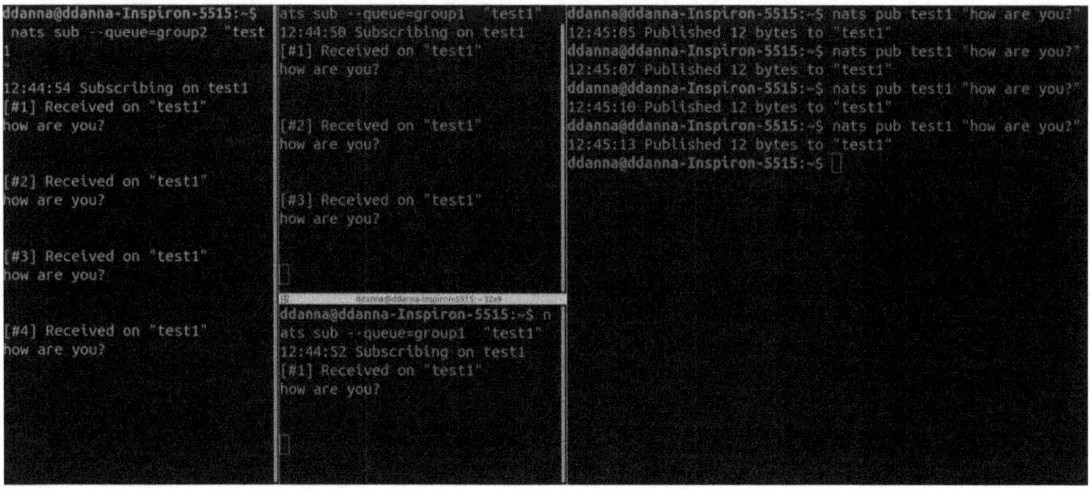

Figure 3-14. Queue groups on CLI

The command to use is

nats sub --queue=group1 "test1"

where the name of the queue could be any string, this will ensure that the subscription is part of the specified group and that the messages are load-balanced across the same group. In Figure 3-14, we have two subscribers belonging to **group1** and one subscriber belonging to **group2**. In the image, we see that four messages are sent, and while the lone subscriber receives all the messages for the topic **test1**, three messages go to one of the **group1** subscribers and one to the other subscriber in the same group. You might have expected the messages to be distributed equally across the two subscribers, but that is not the case. If you were to send hundreds of messages, you would see that the split across the two subscribers would be approaching fifty percent, but that is not strict. The subscriber gets chosen randomly, and simple probability will expect an almost equal distribution across the subscribers.

As you can see, the queue groups allow us to achieve a push/pull topology exactly like we did with mangos. You should not be surprised if you come across a tool that uses a different approach to achieve this topology. While what we've learned through mangos is the approach most similar to the theory, each tool tries to achieve things based on its architecture. NATS is a pub/sub server. Queue groups are used to group the subscribers; no pull socket can be defined.

We've seen how to define queue groups with the CLI; let's now see how to do that with the Go SDK.

We've seen earlier the two functions **Subscribe** and **SubscribeSync**; the SDK provides us with two more functions, **QueueSubscribe** and **QueueSubscribeSync**, which can be used exactly like the previous two. The difference is simply that they will both expect the queue group as the second parameter. Let's see how we modified the code of the original scripts:

```go
package main
................................
for {
        sub, err := nc.QueueSubscribeSync("test1", os.Getenv("QUEUE_GROUP"))
        if err != nil {
            log.Println(err)
        }
        m, err := sub.NextMsg(time.Second)
        if err != nil {
            if !errors.Is(err, nats.ErrTimeout) {
                log.Println(err)
            }
            continue
        }
        fmt.Printf("Received a message: %s\n", string(m.Data))
    }
................................................
```

So, we inject the queue group from an environmental variable. For what concerns the async version, we act similarly:

```go
package main
................................
 // Simple Async Subscriber
```

CHAPTER 3 NATS FUNDAMENTALS

```
nc.QueueSubscribe("test1", os.Getenv("QUEUE_GROUP"),
func(m *nats.Msg) {
    fmt.Printf("Received a message: %s\n", string(m.Data))
})
```

So it is just as simple as that, and our system will be able to work with scalability in mind.

Let's now expand a bit on the scalability issue. When building a distributed system, we create a set of interconnected smaller applications, and we assume that they communicate via messaging.

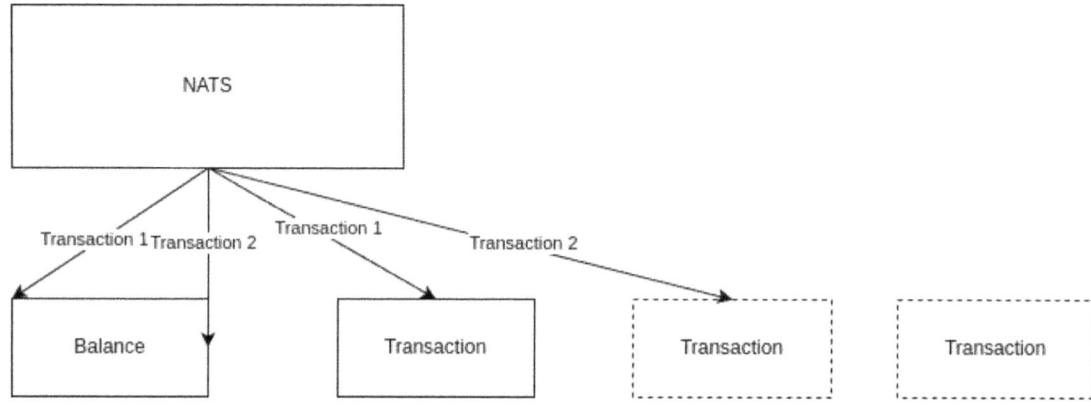

Figure 3-15. *Scaling components*

Let's assume we have developed a banking application, and we have one component that stores an account's balance and one that stores every transaction happening in the account. These two components might be one in a real scenario, but let's now focus on this setup. Let's assume the Transaction component is using almost all its allocated resources, and we will need to replicate it, which means adding more instances of it. The Balance component is healthy and needs no replication. This situation is shown in Figure 3-15, where dotted boxes represent two new instances of the Transaction component. Every time there is a new transaction, a message gets broadcast, and the Transaction component will record the transaction, while the balance component will increase or reduce the balance. If we were not using a queue group, we would store the transaction three times. Using a queue group, all instances, or replicas, of the transaction component will receive different messages, and there won't be duplicate transactions.

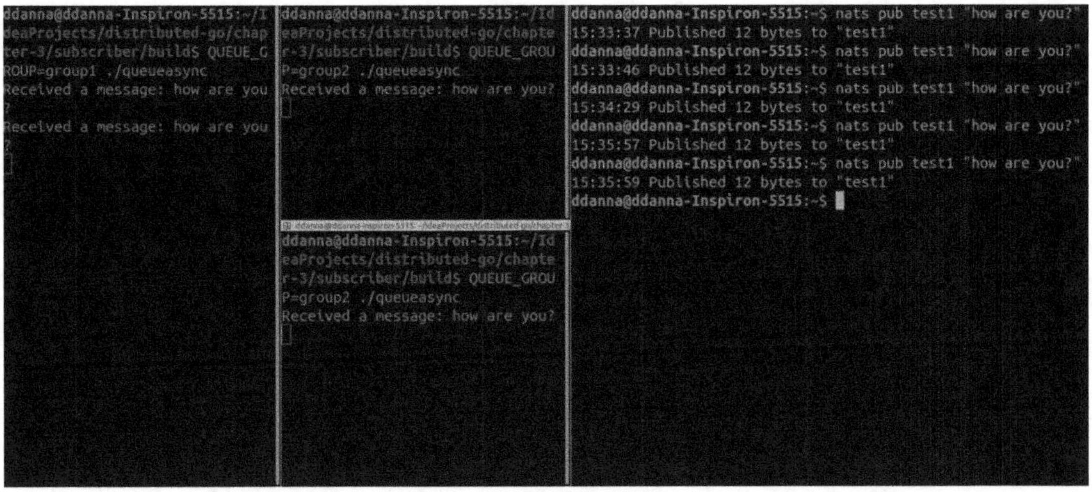

Figure 3-16. Queue groups in the banking app

We can run the applications after we build them in any of the two versions, async or sync, with the queue groups and see that they work exactly like when we used the CLI. Figure 3-16 shows the async version running on a Linux system; the queue groups are passed as environmental variables before calling the built application. In the image, the executable is called **queueasync** and works as expected; the single instance belonging to **group1** receives all the messages, while the two instances with subscribers belonging to **group2** receive one message each.

3.5.3 Req/Rep (Base for Services)

If an ideal system works with asynchronous distributed messages, we need to acknowledge that a user might want to ask something of the system that we are building, and it wants a response. You see this every day when browsing the internet. When you click a link or type a URL, you are actually making a request and then waiting for a reply, which is the page loaded. The same thing happens when you submit a form.

You might have understood that NATS, under the hood, will always use pub/sub and maybe queue groups, but it provides us with a different set of commands and functions to handle this case. In simple terms, it implements a way to make us build a req/rep topology.

As always, we will start with the CLI:

```
nats req test1 "hello"
```

CHAPTER 3 NATS FUNDAMENTALS

This command will say "hello" to whoever is ready to respond to a message delivered to test1. If you run this command now, you will receive a message like in Figure 3-17.

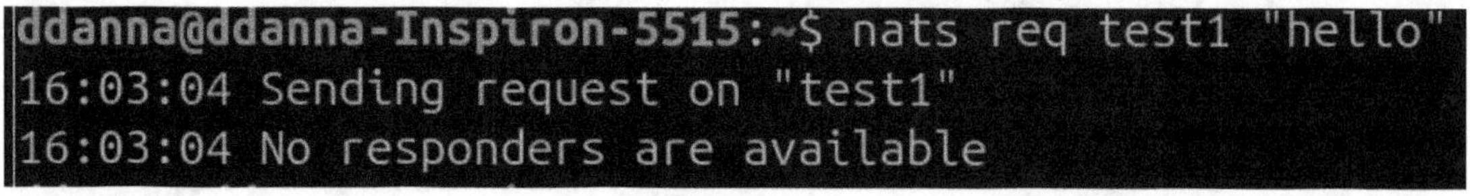

```
ddanna@ddanna-Inspiron-5515:~$ nats req test1 "hello"
16:03:04 Sending request on "test1"
16:03:04 No responders are available
```

Figure 3-17. *No responders available*

The req command needs responders to exist, or the NATS server will notify it that it has no point in asking something, as no responder is available.

To create a responder, which has to be created before asking anything, we use:

`nats reply test1`

We can see what happens when running these commands in a terminal in Figure 3-18.

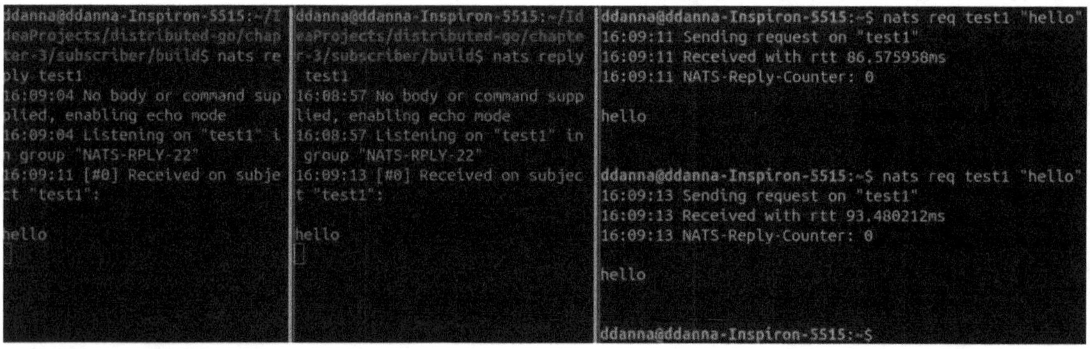

Figure 3-18. *Multiple responders*

We have two responders, and both reply with the same message that they received. Before thinking about the fact that the response, in this case, is just a dumb response, let's focus on the fact that the messages were load-balanced across the responders. We did not define any queue group, but if you see the image well, after running the responder, we get the message:

`16:08:57 Listening on "test1" in group "NATS-RPLY-22"`

This means that NATS automatically created a queue group called **NATS-RPLY-22**, which is used to reply to messages. You could specify a queue group by yourself, but trying to instantiate two responders with different groups on the same subject will result in an error. We must remind you again that the system is also using a pub/sub implementation with queue groups to build the req/rep functionality. The NATS server will ensure consistency and enable a replier to receive only one response. If we allowed multiple responders for a message, we would be in an erroneous state because the responder would only expect one response.

Let's now notice something else in Figure 3-18, which is the message:

`16:08:57 No body or command supplied, enabling echo mode`

The echo mode simply responds with what it just received, which is good for tests but not much in practice. The message hints that there are **body** and **command** options, which might help manipulate the request to send a more meaningful response. Using the command:

`nats reply test1 "thanks"`

We will always reply with thanks to any request, and the "thanks" is the body mentioned above. This is one step toward a more helpful responder but still insufficient.

An option that we have is to use the **–command** flag, which we can use, for example, to echo something we need:

`nats reply test1 -command="echo Thanks for: {{.Request}}"`

This will respond with "Thanks for:" followed by whatever you have sent. In reality, we do not need to use the command in this case because we can just use the **Request** object inside the normal echo response:

`nats reply test1 "Thanks for: {{.Request}}"`

The response string can be used as any Go template, and there are several variables available for you to use inside the template. Running the command:

`nats reply -help`

This will result in thorough documentation for the command **reply,** which includes the following information:

Count	the message number
TimeStamp	RFC3339 format current time
Unix	seconds since 1970 in UTC
UnixNano	nanoseconds since 1970 in UTC
Time	the current time
ID	an unique ID
Request	the request payload
Random(min, max)	random string at least min long, at most max

You can also use any shell command inside your response via the **-command** flag, but you are allowed to use only one command.

Consider now the following reply definition:

```
nats reply test1 "Received {{.Request}} at {{.Time}}, This is the request number {{.Count}} with ID: {{.ID}}, thanks for that"
```

This will notify you that a message with a specific body has been received at a specific time. The request is the n-th request, and it has an internal NATS ID, which is also sent back.

A typical response when requesting "hello" from this replier could be:

```
09:26:27 Sending request on "test1"
09:26:27 Received with rtt 87.148275ms
Received hello at 9:26AM, This is the request number 0 with ID: 5hVHV3TwOOh5MDbYzglou5, thanks for that
```

This starts to be interesting, but unless we are performing some administration or trying to find some bugs, we won't get very far if we don't use the actual SDK and build a service around it.

The Go SDK offers us the following functions: **NC.Request** and **nc.Publish.** For now, we will assume that requests will be sent via CLI, so let's create a script that replies to a request. We will base it on the simple async subscriber. Here is the code for the new version:

```go
package main

import (
    "fmt"
    "github.com/nats-io/nats.go"
    "log"
    "time"
)
func main() {
    // Connect to a server
    nc, err := nats.Connect(nats.DefaultURL)
    if err != nil {
        log.Fatal(err)
    }

    // Simple Async Subscriber
    nc.Subscribe("test1", func(m *nats.Msg) {
        nc.Publish(m.Reply, []byte("Thanks for your message"))
    })
    for {
        time.Sleep(time.Second)
    }
}
```

The code has only one line that is different; inside the **Subscribe's** callback, instead of just printing the received message, we do the following:

```go
nc.Publish(m.Reply, []byte("Thanks for your message"))
```

This instruction will publish a message but will use a topic different from **test1**, which was the topic we subscribed to. The new topic is accessed via **m.Reply**, this is an ephemeral topic created to track the requester so that there will be only one receiver

CHAPTER 3   NATS FUNDAMENTALS

for the reply. This might seem like overkill, but if the publisher is a software component scaled to more than one instance, and all instances were sharing a topic, we wouldn't know which instance sent the request and hence has to receive the response.

We will see later in this book how to create systems without the req/rep topology, but for now, this is the most basic usage in most applications, so we will continue to investigate this protocol.

Imagine we want to create a remote application that does sums—a very basic educational application. We send a request to sum some numbers, and the responder returns the sum.

First, we need to find a way to send the numbers. We will use a comma-separated list of numbers.

The code will be exactly like the last code snippet we've seen, but we will change, again, the callback.

```go
nc.Subscribe("test1", func(m *nats.Msg) {
    d := string(m.Data)
    ss := strings.Split(d, ",")
    sum := 0.0
    for _, s := range ss {
    i, err := strconv.ParseFloat(s, 32)
    if err != nil {
        nc.Publish(m.Reply, []byte("Please only numbers in comma separated list"))
        return
    }
    sum += i
    }
    err := nc.Publish(m.Reply, []byte(fmt.Sprintf("%f", sum)))
    if err != nil {
    log.Fatal(err)
    }
})
```

The instruction:

```
d := string(m.Data)
```

Gets the body of the message and transforms it from bytes to a string. The following instruction:

```
ss := strings.Split(d, ",")
```

Splits the string into chunks, based on the character ",". After that, we just instantiate a 0.0 sum and loop over the strings slice. Each string must be cast into a floating number, and we do it using the **strconv** package from the standard library:

```
i, err := strconv.ParseFloat(s, 32)
```

We chose a 32-bit float; we could use a 64 if we wanted, but we assume small numbers. If the string is not a number, we respond with an error.

We add the current number to the sum and finally send it back using the **publish** method.

Let's now build a command-line app that will accept any number of parameters and send the received parameters as a comma-separated list to the previously created responder. The idea is that we can just use this command-line app to request sums from the responder, using NATS as an internal messaging tool. Here is the simple script:

```go
package main
import (
        "fmt"
        "github.com/nats-io/nats.go"
        "log"
        "os"
        "strings"
        "time"
)
func main() {
        // Connect to a server
        nc, err := nats.Connect(nats.DefaultURL)
        if err != nil {
                log.Fatal(err)
        }
```

```
    numbers := strings.Join(os.Args[1:], ",")
    m, err := nc.Request("test1", []byte(numbers), 1*time.Second)
    fmt.Println(string(m.Data))
}
```

Apart from all the boilerplate code and the connection to NATS, we grab the command line parameters, excluding the first one, which is the program's invocation. We join them into a comma-separated list, and then we send the list via NATS using the **Request** function. The call, with a timeout of one second, will give us back the sum or an error message.

Let's note a couple of things:

1. We have not fully handled all the error messages; we leave that to you.

2. The error returned by the **Request** method is a NATS error. It has nothing to do with your application logic and application errors. You will need to define your errors and the way to send them.

Regarding point number 2, let's mention another way to publish a message. The function **Publish** only allows you to set the subject and a slice of bytes, but there is a way to send a more meaningful message via the function **PublishMsg**.

Let's see how we can change the case when we handle the wrong parameters sent in the responder:

```
if err != nil {
msg := &nats.Msg{
    Subject: m.Reply,
    Header:  nats.Header{},
    Data:    []byte("Please only numbers in comma separated list"),
}
msg.Header.Add("Error", "Wrong parameters")
err := nc.PublishMsg(msg)
if err != nil {
    log.Println(err)
}
return
}
```

Let's see how to use this header now; we will change the command line application to ask for a sum, using this code:

```
package main
.............................
func main() {
.............................
    m, err := nc.Request("test1", []byte(numbers), 1*time.Second)
    if err != nil {
    log.Fatal(err)
    }
    herr := m.Header.Get("Error")
    if herr != "" {
        log.Println(herr)
    }

    fmt.Println(string(m.Data))
}
```

We added some error handling after the **nc.Request** call to make sure we have a message object and not only a **nil** value. Before printing the data, we perform a header check and print the header.

In this example, we are just printing the details, so from a functional perspective, we did not change much. However, being able to discriminate a response, which is a number or an error, might be very important. Our app asks a server for a sum, but another app might need to act on the received response, and if it is not a sum but an error, it must do something other than its normal flow. Using headers is a good option. We might simply return a number or something with a specific format like "Error:". We could just match this string; however, it is much safer and simpler to check if there is an actual error and, if there is, to act upon it. A specific header could be a good way to transmit application logic errors, and we could create a format in, say, JSON with a set of known codes.

3.5.4 More Complex Topologies

With all we have learned, it must be easy to understand how to create more complex topologies.

We can see again a topology with Pub/Sub and then Push/Pull in Figure 3-19, where three messages arrive. Two components, with replications two and three, receive all the messages, but these are load-balanced across the replicas of each component.

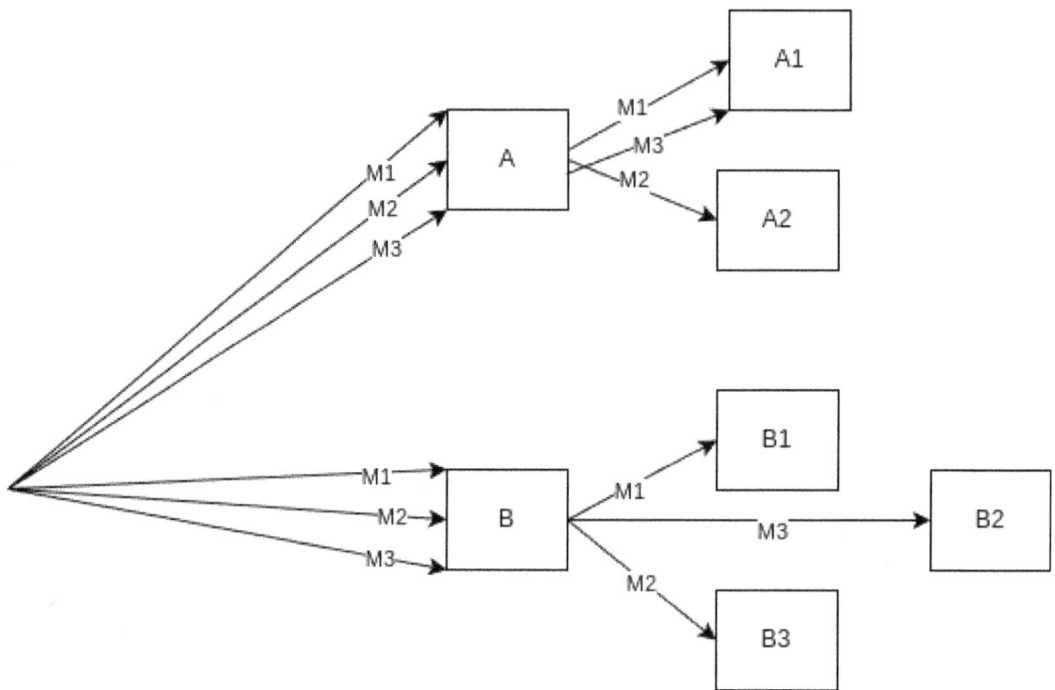

Figure 3-19. *Push/Pull*

When using mangos, achieving this topology meant using a mix of sub, push, and pull sockets, and we can see this exactly in Figure 3-19. With NATS, the situation is much simpler; we've actually seen this already; we can just use queue groups. NATS is, by default, a pub/sub server, so defining five subscribers, where two belong to one group and the other two to another group, achieves this topology.

Other more complex topologies might be created using a mix of manually defined queue groups and automatically created ones via the req/rep functionalities offered by NATS. It goes by itself to say that an application might include subscribers and publishers, so to create very complex topologies, the only limit is our creativity and, of course, our needs.

3.6 Summary

This chapter thoroughly explored the diverse and powerful core capabilities of NATS, a high-performance messaging system central to developing dynamic and efficient distributed systems. We began by understanding NATS's foundational architecture, focusing on its core functionality as a pub/sub streaming server that utilizes subjects for dependable message distribution, a crucial aspect of any distributed setup.

Through practical application, we dove into the NATS Command-Line Interface. This tool aids significantly in sending and receiving messages, allowing us to experiment with and understand various message flows and configurations. Complementing this was an in-depth look at the Go SDK, as Go is the language NATS is written in and the one we focus on in this book. The SDK facilitated our exploration of developing applications that communicate seamlessly with NATS servers using functions like Subscribe and SubscribeSync.

This chapter further expanded our understanding by covering the essential topologies that we had already seen in Chapter 2, "Distributed Communication Basics":

Pub/Sub: We studied this foundational model, in which messages sent to a topic are received by all subscribers. This showcases the central and scalable nature of the pub/sub topology.

Queue Groups: Leveraging these groups, we've learned how to effectively load-balance messages across subscribers. This ensures that each message is processed by only one group member, optimizing resource usage and performance.

Req/Rep Pattern: We dissected the request/reply model, which provides a synchronous communication method, demonstrating its utility in scenarios that require a direct client-server interaction model. We've seen how NATS implements it via queue groups and pub/sub messaging.

Additionally, we explored how to handle errors through headers, enabling applications to process errors gracefully. By combining these NATS components, we've investigated constructing complex and customized messaging patterns designed to meet specific requirements in distributed systems.

This chapter has provided us with a comprehensive understanding of leveraging NATS to build scalable, adaptive, and efficient distributed systems.

CHAPTER 3   NATS FUNDAMENTALS

3.7 Questions

1) **What is the role of subjects in NATS messaging?**

   a) Subjects are used to store messages for future retrieval.

   b) Subjects define the channels through which messages are sent and received.

   c) Subjects are used to encrypt messages.

   d) Subjects balance messages between servers.

2) **How can a subscriber ensure that they receive messages in a synchronous manner using the Go SDK for NATS?**

   a) By calling SubscribeAsync

   b) By using the CLI to poll for messages

   c) By using the SubscribeSync function

   d) By setting a delay on the connection

3) **Which NATS pattern would you use to send a request and wait for a single response from a specific service?**

   a) Broadcast pattern

   b) Pub/Sub pattern

   c) Queue pattern

   d) Req/Rep pattern

4) **What mechanism does NATS provide to balance the load among subscribers processing the same messages?**

   a) Round-robin distribution

   b) Queue Groups

   c) Direct addressing

   d) Subject hashing

CHAPTER 3   NATS FUNDAMENTALS

5) **How do you implement error handling when sending messages in a NATS network?**

   a) Discard all error messages

   b) Use headers to encode error information within the message

   c) Duplicate messages until no errors occur

   d) Convert errors to warnings

6) **Which command-line tool is primarily used to experiment with NATS message flow from the terminal?**

   a) NATTerminal

   b) Go CLI

   c) NATS Command-Line Interface

   d) MessageFlow Tool

CHAPTER 4

Working System

4.1 Introduction

This chapter will guide you through the creation of a complete restaurant ordering and delivery system. This system is composed of several distinct services, each with its own responsibilities, and will use **NATS** for communication between them. The primary components of the system are

- **Restaurant Gateway**: This service is the front-end interface for customers to use to place orders. It provides the restaurant's menu and publishes updates about menu changes and special offers.

- **Order Processor**: The core of the system, this service is responsible for managing the lifecycle of an order. It processes incoming orders, updates their status (e.g., "Preparing," "Out for Delivery," "Delivered"), and interacts with other services as needed.

- **Delivery Tracker**: A service responsible for tracking the status of orders as they progress through various stages. It will update the order's status in real time, allowing customers to track their orders via the customer-facing application.

Additionally, we will build a **command-line application** that simulates the customer's interaction with the system. The app will allow users to:

- View the restaurant's menu.
- Place an order.
- Track the status of their orders, including updates as the order moves from "Preparing" to "Out for Delivery" and eventually to "Delivered."

CHAPTER 4   WORKING SYSTEM

You will be guided through the process of building these services step by step, using **Go** for implementation and **NATS** for communication between the services. We will also explore how to structure and organize the components in a way that simulates the real-world flow of a restaurant's ordering and delivery process.

Finally, we will wrap up by showing you how to deploy the entire system on a local Kubernetes cluster using **Minikube**. This will allow you to run and test the whole application in an isolated environment, ensuring all components interact smoothly and the system behaves as expected.

By the end of this chapter, you'll understand how to build and deploy a distributed ordering and delivery system, from simulating a customer order to real-time tracking of deliveries.

This system demonstrates a few key concepts:

- **Pub/Sub, Req/Rep Messaging using NATS**: Components communicate via NATS, allowing for real-time updates as the order progresses through various stages.

- **Order Tracking**: Tracks each order's status from placement to final delivery, with live updates

- **Command-Line Application**: Simulates the customer experience, enabling menu browsing, ordering, and status tracking.

- **Minimalist Architecture**: Focused on inter-service communication without relying on persistent databases.

The system is intentionally minimalistic, focusing on service interaction. Internal design best practices and full system architecture will be explored in later chapters.

4.2 NATS

If you installed NATS after reading the previous chapter, you should be all set, and the best way to run NATS for a quick test is

```
~$ nats-server
```

Figure 4-1.   Calling the NATS server

CHAPTER 4 WORKING SYSTEM

which means invoking the installed server using the command **nats-server** from the correct installation for your system, as shown in Figure 4-1.

At the end of this chapter, we will use a Kubernetes deployment for it, as we will run the whole system inside **Minikube**, and the code is the same as seen in Chapter 3, "NATS Fundamentals," specifically Section 3.3.3.

For now, just run the command above or run the NATS server as you wish, making sure you are running it on the default port 4222, as the rest of the code will assume that configuration.

4.3 Restaurant Gateway

We will now create the first of our services, the Restaurant Gateway. We will see in further chapters what a real gateway is, but in this chapter, we will use this word more naturally, as the customer's first approach to the restaurant, which will provide a menu and any update on the menu itself or pricing and offers.

The code for the restaurant gateway component is the following:

```go
package main

import (
    "fmt"
    "math/rand"
    "time"

    "github.com/nats-io/nats.go"
)

// Function to generate dynamic menu updates
func generateUpdate() string {
    updates := []string{
        "New item added: Burger for $8!",
        "Half price on Pizza today only!",
        "Buy one Sushi, get one free!",
        "Special offer: Pasta for $7!",
        "Limited time: Ice Cream for $3!",
    }
```

CHAPTER 4 WORKING SYSTEM

```go
        return updates[rand.Intn(len(updates))]
}
func main() {
    // Connect to NATS
    nc, err := nats.Connect(nats.DefaultURL)
    if err != nil {
        fmt.Println("Error connecting to NATS:", err)
        return
    }
     defer nc.Close()

    // Menu with more items
    menu := map[string]int{
        "pizza":     10,
        "sushi":     15,
        "burger":    8,
        "pasta":     12,
        "ice cream": 5,
        "fries":     4,
        "milkshake": 6,
        "hot dog":   7,
    }

    // Request/Reply: Handle customer queries
    nc.Subscribe("restaurant.menu", func(msg *nats.Msg) {
        // Construct a JSON representation of the menu
        menuResponse := `{`
        for item, price := range menu {
            menuResponse += fmt.Sprintf(`"%s": %d,`, item, price)
        }
        menuResponse = menuResponse[:len(menuResponse)-1] + `}`
        // Remove last comma and close JSON
        fmt.Println(menuResponse)
        msg.Respond([]byte(menuResponse))
        fmt.Println("Sent menu to customer.")
    })
```

```go
    // Publish/Subscribe: Publish menu updates periodically
    go func() {
        for {
            time.Sleep(10 * time.Second) // Publish updates every 10 seconds
            update := generateUpdate()
            nc.Publish("restaurant.updates", []byte(update))
            fmt.Println("Published menu update:", update)
        }
    }()

    // Keep the connection alive
    select {}
}
```

Let's see closely what we are doing. Look at this function:

```go
func generateUpdate() string {
    updates := []string{
        "New item added: Burger for $8!",
        "Half price on Pizza today only!",
        "Buy one Sushi, get one free!",
        "Special offer: Pasta for $7!",
        "Limited time: Ice Cream for $3!",
    }
    return updates[rand.Intn(len(updates))]
}
```

This simply holds a list of updates, and one is randomly selected using the random package.

We then have the main function, and inside we have the usual connection to NATS:

```go
    // Connect to NATS
    nc, err := nats.Connect(nats.DefaultURL)
    if err != nil {
        fmt.Println("Error connecting to NATS:", err)
        return
    }
     defer nc.Close()
```

CHAPTER 4   WORKING SYSTEM

After this, we get the menu, which is, in fact, hardcoded:

```
// Menu with more items
    menu := map[string]int{
        "pizza":        10,
        "sushi":        15,
        "burger":       8,
        "pasta":        12,
        "ice cream":    5,
        "fries":        4,
        "milkshake":    6,
        "hot dog":      7,
    }
```

And then we connect to a specific topic so that we can act upon receiving a message:

```
// Request/Reply: Handle customer queries
    nc.Subscribe("restaurant.menu", func(msg *nats.Msg) {
        // Construct a JSON representation of the menu
        menuResponse := `{`
        for item, price := range menu {
            menuResponse += fmt.Sprintf(`"%s": %d,`, item, price)
        }
        menuResponse = menuResponse[:len(menuResponse)-1] + `}` // Remove last comma and close JSON
        fmt.Println(menuResponse)
        msg.Respond([]byte(menuResponse))
        fmt.Println("Sent menu to customer.")
    })
```

In the code above, we subscribe to "restaurant.menu," and we expect a message to arrive asking us for the menu. The message itself will be empty, but we do not care about the message content, as we will always simply return the up-to-date menu.

```
menuResponse := `{`
    for item, price := range menu {
        menuResponse += fmt.Sprintf(`"%s": %d,`, item, price)
    }
    menuResponse = menuResponse[:len(menuResponse)-1] + `}` // Remove
    last comma and close JSON
```

There are several ways to create this message, and we used one that is a bit convoluted, so you can modify it to make the message suit your needs. If you just need to send that map, you could JSON marshal it as it is.

Notice how we send the menu back:

```
msg.Respond([]byte(menuResponse))
```

Using the **msg.Respond** method. We do that because this is a REQ/REP messaging, where a particular client will request the menu, so we do not want to publish the menu to everybody, only to whoever asks for it.

The last part of the code will just send messages to update the customers of current offers:

```
go func() {
    for {
        time.Sleep(10 * time.Second) // Publish updates every
        10 seconds
        update := generateUpdate()
        nc.Publish("restaurant.updates", []byte(update))
        fmt.Println("Published menu update:", update)
    }
}()

// Keep the connection alive
select {}
```

The function **generateUpdate** will select one of the updates in the list, and then the **nc.Publish** function will publish the update to all subscribers.

Consider extending this gateway so that the menu is stored in a database, and you can update the menu and the prices over time. You could also modify it so that when there is an offer, the price on the menu is updated accordingly.

4.4 Order Processor

We now want to see how to process an order. In our distributed system, we can contact each service directly, as we assume we are a client inside a restaurant, and we make our choices via a custom device on our table. We do not care about security, as we are not open to the internet, and the devices can only run the applications we install.

The order processor will accept an order if the menu item is valid; otherwise, it will return an error. We will simulate the preparation and delivery of the order just via a time delay.

To check if the menu is in the menu, we will replicate the same menu in the order processor as a map. We will talk more about this choice later.

Let's present the full code first, and then we will break it down:

```go
package main

import (
    "encoding/json"
    "fmt"
    "time"

    "github.com/nats-io/nats.go"
)

// Order structure to hold the order ID and item
type Order struct {
    OrderID string `json:"order_id"`
    Item    string `json:"item"`
}

// Order Status structure to simulate status updates
type OrderStatus struct {
    OrderID string `json:"order_id"`
    Status  string `json:"status"`
}

func main() {
    // Define the menu with items and prices
    menu := map[string]int{
        "Pizza":    10,
```

```go
        "Sushi":      15,
        "Burger":     8,
        "Pasta":      12,
        "Ice cream":  5,
        "fries":      4,
        "milkshake":  6,
        "hot dog":    7,
    }

    // Connect to NATS
    nc, err := nats.Connect(nats.DefaultURL)
    if err != nil {
        fmt.Println("Error connecting to NATS:", err)
        return
    }
    defer nc.Close()

    // Subscribe to incoming orders
    nc.Subscribe("restaurant.orders", func(msg *nats.Msg) {
        var order Order
        if err := json.Unmarshal(msg.Data, &order); err != nil {
            fmt.Println("Error unmarshalling order:", err)
            return
        }

        // Check if the ordered item is in the menu
        if price, exists := menu[order.Item]; exists {
            // Valid order: Process it
            fmt.Printf("Processing order %s for item: %s (Price: $%d)\n",
            order.OrderID, order.Item, price)

            // Simulate order processing and status updates
            statuses := []string{
                "Preparing",
                "Ready for Delivery",
            }
```

```go
            for _, status := range statuses {
                time.Sleep(5 * time.Second) // Simulate time between
                status updates

                // Publish status updates to the "order.status" topic
                statusUpdate := OrderStatus{
                    OrderID: order.OrderID,
                    Status:  status,
                }
                statusData, _ := json.Marshal(statusUpdate)
                nc.Publish("order.status", statusData)
            }
        } else {
            // Invalid order: Item not on the menu
            fmt.Printf("Order %s for item '%s' is invalid. Item not on
            the menu.\n", order.OrderID, order.Item)

            // Publish an invalid order status
            statusUpdate := OrderStatus{
                OrderID: order.OrderID,
                Status:  "Invalid order: Item not on the menu",
            }
            statusData, _ := json.Marshal(statusUpdate)
            nc.Publish("order.status", statusData)
        }
    })

    // Keep the connection alive
    select {}
}
```

We first create a few useful structs, which we will use to marshal and unmarshal the content of the messages sent and received via NATS:

```go
// Order structure to hold the order ID and item
type Order struct {
    OrderID string `json:"order_id"`
    Item    string `json:"item"`
}
```

```go
// Order Status structure to simulate status updates
type OrderStatus struct {
    OrderID string `json:"order_id"`
    Status  string `json:"status"`
}
```

After that, we make the main loop and define the menu, exactly like in the previous service. We carry on as earlier by connecting to NATS, and then we subscribe to the topic we need:

```go
// Subscribe to incoming orders
    nc.Subscribe("restaurant.orders", func(msg *nats.Msg) {
        var order Order
        if err := json.Unmarshal(msg.Data, &order); err != nil {
            fmt.Println("Error unmarshalling order:", err)
            return
        }
```

After handling the error, we need to check the message and if the ordered item exists in the menu:

```go
        // Check if the ordered item is in the menu
        if price, exists := menu[order.Item]; exists {
            // Valid order: Process it
            fmt.Printf("Processing order %s for item: %s (Price: $%d)\n",
            order.OrderID, order.Item, price)
```

Inside the block, if the item is in the menu, we then simulate the processing of the order:

```go
            // Simulate order processing and status updates
            statuses := []string{
                "Preparing",
                "Ready for Delivery",
            }
            for _, status := range statuses {
                time.Sleep(5 * time.Second) // Simulate time between
                status updates
```

```go
            // Publish status updates to the "order.status" topic
            statusUpdate := OrderStatus{
                OrderID: order.OrderID,
                Status:  status,
            }
            statusData, _ := json.Marshal(statusUpdate)
            nc.Publish("order.status", statusData)
        }
```

Here, we define three statuses and then go through each with a delay of five seconds. After completing each step, we send a notification.

In case the item is not on the menu, we proceed with publishing an error:

```go
    } else {
            // Invalid order: Item not on the menu
            fmt.Printf("Order %s for item '%s' is invalid. Item not on the menu.\n", order.OrderID, order.Item)

            // Publish an invalid order status
            statusUpdate := OrderStatus{
                OrderID: order.OrderID,
                Status:  "Invalid order: Item not on the menu",
            }
            statusData, _ := json.Marshal(statusUpdate)
            nc.Publish("order.status", statusData)
        }
    })
```

Let's now focus on some of the choices made here. First of all, we are simulating the processing of the order. In a real scenario, the chef would send messages about the completion of the orders, so the service would have more subscriptions to different topics to accept orders from customers and update the status via the chef's inputs. We leave to the reader the possibility of implementing something like this. Still, we would not go much in-depth now, trying to build a complex system, because we will need to dig into how to design a full system appropriately in later chapters.

One thing that could be beneficial, though, is to modify this code so that the order processor will generate an order ID. At the moment, this code expects an order to be created and be sent to the processor via NATS; in practice, though, a customer would want to make an order and receive an order number back. In this system, we will build a client app for customers to send orders, and this APP will generate a unique order ID. We will see how to do that later, but we suggest you understand how the system works and try to modify it by playing with messages and replies so that the client app will receive an order number instead of generating it. We believe that showing you this might remove your focus from what we are trying to show you here, but after you understand it, it would be great if you were to extend the system to be more adherent to a real-world scenario.

The last thing to talk about, as you might have guessed, is why we have used the same hardcoded map again for the menu. Let's first think about how this works in a real scenario: The chef knows the menu; it does not pick it up from a database. An order processor component might be used to discard impossible orders, so we might want to share the menu in a shared location with the restaurant gateway. The first thought you will have is to store the menu in the database and have both the Restaurant Gateway and Order Processor pick the menu from there. We will explain this later in this book, but for now, understand that sharing the data between components by reading and writing from the same database is a bad idea. We will enforce the rule that each component owns its own data. We will see how to do this properly later, but the suggestion we want to give you here is that if you do not wish to use a hardcoded map, you let the Order Processor ask the menu at the Restaurant Gateway to check if the order is valid. You have multiple possibilities here, and you will discover later if your chosen approach was correct.

4.5 Delivery Tracker

At this point, we have our order ready and need to deliver it. The order processor was tied to the kitchen and to the chef preparing it. We need to simulate the waiter's actions now. The waiter will pick up the orders and get them ready for delivery. The waiter will walk approximately five seconds to the table. In a real system, the waiter will likely push a button when he picks up the plate. Here, we simply publish the update, as this is a simulation. When the order is delivered, the waiter will publish an update about the delivery.

CHAPTER 4   WORKING SYSTEM

Let's now see the full code for the delivery tracker:

```go
package main

import (
    "encoding/json"
    "fmt"
    "time"

    "github.com/nats-io/nats.go"
)

// Order structure to hold the order ID and item
type Order struct {
    OrderID string `json:"order_id"`
    Item    string `json:"item"`
}

// Order Status structure to simulate status updates
type OrderStatus struct {
    OrderID string `json:"order_id"`
    Status  string `json:"status"`
}

func main() {
    // Connect to NATS
    nc, err := nats.Connect(nats.DefaultURL)
    if err != nil {
        fmt.Println("Error connecting to NATS:", err)
        return
    }
    defer nc.Close()

    // Subscribe to "Ready for Delivery" orders
    nc.Subscribe("order.status", func(msg *nats.Msg) {
        var statusUpdate OrderStatus
        if err := json.Unmarshal(msg.Data, &statusUpdate); err != nil {
```

```go
            fmt.Println("Error unmarshalling status update:", err)
            return
        }

        // Check if the status is "Ready for Delivery"
        if statusUpdate.Status == "Ready for Delivery" {
            fmt.Printf("Order %s is ready for delivery. Starting delivery process...\n", statusUpdate.OrderID)

            // Simulate "Out for Delivery" status
            time.Sleep(3 * time.Second) // Simulate delay before assigning to delivery
            outForDelivery := OrderStatus{
                OrderID: statusUpdate.OrderID,
                Status:  "Out for delivery",
            }
            outForDeliveryData, _ := json.Marshal(outForDelivery)
            nc.Publish("order.status", outForDeliveryData)
            fmt.Printf("Order %s is now out for delivery.\n", statusUpdate.OrderID)

            // Simulate delivery process
            time.Sleep(5 * time.Second) // Simulate delivery time
            delivered := OrderStatus{
                OrderID: statusUpdate.OrderID,
                Status:  "Delivered",
            }
            deliveredData, _ := json.Marshal(delivered)
            nc.Publish("order.status", deliveredData)
            fmt.Printf("Order %s has been delivered.\n", statusUpdate.OrderID)
        }
    })

    // Keep the connection alive
    select {}
}
```

We will now quickly break down this code, but you will see it has nothing surprising or new.

```
// Subscribe to "Ready for Delivery" orders
  nc.Subscribe("order.status", func(msg *nats.Msg) {
      var statusUpdate OrderStatus
      if err := json.Unmarshal(msg.Data, &statusUpdate); err != nil {
          fmt.Println("Error unmarshalling status update:", err)
          return
      }
```

As always, we subscribed to the "order.status" topic and handled any error with the unmarshaling of the message. The next step will be to see if an order is ready for pickup:

```
// Check if the status is "Ready for Delivery"
      if statusUpdate.Status == "Ready for Delivery" {
          fmt.Printf("Order %s is ready for delivery. Starting delivery
          process...\n", statusUpdate.OrderID)
```

And only act in this case, discarding other statuses. We could have used a different technique and used the status inside the topic, like "order.status.ready_for_delivery," and only subscribed to that, but the choice depends on several factors. Feel free to modify the tracker if you want to play with the topics as an exercise.

The code simulates a wait for picking up the order:

```
// Simulate "Out for Delivery" status
 time.Sleep(3 * time.Second) // Simulate delay before assigning to delivery
```

And finally, we publish the order status update: out for delivery:

```
outForDelivery := OrderStatus{
            OrderID: statusUpdate.OrderID,
            Status:  "Out for delivery",
        }
        outForDeliveryData, _ := json.Marshal(outForDelivery)
        nc.Publish("order.status", outForDeliveryData)
        fmt.Printf("Order %s is now out for delivery.\n", statusUpdate.
        OrderID)
```

The last step is to wait five seconds before reaching the table and update the status to "Delivered":

```
// Simulate delivery process
time.Sleep(5 * time.Second) // Simulate delivery time
delivered := OrderStatus{
    OrderID: statusUpdate.OrderID,
    Status:  "Delivered",
}
deliveredData, _ := json.Marshal(delivered)
nc.Publish("order.status", deliveredData)
fmt.Printf("Order %s has been delivered.\n", statusUpdate.OrderID)
```

This component is the last one we needed to build to complete our simulation. If you were building a real system, not a simulation, you would want to have a way for chefs and waiters to update orders manually, and you could do it via a command line interface, a web interface, or again via NATS messaging. You could use this project as a base for your own system, but again, we are very early in our voyage through the design and implementation of distributed systems, and we'd suggest you go further in studying this book before embarking on the design of a fully functional system.

4.6 Customer

The system is now fully built, but we need to test it. As you might have thought, we do not need an actual application to test it because we just use NATS to interact with the system. Let's see, for example, how a customer could request a menu.

Let's assume the NATS server is running, and you run each one of the components manually. We assume you have the code pulled from the GitHub repository connected to this book, so you would run the components this way:

```
go run delivery-tracker/main.go
go run order-processor/main.go
go run restaurant-gateway/main.go
```

CHAPTER 4   WORKING SYSTEM

```
[744372] 2025/01/14 11:22:02.260596 [INF] Starting nats-server      pter-4$ go run delivery-tracker/main.go
[744372] 2025/01/14 11:22:02.260738 [INF]   Version:  2.10.21       Order c713c8dc-af85-4544-8371-0a8a7ede55b4 is ready for deliver
[744372] 2025/01/14 11:22:02.260741 [INF]   Git:      [d3a8868      y. Starting delivery process...
]                                                                   Order c713c8dc-af85-4544-8371-0a8a7ede55b4 is now out for deliv
[744372] 2025/01/14 11:22:02.260744 [INF]   Name:     NBUDT2X5      ery.
FUEEXFL6XGIRNKRNCKMZJWXTEGJGWRTAIBNTCAFRTS2KQOXU                    Order c713c8dc-af85-4544-8371-0a8a7ede55b4 has been delivered.
[744372] 2025/01/14 11:22:02.260746 [INF]   ID:       NBUDT2X5
FUEEXFL6XGIRNKRNCKMZJWXTEGJGWRTAIBNTCAFRTS2KQOXU
[744372] 2025/01/14 11:22:02.261341 [INF] Listening for client
connections on 0.0.0.0:4222
[744372] 2025/01/14 11:22:02.261747 [INF] Server is ready


                                                                   pter-4$ go run order-processor/main.go
                                                                   Processing order c713c8dc-af85-4544-8371-0a8a7ede55b4 for item:
                                                                   sushi (Price: $15)




Published menu update: Half price on Pizza today only!
```

Figure 4-2. *All the components running*

If you use a terminal able to run different split views, you would see something like in Figure 4-2, where NATS and the three other components are active.

If you wanted to get the menu, you could run it on another window of your terminal:

$ nats request restaurant.menu "menu"

and the reply would be shown as

12:26:46 Sending request on "restaurant.menu"
12:26:46 Received with rtt 538.407µs
{"burger": 8,"pasta": 12,"ice cream": 5,"fries": 4,"milkshake": 6,"hot dog": 7,"pizza": 10,"sushi": 15}

Now, we could order a burger by running:

$ nats publish restaurant.orders '{"order_id":"123", "item":"burger"}'

But we would not know unless we read our system logs to see if the order is processing and if it gets delivered. We could also subscribe to the orders' updates:

$ nats subscribe order.status

We need to run the subscriber on another tab or window, and, of course, it has to run before we place any order. If we run the subscriber after placing an order, we might never get the first update because NATS works on a fire-and-forget mode; when messages are sent, they must be captured at that time, or the message will be lost.

Interacting with the system like this might be cumbersome, so we prepared a possible command-line application for a customer to interact with the system.

As the code is quite long and made of several parts, let's start by analyzing its different blocks separately, and then we will show the full code, the opposite of what we've done for smaller scripts.

We first need to define a few structs for our messages:

```go
// Order structure to hold the order ID and item
type Order struct {
    OrderID string `json:"order_id"`
    Item    string `json:"item"`
}

// Order Status structure to simulate status updates
type OrderStatus struct {
    OrderID string `json:"order_id"`
    Status  string `json:"status"`
}
```

We have seen these same structs in the delivery tracker and order processor because they express the common language shared across the components.

We then need to connect to NATS, which we do as always via

```go
// Connect to NATS
    nc, err := nats.Connect(nats.DefaultURL)
    if err != nil {
        fmt.Println("Error connecting to NATS:", err)
        return
    }
    defer nc.Close()
```

CHAPTER 4   WORKING SYSTEM

We now want to track our own orders to not get confused with other people's orders:

```
// Variable to keep track of user orders
userOrders := make(map[string]string) // Key: Order ID, Value: Item Name
```

We then show a menu with command options:

```
fmt.Println("Welcome to the Restaurant CLI!")
fmt.Println("Type 'menu' to view the menu, 'order <item>' to order food or 'exit' to quit.")
```

We will have to implement the commands, so let's start with the loop to capture these commands:

```
// Command-line input loop
scanner := bufio.NewScanner(os.Stdin)
for {
        fmt.Print("> ")
        scanner.Scan()
        command := scanner.Text()
........................................
}
```

We scan from the command line the command, and we store it as text into a variable. The first option will be the exit command:

```
// Handle "exit"
  if command == "exit" {
      fmt.Println("Goodbye!")
    break
}
```

We now want to implement the menu request, where we get the restaurant menu from the restaurant gateway:

```
        // Handle "menu"
        if command == "menu" {
            msg, err := nc.Request("restaurant.menu", nil, nats.
            DefaultTimeout)
```

```go
        if err != nil {
            fmt.Println("Error fetching menu:", err)
            continue
        }
        var menu map[string]int
        if err := json.Unmarshal(msg.Data, &menu); err != nil {
            fmt.Println("Error parsing menu:", err)
            continue
        }
        fmt.Println("Menu:")
        for item, price := range menu {
            fmt.Printf("  %s: $%d\n", item, price)
        }
        continue
    }
```

In here we used the **Request** function of the NATS client:

```go
msg, err := nc.Request("restaurant.menu", nil, nats.DefaultTimeout)
```

Then we unmarshaled the response into a map and printed it to the standard output. Similarly, we can implement the order command:

```go
    // Handle "order <item>"
    if strings.HasPrefix(command, "order ") {
        item := strings.TrimSpace(strings.TrimPrefix(command,
        "order "))
        if item == "" {
            fmt.Println("Please specify an item to order.")
            continue
        }

        // Generate a new Order ID
        orderID := uuid.New().String()
        order := Order{
            OrderID: orderID,
            Item:    item,
        }
```

```
        // Publish the order to the order processor for processing
        orderData, _ := json.Marshal(order)
        nc.Publish("restaurant.orders", orderData)
        userOrders[orderID] = item // Keep track of the order ID
        and item
        fmt.Printf("Order placed for: %s. Your Order ID is %s\n",
        strings.Title(item), orderID)
        continue
    }
```

As seen before, the order processor expects an order ID to be already generated, so we do it, and we create the order message this way:

```
    // Generate a new Order ID
    orderID := uuid.New().String()
    order := Order{
        OrderID: orderID,
        Item:    item,
    }
```

Note that we used

```
nc.Publish("restaurant.orders", orderData)
```

instead of using the **Request** function, because we are not expecting anything back as a response, we just send the order.

We also add our order to the list of orders we make:

```
userOrders[orderID] = item // Keep track of the order ID and item
```

We want to be able to track orders, especially discriminating our orders, and we also want to receive updates from the restaurant with the latest offers. We create, then, two go routines so that they run concurrently while we interact with the application as customers. Let's see the restaurant updates:

```
    // Subscribe to restaurant updates
    go func() {
        sub, _ := nc.SubscribeSync("restaurant.updates")
```

```go
    for {
        msg, err := sub.NextMsg(0) // Blocks until a message is received
        if err == nil {
            fmt.Println("[Update] " + string(msg.Data))
        }
    }
}()
```

Which is pretty straightforward. For the order tracking, we need to subscribe to the correct topic and match the orders with our own orders in the list:

```go
// Subscribe to order status updates (for all orders)
go func() {
    sub, _ := nc.SubscribeSync("order.status")
    for {
        msg, err := sub.NextMsg(0) // Blocks until a message is received
        if err == nil {
            var status OrderStatus
            if err := json.Unmarshal(msg.Data, &status); err != nil {
                fmt.Println("Error unmarshalling order status:", err)
                continue
            }

            // Show update for all orders
            if item, exists := userOrders[status.OrderID]; exists {
                if status.Status == "Delivered" {
                    fmt.Printf("[Your Order %s] %s: Your order for %s has been delivered!\n", status.OrderID, status.Status, item)
                } else {
                    fmt.Printf("[Your Order %s] %s: %s\n", status.OrderID, status.Status, item)
                }
            } else {
```

```
                    // Show updates for other orders
                    fmt.Printf("[Order %s] %s\n", status.OrderID,
                    status.Status)
                }
            }
        }
    }()
```

The first part is similar to the subscription to the restaurant's updates; then we simply match the order with our list of order IDs, and we slightly change the message.

We are simulating here the fact that a customer might be reading the orders updates on a display in the restaurant, and he will keep track of his own orders.

For reference, we give the whole code, which can also be downloaded from the GitHub repository.

```
package main

import (
    "bufio"
    "encoding/json"
    "fmt"
    "os"
    "strings"

    "github.com/google/uuid"
    "github.com/nats-io/nats.go"
)

// Order structure to hold the order ID and item
type Order struct {
    OrderID string `json:"order_id"`
    Item    string `json:"item"`
}

// Order Status structure to simulate status updates
type OrderStatus struct {
    OrderID string `json:"order_id"`
    Status  string `json:"status"`
}
```

```go
func main() {
    // Connect to NATS
    nc, err := nats.Connect(nats.DefaultURL)
    if err != nil {
        fmt.Println("Error connecting to NATS:", err)
        return
    }
    defer nc.Close()

    // Variable to keep track of user orders
    userOrders := make(map[string]string) // Key: Order ID, Value: Item Name

    fmt.Println("Welcome to the Restaurant CLI!")
    fmt.Println("Type 'menu' to view the menu, 'order <item>' to order food or 'exit' to quit.")

    // Subscribe to restaurant updates
    go func() {
        sub, _ := nc.SubscribeSync("restaurant.updates")
        for {
            msg, err := sub.NextMsg(0) // Blocks until a message is received
            if err == nil {
                fmt.Println("[Update] " + string(msg.Data))
            }
        }
    }()

    // Subscribe to order status updates (for all orders)
    go func() {
        sub, _ := nc.SubscribeSync("order.status")
        for {
            msg, err := sub.NextMsg(0) // Blocks until a message is received
            if err == nil {
                var status OrderStatus
```

CHAPTER 4   WORKING SYSTEM

```go
            if err := json.Unmarshal(msg.Data, &status); err != nil {
                fmt.Println("Error unmarshalling order status:", err)
                continue
            }

            // Show update for all orders
            if item, exists := userOrders[status.OrderID]; exists {
                if status.Status == "Delivered" {
                    fmt.Printf("[Your Order %s] %s: Your order for %s has been delivered!\n", status.OrderID, status.Status, item)
                } else {
                    fmt.Printf("[Your Order %s] %s: %s\n", status.OrderID, status.Status, item)
                }
            } else {
                // Show updates for other orders
                fmt.Printf("[Order %s] %s\n", status.OrderID, status.Status)
            }
        }
    }
}()

// Command-line input loop
scanner := bufio.NewScanner(os.Stdin)
for {
    fmt.Print("> ")
    scanner.Scan()
    command := scanner.Text()

    // Handle "exit"
    if command == "exit" {
        fmt.Println("Goodbye!")
        break
    }
```

```go
// Handle "menu"
if command == "menu" {
    msg, err := nc.Request("restaurant.menu", nil, nats.
    DefaultTimeout)
    if err != nil {
        fmt.Println("Error fetching menu:", err)
        continue
    }
    var menu map[string]int
    if err := json.Unmarshal(msg.Data, &menu); err != nil {
        fmt.Println("Error parsing menu:", err)
        continue
    }
    fmt.Println("Menu:")
    for item, price := range menu {
        fmt.Printf("  %s: $%d\n", item, price)
    }
    continue
}

// Handle "order <item>"
if strings.HasPrefix(command, "order ") {
    item := strings.TrimSpace(strings.TrimPrefix(command,
    "order "))
    if item == "" {
        fmt.Println("Please specify an item to order.")
        continue
    }

    // Generate a new Order ID
    orderID := uuid.New().String()
    order := Order{
        OrderID: orderID,
        Item:    item,
    }
```

```
            // Publish the order to the order processor for processing
            orderData, _ := json.Marshal(order)
            nc.Publish("restaurant.orders", orderData)
            userOrders[orderID] = item // Keep track of the order ID
            and item
            fmt.Printf("Order placed for: %s. Your Order ID is %s\n",
            strings.Title(item), orderID)

            // No need to simulate sending order status updates here; this
            will be done by the Order Processor.

            continue
        }
        // Unknown command
        fmt.Println("Unknown command. Try 'menu', 'order <item>', 'track
        <order_id>', or 'exit'.")
    }
}
```

4.7 Summary

In this chapter, we've developed a distributed system to handle a restaurant's customer interaction. It handles delivering a menu on request and providing updates on offers, ordering foods and drinks, and their delivery. We've used NATS for streaming messages to allow communication between customers and services, services with each other, and the broadcasting of updates to all the customers connected.

The system does not use a storage engine; it relies on direct communication to share information and memory to handle orders and deliveries. The system could be improved, and a storage engine could be beneficial in some of its parts. We mentioned, however, that sharing data between components via a database accessed by multiple components is not a good idea, and we will dig into this in the following chapters of this book.

We used several topologies in this project, and you could have fun rewriting it using mangos instead of NATS as an exercise. One thing that you noticed, though, is that we have run only one instance of each component, and we couldn't do otherwise. If we were running multiple Gateways, we would get the same update multiple times; if we were running multiple order processors, we would prepare the same order multiple times; and by running multiple instances of the delivery tracker, we would deliver the same order multiple times. Without somehow synchronizing the restaurant updates, we cannot run multiple gateways, but let's say this component might be a single instance, as it does not do much and will likely not have many requests. We would like, however, to have multiple order processors and delivery trackers. We could achieve this by simply changing our subscriptions in the code with a queue subscription, i.e.,

```
nc.QueueSubscribe("restaurant.orders", "order-processor-group", func(msg *nats.Msg) {
```

So that all the instances of the order processor will load-balance the orders.

4.8 Full Example with Minikube

It should be clear by now that even such a small system is difficult to manage, with many components running as command-line processes, each one possibly failing and crashing at some point in time. We will now see how to run everything inside Minikube after dockerizing each component.

We will assume that you have your code in a folder following the structure of the GitHub repository for this book, which is

```
├── distributed-go
│   ├── chapter-4
│   │       ├── restaurant-gateway
│   │       │   └── main.go
│   │       ├──order-processor
│   │       │   └── main.go
│   │       ├──delivery-tracker
│   │       │   └── main.go
```

We need to dockerize every one of these three components so that we can run them in our minikube. In order to do so, we can add a Dockerfile in each one of those three components so that we have this structure:

```
├── distributed-go
│       ├── chapter-4
│                 ├── restaurant-gateway
│                 │        ├── docker
│                 │        │       └── Dockerfile
│                 │        └── main.go
```

The content of the Dockerfile can be something like this:

```
FROM golang:1.23-bookworm AS build

WORKDIR /app

RUN ls
COPY chapter-4/go.mod ./
COPY chapter-4/go.sum ./
RUN go mod download

COPY ./chapter-4/restaurant-gateway ./
RUN pwd
RUN ls

RUN go build -o /server ./main.go

##
## Deploy
##
FROM gcr.io/distroless/base-debian12

WORKDIR /

COPY --from=build /server /server

USER nonroot:nonroot

ENTRYPOINT ["/server"]
```

This Dockerfile assumes the file structure above, but you can change accordingly the line:

```
COPY ./chapter-4/restaurant-gateway ./
```

to suit your needs.

This file also assumes that you have a go mod file in the folder you run the **docker build** command from, which is above the **chapter-4** folder. If you are using a different setup, you need to change the file accordingly. We will not dig much into how Docker works, but to give an idea, if you have a folder with just the code of this chapter, you will need to have go mod initialized there, you will run **docker build** from that same folder, and you will have the Dockerfile line be:

```
COPY ./restaurant-gateway ./
```

You will need to learn how to use Docker following the official documentation for your operating system.

Once you have replicated the same Dockerfile for each one of the three components, you will be able to run the command:

```
docker build . -f ./chapter-4/restaurant-gateway/docker/Dockerfile --tag restaurant-gateway-1
```

and

```
docker build . -f ./chapter-4/order-processor/docker/Dockerfile --tag order-processor-1
```

and

```
docker build . -f ./chapter-4/delivery-tracker/docker/Dockerfile --tag delivery-tracker-1
```

So that you can build all three images. The GitHub repository also contains the three images already built for you to use to test everything directly; you can just pull those.

Once you have the image steady, you can create deployment files for Kubernetes. We will show here how to do it for the restaurant gateway as an example:

```
apiVersion: apps/v1
kind: Deployment
metadata:
  labels:
    app: restaurant-gateway
    name: restaurant-gateway
  name: restaurant-gateway
```

CHAPTER 4   WORKING SYSTEM

```yaml
spec:
  replicas: 1
  revisionHistoryLimit: 4
  selector:
    matchLabels:
      name: restaurant-gateway
  strategy:
    rollingUpdate:
      maxSurge: 1
      maxUnavailable: 1
    type: RollingUpdate
  template:
    metadata:
      labels:
        name: restaurant-gateway
    spec:
      containers:
        - env:
            - name: NATS_URL
              value: "nats://nats:4222"
          image:   restaurant-gateway-1
          imagePullPolicy: Always
          name: restaurant-gateway
          resources:
            limits:
              cpu: "0.5"
              memory: "100M"
            requests:
              cpu: "0.2"
              memory: "50M"
      dnsPolicy: ClusterFirst
      imagePullSecrets:
        - name: regcred
      restartPolicy: Always
```

Let's now dissect this file:

```
apiVersion: apps/v1
kind: Deployment
```

Defines the type of item to deploy to Kubernetes as a deployment.

```
metadata:
  labels:
    app: restaurant-gateway
    name: restaurant-gateway
  name: restaurant-gateway
```

These are simply metadata used to tag the deployment object to the orchestrator (Kubernetes).

```
spec:
  replicas: 1
```

Defines only one instance of the deployment; you can set it to more, but you need to have an image that uses the **QueueSubscribe** method, as explained earlier.

```
  selector:
    matchLabels:
      name: restaurant-gateway
```

Defines how it will be possible to select this component by other components in the cluster.

```
  spec:
    containers:
      - image: restaurant-gateway-1
```

This is where we define which image we are pulling; if you wish to use the images in the GitHub package registry, you can change this line accordingly.

The rest of the file defines some resource limits and other less important information.

You can try to create a deployment file for the other two components, and you can use the deployment file provided in Chapter 3, "NATS Fundamentals," for running NATS.

CHAPTER 4   WORKING SYSTEM

Before you can be ready to go, however, you have another issue. In the deployment files, you've seen these lines:

```
- env:
        - name: NATS_URL
          value: "nats://nats:4222"
```

Which you might not have noticed, but they are very important. The code we've seen till now assumes that NATS is running on the default port 4222, but also at the IP 127.0.0.1. Let's assume you want, now, to run NATS in your local machine using your local NATS server installation. You could, after doing that, run your freshly created containers with a command like this:

```
docker run restaurant-gateway-1
```

The result of your command would most likely be:

```
Restaurant gateway starting
Error connecting to NATS: nats: no servers available for connection
```

This is because your image is running inside a Docker container, which has no access to your host machine's network. You can easily fix that by using this command instead:

```
docker run -network host  restaurant-gateway-1
```

which tells Docker to share the local network of the container with your machine's (the host's) network. This will work, but unfortunately, when using Kubernetes, this won't be possible. We can change, then, all our components' code to be like this:

```
........................................
nu := os.Getenv("NATS_URL")
    if nu == "" {
        nu = nats.DefaultURL
    }
    ...........................
    // Connect to NATS
    nc, err := nats.Connect(nu)
```

CHAPTER 4 WORKING SYSTEM

This way, we use the default URL, which is **nats://127.0.0.1:4222,** unless a different one is provided via an environmental variable called **NATS_URL**.

You can perform this change and rebuild all your images so that they are aware of this environmental variable. If you are using the code pulled via the GitHub repository, this won't be necessary, as the code already contains this line.

You can now create a Minikube cluster. If you haven't installed Minikube, do it now, following instructions provided in Chapter 3, "NATS Fundamentals."

To create the cluster, do

```
minikube start --cpus='2' --memory='2g' --kubernetes-version='1.25.3' -p chapter-4
```

this command will automatically switch your **kubectl**-pointed cluster to the newly created one, but you can check by running:

```
minikube profile list
```

if you are in the correct cluster, you will see a * next to the profile chapter-4. if you are not in the correct profile, you can change it with:

```
minikube profile chapter-4.
```

Once you are sure that **kubectl** is pointing to the correct cluster, you can run:

```
kubectl apply -f ./chapter-3/nats-template/templates/nats/deployment.yml
```

Where you should change the path to your NATS deployment file according to your local file system.

If you now run

```
$ kubectl get deployments
```

you should see something like in Figure 4-3, with only the NATS deployment available.

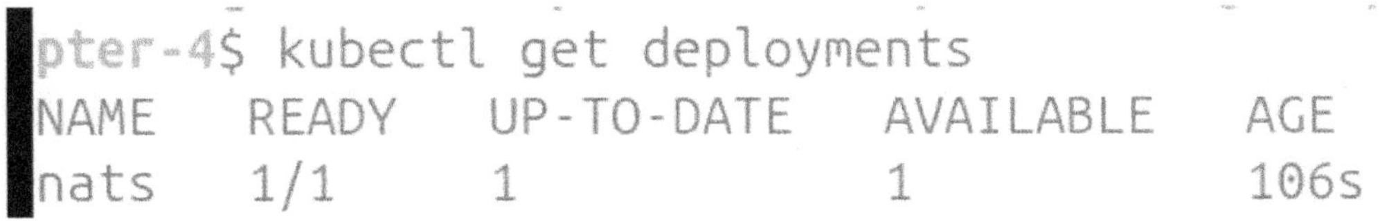

```
pter-4$ kubectl get deployments
NAME    READY   UP-TO-DATE   AVAILABLE   AGE
nats    1/1     1            1           106s
```

Figure 4-3. *NATS deployment running*

155

CHAPTER 4   WORKING SYSTEM

You can apply the deployment files for the other three components, i.e.,

`kubectl apply -f ./chapter-4/restaurant-gateway/k8s/2-restaurant-gateway.yml`

At this point, you might still encounter a problem: although the restaurant-gateway image is configured to connect to **nats://nats:4222**, and the **NATS** deployment is running a pod, the gateway service is unable to connect.

This is because the NATS pod is not yet exposed via a Kubernetes Service, meaning there's no consistent network address (NATS) that other pods can resolve.

If you've cloned the code from the GitHub repository, you will find a file called service.yml in the **chapter-3** folder under templates. This file defines a Kubernetes service that exposes NATS at a stable URL, allowing other components in the cluster to communicate with it reliably.

Even though we currently only have one NATS pod, a service is still necessary to ensure discoverability and consistent communication.

We show here the content of that file:

```yaml
apiVersion: v1
kind: Service
metadata:
  name: nats
  labels:
    name: nats
spec:
  selector:
    app: nats
  clusterIP: None
  ports:
  - name: client
    port: 4222
  - name: cluster
    port: 6222
  - name: monitor
    port: 8222
  - name: metrics
    port: 7777
```

```
  - name: leafnodes
    port: 7422
  - name: gateways
    port: 7522
```

It is simply defining a service:

```
apiVersion: v1
kind: Service
```

With its metadata:

```
metadata:
  name: nats
  labels:
    name: nats
```

and a crucial thing:

```
spec:
  selector:
    name: nats
```

Inside the specs, we have a selector, w, which needs to match the label selector defined in the deployment file, which was:

```
  selector:
    matchLabels:
      name: nats
............................
  template:
    metadata:
      labels:
        name: nats
```

If you apply now, this file via kubectl:

```
kubectl apply -f ./chapter-3/nats-template/templates/nats/service.yml
```

You will have the NATS service exposed correctly, and your restaurant gateway should run smoothly. If it does not, just restart the deployment:

CHAPTER 4 WORKING SYSTEM

```
kubectl rollout restart deployment restaurant-gateway
```

At this point, you can apply the Kubernetes deployment files to the remaining components: order processor and delivery tracker. Make sure that you have updated and rebuilt the images so that they accept the NATS_URL environmental variable.

When you've done all that, you should run the command:

kubectl get pods, and you should see something like

NAME	READY	STATUS	RESTARTS	AGE
delivery-tracker-7865598759-n6vzk	1/1	Running	0	114s
nats-7886bb5f76-5mw96	1/1	Running	0	18m
order-processor-5445896c6c-s2czw	1/1	Running	0	97s
restaurant-gateway-6c489cdb6c-x6jtj	1/1	Running	0	5m50s

You want, now, to test your system. You have a customer component, which you ran manually, and you could still do so. You need, however, to be able to send messages to the NATS installation running inside your cluster. You can do this easily, and all you need are two terminals. In the first terminal, you can run this command:

```
kubectl port-forward svc/nats 4222:4222
```

You should see now that the NATS service is properly forwarded to port 4222 in your local machine. Assuming now that you are, with the second terminal, in the **chapter-4** folder with your customer folder inside, you can run this command:

```
go run customer/main.go
```

And you should be able to ask for a menu and make any order. You could forward the service to another port, for example 5200, and you would have to do:

```
kubectl port-forward svc/nats 5200:4222
```

This forwards the service's internal port 4222 to port 5200 on your host machine. On top of that, you should make sure that you have added the lines:

```
nu := os.Getenv("NATS_URL")
    if nu == "" {
        nu = nats.DefaultURL
    }
    ..............................
```

```
// Connect to NATS
nc, err := nats.Connect(nu)
```

Also to your customer component code, so that you could do:

`NATS_URL=nats://127.0.0.1:5200 go run customer/main.go`

To run your component and connect to that different local port.

As the last option, you could also build your customer component and run it inside your Kubernetes cluster. You can figure out what the Kubernetes deployment would look like if you haven't done it yet and apply the deployment.

You need, now, a way to interact with the customer component, as it is running, but it is inside the cluster. In order to do so, you first need to find your pod. You can find it by running:

```
$ kubectl get pods
NAME                                    READY   STATUS    RESTARTS   AGE
customer-5fc6667454-p6zfg               1/1     Running   1          9m11s
delivery-tracker-7865598759-xggkh       1/1     Running   0          15m
nats-7886bb5f76-5mw96                   1/1     Running   0          79m
order-processor-5445896c6c-s2czw        1/1     Running   0          63m
restaurant-gateway-6c489cdb6c-x6jtj     1/1     Running   0          67m
```

In the example above, the pod you need is **customer-5fc6667454-p6zfg,** which, in your case, will have a different name.

Substitute your pod name now in the following code:

`kubectl attach -it customer-5fc6667454-p6zfg`

And run it in your terminal.
You might see a message like

`If you don't see a command prompt, try pressing enter.`

Do that, and you will be inside your application, which you can interact with by simply typing the expected commands: menu, order, and exit.

In this chapter, we built a distributed system made of small, self-contained services that communicate through NATS messaging. We containerized the services and deployed them in a Kubernetes cluster using Minikube.

CHAPTER 4   WORKING SYSTEM

You now have a working system, but as you may have noticed, each service fits into a single file. In the next chapter, we'll explore how to structure components properly for production-grade distributed systems—including concerns like modularization, persistence, configuration, and scalability.

PART II

Inside a Service: Core Architecture

CHAPTER 5

Anatomy of a Service

5.1 Foreword to Part 2

In the previous part, we explored the low-level components of a distributed system, including how they communicate and the topologies they can form. Until now, we did not care how a component was designed, and we simply put some logic around a **socket**. The component itself looked like a small script connecting to other components via something like Mangos or NATS. We will now shift focus to how a component should be designed and what good practices and architectural patterns we should use.

It might seem out of scope in a book devoted to presenting a distributed system to have a whole part on how to design a single component. The truth is, although some concepts and practices are common for designing any good software system, some things work better for a distributed system and some things, even though they apply everywhere, are critical when designing a component that has to fit into an overall system, especially when the system is distributed.

This means that each component must be designed to fulfill its immediate purpose and integrate cohesively within a larger ecosystem. Whether you're building a monolithic service, a microservice, or something in between, understanding the anatomy of a service is crucial for crafting robust, maintainable, and future-proof systems. Here, we will focus on general and specific techniques for building components as part of a larger distributed system.

This part begins by exploring the anatomy of a service and the transition from low-level components to complete service architectures. In this chapter, we will see what a service is and how it differs from a component to a microservice.

It then provides an in-depth analysis of a service, providing the base for understanding the layers, components, and roles that define an effective service architecture. From there, we explore Domain-Driven Design (DDD), a powerful approach that aligns technical implementations with business needs. By putting the business and its language first, DDD helps create systems that are both technically sound and relevant to stakeholders. It also makes the system easier to discuss, ensuring that engineers and businesspeople can communicate without misunderstandings.

After that, we will explore hexagonal architecture, an architectural style that advocates for clear boundaries and well-defined communication paths between a service's core logic and external dependencies. This approach ensures that services remain adaptable and resilient in the face of change, making them easier to maintain and extend.

As with the previous part, we'll conclude with a complete example that puts these principles into practice, showing how to design a service from the ground up using everything we've covered.

5.2 From Low-Level Building Blocks to Services

At the heart of every complex system lies a foundation of simple components. Consider, for example, a script communicating via a socket or a lightweight NATS-based message exchange. These low-level building blocks perform specific tasks but operate in isolation, handling narrowly scoped responsibilities. While such components are effective at their scale, they lack the structure and cohesion required to function as an organic part of a larger system.

A service, in contrast, represents a higher level of abstraction. Unlike a standalone component, a service integrates multiple responsibilities to deliver meaningful, cohesive functionality. It bridges the gap between low-level operations and high-level system requirements by orchestrating communication, maintaining state, and exposing interfaces that align with business needs. Where a component might simply send or receive data, a service transforms, processes, and contextualizes that data to deliver actionable outcomes.

This transition from a low-level component to a service is not merely about adding functionality but also about embracing a design philosophy. Services are designed with the understanding that they are part of an ecosystem. They account for concerns such as scalability, reliability, and observability. A service communicates with other parts of the system using well-defined protocols, ensuring it can evolve independently while remaining interoperable.

By moving from components to services, we shift from thinking about isolated, task-specific operations to designing cohesive units that provide value within a larger system. This progression sets the stage for exploring service-oriented principles, ultimately enabling the creation of systems that are both robust and adaptable.

The chapters ahead are designed to answer key questions:

> What constitutes a well-designed service?
>
> How do principles like DDD and hexagonal architecture shape modern service design?
>
> How do we layer, persist, and expose data in a service to ensure scalability and maintainability?
>
> What does a complete service implementation look like in practice?

By the end of this part, you will have a deeper understanding of how to design, implement, and maintain individual services that form the foundation of distributed systems. You'll also gain insights into the challenges and trade-offs inherent in service design, preparing you for the practical aspects of building scalable systems.

Let's dive into the anatomy of a service and explore what lies at the heart of effective system architecture.

5.3 Service or Microservice

You may already know what a microservice is—or believe you do. Some consider it not even a standalone term, arguing the proper name is "Microservices Architecture." Others have firm ideas about what a service is and what defines a microservice. Perhaps you've learned the key differences and see a microservice either as unrelated to services or as a special case of one. If you already have your idea about that, I do not want to dismantle it with mine, because, after all, there is so much on the internet, and if one view were the correct one, we would know, and no other opinion would be accepted. Here, we will present a logical view of the topic and make things clear, but we will dive deep into a microservice in the following chapters.

When creating a complex piece of software, be it distributed or not, we use the old wisdom *divide et impera,* divide and conquer, which is often our best weapon. We, as humans, can process a considerable amount of data, but it is evident that a smaller set of

CHAPTER 5   ANATOMY OF A SERVICE

data is easier to handle than a bigger one. Taking a complex system and dividing it into smaller parts is how we can keep our head around such complexity, treating each part separately.

This leads us to several ways to operate our subdivision of a complex system, and building some components of a manageable size is one key step to achieve that. We can call some components services, let's say, because they serve some specific purpose, and each service will be made of other smaller components. Services communicate with each other; services have duties, and they act on some particular data and types and on specific domains of the system.

You can understand that apart from a manageable size, which can be somewhat intuitive, these services might be organized with a very different degree of communication with each other in terms of how much they communicate, how often, and whether they can function without communicating. Shall we actually let them communicate at all? Shall they share data? How should they share data?

You can see that there are a lot of questions, and unfortunately, there is no single answer; it sort of depends on what you want to do, what your goal is, and your trade-offs. If you look online, some websites will tell you that you can build microservices and pretty much do whatever you want in terms of the aforementioned questions, but most will disagree with that, and we do too.

The truth is that software engineering has evolved, and many different architectural styles have been developed. Some are still in use, while others have been abandoned. We will study in the rest of this book what microservices look like, what their boundaries are, what their data strategy is, and how they are built internally.

When services started being a thing, we developed a way to split a system into services where these components were very much interconnected and dependent on each other; they had a lot of communication going on between them, and even services whose only duty was to make other services communicate. You could see it as some company departments, say marketing and sales, and another department was called the sales-marketing communication department. This all made sense, but it raised even more concerns about complexity, which led to abandoning this approach. Services, however, were not abandoned as a concept. Over time, a new architectural style emerged, called microservices, in which services have very specific characteristics—often quite different from those in older service-based architectures. For this reason, the older style, known as Service-Oriented Architecture (SOA), was largely abandoned and is now considered distinct from the modern microservices architecture. This again led to the fact that some see the microservices as part of service-oriented architecture, and some others see it as a totally different thing. It all boils down to the fact that for some, any service-based architecture is a service-oriented architecture (SOA), and for some others, SOA is structured in a very specific way.

We will not care about this, but we had to make clear that we are exposing a way of building distributed architecture. We are using some conventions and a point of view; yet, the whole matter and the software architecture world are still evolving and improving.

5.4 Developer vs. Engineer

The world of software is highly diverse in terms of technologies and techniques used, as well as job titles and positions. Most people who write code tend to call themselves coders, programmers, or software developers. There is an overall emphasis on crafting code as if it were an art, and the focus is essentially on the code written. This might feel very satisfying to the "coder," but it often ends in engineering teams being siloed and separated from the rest of the teams in the companies they work for, and the amount of misunderstandings and lack of effective communication between functions inside a company is astonishing when comparing programmers and any other function. Programmers, coders, and software developers often have as their only interest writing code and are drawn more to the perceived "beauty" or "correctness" of their code than the effect their code has on the business.

This is quite a generalization, and not all programmers or software teams are like that, but it is a widespread problem that these teams have almost no intellectual contact with the rest of the company.

In summary, businesspeople speak a totally different language from the people on the "engineering team." This, however, is due to the simple fact that engineering teams are not engineering teams but coding teams, much like a coding factory inside a company, rather than one of the many teams.

To give a quick example of this high degree of difference between an average engineering team and any other team, like marketing, you might notice, and maybe experience, directly or indirectly, that in any other team, people start in a position like a junior marketing associate, and then they go up on the ladder by managing more and more, taking on more responsibilities, most of which involve people management.

Coders, programmers, and software developers are generally allergic to management. They want to write their code and make the best code in terms of engineering practices, paradigms, architectural styles, and so on.

This seems all correct, but there is one catch. We surely want to write a code that follows the best principles and is maintainable and scalable, but ultimately, the company needs business value from the software developed.

Here is the key point of this paragraph and this whole part in this book: Companies need software engineers, not coders, programmers, or developers.

A software engineer understands business needs and the impact of his work on the overall business. He can speak with non-technical people and understand their point of view; he speaks their language but has a specific skillset that is different from sales, marketing, and other functions.

This book is not about software engineering in general; it is about distributed systems. However, it is important to understand that any good architecture is not purely technical. It needs to build value, business value, and it is due to undergo constant change due to business needs.

It should be clear, then, that when we build software, we mimic business entities, and businesspeople see the software as precisely that, an implementation of business needs, a business product. The more the relation between the pieces of code and the business entities are clear to both engineers and businesspeople, the easier it is to build what is needed and change it when necessary.

What we will stress in the next chapter is how to achieve exactly that, which is the key to start building a system. We can't adapt to business needs and vision later on; we need to start on the right foot. That's why we will spend time digging into DDD, and we will make sure that you will think like an engineer and not like a mere coder because code that is syntactically perfect but does not align with the business is not just far from perfect but is completely wrong in its purpose.

As a software engineer, whatever your position—developer, architect, or even DevOps engineer—you will need to start your work by understanding the business needs and translating them into what you build.

5.5 Summary

In this part, we shift our focus from low-level communication between components to the design and architecture of services within a distributed system. Until now, we have treated components as simple scripts communicating via sockets or message brokers, but now we explore what makes a component a service and how to design it effectively.

A service is more than a simple component—it orchestrates multiple responsibilities, ensures cohesion, and integrates into a larger system while maintaining scalability, reliability, and business alignment. It is, in fact, something very complex that needs careful analysis and implementation.

We will soon introduce foundational architectural principles such as Domain-Driven Design (DDD), which emphasizes modeling software based on business needs and shared language, ensuring that technical implementation directly reflects the domain it serves. We'll also explore hexagonal architecture, which advocates for clear boundaries between a service's core logic and its external dependencies, making the system more adaptable and maintainable.

Furthermore, this chapter discussed the evolution of service-based architectures, distinguishing between traditional Service-Oriented Architecture (SOA) and microservices, highlighting how the latter emerged as a response to the challenges of tightly coupled services.

While different perspectives exist on whether microservices are a subset of SOA or a separate paradigm, we focus on practical approaches to building distributed systems.

We emphasized the distinction between coders and software engineers, noting that software development is about writing elegant code and understanding and delivering business value. A software engineer bridges the gap between technical implementation and business needs, ensuring that the system is not only robust but also aligned with its intended purpose.

We strive to have the reader embrace an engineering mindset rather than a crafting mindset so that it will provide business value and build systems that are meaningful to the business.

With these concepts in place, we now move forward to explore in depth how to design and implement services that form the backbone of scalable and efficient distributed architectures.

CHAPTER 6

Domain-Driven Design (DDD)

6.1 Business First

6.1.1 A New Approach

Traditional software development often begins with technical considerations—choosing frameworks, setting up infrastructure, and structuring the codebase based on programming paradigms. However, any software development process is the response to a business need. For example, a bank may request a system to process loan applications automatically. Engineering teams do not build things out of nowhere; they have specific requests to build something. You might be familiar with the software engineering process of gathering requirements, requirements elicitation, and so on. Once the requirements get translated into user stories (if you follow this approach), the connection between the engineering team and the business teams is lost, and only figures like the product owner, project manager, and so on are keeping this link. In fact, these people are seen, from the perspective of the engineers, as the ones who interact with the non-technical people and relieve them from the burden of meaningless chats about things that businesspeople would not understand. From the perspective of businesspeople, these figures are the ones who try to help them make some sense with the engineering team and explain to them what the problems are and why things are not like they expected.

Many people seem to think this is the way forward. However, project managers need to manage projects, and product managers need to work on products. If mediating between different teams is part of the job, putting too much effort into it derails them from their actual job.

This creates a dichotomy between engineering and business functions, which in turn creates an overall dissatisfaction and reduces not only productivity but also happiness.

How can we mitigate these problems, have people understand each other, and yet focus on what they really care about, which is marketing for the marketing team, sales for the sales team, and building software for a software engineering team?

Fortunately, there is a solution, but it is not a silver bullet, cannot be applied everywhere, and is also quite complex. This solution is called Domain-Driven Design, generally addressed as DDD.

It works by defining a common domain that the whole company will refer to, whatever the function, and a set of smaller domains related to specific functions, like marketing and sales. Each domain will have a domain language, which includes entities (e.g., a customer or order) and value objects (e.g., a money amount or address), among other things.

Let's understand that this language is focused on being easily translated into architecture and software design, but it also adheres closely to business needs and how the business sees that the product should work.

In a distributed system, and especially when applying Domain-Driven Design (DDD), the traditional approach seen at the beginning of this paragraph is reversed: business needs come first. A system exists to serve a purpose, and that purpose is rooted in the domain within which it operates. This means that before writing a single line of code, we must first understand the business goals, the key problems being solved, and how different parts of the system contribute to delivering value.

In this approach, software is not just a collection of services and data flows but a reflection of real-world business processes and operations. By engaging with domain experts early on, engineers gain a deep understanding of the business, ensuring that the system is designed around actual needs rather than assumptions. This shift in mindset allows teams to avoid unnecessary complexity and instead create efficient and meaningful software.

We shape our technical design around business operations rather than forcing business requirements into rigid technical models. This leads to a more natural and maintainable architecture, where changes in business strategy can be accommodated without unnecessary refactoring. A business-first approach also promotes collaboration between developers, product teams, and stakeholders, breaking down silos and ensuring that all parties contribute to shaping a system that truly aligns with its intended purpose.

By adopting this new perspective, we lay the foundation for a more cohesive, adaptable, and purpose-driven software system that evolves alongside the business rather than becoming an obstacle to its growth. In the following sections, we will explore how this philosophy fosters stronger cohesion between disciplines and how language is crucial in maintaining alignment across teams.

6.1.2 Cohesion Across Crafts

Let's spend a few more words on the relation between different crafts. If you have ever worked in a team, especially a mixed team, you might have been in one of the following positions:

1) As a backend engineer, you didn't really care about what front-end people needed; you were building an API focusing on data transfer economy and database structure and strongly opposed giving more data, which you deemed unnecessary, to the front-end.

2) As a front-end engineer, you wanted to structure your code according to your best practices and get all the data you wanted. Maybe you enjoyed GraphQL for the autonomy it gives you, but you fought with back-end engineers for not receiving the data you wanted.

3) As a programmer, you fought with QA engineers because what you built is perfect from your perspective, and QA engineers are just so picky and cannot read between the lines of what is really needed.

4) As a project manager or product manager nowadays, you always see engineers too focused on technical issues without even knowing about business needs, so you need to work as a cushion between business and engineering, trying to translate the needs of both, avoiding providing too much information to either party. If you read this book, you most likely are a technical manager, and you are not even able to cushion very well, and if you have never managed, you might see the struggle in your manager even if you do not realize how big it is.

5) You might have struggled interacting with marketing people, salespeople, and even HR on matters that seem not to bother anybody from these teams when they interact between them.

In general, you might have noticed that the farther the craft of the person you interact with is from yours, the worse the understanding is, and the more frustration arises. Of course, we are focusing on work-related matters, not small talk, but the stress might get very high when talking about work because the misunderstandings build up.

Now pause for a moment and think about what would happen if you could talk to anybody about work the same as you would with your favorite colleague. Whenever you build something, everybody is happy that you built exactly what they were thinking. If there is an issue with the product, all of you agree to the fact that there is a problem, and you are happy to fix it.

When we talk about cohesion between crafts, we are not talking about giving unnecessary technical details to non-technical people, nor are we talking about having engineers understand everything about other crafts; this would be very impractical for either party. What we need is a way to bridge the gap as easily as possible so that the people won't speak different languages.

This might seem now a bit of a joke, but essentially, as people from different teams speak, figuratively, different languages, that's exactly where we can act upon and start building an actual language that is shared between the teams.

Cohesion across crafts ensures everything is aligned between teams, functions, and hierarchies. Increased communication and understanding helps not only with mood but also with productivity, time to market, and anything else work-related.

All this might seem not very related to distributed systems, and, in fact, it is not applied only to distributed systems, but the most common systems now developed are distributed. These systems are pretty complex, so the techniques and strategies explained in this chapter are highly beneficial to the subject. In a nutshell, they check all the boxes for being applied in this context.

6.1.3 The Importance of Language

In many posts about DDD, there is a lot of focus on how to structure the code, the layers, and the code artifacts like entities and value objects. What many people take from full DDD books are design strategies and patterns, a way to better craft their code, a way that is more maintainable and that somehow helps with communication with the business.

It is not hard to understand the reason: these books and articles are picked up by coders whose only interest is to craft code. They buy the narrative that DDD will help them with their system, and they will get the side effect of pleasing the business. It is not surprising that the business will still not understand them, and the frustration will be the same.

As mentioned earlier, DDD is for software engineers who are not merely coders. If you pick up any DDD book, you will see the first chapters talking about the relation between software and business and how to model code to match the business, and it all starts with language.

With a language, we communicate with others, be it a programming language that we use to communicate with a machine or with a colleague. Furthermore, it is pretty much established that the code with which we write software has to be understandable also to other programmers so that they can modify it.

The next step is to understand that language is the key to communicating business needs and requirements, as well as struggles with how something works. All books about DDD start with this, and yet the subject is often overlooked, and people say things like: We are doing DDD, but just the design part. The key point is that there is no design part, or at least there is no design part without the language part.

At times, people will define a domain folder for their project, and yet, that will be a set of shared entities and interfaces, which might still be far from an actual representation of the business as a non-technical person would understand it.

The reason for implementing DDD is to connect engineering with other functions, so it is crucial that a common ground is set between them, and, as said, this common ground must be the language so that people can understand each other.

DDD introduces a powerful concept about this communication issue and the shared language: the **Ubiquitous Language**. This isn't just about using the right technical terms; it's about creating a consistent, business-centric vocabulary that developers, product managers, domain experts, and other stakeholders all understand and use—in meetings, in documentation, and even directly in the codebase.

The key traits of a good Ubiquitous Language are

> **Consistency Across Teams:** Everyone uses the same terms in discussions, documentation, and code.
>
> **Business-Centric:** The language reflects the business domain and helps align software with business goals.

In other words, if cohesion across crafts is the goal, then shared language is the vehicle that gets us there. When developers interpret requirements differently from business analysts, or when domain experts explain a concept one way but the code reflects it another, the system diverges from the business's needs. By establishing a shared language, we reduce the translation layers between crafts. Product managers no longer need to act as interpreters, developers no longer make incorrect assumptions, and domain experts see their knowledge directly represented in the system's design.

A well-crafted Ubiquitous Language has two key traits: it's rooted in the business domain, and it evolves alongside the domain. This means the language should reflect the way the business operates—using the same terms stakeholders use—and should adapt as the business itself changes. For example, if a retail company refers to "customers" as "clients" and "orders" as "purchases," the system should mirror those terms precisely. This keeps everyone on the same page and ensures the software models reality accurately.

At the same time, the language should live in the code. Class names, method names, and module boundaries should reflect the same language spoken by the business. If the domain expert talks about "booking a reservation," the code should contain a `ReservationBookingService`, not a vague `ProcessHandler`. This makes it easier to discuss and modify the systems over time.

Ultimately, by prioritizing a shared language, we transform cross-functional collaboration from a painful exercise into a productive dialogue.

6.1.4 Product Focus

When working on something, whatever it is, we tend to focus on our specific job or our area of expertise and forget much of what lies around. It is normal. Otherwise, there would not be different functions in a company, and everybody would know everything about every aspect of the business. We do generally understand that we have to know something that borders on our work, and, of course, we do not go much further.

We are not implying that this is wrong, and it is very important to understand that we have very clear duties and that we need to focus and excel in our functions. The aim of this chapter is not to tell you that you need to be both a software engineer and a marketer and also a salesman and so on.

We introduced and will see in more detail how gathering and building a common language is the key to being as productive as we were omniscient in all the functions of the business without actually having to be, but one thing is very important to understand: the product is the most important thing.

We've seen how product management has taken on more and more importance in recent times; this is because there has been a shift from focusing on procedures and management to actually delivering value, so putting all efforts into making the best product is what has proven to give the best results for a company.

This is no different for a software engineer; understanding what you are building and why is crucial and helps make sense of the language that will be built together with you.

Good code, great design, and wonderful architecture are all must-haves, but before that, they need to be based on solid ground: value.

This is why, independently of your function in a company, you must put the product above all, obviously working-wise.

In this narrative, a "product first" mindset means shifting the focus from internal technical considerations to the external impact—what the product achieves for the business and its users. This doesn't mean abandoning technical quality or maintainability; instead, it means prioritizing decisions based on how they contribute to the product's success.

In a DDD context, this involves continuously aligning the software model with evolving business goals. A product-first approach ensures that every decision, from data structures to API design, serves the product's core value proposition. It encourages teams to engage more deeply with product managers, domain experts, and even customers to understand the "why" behind features—not just the "how." Engineers should ask: *Is this feature solving the right problem? Does this model represent the domain in a way that supports product growth and change?*

Moreover, a product-first mindset helps balance technical debt and delivery speed. It's easy to over-engineer for a future that may never come or to hack together a quick fix that later cripples the system. By keeping the product at the center, teams can also make better trade-offs.

At the end, DDDD is not just about building better software; it's about building better software that supports a better product. Prioritizing the product fosters stronger collaboration between functions inside the business, creating a shared sense of purpose. When the product wins, everyone wins—and the software becomes a true reflection of the business's success.

6.2 The Domain
6.2.1 Introduction

We will now see how this language, shared across teams, is created. To create a set of practical processes, you might envision a few options, like meetings, more informal discussions, or whatever brings people together. It is good to have a schematic process, but the specifics will depend on when you start all this, at which stage of your project. Ideally, you will build this from the beginning and follow along, but sometimes, you might be rewriting an already existing system, so people will feel that they have already discussed enough about the product, but it surely won't be enough.

One suggestion is to schedule a set of meetings to go through the analysis of the system. You might already have documents like tasks or product specifications, and you could use that as a starting point to define a set of words that you are going to use throughout your project. You can write that down on a document and then show it to the people attending the meeting so that you can start with them building a vocabulary that makes sense to everybody.

You will need definitions for all the elements that are going to be part of the product, hence, the language. You will have actors, actions, functionalities, and whatever is specific to the project. If you start from scratch, you will have a product description with the functionalities and the actors for the product, so it should be easy to extract them. A backlog of tasks, maybe user stories, might help too, but if that has been created before the definition of a domain language, these tasks will have to be updated to match what's already been defined.

All this might seem very straightforward to you, but let's have a look at what happens with a practical example, a very common example: You need to build a booking system for a health practice. Engineers tend to start with a registration/login system, which is pretty standard. You, as an engineer, will start by designing something like "user" registration or login; then, you might think about user details and so on.

The director of the practice, who is the one who commissioned the product, is a doctor and will ask you, "So, where do the patients register?" Of course, you will show him the form and everything else and will reply, "So here is where the users..."

It is very normal for you to understand that when the doctors talk about patients, they are actually referring to the users of the system. This is pretty straightforward, but the thing will replicate for many terms, and a patient is not exactly the same thing as a user. Surely, they will both fit into the definition of who books an appointment, but they are two different concepts. Imagine now that marketing teams will join the conversation, and, talking about potential patients, they will call them "leads," which will register to the system. The actual users, already registered and using the service, will be the subscribers.

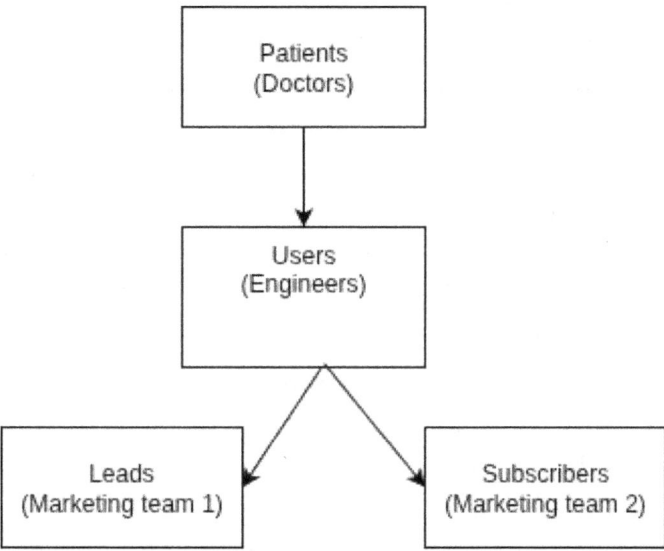

Figure 6-1. *Different naming on patient's concept*

You will see that while the marketing people will start using all these terms and making assumptions on how the system will have to be different depending on if a person is a lead, a subscriber, or a visitor, the doctors will most likely just call all of them patients, possibly even if they have not registered yet. The engineers will jump in, explaining that there is no difference between many of these personas, as they are users anyway. This situation is depicted in Figure 6-1, where the same concept of patient is expressed with several different names, even inside the same department, like in the marketing case.

You can see where this is going. This scenario might seem slightly exaggerated, but you would be surprised by how often this situation happens.

It is clear, then, that everybody needs to have clear in their mind how to call things so that there is no ambiguity and that nobody expects different things to happen in the system to be built.

In the same meeting, people from every team must understand precisely what everybody is talking about, and the only way to do that is to have a ubiquitous language, a general domain language that applies to all aspects of the product.

We are not here to tell you in your specific situation what the correct names are, and even in this booking system, we cannot provide a final correct answer, as it will depend on the teams involved and actual features to be built, but we will not go into this detail here.

We will assume, in this case, that "patient" is what everybody will understand; it is a health practice, after all, so whoever is going to use it is going to be a patient.

This will mean that you must have a definition in your domain language for a patient, and you will have some struct in your Go code called ***patient***. You might not start thinking that a patient must be there but maybe a user is something else and should still exist, and you will soon understand that when building the part of the product related to marketing the practice, there will be a need for discriminating between leads, prospects, and subscribers, for example.

Here, things start to get complicated because **a common language cannot include everything needed by every single team or function**. If we were to do that, people would still use their terms, and nothing would change for the initial chaos. If we don't give marketers the possibility to talk about their entities of interest, however, they won't be able to perform their duties.

You can clearly understand that a common language is needed to talk about shared things, while each function of the business needs a specific language tailored to its needs.

At this point, you might think that these different teams can still use their language and that language does not have to be documented by you, as you won't have to touch marketing, sales, or doctor's language.

This is not true; if every team has some overlap with some other teams and needs to get part of their specific language, the chance is that at least a small part of the product you will build will be related to any of the existing team's area of action.

In a very big system, different engineering teams will handle the software part of the product related to specific business functions. You might find that one or more teams will work on building software features related to marketing, some teams will work on sales features, and so on. The way the teams will be divided, if they are, depends on specific situations that we will not address here, but it's clear that if a team works on marketing features, they need to incorporate in their language things like leads, prospects, etc.

This will, in fact, reflect in their code. You will see that a team working on marketing features will most likely include Go structs called ***Lead, Prospect, and Visitor.*** In an ideal, well-structured scenario, only those teams will have a codebase incorporating these structs. There might be the case that some of these concepts are more general, so they will be pushed up to the general domain language of the product, but everything else will lie in a specific domain language.

To summarize, we will have a ubiquitous language understandable by everybody in the company, in this case a health practice, which expresses a domain shared by every employee across every function, and then some other domain languages specific to an area of the business, which will reflect in how the product should work and in the actual code written.

Bear in mind that while the company-wide domain language should be understood by everybody, a marketing-specific domain language needs to be understood only by the people who work within the marketing domain. Please don't be fooled by "within the marketing domain" because this also includes the software engineers, now we can call them that, who work towards marketing-related features.

You can understand that this idea of creating languages for different layers of people in the company highly focuses on business structure and goes in a different direction with respect to what engineering teams often look like or how they are generally structured. In other words, applying DDD has an impact not only on the code you will write but also on the structure the engineering departments will have. If all engineers work on every single bit of the platform, they will need to know all the domain languages specific to every domain, at which point this will help non-technical people but will be very complicated for the engineering team. We will not dig into how engineering teams should be structured and how the whole department should be structured; we suggest, however, having a look at the Spotify model for agile teams. It is important to stress that this model is not even really applied by Spotify itself, but it gives quite a lot of good ideas about structuring a whole company. You might find yourself in a company that already utilizes some of these ideas.

A key principle is to divide the engineering teams into domains, which is already a name that links to DDD. A domain might be marketing or sales, but it could also be growth or advertising. In a company with a worldwide presence, it might make sense to have country-specific domains. Looking at how the business is already structured, it might be easy to guess what the domains are. We are not saying that every company is well-structured and has clear domain separations, but let's assume you are in one of those or that you might help reshape the company structure into something that is more productive.

Once the domains are clearly defined, it is easy to create domains within the engineering function. We are not discussing if engineering is going to be under a whole function or if each engineering team will be part of a domain; that is left to the company to decide, but ideally, one or more engineering teams will be working only on features for a specific domain.

You might wonder what will happen to backend engineers, frontend engineers, and so on, because they will need to communicate and share information. This book is not about company organization, but there are ways to keep engineers up to date with what happens in their field. We are focusing here on how to structure an engineering department to have access to specific business-related domain languages, giving to everybody as little as possible knowledge outside of their field of action: software engineering.

We hope this introduction will trigger your interest in shaping teams, as it is often an underlooked problem in software engineering, and that this will make you more of an engineer than a coder.

6.2.2 Data Structures

Once a shared language is established, the next step is to **reflect that language in the code**. The structure of data within a system is not just a technical concern—it is a direct **representation of the domain** and the **concepts** agreed upon by all stakeholders.

When defining data structures, the first instinct of many engineers is to focus on **database schemas** or **how data will be stored**. However, it is crucial to take a **domain-first approach**, ensuring that the structures in the codebase match the business **concepts** rather than prematurely optimizing for storage or performance.

For example, if we continue with our **health practice booking system**, we have already established that the term **"patient"** is the shared language term used across teams. That means our code should explicitly define a **Patient** data structure, not a generic **User** that might lead to confusion. However, marketing still needs to distinguish between **leads, subscribers, and visitors**, so these concepts should also be reflected in the data structures but within the context of their specific domain.

A **well-structured domain model** does not just capture data; it captures **behavior**. A patient is not just a set of attributes (name, date of birth, contact details); they also **interact with the system**—booking appointments, updating medical history, or making payments. Structuring data **only as flat database records** ignores these behaviors and risks making the domain logic harder to manage.

Instead of immediately mapping domain concepts to database tables, we should define **rich data structures** that accurately **express intent**. In Go, for instance, instead of treating a patient as a plain struct with getters and setters, we can define **methods** that encapsulate business logic; for example, we could think, for now, to do something like this:

```
type Patient struct {
    ID              string
    Name            string
    BirthDate       time.Time
    Email           string
}

func (p *Patient) BookAppointment(date time.Time) (*Appointment, error) {
    // Business logic for booking an appointment
}
```

This approach ensures that the data structure is not just a passive container but an **active part of the domain logic**.

Moreover, each business domain within a company might require **different representations of the same concept**. In the **marketing domain**, a patient may be represented as a **Lead**, while in the **medical domain**, the same individual is a **Patient**. Rather than trying to create a one-size-fits-all data structure, it is better to model these separately while ensuring that they remain **logically connected**.

By carefully designing data structures around the **ubiquitous language** and **business behaviors**, we ensure that our system remains **flexible, maintainable, and aligned with business goals**.

What we've just seen with the **Patient** structure is called an **entity** in DDD. An entity is a basic data structure together with **value objects**, which are defined in a domain language.

Both entities and value objects express the elements of the business, the things we act upon in our product. Before getting into the details of how they differ, let's take a step back and think of what we've said at the beginning of this paragraph: that we do not start with the database in order to define the data structure, but the business. You might have shaken at this statement, but fear not, all the things you know about databases will still apply here, and you will still be able to create your data as it makes sense to get performant software. We will see, later, how to create different layers, but bear in mind that no businessperson will ever care about what happens deep inside your code; they will focus on the functionalities provided and the ones they want to be built. You might start understanding that we are creating an interface for external communication that mimics the business processes, but that does not mean that this is a facade and that you can then feel free to write your usual code, as long as the interface is kept. It is not like that. The thing is, in a big project, otherwise there wouldn't even be the need for it to be distributed; you cannot think it is simply a set of CRUD service. Each service, or microservice, will perform some duties that are not merely adding or deleting some data as from a direct request. Still, deep down, there will be some CRUD functionalities. At the end of the day, a patient will need to book an appointment, the patient will be stored in the database, the booking will be there too, and the appointment, if it is a different entity than the booking, will be in the database too.

The thing is, all you might ask the service to do is to create a booking for a patient; that is the business action. The business will want a booking number after the patient has booked an appointment. The fact that an appointment will be created too and then added to the database and the fact that many other things will happen to other services or any table is irrelevant to the business and to the domain. A businessperson will never ask you about the booking struct, or the bookings table, or if it is the same thing or not as the appointment inside the database; they will stand by what is available in the domain language, which you will need to gather from them.

In the earlier example, the code shows a **Patient** struct with a method **BookAppointment,** but there was no code specified for that method. We will now change a bit and then complete that code:

```go
// The Patient entity itself has business logic
type Patient struct {
    ID           string
    Name         string
    BirthDate    time.Time
    Email        string
    Appointments []Appointment
}

func (p *Patient) BookAppointment(date time.Time, reason string) (*Appointment, error) {
    // Business logic for booking an appointment
    appointment := &Appointment{
```

```
        PatientID: p.ID,
        Date:      date,
        Reason:    reason,
    }

    // Add to the Patient's appointments list
    p.Appointments = append(p.Appointments, *appointment)

    return appointment, nil
}
```

The above code encapsulates the appointments inside a patient, which could be a good option. Your service will receive a request about booking an appointment for a specific patient; you will need, somehow, to retrieve the patient details, which is the related struct, and then apply the method to add the appointment.

You might realize a few problems here:

1. We didn't see how to retrieve the patient.

2. We didn't see how to persist the bookings.

3. We didn't see if any slot with a specific doctor is available; we didn't even mention a doctor.

Bear in mind that we do not know, in this case, the specifics of the healthcare app. We have been a bit vague, but this is intended so that we can explore different possibilities and help you make a design for your specific case.

Your app might have one single doctor, so it is not necessary to specify one. The practice might not have issues with bookings, as it has a virtually unlimited supply of doctors, so one will always be available, and we simply need to check which one it is. This is to say that these issues will have to be addressed, and the code modified, but we can't say how exactly, and we leave the ideas to you.

Imagine, for illustration purposes, that the practice works like an ER, and we only know that we have a capacity of twenty bookings per hour. We will need, somehow, to get this information, but we won't care about the specific doctor, as one will be available if we haven't exceeded capacity.

Another important thing to think about is that you will be able to give suggestions. We are assuming a business is correctly administered, but if the practice is not afraid of overbookings, you might not even care about this detail, and the code will be perfectly fine as you have seen it. We are not suggesting you build a bad product; however, although an engineer's role is to also offer suggestions and to understand the business well, unfortunately, some decisions are out of your reach, and you need to make the best product out of the requirements and specifications.

Let's now address the question of persistence. We have just stored the appointment in the memory, and we haven't even persisted it in an in-memory list. The change, which happens via an external request to the service made asynchronously via NATS, will run inside a function and then be lost. We will not care about persistence in this paragraph, but we will see later how to do it. What you need to know at the moment is that we are defining the domain of this application; we are translating the domain language, which you and the business have defined earlier, into actionable code, but we are focusing here only on what is included in the domain language. The domain language won't have anything to do with databases or HTTP requests; it is all about the actors and their actions. There will be space for all the rest, but we are focusing now on the **domain** only, so everything that is of importance to the business.

Again, to reiterate what we said earlier, the businesspeople will not care about how data structures are stored in the database and which database, but they will care that there is a patient, there is a booking, and that a patient can make bookings.

You can now see why these structures and methods are important, but be careful to include this information only in the domain and to not add anything that is not of relevance to the business.

One thing that might not be clear is where we will add all these data structures inside our codebase. Practically, where do they lie in our folders or packages? We will see this better later, in the next chapter, but imagine that all the code of the domain must be clearly separated, so we will have a package called **domain** or whatever you want, with specific subfolders/subpackages if needed. We will call these elements like entities or whatever else via something like

```
domain.Patient
```

Before discussing the other data structure types available in the domain and how they differ from each other, we will anticipate that communication between different layers of the system in DDD is restricted. The different layers are not necessarily to be considered one on top of the other; we will see a better layering later; they are more like different packages, and the communication between these packages is somewhat restricted. The key principle to keep in mind is that the domain is used as the only way to communicate between different layers: the presentation layer, for example, will ask the app layer to perform actions but will send or receive domain structures from the app layer. Each layer can hold its structure but cannot share its layer-specific structures with any other layer. We will see this better later; for now, consider the domain as the layer or package holding all the shareable data and operations between different application parts.

It is now the moment to see the other data structure and distinguish it from the entities. These other data structures are called **value objects**. As the name states, these are objects (in Go that will be represented by a struct) that hold values but have no identity.

It seems a bit confusing, as entities also hold values, but there are key differences in the focus. A value object has no identifier. As a rule of thumb, if the concept you need to translate into a struct needs an ID and needs to be retrieved by an ID that is itself an identity, and struct will represent an entity. If the struct will represent a concept that has no ID, then it will be a value object.

You can now create your code with this in mind, but the next important thing is that value objects are immutable. If you need some details about a bank account or a patient, but you are bit interested in the patient itself of its identity, and you are making some statistics, or whatever else is needed, you won't need to change its values.

Let's consider a very basic example: an amount of money. You might want to multiply an amount of money or something, and you might want to use it in calculations, but you do not need to modify that variable's value.

A value object holds some values that you can use in calculations, but you do not need to change it. Let's review and modify the earlier example with appointments:

```go
func (p *Patient) BookAppointment(date time.Time, reason string) (*Appointment, error) {
    // Business logic for booking an appointment
    appointment := &Appointment{
        PatientID: p.ID,
        Date:      date,
        Reason:    reason,
    }
}
```

```
        // Add to the Patient's appointments list
        p.Appointments = append(p.Appointments, *appointment)

        return appointment, nil
}
```

You see that the appointment has a patient ID but not an ID itself. We might argue that we do not even need, most likely, a patient ID, but surely we do not need, in this case, an appointment ID. We are creating this struct, and we can use it as a value object because it simply holds some values. If we want to modify an appointment, we can simply override it with a new appointment.

Bear in mind that you can enforce immutability via lowercase attributes, a **NewAppointment** function, and getters, but the point of DDD is not to force your code. You can use naming conventions, documentation, and everything you want in order to keep value objects immutable.

For what concerns immutability, entities are not necessarily immutable. Most of the time, you'll have mutable entities because a patient will change his email address, will make bookings, and so on.

Bear in mind that this mutability is more of a concept and might not be reflected in the code. Let's take, for example, the case of the patient booking. The function might actually follow a more functional style and do

```
func (p *Patient) BookAppointment(date time.Time, reason string) (Patient, error) {
    // Business logic for booking an appointment
    appointment := &Appointment{
        PatientID: p.ID,
        Date:      date,
        Reason:    reason,
    }

    //New Patient
    np := Patient(p.ID, p.Name, p.BirthDate, p.Email, p.Appointments)
    // Add to the Patient's appointments list
    np.Appointments = append(p.Appointments, *appointment)

    return np, nil
}
```

In this case, the BookAppointment method will return a new patient with the updated booking list. We did not modify the original patient, and we might want to do it for some specific reasons in our business logic.

With this, we completed the data structures, which you can define inside your domain, and we will pass them to the services.

6.2.3 Services

The domain of your project, be it the language or the code itself, is not just a set of data structures and their methods. A domain also includes operations and processes, which are encapsulated in **Services.** A service is an operation or a container of operations performing domain logic. As we've talked only about domain, you might still be confused by what does not go inside the domain; you only know that no database interaction and database-related structures will go inside that, but now we are talking about domain logic, and you might start thinking about methods and operations that might be part of different layers. Let's stick with the domain, its language, and the business-related logic.

We were talking about bookings and appointments. We've seen that a Patient entity can book appointments, which are value objects, from the perspective of the domain, but there might be other pieces of information needed for the Patient to be able to book an appointment. In reality, booking an appointment is no trivial task, and yes, we can have a method to add an appointment to a patient, but unless a patient has embedded inside itself data like insurance (for example), or dates with availability (if applicable), or doctor's information, it will be unlikely that a simple entity will be able to perform this action. We could pass all these pieces of information as parameters, but still, think business-wise: a patient might perform the action of booking, but the practice will do the actual booking. You might actually design it as you think is better; we are only providing possible options, but it is fair enough to think that you might need some sort of structure, which does not represent concepts or actors but action performers, which essentially are services that also incorporate other services and can perform actions on entities and value objects.

Let's carry on along the line that a patient might book an appointment; they will need a date, among the available dates, and most likely they will have selected a date they found available in the system. We do not know if the system is supposed to display possible dates and block them till the user decides or abandons the system or if the dates might be taken and changed in availability during the process. Those are things to consider and gather via requirements. What we know, in this instance, is that there is a set of available dates and a chosen date. We can think of building a service that will match the requested date against the available ones and then add the booking to the patient. We will add the constraint that the user cannot book more than a week in advance and that the practice works from 7 AM till 10 PM. This will total 22 one-hour slots for appointments, and we will consider here two doctors per slot. This will bring us to 308 slots. We will have a service holding all the available slots among these 308 minus the booked ones. This means that we can have an entity representing an available slot and a service providing slots in a specific time range or exact time.

Then we can have a service for booking appointments, which includes the appointment slots service plus the patient entity, and use these pieces of information to accept or not the booking. Let's see it practically:

```go
// Appointment represents a booked appointment
type Appointment struct {
    PatientID string
    DateTime  time.Time
}

// AppointmentSlot represents an available time slot
type AppointmentSlot struct {
    DateTime time.Time
}

// AppointmentSlotService manages available slots
type AppointmentSlotService struct {
    AvailableSlots []AppointmentSlot
}

// NewAppointmentSlotService initializes slots
func NewAppointmentSlotService() *AppointmentSlotService {
    slots := generateAvailableSlots()
    return &AppointmentSlotService{AvailableSlots: slots}
}
```

```go
// GetAvailableSlots generates slots for the next week
func GetAvailableSlots() []AppointmentSlot {
    var freeSlots []AppointmentSlot
    // Return a copy of available slots
    for _, slot := range s.AvailableSlots {
        freeSlots = append(freeSlots, slot)
    }
    return freeSlots
}

// BookSlot removes the slot from the available slots
func (s *AppointmentSlotService) BookSlot(dateTime time.Time) error {
    for i, slot := range s.AvailableSlots {
        if slot.DateTime.Equal(dateTime) {
            // Remove the slot by appending the slices before and after
                the slot
            s.AvailableSlots = append(s.AvailableSlots[:i],
            s.AvailableSlots[i+1:]...)
            return nil
        }
    }
    return errors.New("slot not available")
}

type AppointmentBookingService struct {
    SlotService *domain.AppointmentSlotService
}

/ NewAppointmentBookingService initializes a new appointment booking service
func NewAppointmentBookingService(slotService *domain.AppointmentSlotService) *AppointmentBookingService {
    return &AppointmentBookingService{
        SlotService: slotService,
    }
}
```

```go
// BookAppointment books an appointment for a specific patient
func (s *AppointmentBookingService) BookAppointment(patient *domain.
Patient, dateTime time.Time) error {
    // Get all the available slots
    availableSlots := s.SlotService.GetAvailableSlots()

    // Check if the requested slot is available
    var slotToBook *domain.AppointmentSlot
    for _, slot := range availableSlots {
        if slot.DateTime.Equal(dateTime) {
            slotToBook = &slot
            break
        }
    }

    // If the slot is not available, return an error
    if slotToBook == nil {
        return errors.New("slot not available")
    }

    // Book the slot by removing it from the available list
    _, err := s.SlotService.BookSlot(dateTime)
    if err != nil {
        return err
    }

    // Add the booked slot to the patient's bookings
    patient.BookAppointment(slotToBook)

    return nil
}
```

In this scenario, we have a service that returns the available slots:

```go
// AppointmentSlotService manages available slots
type AppointmentSlotService struct {
    AvailableSlots []AppointmentSlot
}
```

We can use this to get all the available slots. We assume that the list returned by the **GetAvailableSlots** function will only return the free slots for the next seven days. We do not care how we get these data; somehow, we will inject them into this service.

We will have another service to perform bookings:

```
type AppointmentBookingService struct {
    SlotService *domain.AppointmentSlotService
}
```

Which will use the previous service to get the available slots.

This service will have a method:

```
func (s *AppointmentBookingService) BookAppointment(patient *domain.Patient, dateTime time.Time) error {
```

Which will use the Slotservice first, get the slots, check availability, and then use the patient to add the actual booking and the slot service to remove the slot from the available ones.

Let's now think about this approach; we have everything that is part of the domain, everything that a businessperson might understand or care about. In a different scenario, with different colleagues, that might not be the case, but in this case, we assumed that all these services exist in the domain because businesspeople across all departments need to talk about bookings, and they see, together with the engineers, the process like this. If there was no need for those people to understand or talk about this process, it could be somewhere else, hidden from non-technical people, but in this case, they want to know it; it is part of their process, and they use it for marketing or other purposes.

You might think that this is not performant, and it might not be, and your task is actually trying to make it performant, but not inside the domain. What we assumed here is that something else, outside of the domain, will make sure to provide the AppointmentSlotService with only the necessary data. The database might hold data for the next thousand years, but something needs to pull only the needed data and pass them to the AppointmentSlotService. We will see how to get these data in a different paragraph, but for now, we focus on the domain.

The services you've seen are domain services; they only use domain structures like entities and value objects and perform calculations and manipulations on them. All the data they manage are available to them and part of the domain.

CHAPTER 6   DOMAIN-DRIVEN DESIGN (DDD)

Technically, you might not even need, in your specific case, to remove an available slot from the list, but we assume that this is important because marketing needs to think about it and possibly do something about it during a booking.

We are not analyzing here a full real case scenario; we do not have all the answers. We are simply seeing how you might find yourself inside a real case scenario, so we will not focus on why we need to remove that slot from the AppointmentSlotService, but we assume that for some reason we have to. It is not about what you find logical based on the few things you know; it is about the domain language and the domain processes, business processes, in place. We assume that this requirement has been validated and added to the domain language for a specific reason.

To summarize, there is no silver bullet to create a domain language, but the following points are crucial:

1. The domain language has to be created with very tight collaboration between crafts; it's not a coding exercise or a good coding practice; it is an engineering process where you need to be holistic.

2. There are different domain languages for each domain and subdomain. The company-wide domain is what defines the higher-level ubiquitous language.

3. When creating the code for any function or any service inside the domain-related code, performance and optimization are purely about domain logic, not about data gathering, database, or internet communication; it is all self-contained.

4. No assumption has to be made on the functionality based on engineering practices, domain language, and its related code; it is all about business and how the product is seen working from a non-technical perspective.

We know that this is not a comprehensive introduction to DDD and to the domain language, but it gives you some principles and some key points to dig more into it.

6.3 App Layer

Let's now discuss the **app** layer, which is, as the name says, focused on the application itself. We need to understand what "application" means and how it is distinguished from the domain.

We highly stressed the connection between engineers and the rest of the business since the beginning of this second part of the book, how even the code needs to represent business language and processes, but it would be foolish to think that to align with the business we need to make sure nontechnical people have an understanding of everything that happens inside the code we write. This is fortunately not the case.

A businessperson might have an idea of how a web interface will affect the usage of an application. Still, it will reflect, to some extent, the business processes defined inside the domain. Surely, though, businesspeople or the business itself should not care about how data are stored and in what database engine.

We have, then, several layers in our application, and the business should only care about the business-related layer, the part of the application that performs business-related logic. It is straightforward to understand what a presentation or persistence layer might be about and what goes inside, although we will analyze those layers too, but when talking about application and domain, things might appear a bit blurry or confusing.

The application layer is about the application logic, but you might see it as if it is not about the business logic, or about the data persistence, or about how we interact with the application from outside, then it must be application logic. Thinking this way might help in understanding where we should put some code and where it belongs, but we can also give a practical example. We've seen earlier our booking app, and we've used the domain to perform some business logic, but these services and entities had to be somehow set up with the needed data.

Let's stop for a moment here and make some considerations. This book is not a book about DDD; it is about building distributed systems. In this chapter, we focus on DDD in order to provide some principles that are very useful when designing a complex system. We are not extensively teaching DDD, and we would like you to take these pieces of information, these inputs, and use them as you think is good. We will also provide, in the next chapter, a way to organize the layers and the way they communicate and interact that is proven to be effective. This is not, however, written in stone. You might decide to let different layers communicate or even to exclude some layers. This will result in you not fully following DDD principles and possibly lead to problems. We'd suggest you dig more into DDD if you can; otherwise, be advised that what we provide here are the standard practices that have been proven to be effective at creating robust systems. You might surely come up with a different configuration and structure based on these principles, but you would be in an uncharted area.

Now, let's go back to our booking app and the domain services and entities. We said that they must be filled with data and that the entities should be instantiated, but who would do that? Where? The answer, as you might have guessed, is inside the application layer, or app layer.

One thing that should be clear is that anything outside of the domain layer can use domain elements, such as entities, services, and value objects. The domain itself, however, cannot use anything external; it is completely self-contained.

Other layers need to communicate with each other, and the application (app) layer controls the application flow. It manages whatever is needed for each layer to do its job.

The persistence layer is responsible for gathering and storing data, which is used to instantiate domain services and entities. But who uses the persistence functionality to instantiate domain elements and execute business logic? That responsibility belongs to the app layer.

Let's see an example of code that does exactly what we just said and that lies inside the app layer:

```go
type BookingAppService struct {
    PatientRepo           PatientRepository
    AppointmentSlotService *AppointmentSlotService
}

func (svc *BookingAppService) BookAppointment(patientID string, date time.Time) error {
    patient, err := svc.PatientRepo.FindByID(patientID)
    if err != nil {
        return err
    }

    // Use domain service logic
    err = svc.AppointmentSlotService.BookSlot(date)
    if err != nil {
        return err
    }
```

```
    // Let the entity handle internal rules
    err = patient.BookAppointment(date)
    if err != nil {
        return err
    }

    return svc.PatientRepo.Save(patient)
}
```

As you can see, this service works in such a way that allows for instantiation and calls to whatever is inside the domain, allowing the business logic to run, but uses other layers to gather all the information necessary to run the application. Services in the app layer manage and control what happens in other layers.

One thing to understand, however, is that although there are some interactions between layers, the shared structures are minimal. Whatever function lies inside the infrastructure layer, it will have to use, as parameters and result values, either primitive types or domain structures. This ensures that no structure that is owned by a layer ever goes out of that layer. If we need a patient, and there is a Patient entity in the domain, and we need to retrieve that entity, the infrastructure repository that will return a patient should return a domain Patient, which is accessible by any layer, as they all speak the domain language.

In other words, business logic stays inside the domain layer, but the domain is also defining a shared language that everybody, be they people or pieces of code, will have access to. Domain structures, like entities and value objects, are part of the shared language.

As with everything, there are some exceptions when it makes sense. If a layer needs to return data that are totally application-related and not business-related, although that is a very uncommon case, infrastructure or presentation can use application-specific data structures.

Bear in mind that the reason for a domain language and sharing information through that language also has a technical reason: reduce dependencies and with that what is commonly referred to as spaghetti code. If every layer holds its data structure but exchanges only structures belonging to the domain, we abstract our code so that every service effectively has an API that is independent of infrastructure or presentation or application-specific details and only allows interaction via domain language.

CHAPTER 6   DOMAIN-DRIVEN DESIGN (DDD)

Having said that, there are cases where you might want a repository in the domain layer if that has a meaning in the business logic, and there are many cases where this applies too.

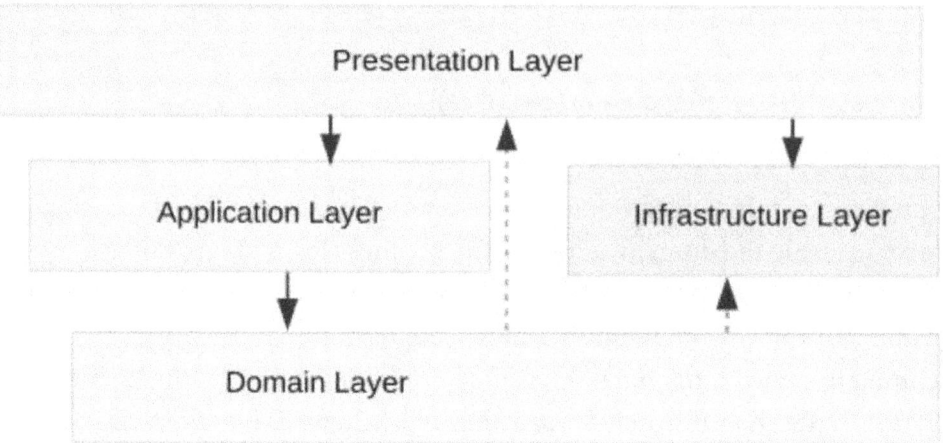

Figure 6-2. Dependency diagram

In order to understand the dependency chain and order in a general DDD application, you can have a look at Figure 6-2. The domain layer is used directly by the application layer, which can instantiate structures and services. The presentation layer can use application and infrastructure services and whatever is needed, but not directly domain services; it can, however, and should, make use of application and domain entities and structs in order to interact with other layers. Infrastructure cannot use anything directly but can accept and return domain and app entities.

6.4 Infrastructure Layer
6.4.1 Introduction

We have seen how business logic gets handled, and we've seen that application logic goes into the app layer. Still, application logic can gather and receive information from external sources but has no ability to actually contact these sources directly. Neither domain nor application knows what external sources are; they both know only whatever is related to the application, and yet they need data from a database, a messaging system, an HTTP request, and whatever else you can think of.

As you might understand, even though we want to use domain or application structures for our business and application logic, that's not necessarily what we will receive from external sources. In order to get the data related to a specific patient's identity, we will need, in practice, to get it from a database like MySQL, MongoDB, ArangoDB, or any other. The data in such databases are stored in different formats and might be spread across different collections or tables, and we need to gather them into one single Patient struct. The domain and the application layers will not have to know at all how the data are stored inside a database; they will always only need to use and receive primitive types or the structs they know. Somewhere, however, there will have to be some knowledge of how and where the data are stored, how to connect to the data source, and how to gather all the data to produce structures understandable by the above-mentioned layers.

The place where this happens is the infrastructure layer, often also called the persistence layer, although persistence might be a simplification.

The infrastructure is where the "real-world" code lies. Whatever the business logic or the application logic, you will need to contact something that is external to the application and will be part of some sort of infrastructure. The infrastructure code will perform anything that your application or business logic will require to be done outside of its scope. If you need data, the infrastructure will provide the necessary connections to get the data. If you need to send or receive messages, the infrastructure layer will provide the necessary clients or servers. Some data manipulation might occur in the infrastructure layer, but that's not data manipulation for any business or application logic; it is simply a transformation meant to provide data in an exchangeable format across the layers, hence domain or app structs.

6.4.2 Database

When getting into DDD, we often hear about the persistence layer, and it is commonly assumed that this is a layer where data are stored or retrieved. In reality, persistence is just one part of the infrastructure, or infra, layer. The infrastructure layer is where things related to interacting with external resources are implemented, and the database is one of them.

When using a specific database like Postgresm MtSQL, MongoDB or ArangoDB you will have a driver provided by the community or the organization maintaining the database engine, and that will generally be in your vendor folder. Generally, you will need some code to use the driver, like instantiating a connection, and that will be your database client, which is still a pretty low-level client.

Your application will need data and will define ways to gather this data via interfaces, which can be located either in the domain or app layer.

The key artifact used to retrieve and store data is a repository, and we saw that in the earlier paragraphs. We encountered, in fact, the **PatientRepository**, which is used inside the application layer to gather patient data. The PatientRepository is defined as an interface inside the app layer and implemented inside the infrastructure layer under the **persistence** subfolder. You might organize your folders as you want and have a database-specific folder under persistence, but essentially, you will have a repository implemented for a specific database that retrieves patients' data.

Let's assume, for now, that your database of choice is ArangoDB, so you will have a repository that will have

```
func (r *ArangoPatientRepo) FindByID(patientID) (domain.Patient, error)
```

This is straightforward, and inside the app layer, a service can use the PatientRepositoryInterface, which in turn is injected into the service as a concrete ArangoDB implementation.

Bear in mind that there is no real need to call the interface with the explicit name **PatientRepositoryInterface**, as the concrete implementations will be called via their package, so you could have a **PatientRepository** in the app layer, which gets injected an **arangodb.PatientRepository,** which is its concrete implementation.

All this might seem cumbersome, and it certainly is if you are building a simple CRUD application. We stress that even in a complex distributed system, you might still need some simple services that do not really need full DDD design. We could argue that a domain language is still needed, and it might be true, but all this layering might be too much for a simple CRUD service.

Going back to our actual scenario, where a service is complex enough to justify this design and DDD usage, we must stress that the case we just showed you is actually the simplest situation where you need data from a single source. You might get patient personal data from an SQL database and appointments or other types of data from a graph database like Neo4j. We gave an example with ArangoDB because it is a multi-model database, but in practice you might have data spread across different data sources for different reasons.

What would seem most likely natural to you is that you will define a repository interface for each data type, like PatientRepository, PatientAppointmentsRepository in the app layer, and then have the concrete implementations inside the infrastructure layer under persistence.

If you think about this, however, the two repositories will actually be shaped inside the application layer because of specific infrastructural needs. Essentially, as you know, you have two data sources; you will implicitly put this information inside the app layer, which will depend on the actual infrastructure, although this is hidden and disguised as an architectural and design decision. In your data model, in your Business or Application logic, there might not be a need at all to have two repositories for patient's details and their bookings. The repository, hence, should be just one, providing all the data. Let's see how we would handle this situation now.

We are not saying, however, that you would never need two different repositories if you are handling patients and their bookings; we are saying that you should focus, in the application layer, on shaping your data access so that it is meaningful for your application logic and not based on your infrastructure needs. Every case will be specific, but you should not create your app layer thinking about your infrastructure; in fact, you should try to build your infrastructure layer afterwards.

Let's see, practically, how we would now handle the case where we have one repository and multiple data sources. First of all, we need an interface in the app layer to define our data retrieval:

```go
// app/repositories/patient_repository.go

package repositories

import (
    "myapp/domain"
)

type PatientRepository interface {
    FindByID(id string) (*domain.Patient, error)
    Save(patient *domain.Patient) error
}
```

Now, creating a concrete implementation of this will be our final goal, and it will happen inside the infrastructure layer, under a specific subfolder of the persistence package. We know that a patient's details are stored inside a MySQL database, for example, so here is a Go implementation of this situation:

```go
// infra/mysql/mysql_patient_repository.go

package mysql

import (
    "database/sql"
    "myapp/domain"
)

type PatientRepository struct {
    db *sql.DB
}

func NewPatientRepository(db *sql.DB) *PatientRepository {
    return &PatientRepository{db: db}
}

func (r *PatientRepository) FindPersonInfoByID(id string) (*domain.PatientPersonInfo, error) {
    var info domain.PatientPersonInfo
    err := r.db.QueryRow("SELECT id, name, email FROM patients WHERE id = ?", id).Scan(&info.ID, &info.Name, &info.Email)
    if err != nil {
        return nil, err
    }
    return &info, nil
}

func (r *PatientRepository) SavePersonInfo(info *domain.PatientPersonInfo) error {
    _, err := r.db.Exec("UPDATE patients SET name = ?, email = ? WHERE id = ?", info.Name, info.Email, info.ID)
    return err
}
```

CHAPTER 6   DOMAIN-DRIVEN DESIGN (DDD)

As you can see, this repository includes two methods, **FindPersonInfoByID** and **SavePersonInfo**, which are not in the original app layer interface. In fact, this is not a concrete implementation of an interface present in another layer but simply a repository to access some patient's personal data; this repository shall not be used outside of the infrastructure layer.

We still need bookings, and these are stored inside a MongoDB database, so let's see how we can retrieve those:

```go
// infra/mongodb/mongo_patient_booking_repository.go

package mongodb

import (
    "context"
    "myapp/domain"
    "go.mongodb.org/mongo-driver/mongo"
)

type PatientBookingRepository struct {
    collection *mongo.Collection
}

func NewPatientBookingRepository(collection *mongo.Collection) *PatientBookingRepository {
    return &PatientBookingRepository{collection: collection}
}

func (r *PatientBookingRepository) FindBookingsByPatientID(id string) ([]domain.Booking, error) {
    ctx := context.Background()
    var bookings []domain.Booking
    cursor, err := r.collection.Find(ctx, map[string]interface{}{"patient_id": id})
    ..................................................
    return bookings, nil
}
```

CHAPTER 6   DOMAIN-DRIVEN DESIGN (DDD)

```go
func (r *PatientBookingRepository) SaveBookings(patientID string, bookings
[]domain.Booking) error {
        ctx := context.Background()
    _, err := r.collection.DeleteMany(ctx, map[string]interface{}{"patient_
id": patientID})
        ......................................................
    return err
}
```

We did not put the full code, as we do not need to show you how to use MongoDB driver. As you can see, like in the previous case with MySQL, we have again two methods not available in the original interface: **FindBookingsByPatientID** and **SaveBookings**. We will see now how we can combine these two repositories to actually provide a concrete implementation of the app layer's repository interface.

```go
// infra/composite_patient_repository.go

package infra

import (
    "myapp/domain"
    "myapp/app/repositories"
    "myapp/infra/mysql"
    "myapp/infra/mongodb"
)

type CompositePatientRepository struct {
    mysqlRepo *mysql.MySQLPatientRepository
    mongoRepo *mongodb.MongoPatientBookingRepository
}

func NewCompositePatientRepository(mysqlRepo *mysql.
MySQLPatientRepository, mongoRepo *mongodb.MongoPatientBookingRepository)
*CompositePatientRepository {
    return &CompositePatientRepository{
        mysqlRepo: mysqlRepo,
        mongoRepo: mongoRepo,
    }
}
```

```go
func (r *CompositePatientRepository) FindByID(id string) (*domain.Patient,
error) {
    personInfo, err := r.mysqlRepo.FindPersonInfoByID(id)
    if err != nil {
        return nil, err
    }

    bookings, err := r.mongoRepo.FindBookingsByPatientID(id)
    if err != nil {
        return nil, err
    }

    return domain.NewPatientFromData(personInfo, bookings), nil
}

func (r *CompositePatientRepository) Save(patient *domain.Patient) error {
    err := r.mysqlRepo.SavePersonInfo(patient.PersonInfo())
    if err != nil {
        return err
    }

    return r.mongoRepo.SaveBookings(patient.ID, patient.Bookings())
}
```

As you can see, this implementation implements the actual interface but uses infra-specific repositories to retrieve the data. It also uses domain entities as expected and provides a way to access infrastructure-specific data without explicitly needing to know them when using it. It all happens behind the scenes, from an app layer's perspective.

The app layer, at this point, can simply use the interface's concrete implementation as

```go
// app/services/booking_service.go

package services

import (
    "myapp/app/repositories"
    "time"
)
```

CHAPTER 6   DOMAIN-DRIVEN DESIGN (DDD)

```go
type BookingService struct {
    PatientRepo repositories.PatientRepository
}

func NewBookingService(repo repositories.PatientRepository)
*BookingService {
    return &BookingService{PatientRepo: repo}
}

func (s *BookingService) BookAppointment(patientID string, date time.Time) error {
    patient, err := s.PatientRepo.FindByID(patientID)
    if err != nil {
        return err
    }

    err = patient.BookAppointment(date)
    if err != nil {
        return err
    }

    return s.PatientRepo.Save(patient)
}
```

As you can see, the App service will use the **repositories.PatientRepository,** which is an interface, and will have no clue of how data are actually retrieved. To provide an actual concrete implementation, we will have a main go file like

```go
// main.go

package main

import (
    "myapp/infra"
    "myapp/infra/mysql"
    "myapp/infra/mongodb"
    "myapp/app/services"
    "database/sql"
    "go.mongodb.org/mongo-driver/mongo"
)
```

```go
func main() {
    var mysqlDB *sql.DB              // assume you initialized this
    var mongoCollection *mongo.Collection // assume you initialized this

    mysqlRepo := mysql.NewPatientRepository(mysqlDB)
    mongoRepo := mongodb.NewPatientBookingRepository(mongoCollection)
    compositeRepo := infra.NewCompositePatientRepository(mysqlRepo,
    mongoRepo)

    bookingService := services.NewBookingService(compositeRepo)

    // Now you can book an appointment
    err := bookingService.BookAppointment("patient123", /*some date*/)
    if err != nil {
        panic(err)
    }
}
```

which means that, essentially, we will provide the composite repository as

`bookingService := services.NewBookingService(compositeRepo)`

but inside the app layer, we will just refer to the interface we know.

You might think to implement some more complex concrete repository inside the app layer, which could be fine. Be careful, however, that this should still be designed around proper app logic and abstracted from infrastructural needs.

As an example of bad choices, let's imagine you were to implement the composite repository inside the app layer. This repository would have to use two repositories to access patient data and bookings data. We will, again, fall into the trap of unneeded PatientRepository and BookingsRepository interfaces, which are tied to the database structures.

We will stress again that in some other cases you might need, in fact, a patient and a bookings repositories; it might make perfect sense, but only if that logic is an application logic and is not defined based on the underlying infrastructure. You might, of course, be thinking about performance issues, and you are correct, but these should be addressed at the infrastructure level. Any trade-off must be implemented with in mind the fact that app layer should be independent of the underlying infrastructure.

To give an example of why we affirm this, think about what happen if you need to change your database structure and data sources: you will change your infrastructure layer's code, but you must be able to not change at all your other layers.

6.4.3 External Services

When we speak about architecture, as we've mentioned earlier, we are not just talking about data and database interactions. We might use a messaging system like NATS, we might contact REST APIs, we might provide gRPC or HTTP servers, we might want to interact with Docker or Kubernetes, and we might want to send logs. Everything that is outside of the application we are building, everything external, will be contacted via some infrastructure-specific code, which will have to lie inside the infra layer. We will not show here how microservices should interact with each other; we will see this later on, but we have to stress that even interactions with other services must have some connectors, or drivers, or client libraries, which will lie inside the infra layer. Some of this code will have a corresponding interface in the app or domain layer, as we've seen for the database, but some other code will stay inside the infra layer or will be used by the presentation layer, which we will see later.

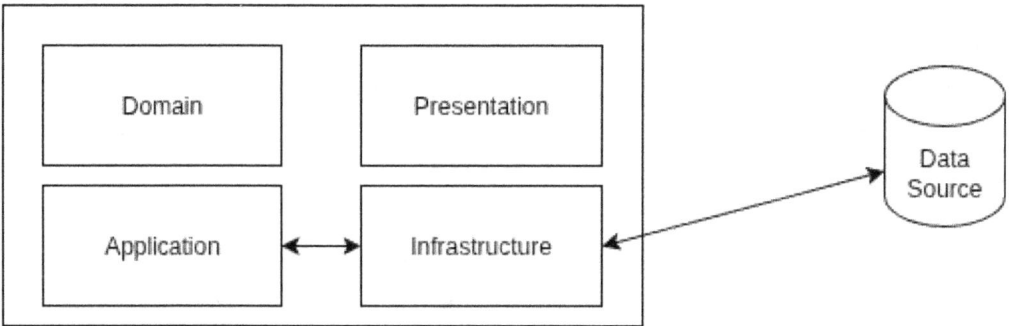

Figure 6-3. *External services communication*

We will see in the next chapter a very good way of organizing the different layers and how they should communicate. For now, we give a simple idea in Figure 6-3, where the infrastructure layer is the connector to the external services and is commanded by the application layer.

Let's now say we have an external service that will provide us with the patient's preferences, which for some reason is not inside a database or, as it might make more sense, will be available inside the patient preferences microservice. It is not a matter of this chapter, or even this part, to decide whether getting data from another service is a good or a bad idea. In any case, you might face this scenario. Let's say you need to gather some personal preferences. Here is what you will have inside the infra layer:

```go
// infra/restclient/patient_preferences_client.go
package restclient

import (
    "encoding/json"
    "fmt"
    "net/http"
    "myapp/app/services"
)

type PatientPreferencesClient struct {
    BaseURL    string
    HTTPClient *http.Client
}

func NewPatientPreferencesClient(baseURL string) *PatientPreferencesClient {
    return &PatientPreferencesClient{
        BaseURL:    baseURL,
        HTTPClient: &http.Client{},
    }
}

func (c *PatientPreferencesClient) GetPreferences(patientID string) (*services.PatientPreferences, error) {
    url := fmt.Sprintf("%s/patients/%s/preferences", c.BaseURL, patientID)

    resp, err := c.HTTPClient.Get(url)
    ...............................................
    var prefs services.PatientPreferences
    if err := json.NewDecoder(resp.Body).Decode(&prefs); err != nil {
        return nil, fmt.Errorf("failed to decode preferences response: %w", err)
    }
```

```
    return &prefs, nil
}
```

This code represents a client to interact with an external REST API and can be used inside another repository or app service interface like this:

```
// app/services/patient_preferences_service.go

package services

type PatientPreferences struct {
    Language string
    ContactMethod string
}

type PatientPreferencesService interface {
    GetPreferences(patientID string) (*PatientPreferences, error)
}
```

You can also imagine you want to create an HTTP server, or you might want to respond to a NATS req message. We can create inside the infra layer a NATS REP server, which will reply to a booking request:

```
// infra/messaging/nats_booking_server.go
type NATSBookingServer struct {
    conn            *nats.Conn
    bookingService  application.BookingService
}

func NewNATSBookingServer(conn *nats.Conn, bookingService application.
BookingService) *NATSBookingServer {
    return &NATSBookingServer{
        conn:           conn,
        bookingService: bookingService,
    }
}

func (s *NATSBookingServer) Start() error {
    ........................
}
```

As you can see, the app layer will define a service that actually does things, while infrastructure is using it and gets injected with an actual service instance at instantiation time, in the **main.go** file.

This should give you an idea of how to use the infrastructure layer to contact external services and how to use these connectors inside your application.

6.5 Presentation Layer

Here, we will see the last layer, which you will need to learn: the presentation layer. After seeing how the infrastructure layer connects our application to the external world through databases, message brokers, and other services, it is time to introduce the presentation layer. If the infrastructure layer allows the system to **reach outward** and gather or store data, the presentation layer is the **entry point for inbound communication** coming from clients or external systems. Whenever an external entity wants to interact with our service—whether through HTTP requests, NATS messages, WebSocket connections, CLI commands, or anything else—the presentation layer is where the request is first received and processed.

The presentation layer has the specific task of handling external communication protocols and ensuring that data is correctly mapped into forms understandable by the application layer. It does not contain any business logic or application logic itself; its responsibility is strictly limited to interaction, validation, transformation, and delegation. The transformation step is key: external systems often use formats or structures that are not aligned with the domain models of the application, and the presentation layer is responsible for reshaping this incoming data into well-formed structures that can be safely handed off to application services. Similarly, it transforms outputs from the application into appropriate response formats for the client.

In practice, when dealing with an HTTP API, this means parsing request bodies, validating input parameters, handling authentication tokens, mapping incoming data into DTOs, and calling application services with that data. When dealing with a messaging system like NATS, it means subscribing to specific subjects, unmarshalling message payloads, performing minimal protocol-related validation, and triggering application logic accordingly.

The presentation layer depends directly on the application layer, and it interacts only with the application layer's interfaces and types. It does not, and must not, directly interact with the domain or infrastructure layers. The presentation is agnostic of how persistence works or what external services the application uses internally; its concern is solely how to accept input and deliver output according to the agreed communication protocols.

It is important to note that the presentation layer might itself need to define small, protocol-specific data models—for example, request and response structs for an HTTP API. These structures should stay confined within the presentation layer and should not leak into application or domain layers. The transformation from these structures into domain or application structures is handled inside the presentation so that the application layer remains completely clean and independent of external protocols.

Another point to understand is that the presentation layer is often composed of multiple types of entry points. A service could simultaneously expose an HTTP API, consume messages from a queue, and provide a WebSocket endpoint for real-time updates. Each of these will be separate submodules inside the presentation layer, but all will share the same fundamental principle: map external communication into application-level calls and ensure that domain and business rules remain untouched.

Finally, the presentation layer must also take care of error handling at the protocol level. It translates application and domain errors into proper HTTP status codes, NATS replies, or gRPC error statuses, depending on the protocol. Errors must be communicated in a way that makes sense for the client without exposing internal system details.

As we can see, the presentation layer plays a critical role in separating the external world's concerns from the internal consistency and purity of our application's core logic. It acts as a protective shield, absorbing the complexities of communication while keeping the application's inner workings clean, decoupled, and resilient to changes in external APIs.

One thing that might seem a bit awkward is the knowledge the presentation layer might have about external information that is not present in the app or domain layers. We've seen in the previous paragraph that the infrastructure, or infra layer, is where external knowledge exists. In reality, the presentation, as we've said earlier, is an entry point, and it contains abstraction on the infrastructural part that concerns connecting to external resources, but it will have knowledge of how messages will look like when reaching it. The presentation layer will know if it is handling an HTTP request or something else. We could actually abstract also that if we really need to, but again, it is the responsibility of the presentation to "present the microservice to the world." Data manipulations and calls to application services are what the presentation will do, and also replying, as previously stated, with proper error messages.

6.6 Summary

This chapter introduced and explored the principles of Domain-Driven Design (DDD), emphasizing a **business-first** approach to building software systems. Instead of starting from technical considerations, DDD advocated that the development of any software project should be firmly grounded in an understanding of the **business domain**. This inversion of the traditional development process—where infrastructure and technical decisions usually came first—led to more meaningful, robust systems that directly reflected and served the underlying business goals.

By prioritizing the business domain, DDD naturally brought technical and non-technical stakeholders closer together, reducing the traditional gaps and misunderstandings between business analysts, developers, and other participants. A key tool in this bridging effort was the adoption of a **Ubiquitous Language**, a shared vocabulary that was used consistently by all parties when discussing the domain. This language was not only for conversations but was directly reflected in the system's code and architecture, ensuring that the way developers thought, spoke, and coded was tightly aligned with the real-world processes and terminology of the business.

The chapter then systematically explored the organization of a project into well-defined **layers**, each responsible for distinct concerns but collaborating through carefully crafted protocols. The **Domain Layer** sat at the heart of the system and encapsulated the core business rules and policies. It was composed of **Entities** and **Value Objects**, each representing concepts from the Ubiquitous Language and modeling the most important parts of the business without any technical contamination. The domain layer was intentionally isolated from infrastructural or application concerns, preserving the purity and longevity of the core business model.

Above the domain, the **Application Layer** orchestrated use cases and business processes. It acted as a thin coordination layer that delegated work to domain objects but did not itself contain business rules. It defined **service interfaces** and **use case handlers** that external layers could invoke, ensuring a consistent and decoupled interaction with the domain.

The **Infrastructure Layer** provided concrete implementations needed to interact with the outside world, such as databases, messaging systems, and external APIs. While the application and domain layers defined abstractions and business contracts, the infrastructure layer implemented them, allowing the core logic to remain agnostic about how and where data was stored, retrieved, or sent. It was where the complexity of real-world systems—such as network failures, storage peculiarities, or protocol details—was hidden from the upper layers.

Finally, the **Presentation Layer** served as the primary entry point into the system. Whether it handled HTTP requests, incoming NATS messages, WebSocket connections, or any other client interaction, the presentation layer's role was to receive external input, validate it, map it into the system's internal structures, and delegate the processing to the application layer. It isolated the external communication protocols from the application's inner workings, ensuring that the business and application logic did not leak details about HTTP, NATS, gRPC, or any other external dependency.

Throughout the chapter, a strong emphasis was placed on maintaining a **clean separation of concerns** between these layers. Communication across layers was achieved exclusively through well-defined interfaces and contracts, ensuring that changes in infrastructure or external APIs did not ripple into the domain or application layers. This strict separation allowed the system to evolve over time without becoming entangled or brittle, maintaining adaptability in a changing business and technological landscape.

By organizing software projects around **business logic** rather than **technical structure**, Domain-Driven Design ensured that systems remained aligned with the organization's needs, improving maintainability, clarity, and strategic flexibility. It transformed the software from a mere technical artifact into a faithful, living model of the business itself.

6.7 Questions

1) **What is the primary focus of Domain-Driven Design (DDD)?**

   a) Understanding technical constraints first

   b) Aligning software architecture with core business functions

   c) Prioritizing graphics and UI design

2) **Why is the use of Ubiquitous Language critical in domain-driven design?**

   a) It fosters effective communication across teams.

   b) It provides a coding language for optimization.

   c) It is used solely for project documentation.

CHAPTER 6   DOMAIN-DRIVEN DESIGN (DDD)

3) **How does DDD propose to connect the engineering team with business objectives?**

   a) By using shared domain languages and engaging experts

   b) By implementing software without business input

   c) By focusing purely on code efficiency

4) **What role do services play in the domain-driven approach?**

   a) Services are used to hard-code business logic.

   b) Services are added for aesthetic purposes.

   c) Services perform domain-specific operations.

5) **What are the main components of the domain layer in DDD?**

   a) Databases and data warehouses

   b) Entities, value objects, services, and Ubiquitous Language

   c) Mobile interfaces and graphical UI elements

6) **How does DDD accommodate different teams with specific domain languages?**

   a) By creating isolated projects for each team

   b) By allowing specific languages to be integrated into Ubiquitous Language

   c) By ignoring team-specific needs

CHAPTER 7

Hexagonal Architecture

7.1 Layered Systems

As you've seen in the previous chapter, organizing the structure of a service is a complex matter: the number of parts, what duties they should have, the boundaries between them—it all has to be carefully considered. The focus of DDD was mainly on language and boundaries and cooperation between domain experts and tech experts, but it also offered some sort of direction on how to organize the code. In fact, we talked about layers, but we never explained what they are and let you have an instinctive idea of what they mean.

Let's take a step back for a second and think of how people have been organizing code. We will not give a full history here, as we are showing a modern approach to architecting and designing systems, but it is interesting to see how the human mind instinctively tries to organize components and make sense out of chaos.

One of the oldest ways to do that was by grouping similar components together. If you have repositories, just put them in the same folder. Do you have services? All are in the same folder. In some projects, you might call things *Controllers* or *Handlers*. Guess what? They were all put in the same folder: the Handlers folder, the Controllers folder, etc. There would be no distinction between business, application, and infrastructure as application areas with clear boundaries, but the division was pretty simple. This way of setting up a project is also what was used in older MVC projects. If you are not familiar with MVC, this is a way to design a system where there are three logical parts of an application: the model, the view, and the controller.

A view is what appears to the user, for example, a graphical interface, an HTML page, and so on; the model is what acts on data: retrieves and stores them. The controller is what manages the interaction between the views and models, so it is what receives the requests parsed by a view and decides which model will handle and spit back the data needed. We will not dive deep into how these parts work, but you must understand a few things: There are multiple views, controllers, and models; the system is layered with three layers; the set of views is what makes the view layer; and so on. The MVC is a pattern, a design, and an architectural style. If you think about DDD and its layers, you will see that the presentation layer matches pretty well what the view does in MVC.

This is not to say that everything in MVC matches what is in a DDD app; that's far from reality, but it makes sense that a way of interacting with users is a layer of its own. We have several ways of splitting applications into layers, and we still have several n-layered architectures. Layering is a common feature of many architectural and design styles. If entities, services, or any data structure has specific duties and a domain of action, grouping them into sets helps us make sense of a big application and group duties together. What we need to understand now is why we call them layers and not simply sets or groups.

If you think about anything layered in real life, like an onion or the earth, you will notice that layers are in contact only with neighboring layers, the one above and the one below. This can be easily visualized in Figure 7-1, where each layer is in contact only with the one directly surrounding it.

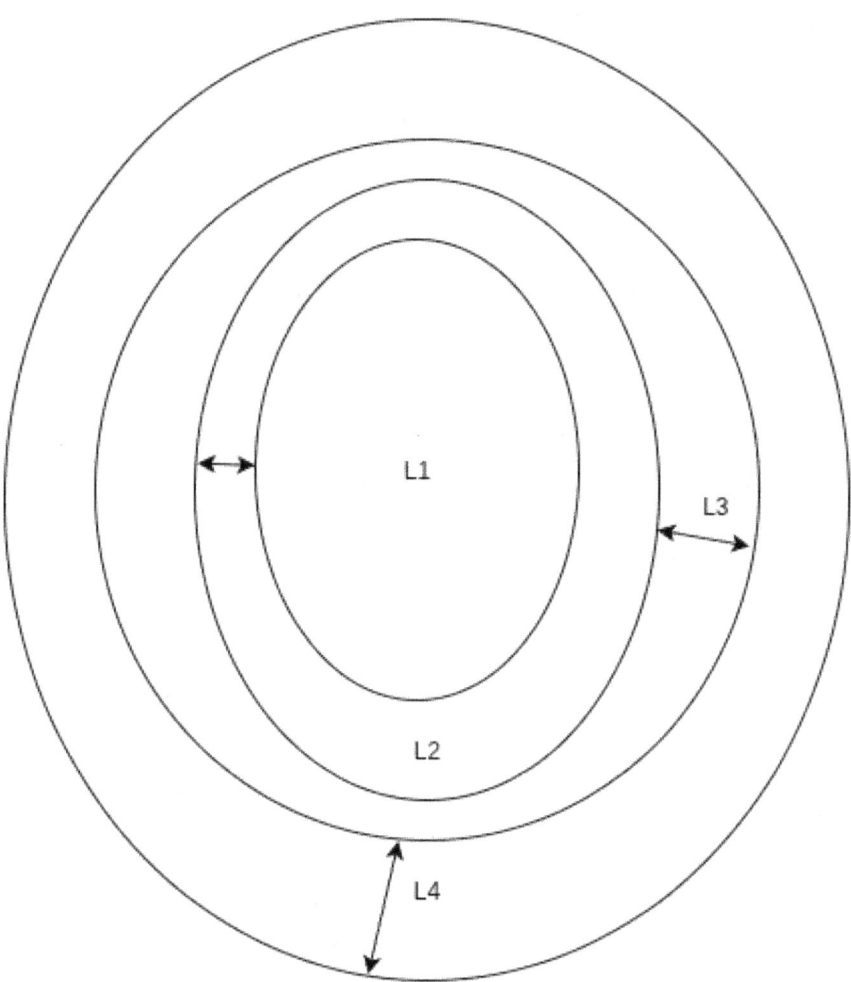

Figure 7-1. *Layered boundaries*

This structure keeps specific boundaries and borders, and it is not casual but has a purpose. If we had groups scattered around or all bordering with each other, the boundaries would have a logical but not practical meaning, as what most likely will happen is that sets interact with each other, and interacting with a neighboring set is easy, and it can be abused. What layers enforce is a specific set of boundaries not only on duties but also on how these sets communicate with each other.

This way of architecting a service or a system is not the only possible one, but one thing to bear in mind is that more communication and more interactions of any sort mean more complexity. We are trying to tackle complexity and put some order in something potentially big, which can easily grow into something chaotic. For example, if in one project, every service was allowed to call every other service directly, that would lead to a web of dependencies that makes even a small change risky and time-consuming. Having fewer points of contact and making some sort of hierarchy between layers with direct contact only between neighboring layers simplifies the whole system.

7.2 Layered Communication Styles

Once we have accepted the idea of layers in software architecture, the natural next step is to ask how these layers should interact. It's not enough to say that each layer has a specific responsibility or domain of concern—we need to understand how information and control flow between them and what kind of mechanisms we should put in place to preserve the benefits of layering. Communication across layers is not a casual process. It requires careful consideration of directionality, boundaries, and stability, and it plays a crucial role in shaping the way we can maintain the whole system.

Layers in a system typically sit on top of one another in a logical stack, with each layer calling only the one directly below it. This downward communication is straightforward: one layer invokes functionality the one beneath it offers. For example, a handler might call a service, and the service might, in turn, call a repository. What matters is that the flow is unidirectional and that each layer is isolated from the internal details of the others. The upper layer doesn't need to know how the lower one works—it just needs to know what interface it exposes. This should be clear from Figure 7-2, where stacked layers can communicate with each other only between contiguous layers, but communication can start from one layer and reach the farthest layer thanks to layer-to-layer interaction.

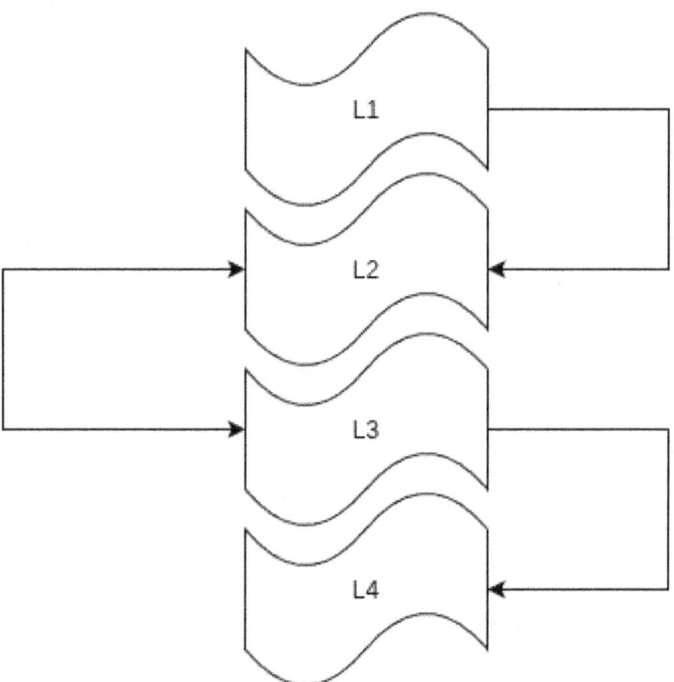

Figure 7-2. *Stacked layers communication*

This is where contracts and abstractions come in. A layer does not expose its full internal state or implementation; it defines clear interfaces or APIs that the layer above can rely on. These interfaces form the communication protocol between layers, and they serve a critical purpose: they decouple the implementation from its usage. The underlying layer can change its internal logic, replace a third-party library, or shift from SQL to NoSQL, without the upper layers needing to know—as long as the interface remains consistent.

In some systems, this abstraction is taken a step further through dependency inversion. Rather than having the upper layer import a concrete implementation from the lower one, it defines the interface itself, and the lower layer implements it. This flips the dependency, allowing the upper layer to remain completely agnostic about the lower layer's implementation details. This principle is particularly useful when it comes to testing and flexibility, as it allows mocking or swapping implementations with minimal friction. We've seen this approach when analyzing repositories in the previous chapter about DDD. We've seen interfaces defined in the app or domain layer and the concrete implementations being located in the infrastructure layer.

It is also important to stress that communication between layers is not always symmetrical. While a higher layer can call into a lower one synchronously through a function or method, the inverse is not typically true. Lower layers should not call upward—that would break the hierarchy and introduce tight coupling. However, in some architecture, we allow lower layers to notify upper layers through callbacks, event dispatchers, or message passing, always taking care to keep the boundaries clean and avoid circular dependencies. You might have encountered these approaches, but we will not really see them here, and we will not suggest their usage.

There is also the question of data formats and structures. Often, the data used inside one layer isn't suitable to be passed directly to another. Each layer has its own context and its own purpose and thus may require data in a specific form. This is why transformation and adaptation are essential steps when passing data between layers. A good architectural approach avoids leaking internal representations across layers and ensures that what is passed upward or downward is shaped specifically for the recipient layer's needs—and nothing more. Again, we've seen this when dealing with domain entities and database-specific structs.

Ultimately, the style of communication between layers defines how resilient a system is to change. The more explicit, stable, and one-directional the interaction, the easier it is to isolate changes, evolve parts independently, and maintain long-term clarity in a growing codebase. Whether you're building a tiny RESTful service or a sprawling distributed system, clean and well-thought-out communication between layers will determine how well the system holds up over time—both in terms of performance and in terms of human understanding.

7.3 Hexagonality

Software architecture is an evolving field, and even though some things have been hanging around long enough and improved upon, new ideas can still come in. Layering, even if still popular nowadays, is not the only concept that improves our system design.

At some point, a new way of logically organizing a service came up and did not consider layers at all. This new style was called hexagonal architecture. Before seeing why it is called hexagonal, let's analyze the key characteristics and then see if it is really something that hasn't got anything to do with layers.

The main assumption is that a system will have an internal way of thinking/operating and need to access external resources. A hexagonal architecture is constructed by a kernel with business and application logic, which exposes some ports to the external world. These ports are connected via some adapters to the concrete external resource.

A port is anything that requires incoming or outgoing information, which means it will provide a contract in order to get or send information. For now, you can think of, for example, a repository interface as the port that allows for data exchange with an external database engine. The interface is generic, and it allows incoming and outgoing data flow, but in order to work, there is a need for an actual adapter that will connect to the real database. The concrete implementation of the repository interface is the adapter, which will do all the actual work of interacting with what's outside of the application/service.

We referenced what we learned about DDD because we are not providing here a new alternative to DDD but rather something that can be used in conjunction with it. Although hexagonal architecture can live without DDD, we believe that those two can work together to give the software architect the best experience.

To give some more details, we are free to create our application's kernel, and this means we can use DDD and make our application code built with a domain and an application part, which we had previously called layers, and around that we can have all the connectors, or adapters, for the external world. In a way, a properly made DDD application is already hexagonal, although, on average, a bit more complex than just that.

Let's now understand why it is called hexagonal. In general, we could simply see this style as an onion architecture, like in Figure 7-3. In this case, a big core or kernel contains all that the application needs in order to work, and the adapters around it connect it to the external services.

CHAPTER 7 HEXAGONAL ARCHITECTURE

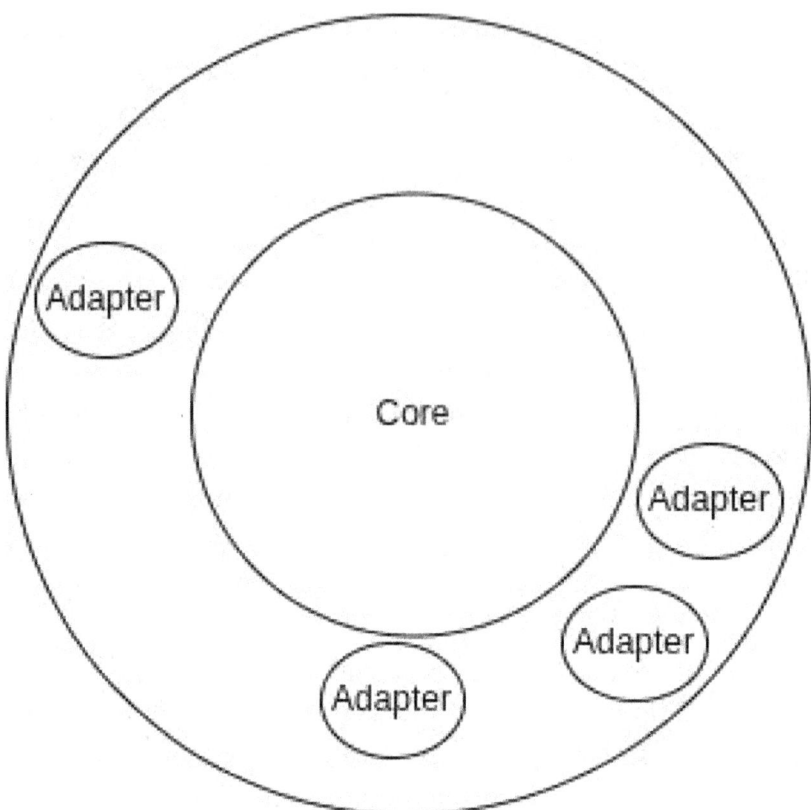

Figure 7-3. *Onion architecture*

The name is hexagonal, however, and this is not really because this shape somehow comes into place but simply because there is a common way to see these adapters grouped into specific areas of action, and these groups could be visualized as edges of a geometrical shape.

Let's see a first way to group these adapters. Let's say we have a UI to gather inputs and show outputs and a set of data sources to get and store data.

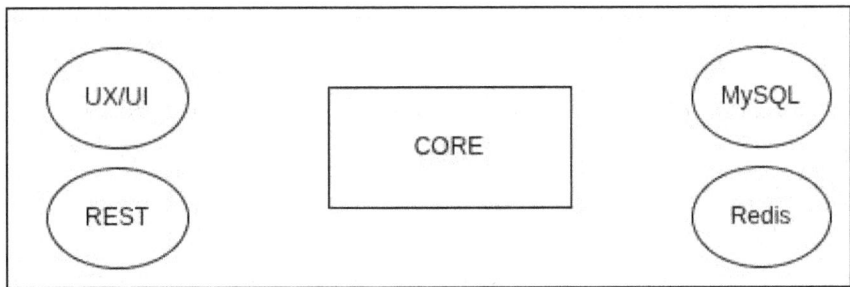

Figure 7-4. *Rectangular architecture*

In the case mentioned above, we could visualize everything related to user interaction, a graphical UX/UI, and a REST API as part of the user interaction group. While any interaction with Redis or MySQL is a persistence group. This is clearly visualized in Figure 7-4, where we have the user, human or synthetic, interaction group on the left and the data interaction group on the right.

By using a rectangle from the concentric circles, we gave a more organized view, but we can still increase the number of edges and, finally, have a hexagon.

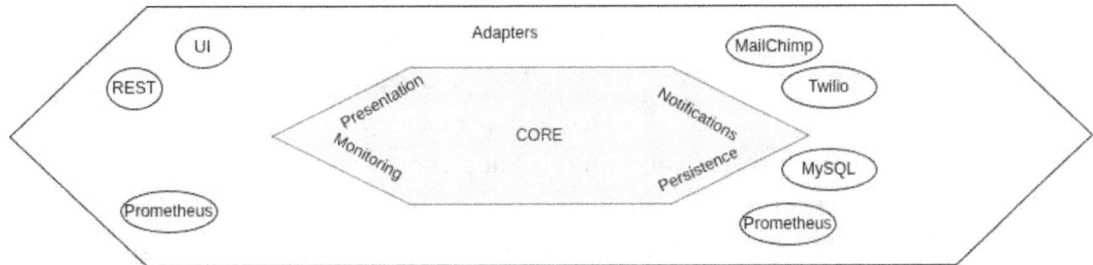

Figure 7-5. *Hexagonal architecture diagram*

We can, essentially, define some logical areas for which the application needs some connection to the external and add all the adapters we need in each one of these areas.

In Figure 7-5, we see an example where four areas, or scopes, are defined, and adapters belonging to those areas—Presentation, Monitoring, Notifications, and Persistence—are placed. These are pretty common areas, but you can define your own ones. We still see two extra edges that we could use, and you could define two extra areas for adapters to be defined. In theory, you could have n areas, making your architecture an N-edged shape. In practice, allowing anybody to define as many areas as they want would lose purpose, and groups would become way too specific. The number six has been generally agreed upon as a decent number of edges, which allows you to define a

CHAPTER 7   HEXAGONAL ARCHITECTURE

set of groups that are logically separated enough from each other but not so specific as to lose meaning. This number, as you might appreciate, is neither mystical nor analytically derived; it is an empirical value based on practical experience and informed judgment. Although the number is descriptive, we strongly encourage you not to exceed the maximum number of areas of six, but also, do not force yourself to have exactly six areas because, depending on your application, you might need less than that.

You shall see the application ports as ports in an electronic circuit, such as your Raspberry Pi. There is a limited number of connectors, and you can have some empty ones.

It's important to emphasize that there are no fixed group names you must use—such as *Persistence* or *View*. How you organize your groups, including the names you choose for them, is entirely up to you. What matters is that the grouping makes sense for your specific application. For example, while many applications might include a persistence-related group to handle database connections, this is not a requirement—you may find a different structure that fits your needs better.

In many common grouping examples, you will see that Persistence and business events are common names for application areas that need external ports and adapters to be attached. Do not take this as an absolute rule, because, for example, it is perfectly fine that you have a presentation area and a related group of ports and adapters.

Another reason for the hexagonal shape is that we can put our areas of action on the left and right sides of the hexagon, and this also has a conventional meaning. You might notice that, in fact, every connection to a potential incoming request, like UI or REST API, is on the left, while generally, things that are sent by the system or requested from it are on the right.

7.4 Communication in Hexagonal Systems

Now that we have a clear understanding of how a hexagonal system is structured, it's time to explore how communication flows within it. In the end, the success of any architecture relies on how its components interact, and in hexagonal architecture, these interactions are managed in a very specific way.

At the heart of a hexagonal system is the **kernel**, which contains the core business and application logic. This is where the real "thinking" happens. The kernel interacts with the outside world not directly but through a set of well-defined **ports**. These ports are like entry or exit points for the data and events flowing into or out of the system. They define what type of data is needed and what is expected in return, but crucially, they don't concern themselves with *how* the communication is handled.

For the actual communication to happen, we need **adapters**. Adapters sit between the ports and the external world, transforming requests, responses, or data formats so that they are understandable to the system and vice versa. These adapters are the components that make external interactions possible—whether it's talking to a database, sending an email, or receiving a request via REST.

So, to clarify, **ports** are the contracts or interfaces that the kernel exposes, and **adapters** are the components that implement those contracts, adapting the real-world communication to fit the system's internal needs.

To put this into context, let's consider a few examples:

- A **REST controller** might be an **inbound adapter**, receiving HTTP requests and converting them into method calls to the application via the exposed port.

- A **repository** interface could be a **port**, defining how the kernel expects to interact with data storage, without worrying about whether it's a relational database, NoSQL, or something else.

- An **outbound adapter** could be a class that knows how to persist data in a PostgreSQL database, implementing the repository interface that was defined in the port.

The communication model within hexagonal architecture can be broken down into **inbound** and **outbound** flows, and this is a key part of its flexibility.

- **Inbound communication** is anything that triggers an action within the application. This could be a user interaction through a UI, a REST API call, or a message from another service. These inbound events come into the system via **inbound adapters**, which translate them into the internal format the application understands.

- **Outbound communication**, on the other hand, is how the application sends out requests or notifications. This might include things like saving data to a database, calling an external API, or publishing an event. These actions are handled through **outbound adapters**, which implement the outbound ports defined by the kernel.

It's important to note that the kernel itself doesn't need to know how the adapters work. The kernel simply defines the expectations through ports. Whether it's a web request or a command from a job queue, the system's internal logic doesn't need to care about how that request is received. It only knows that the request must pass through a port, and the adapter will handle the rest.

This separation of concerns gives hexagonal architecture its core benefits: **decoupling** and **flexibility**. Want to change the way the system interacts with the outside world? Just change the adapter. The core logic stays the same.

The beauty of hexagonal communication lies in the ability to swap or mock out external systems without touching the application's core logic. Want to change the database? Build a new adapter. Need to swap from a REST API to a GraphQL interface? Again, create a new adapter. This makes the system flexible and easy to evolve without causing ripple effects throughout the application.

In summary, communication in hexagonal systems works as follows:

1. **Inbound adapters** handle incoming requests or events and pass them to the core via the appropriate **port.**

2. The **core logic** processes the request and may interact with external systems via **outbound ports**.

3. **Outbound adapters** handle communication with external systems like databases, message brokers, or other services.

Through this clear division of roles—ports defining the interface and adapters implementing the communication—hexagonal architecture ensures that the core application remains clean, decoupled, and easy to modify as external technologies evolve.

You might wonder how different all this is from the DDD, as we've analyzed it earlier. The first thing to consider is that hexagonal architecture does not enforce any domain language, so a service written with hexagonal architecture might simply not have that, and it does not enforce any cooperation between different functions inside the company. Hexagonal architecture is, in fact, an architectural style. DDD is a way to design a system that encompasses some architectural guidelines, but it is fully compatible with different architectural styles, including hexagonal architecture. By combining the two, actually, we can build very solid services, or any application really, that are also very maintainable.

One more note is how the hexagonal architecture might be similar to a kernel architecture. We've mentioned this style in Chapter 1, "Overview of Distributed Systems," but that is generally used for system applications or even desktop applications, like IDEs, where a kernel is handling the core of the application and plugins are plugged in via some openings. The two things are not the same; they have different scopes of action. An adapter focuses on connecting the system to an external interface or dependency, translating one contract into another. A plug-in, on the other hand, can contain its own logic and perform internal functionalities without necessarily interacting with the external world. For instance, a plug-in might provide additional reporting features within the system itself, while an adapter would mainly be used to link the system with an external payment gateway or database. Nonetheless, the core part and some ports that interact with an added component are somewhat similar to the way a hexagonal system works.

It should be easy now to ensure that our application, as seen in the previous chapter, also follows hexagonal architecture.

We will first make sure that the domain layer is inside the core and that the application layer can fully use the domain.

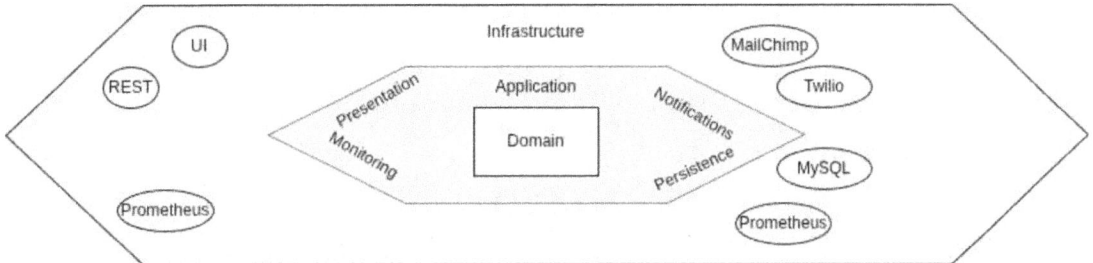

Figure 7-6. *Hexagonal DDD*

In Figure 7-6, you can see that the core is made of the Domain layer, and around there is the Application layer. The domain tends not to have interfaces for external access in order to work, while the application logic, which embeds the business logic (domain), completes the application's core and exposes ports for interaction with the external world. The different areas of the application layer can be organized into subfolders or packages to give a better separation of scopes. The external ring in the hexagon is actually the infrastructure layer, which, again, can be divided into folders/packages related to the ones seen inside the inner hexagon.

It should be clear from all we said that, of course, the way the adapters only interact with the core via the interfaces it exposes is compliant with the way DDD lets layers communicate. The core ports, exposed as interfaces, also include Domain and

Application structs; hence, the adapters, like any concrete implementation of domain and application interfaces, can use these structs, but the core cannot directly use any adapter. The core is, in fact, adapter agnostic.

As we did show both concepts, DDD and hexagonal architecture, you might wonder why we even showed them both and why DDD wasn't enough. In reality, any application built with DDD will most likely also be hexagonal, but not always. The four groups lying at the edges of the hexagon are not necessarily present in a DDD system, which does not enforce hexagonality specifically; there might not be groups after all, or too many might be present. We believe that hexagonality offers an added layer of good practices to keep things clean and manageable, but what about a hexagonal system that does not implement DDD?

As previously stated, it is difficult that a distributed system won't be complex enough to justify the usage of DDD, but this is not always the case. If you are building a small service, maybe a CRUD service, or any other very simple part of a big distributed system, DDD or the full DDD approach might be overkill. Keeping the service at least hexagonal is not so cumbersome, does not involve so many people, and could be a good trade-off when needed.

7.5 Summary

In this chapter, we have thoroughly explored two prominent architectural styles for organizing and structuring software systems: layered architecture and hexagonal architecture. Both approaches aim to address complexity and enhance maintainability, but they do so in distinct ways.

We began by examining layered architecture, which has been a popular method of organizing code for decades. The core idea behind layering is to divide the system into logical groups or sets of components, each with a specific responsibility. This division enforces clear boundaries between different parts of the application, such as business logic, application logic, and infrastructure. The system's layers interact in a unidirectional manner, meaning that each layer communicates only with the one directly beneath it. This ensures that the upper layers remain agnostic of the lower ones' internal workings, reducing dependencies and enhancing flexibility. We discussed how these layers are defined through clear interfaces and contracts, which provide a means of communication without exposing the internal state or implementation of a given layer. The concept of dependency inversion was also introduced, where upper layers define the interfaces, and lower layers implement them, allowing for greater decoupling and easier testing and maintenance.

We then transitioned to hexagonal architecture, which represents a shift away from the traditional layered approach. Rather than structuring the system in strict layers, hexagonal architecture revolves around a central core containing the business and application logic. This core interacts with the external world through ports, which define the expectations of the system's interactions. These ports are not concerned with how the communication is handled but simply define what needs to be received or sent. The actual handling of external interactions is done by adapters, which connect the ports to real-world systems like databases, APIs, or message queues. This separation between the core logic and the external systems allows for greater flexibility, as adapters can be easily swapped or modified without impacting the core logic of the system.

Hexagonal architecture introduces the concept of inbound and outbound communication. Inbound adapters handle incoming requests, such as user inputs through a UI or HTTP requests via a REST API, and translate them into the internal format the system understands. Outbound adapters, on the other hand, manage the communication going out of the system, such as saving data to a database or calling an external API. This clear division between the internal logic and external systems makes it easy to adapt to changing requirements and technologies without significant rework. One of the primary benefits of this approach is its ability to decouple the application from the external technologies, ensuring that changes to the external world—such as switching databases or replacing an API—do not require changes to the core business logic.

A key takeaway is that hexagonal architecture does not dictate how the business logic should be structured or the design patterns to be used. It is an architectural style, meaning that it can be used with a variety of design approaches, including Domain-Driven Design (DDD). DDD emphasizes the importance of aligning the system's design with the business domain, ensuring that the codebase reflects the real-world concepts and processes. Hexagonal architecture complements DDD by allowing the business logic (domain) to remain isolated from external concerns while still providing clear ports and adapters to facilitate communication with the outside world.

We also explored how both layered architecture and hexagonal architecture can work together. In a DDD context, the core domain logic can be seen as the central kernel of a hexagonal system, with the application layer and infrastructure layer surrounding it. This allows for a clean separation between the domain and other concerns such as persistence, user interaction, and external integrations. By combining DDD with hexagonal architecture, we can create systems that are both highly maintainable and flexible, capable of evolving over time without losing clarity or coherence.

Ultimately, both layered and hexagonal architectures strive for the same goal: creating systems that are easily maintainable, adaptable to change, and resilient in the face of evolving technologies and business requirements. By understanding these architectural styles and their respective benefits, software architects can make informed decisions on how to structure their systems to best meet the needs of the business while ensuring long-term sustainability.

7.6 Questions

1) **What is the primary focus of hexagonal architecture?**

    a) Enhancing graphical performance in applications

    b) Decoupling the core business logic from external systems

    c) Promoting efficient storage solutions

2) **In hexagonal architecture, what roles do ports serve?**

    a) They act as storage units for application data

    b) They define interfaces for core application communication

    c) They are responsible for user authentication

3) **What advantage does hexagonal architecture offer over traditional layered architecture?**

    a) It allows for creating several user interfaces simultaneously

    b) It ensures complete isolation of business logic from user interaction

    c) It facilitates flexibility and adaptability when integrating with external systems

CHAPTER 7   HEXAGONAL ARCHITECTURE

4) **How does hexagonal architecture enhance testability in systems?**

   a) By eliminating the need for any adapters

   b) Through clear interface definitions that allow independent component testing

   c) By using monolithic database structures

5) **What is a potential challenge when implementing hexagonal architecture?**

   a) Increased graphical load on the user interface

   b) Difficulty in defining appropriate abstraction levels for ports

   c) The requirement for a single-layered application structure

CHAPTER 8

Sample Service

8.1 Introduction

In Chapter 4, "Working System," we built a basic restaurant ordering system; we did it focusing on the communication topologies and not on how the components should have been properly designed one by one. This was a deliberately stripped-down design that focused more on how services talked to each other (using NATS) than on how they were structured internally. It worked, but it was never meant to be production-grade. In this chapter, we revisit one of its most important pieces: the Order Processor. And this time, we're doing it properly, following the principles about DDD and hexagonal architecture learned in the previous chapters of this part.

The Order Processor can be considered the heart of the restaurant's flow, as it's the part that owns the full lifecycle of an order, from the moment a customer places one all the way through fulfillment. In Chapter 4, "Working System," this service lacked real persistence, a hardcoded menu, and minimal separation of concerns. That made it easy to follow, but it also made it fragile, hard to test, and tightly coupled to the environment around it. Now, we're going to fix that by bringing in domain-driven design (DDD) and Hexagonal Architecture to reshape the service from the inside out.

The first goal is maintainability. Clean boundaries between business logic and infrastructure ensure that changing one thing doesn't break another, because the logic of one layer doesn't spill over into another layer. You can update a database driver or refactor the logic without fear of causing weird side effects in unrelated parts of the system. This kind of separation is what layered and hexagonal designs are all about, making sure each part of the system knows exactly what its job is and nothing more.

Next comes testability. When your business rules aren't buried under framework glue or database calls, testing them becomes dead simple. No need to spin up containers or run full integration suites just to check if discounts apply correctly. You swap in mocks, run your tests, and move on. That's the benefit of isolating the core: fast feedback, lower overhead, and fewer surprises.

Flexibility is another key win. Once the core logic is decoupled, you can swap out the tech stack without touching the core of the system. Whatever you decide to change, a database or a different message queue won't cause any problems. The core remains the same, and we simply wire in new adapters at the edges. That kind of plug-and-play architecture pays off greatly when requirements or infrastructure shift over time.

There is, however, more to this than clean code. Good architecture should reflect how the business actually works. By using the language of the restaurant, such as orders, menus, tickets, and fulfillment, directly in the codebase, we're narrowing the gap between domain experts and developers. That "Ubiquitous Language" is more than just a DDD buzzword, as we've stressed and will continue to stress until exhaustion, because that's how teams stay aligned and how software stays grounded in reality.

Back in Chapter 4, "Working System," we called the Order Processor "the core of the system," and it is. In DDD terms, it's the Core Domain, the part of the system that deserves the most attention and the cleanest boundaries. As we refactor it, we're also implicitly carving out a Bounded Context, a concept we'll go deeper into in Chapter 10, "DDD for Systems." By building one clean, focused service around a clear domain model, we're laying the groundwork for thinking about the larger system in modular, domain-aligned terms.

What we will analyze in this chapter, essentially, isn't a throwaway example, but it's a pattern to follow. We will present one service, properly shaped, which can serve as a reference point for everything that comes later.

In the pages ahead, we will start by revisiting the domain of the Order Processor and clarifying the responsibilities it truly owns. From there, we'll introduce a proper domain model and wrap it in a hexagonal architecture, isolating the core logic from its surrounding infrastructure. As the chapter unfolds, you'll see how persistence and messaging are plugged in as adapters, how the design makes testing straightforward, and finally how the refactored processor integrates back into the restaurant system we built earlier. Each step builds upon the last, gradually transforming a minimal working example into a robust, maintainable service.

8.2 Domain Layer

The domain layer is the core part of the Order Processor service, which defines how things should be structured from a business perspective. It implements the business logic as the business people would understand it. Its primary function is to maintain the essential business rules and ideas related to restaurant order processing. This layer is made to be "self-contained" and "pure," which means it works completely separate from outside concerns like databases or messaging systems. This is where the "Ubiquitous Language" of the restaurant domain is directly turned into working code.

We reiterated here what was mentioned in Chapter 6, "(DDD) Domain-Driven Design": the domain layer focuses purely on the business, its participants, and its processes, without any technical distractions. It represents the common language that everyone involved, both technical and non-technical, understands and uses.

We will now analyze the core concepts of the domain again, and we will see how they can be implemented in the order processor:

Order Entity

In Chapter 4, "Working System," the order was a rudimentary data structure. Within a DDD framework, it transforms into a rich entity, possessing a unique identity (OrderID) and encapsulating the behaviors that govern its lifecycle and state transitions. A significant enhancement in this re-architecture is that the OrderID is now generated internally by the Order Processor, directly addressing a previous suggestion to shift this responsibility from the customer application. The Order entity now comprises **MenuItem** (as a Value Object), **Quantity**, and **Status**. Methods such as **MarkAsPreparing()**, **MarkAsReadyForDelivery()**, **MarkAsOutForDelivery()**, **MarkAsDelivered()**, and **MarkAsInvalid()** are integral to this entity, encapsulating the business rules that dictate valid state changes for an order.

```go
// domain/order.go
package domain

import (
    "errors"
    "time"
)
```

CHAPTER 8　SAMPLE SERVICE

```go
type OrderStatus string

const (
    OrderStatusPending         OrderStatus = "Pending"
    OrderStatusPreparing       OrderStatus = "Preparing"
    OrderStatusReadyForDelivery OrderStatus = "Ready for Delivery"
    OrderStatusOutForDelivery  OrderStatus = "Out For Delivery"
    OrderStatusDelivered       OrderStatus = "Delivered"
    OrderStatusInvalid         OrderStatus = "Invalid"
)

// Order is an Entity because it has an identity (OrderID) and a lifecycle.
type Order struct {
    OrderID   string
    MenuItem  MenuItem // Value Object
    Quantity  int
    Status    OrderStatus
    CreatedAt time.Time
    UpdatedAt time.Time
}

func NewOrder(orderID string, item MenuItem, quantity int) (*Order, error) {
    if orderID == "" || quantity <= 0 {
        return nil, errors.New("order ID and quantity must be valid")
    }
    return &Order{
        OrderID:   orderID,
        MenuItem:  item,
        Quantity:  quantity,
        Status:    OrderStatusPending,
        CreatedAt: time.Now(),
        UpdatedAt: time.Now(),
    }, nil
}
```

```go
func (o *Order) MarkAsPreparing() error {
    if o.Status != OrderStatusPending {
        return errors.New("order must be pending to be marked as
        preparing")
    }
    o.Status = OrderStatusPreparing
    o.UpdatedAt = time.Now()
    return nil
}

func (o *Order) MarkAsReadyForDelivery() error {
    if o.Status != OrderStatusPreparing {
        return errors.New("order must be preparing to be marked as ready
        for delivery")
    }
    o.Status = OrderStatusReadyForDelivery
    o.UpdatedAt = time.Now()
    return nil
}

func (o *Order) MarkAsOutForDelivery() error {
    if o.Status != OrderStatusReadyForDelivery {
        return errors.New("order must be ready for delivery to be marked as
        out for delivery")
    }
    o.Status = OrderStatusOutForDelivery
    o.UpdatedAt = time.Now()
    return nil
}

func (o *Order) MarkAsDelivered() error {
    if o.Status != OrderStatusOutForDelivery {
        return errors.New("order must be out for delivery to be marked as
        delivered")
    }
```

CHAPTER 8   SAMPLE SERVICE

```go
        o.Status = OrderStatusDelivered
        o.UpdatedAt = time.Now()
        return nil
}

func (o *Order) MarkAsInvalid(reason string) {
        o.Status = OrderStatusInvalid
        o.UpdatedAt = time.Now()
        // In a real system, the reason might be stored or an event published.
}
```

MenuItem Value Object:

This is an item on the restaurant menu. Unlike an order, a MenuItem doesn't have its own unique identity separate from its attributes (name, price). It's treated as an immutable value, essentially just a description, rather than something tracked by IDs. This setup fixes the hardcoded menu problem from Chapter 4, "Working System," by giving menu items a proper domain model.

```go
// domain/menu_item.go
package domain

import "errors"

// MenuItem is a Value Object because it's identified by its attributes (Name, Price)
// and has no independent identity. It should be immutable.
type MenuItem struct {
    Name  string
    Price float64
}

func NewMenuItem(name string, price float64) (MenuItem, error) {
    if name == "" || price <= 0 {
        return MenuItem{}, errors.New("menu item name and price must be valid")
    }
    return MenuItem{Name: name, Price: price}, nil
}
```

240

The way we defined the MenuItem reminds us of Chapter 6, "(DDD) Domain-Driven Design," and the key role of the "Ubiquitous Language": a shared vocabulary everyone uses. By defining Order as an entity and MenuItem as a value object in the domain package, we're not just writing Go structs. We're directly turning how the business thinks about "what an order is" and "what a menu item is" into code. This means when someone from the business talks about an order, the engineer instantly knows exactly what **domain.Order** means and how it works. This bridges gaps, so everybody is on the same page.

As we complete with our models, we will start implementing our services:

MenuService Domain Service

This service holds the current menu, usually loaded from the application layer, and provides methods to check if a menu item exists and to retrieve it.

```go
// domain/menu_service.go
package domain

type MenuService struct {
    // This service holds the current menu, typically populated from the
        application layer.
    menu map[string]MenuItem
}

func NewMenuService(items []MenuItem) *MenuService {
    m := make(map[string]MenuItem)
    for _, item := range items {
        m[item.Name] = item
    }
    return &MenuService{menu: m}
}

func (s *MenuService) IsItemValid(itemName string) bool {
    _, exists := s.menu[itemName]
    return exists
}

func (s *MenuService) GetMenuItem(itemName string) (MenuItem, bool) {
    item, exists := s.menu[itemName]
    return item, exists
}
```

CHAPTER 8   SAMPLE SERVICE

OrderFactory (Domain Service/Factory)

The OrderFactory is responsible for creating valid Order entities. It handles generating unique OrderIDs and validating items via MenuService. This shifts ID generation from the customer app (Chapter 4, "Working System") to the core Order Processor, ensuring orders comply with domain rules from the moment of creation.

```go
// domain/order_factory.go
package domain

import (
    "errors"
    "github.com/google/uuid"
)

type OrderFactory struct {
    menuService *MenuService
}

func NewOrderFactory(ms *MenuService) *OrderFactory {
    return &OrderFactory{menuService: ms}
}

func (f *OrderFactory) CreateOrder(itemName string, quantity int) (*Order, error) {
    menuItem, exists := f.menuService.GetMenuItem(itemName)
    if !exists {
        return nil, errors.New("item not found on menu")
    }
    if quantity <= 0 {
        return nil, errors.New("quantity must be positive")
    }
    orderID := uuid.New().String() // Order Processor generates a unique ID
    return NewOrder(orderID, menuItem, quantity)
}
```

Chapter 4, "Working System," showed how hardcoded menus duplicated data across services and suggested that the Order Processor fetch the menu from the Restaurant Gateway. Here, the MenuService keeps a local, consistent menu snapshot, implying asynchronous updates from the Restaurant Gateway and embracing eventual consistency and data ownership principles in distributed systems.

Table 8-1. Core domain entities and value objects

Concept	Type	Key Attributes	Key Methods	Why
Order	Entity	OrderID, MenuItem, Quantity, Status	NewOrder(), MarkAsPreparing(), MarkAsReadyForDelivery(), MarkAsOutForDelivery(), MarkAsDelivered(), MarkAsInvalid()	Unique identity and lifecycle, encapsulates order state and transitions
MenuItem	Value Object	Name, Price	NewMenuItem()	Identified by attributes, immutable descriptive value
MenuService	Domain Service	menu (map of MenuItem)	NewMenuService(), IsItemValid(), GetMenuItem()	Holds menu data and provides validation beyond single entities
OrderFactory	Domain Service/ Factory	menuService	NewOrderFactory(), CreateOrder()	Creates valid Orders, handles ID generation and validation

Table 8-1 provides a simple and clear overview of the main decisions made when modelling the domain. It helps everyone, whether they're tech-savvy or not, get a quick and clear picture of how the business works in the code. It's like a shared cheat sheet that keeps everyone on the same page. Seeing these concepts laid out makes those architectural ideas feel real and easy to understand.

8.3 Application Layer

The application layer acts as the coordinator for the service's specific use cases. It is a thin layer that manages communication between the presentation layer, which handles incoming requests; the domain layer, where the core business logic resides; and the infrastructure layer, which handles access to external resources. A key role of this layer is to define interfaces, often referred to as "ports" in Hexagonal Architecture that handle interactions with external systems. These interfaces describe what the application needs to do, while their actual implementations sit in the Infrastructure Layer. The previous chapter explains that "ports" are the interfaces exposed by the kernel, which include both the domain and application layers, enabling the system to interact with the outside world.

Application Services

The main elements in this layer are the application services, which represent the specific functions the service provides.

The OrderProcessingService is the core application service for the Order Processor. Its duties include:

- Receiving requests from the Presentation Layer, like new order submissions.

- Using the OrderFactory from the Domain Layer to create new Order entities, making sure domain rules are enforced right from the start.

- Working with the OrderRepository interface, defined in this layer but implemented in the Infrastructure Layer, to handle saving and retrieving order data.

- Using the OrderStatusPublisher interface, also defined here and implemented in Infrastructure, to broadcast updates about order status to other services.

- Managing the entire order process, including initial checks via the MenuService from the Domain Layer, and handling status changes as the order progresses.

```go
// application/order_processing_service.go
package application

import (
    "errors"
    "fmt"
    "myapp/domain"
)
```

```go
// Interfaces (Ports) for external dependencies, implemented by
Infrastructure.
// These define WHAT the application needs, not HOW it gets it.
type OrderRepository interface {
    Save(order *domain.Order) error
    FindByID(orderID string) (*domain.Order, error)
    // Potentially other methods like FindByStatus,
        UpdateStatus, etc.
}

type OrderStatusPublisher interface {
    PublishOrderStatus(orderID string, status domain.OrderStatus,
    item string) error
}

// OrderProcessingService is an Application Service that
    orchestrates use cases.
type OrderProcessingService struct {
    orderRepo       OrderRepository
    orderFactory    *domain.OrderFactory
    menuService     *domain.MenuService
    statusPublisher OrderStatusPublisher
}

func NewOrderProcessingService(
    repo OrderRepository,
    factory *domain.OrderFactory,
    menuSvc *domain.MenuService,
    publisher OrderStatusPublisher,
) *OrderProcessingService {
    return &OrderProcessingService{
        orderRepo:       repo,
        orderFactory:    factory,
        menuService:     menuSvc,
        statusPublisher: publisher,
    }
}
```

CHAPTER 8 SAMPLE SERVICE

```go
// ProcessNewOrder is a specific use case method.
func (s *OrderProcessingService) ProcessNewOrder(itemName string, quantity int) (string, error) {
    // Application logic: First, check if the item is valid using
        the Domain's MenuService.
    if !s.menuService.IsItemValid(itemName) {
        // Publish an invalid status update immediately, even
            before order creation.
        s.statusPublisher.PublishOrderStatus("N/A", domain.
        OrderStatusInvalid, fmt.Sprintf("Item '%s' not on menu",
        itemName))
        return "", errors.New("item not on menu")
    }
    // Application logic: Use the Domain's OrderFactory to create
        a new Order entity.
    order, err := s.orderFactory.CreateOrder(itemName, quantity)
    if err != nil {
        s.statusPublisher.PublishOrderStatus("N/A", domain.
        OrderStatusInvalid, fmt.Sprintf("Failed to create order
        for '%s': %v", itemName, err))
        return "", fmt.Errorf("failed to create order: %w", err)
    }
    // Application logic: Persist the new order using the
        OrderRepository (Infrastructure via port).
    if err := s.orderRepo.Save(order); err != nil {
        s.statusPublisher.PublishOrderStatus(order.OrderID,
        domain.OrderStatusInvalid, fmt.Sprintf("Failed to save
        order '%s': %v", order.OrderID, err))
        return "", fmt.Errorf("failed to save order: %w", err)
    }
    // Application logic: Publish the initial status update
        (Infrastructure via port).
    s.statusPublisher.PublishOrderStatus(order.OrderID, order.
    Status, order.MenuItem.Name)
    return order.OrderID, nil
}
```

```go
// UpdateOrderStatus is another use case method, potentially
triggered by an internal event (e.g., from Delivery Tracker).
func (s *OrderProcessingService) UpdateOrderStatus(orderID string,
newStatus domain.OrderStatus) error {
    // Application logic: Retrieve the order from persistence.
    order, err := s.orderRepo.FindByID(orderID)
    if err!= nil {
        return fmt.Errorf("order %s not found: %w", orderID, err)
    }
    // Check if the order is already in the requested status.
    // If so, no state transition is needed, and we can
      return early.
    if order.Status == newStatus {
        fmt.Printf("Application Layer: Order %s is already in
          status '%s'. No transition needed.\n", orderID, newStatus)
        return nil
}

    // Delegate status change to the domain entity
      (business logic).
    var statusErr error
    switch newStatus {
    case domain.OrderStatusPreparing:
        statusErr = order.MarkAsPreparing()
    case domain.OrderStatusReadyForDelivery:
        statusErr = order.MarkAsReadyForDelivery()
    case domain.OrderStatusOutForDelivery:
        statusErr = order.MarkAsOutForDelivery()
    case domain.OrderStatusDelivered:
        statusErr = order.MarkAsDelivered()
    case domain.OrderStatusInvalid:
        order.MarkAsInvalid("External invalidation")
        // Direct call if no specific transition rules
    default:
        return errors.New("invalid status transition")
    }
```

```
            if statusErr!= nil {
                return fmt.Errorf("failed to update order status: %w",
                statusErr)
            }
            // Application logic: Save the updated order.
            if err := s.orderRepo.Save(order); err!= nil {
                return fmt.Errorf("failed to save updated order: %w", err)
            }
            // Application logic: Publish the updated status.
            s.statusPublisher.PublishOrderStatus(order.OrderID, order.
            Status, order.MenuItem.Name)
            return nil
        }
```

The **OrderRepository** and **OrderStatusPublisher** are explicitly defined as Go interfaces within the application package. This clearly represents the concept of "ports," drawing a firm line between what the application aims to do, such as persisting orders or publishing status updates, and how these tasks are actually performed, for example, using a specific database or messaging system. This architectural decision is a straightforward application of the dependency inversion principle, ensuring that the application layer remains independent from the concrete details of its infrastructure. By defining abstract interfaces (ports) in the application layer, the application logic is effectively decoupled from the implementation specifics of external systems.

Chapter 6, "(DDD) Domain-Driven Design," describes the role of the application layer as orchestrating use cases and managing the overall flow of the application. The methods **ProcessNewOrder** and **UpdateOrderStatus** within the **OrderProcessingService** fulfill this function precisely. These methods do not contain business rules themselves, as those are encapsulated within the **domain.Order** entity or the **domain.MenuService**. Instead, they coordinate the necessary steps: creating an order, carrying out initial validation, persisting the order, and publishing relevant updates. This clear separation distinguishes the application-specific orchestration logic from the core domain logic, which governs business rules and behaviors. The application layer acts as an interpreter of high-level use cases, for example, processing a new order from an external request and translating it into a sequence of domain-driven actions such as validating the item, creating the order entity, saving it, and publishing the status. It bridges the gap between external commands and internal business logic, defining the application's functional capabilities in terms of business processes.

Chapter 4, "Working System," noted that originally, the customer application was responsible for generating the **OrderID**. By moving this responsibility into the **OrderProcessingService** within the Application Layer and delegating **OrderID** generation to the **OrderFactory** in the Domain Layer, there is a fundamental shift in ownership. This is more than simply moving code; it makes the Order Processor service more self-contained and authoritative over its domain entities. This ensures that order IDs are created and managed consistently within the service's own boundaries, aligning fully with domain-driven design principles of entity management.

8.4 Database Layer

The database layer, mentioned in the Table of Contents, is part of the wider Infrastructure Layer. At first, this might seem to conflict with the usual Hexagonal Architecture diagrams, where persistence is just one type of adapter inside the infrastructure. However, by organizing the code clearly into an infrastructure/persistence package, the relationship becomes obvious. It shows that database code is a specialized adapter responsible for persistence within the infrastructure. This section explains how the OrderRepository and MenuItemRepository interfaces, which were defined earlier in the Application Layer, are implemented. This solves the problem of not having persistent storage in the system discussed in Chapter 4, "Working System," and follows the DDD idea that each part owns its own data.

Implementation of OrderRepository

In order to keep things simple and focus on the architecture without the burden of dealing with an external database, we will, for our implementation, use an in-memory store to save the orders. This demonstrates how the repository interface is constructed, keeping the application layer unaware of how data is stored. Choosing the in-memory store also highlights a big advantage of Hexagonal Architecture, which is easier testing. The in-memory store can be swapped out for a real database like PostgreSQL or MongoDB in production without changing the application code. This working example proves that the architecture is flexible but robust. If the core logic works well with the in-memory store, it means the system is ready to use any real database by just switching the adapter. This moves the tricky parts from architecture to handling specific technology details.

CHAPTER 8   SAMPLE SERVICE

```go
// infrastructure/persistence/inmemory_order_repository.go
package persistence

import (
    "errors"
    "myapp/domain" // Depends on domain layer
    "sync"
)

// InMemoryOrderRepository implements the application.OrderRepository
//   interface.
type InMemoryOrderRepository struct {
    orders map[string]*domain.Order
    mu     sync.RWMutex // Mutex for concurrent access
}

func NewInMemoryOrderRepository() *InMemoryOrderRepository {
    return &InMemoryOrderRepository{
        orders: make(map[string]*domain.Order),
    } // Corrected brace position
}

// Save adds or updates an order in the repository.
func (r *InMemoryOrderRepository) Save(order *domain.Order) error {
    r.mu.Lock()
    defer r.mu.Unlock()

    // Ensure the order has an ID to be used as the map key
    // Using .ID as per domain/order.go
    if order.OrderID == "" {
        return errors.New("order ID cannot be empty")
    }

    r.orders[order.OrderID] = order // Correctly assign the order to the
    map using its ID as the key
    return nil
}
```

```go
// FindByID retrieves an order by its ID.
func (r *InMemoryOrderRepository) FindByID(orderID string) (*domain.Order, error) {
    r.mu.RLock()
    defer r.mu.RUnlock()

    order, exists := r.orders[orderID] // Correctly access the map using the orderID key
    if !exists {
        return nil, errors.New("order not found")
    }

    // Return a deep copy to prevent external modification of the
        stored object,
    // reinforcing domain purity (though a simple struct copy suffices for
        this example).
    // This creates a *new* struct with copied values.
    copyOrder := *order
    return &copyOrder, nil
}
```

Implementation of MenuItemRepository

Similarly, we use an in-memory store for storing MenuItem data. This demonstrates how menu information, previously hardcoded and duplicated across services in Chapter 4, "Working System," is now managed through a dedicated repository. This follows the principle of data ownership, whereby the Order Processor maintains its own consistent view of the menu, potentially synchronized from an external source.

```go
// infrastructure/persistence/inmemory_menu_item_repository.go
package persistence

import (
    "myapp/domain" // Depends on domain layer
)

// InMemoryMenuItemRepository implements an interface (implicitly or
    explicitly defined in application layer)
```

```go
// for fetching menu items.
type InMemoryMenuItemRepository struct {
    items []domain.MenuItem
}
func NewInMemoryMenuItemRepository(initialItems []domain.MenuItem)
*InMemoryMenuItemRepository {
    return &InMemoryMenuItemRepository{
        items: initialItems,
    }
}

func (r *InMemoryMenuItemRepository) GetAll() ([]domain.MenuItem, error) {
    // Return a copy to ensure immutability from external changes,
        protecting the internal state.
    copiedItems := make([]domain.MenuItem, len(r.items))
    copy(copiedItems, r.items)
    return copiedItems, nil
}

func (r *InMemoryMenuItemRepository) FindByName(name string) (domain.
MenuItem, bool) {
    for _, item := range r.items {
        if item.Name == name {
            return item, true
        }
    }
    return domain.MenuItem{}, false
}
```

The previous chapter has shown that Hexagonal Architecture can hugely improve testability by allowing external resources to be easily mocked or swapped. We've shown this directly by using the **InMemoryOrderRepository** and **InMemoryMenuItemRepository**. The **OrderProcessingService** in the Application Layer only depends on the **OrderRepository** interface, rather than any of its specific implementations. This means we can replace the in-memory version with a mock during tests or use a full database in production, all without changing the application logic. This is not just a theoretical benefit but a practical example of the flexibility and testability that this style of architecture offers.

Furthermore, in Chapter 6, "(DDD) Domain-Driven Design," we introduced a key architectural rule: each component must own its own data. This example follows that rule closely.

By implementing its own **OrderRepository**, even in memory, the **Order Processor** takes full responsibility for its order data. It also maintains its own **MenuItemRepository**, which could be kept up to date by subscribing to changes from a separate menu service. This avoids the problem of shared databases and prevents other services from directly modifying the same data. In doing so, the Order Processor becomes the single source of truth for its own domain.

This design reduces dependencies between services, keeping each part of the system loosely coupled and independently manageable.

8.5 Presentation Layer

The presentation layer acts as the main entry point for incoming communication into the Order Processor service. Its core responsibility is to manage external communication protocols and ensure that incoming data is correctly translated into a form the application layer can understand. This layer functions as an inbound adapter in the Hexagonal Architecture, receiving requests from outside and converting them into calls to the core application logic.

For the Order Processor, as explained in Chapter 4, "Working System," incoming orders typically arrive as NATS messages at the "**restaurant.orders**" subject. The presentation layer handles the NATS subscription, unmarshalling the raw message payloads into Data Transfer Objects (DTOs) that represent the incoming requests in a protocol-specific format. These DTOs are then converted into the appropriate domain or application structures before being passed to the OrderProcessingService in the Application Layer.

Importantly, the Presentation Layer contains no business or application logic. Its responsibilities are strictly limited to

- Receiving external input by subscribing to NATS subjects for new orders
- Performing minimal protocol-related validation on the incoming message format

CHAPTER 8   SAMPLE SERVICE

- Transforming raw NATS message data into structured DTOs and then into the domain or application types expected by the OrderProcessingService

- Delegating by invoking the correct methods on the OrderProcessingService to handle the request

- Handling errors by converting any application or domain errors into a client-appropriate format, such as a NATS reply indicating an invalid order, without exposing internal system details

This approach ensures that the core business logic within the domain and application layers remains fully isolated from how external requests are received. For example, if the Order Processor were to add an HTTP API for placing orders in the future, a new HTTP adapter would be introduced within the Presentation Layer while the OrderProcessingService would stay unchanged. This strict separation preserves the integrity and independence of the application's core, making it robust against changes in external communication methods.

Below are code examples illustrating NATS inbound adapters in the presentation layer.

```go
// presentation/nats_order_receiver.go
package presentation

import (
    "encoding/json"
    "fmt"
    "myapp/application" // Depends on application layer
    "myapp/domain"      // Depends on domain layer for OrderStatus type
    "github.com/nats-io/nats.go"
)

// OrderRequestDTO represents the data structure for an incoming new order request.
// It mirrors the expected payload from external clients (e.g., the
    customer application).
type OrderRequestDTO struct {
    Item     string `json:"item"`
    Quantity int    `json:"quantity"`
```

```go
        // OrderID could optionally be included here if the client provides a
           correlation ID,
        // but the Order Processor will generate its authoritative OrderID.
        // OrderID string `json:"order_id,omitempty"`
    }
    // NATSOrderReceiver is an Inbound Adapter for receiving new order requests
       via NATS.
    type NATSOrderReceiver struct {
        nc                 *nats.Conn
        orderProcessingSvc *application.OrderProcessingService
    }

    func NewNATSOrderReceiver(nc *nats.Conn, ops *application.
    OrderProcessingService) *NATSOrderReceiver {
        return &NATSOrderReceiver{
            nc:                 nc,
            orderProcessingSvc: ops,
        }
    }
    // Start subscribes to the NATS subject for new orders (Pub/Sub style).
    // It receives order requests, unmarshals them, and delegates to the
       application layer.
    func (r *NATSOrderReceiver) Start() error {
        _, err := r.nc.Subscribe("restaurant.orders", func(msg *nats.Msg) {
            var orderReq OrderRequestDTO
            if err := json.Unmarshal(msg.Data, &orderReq); err!= nil {
                fmt.Printf("Presentation Layer: Error unmarshalling order
                request: %v\n", err)
                // For Pub/Sub, typically just log and return. No direct
                   response to the sender.
                return
            }

            fmt.Printf("Presentation Layer: Received new order request for
            item: '%s', quantity: %d\n", orderReq.Item, orderReq.Quantity)
```

CHAPTER 8   SAMPLE SERVICE

```go
            // Delegate to the Application Layer for processing.
            // The application service handles domain logic and publishing
                status updates.
            orderID, err := r.orderProcessingSvc.ProcessNewOrder(orderReq.Item,
            orderReq.Quantity)
            if err!= nil {
                fmt.Printf("Presentation Layer: Failed to process order for
                '%s': %v\n", orderReq.Item, err)
                // The application service already publishes an 'Invalid'
                    status if creation/save fails.
            } else {
                fmt.Printf("Presentation Layer: Order for '%s' (ID: %s)
                successfully initiated.\n", orderReq.Item, orderID)
            }
        })
        if err!= nil {
            return fmt.Errorf("failed to subscribe to 'restaurant.orders'
            subject: %w", err)
        }
        return nil
}

// OrderStatusUpdateDTO represents the data structure for an incoming order
    status update.
// This is typically received from other internal services (e.g., Delivery
    Tracker).
type OrderStatusUpdateDTO struct {
    OrderID string `json:"order_id"`
    Status  string `json:"status"`
    Item    string `json:"item"` // For context, though not strictly needed
                                    for status update logic
}
```

```go
// StartOrderStatusUpdater subscribes to NATS for status updates (e.g.,
from Delivery Tracker)
// and delegates to the application layer to update the order status.
// This acts as an inbound adapter for internal service communication.
func (r *NATSOrderReceiver) StartOrderStatusUpdater() error {
    _, err := r.nc.Subscribe("order.status", func(msg *nats.Msg) {
        var statusUpdate OrderStatusUpdateDTO
        if err := json.Unmarshal(msg.Data, &statusUpdate); err!= nil {
            fmt.Printf("Presentation Layer: Error unmarshalling status
            update: %v\n", err)
            return
        }

        fmt.Printf("Presentation Layer: Received status update for Order ID
        '%s': %s\n", statusUpdate.OrderID, statusUpdate.Status)

        // Convert DTO status string to domain.OrderStatus type
        domainStatus := domain.OrderStatus(statusUpdate.Status)

        // Delegate to the Application Layer to update the order status.
        err := r.orderProcessingSvc.UpdateOrderStatus(statusUpdate.OrderID,
        domainStatus)
        if err!= nil {
            fmt.Printf("Presentation Layer: Failed to update status for
            Order ID '%s': %v\n", statusUpdate.OrderID, err)
        } else {
            fmt.Printf("Presentation Layer: Order ID '%s' status updated to
            '%s' successfully.\n", statusUpdate.OrderID, domainStatus)
        }
    })
    if err!= nil {
        return fmt.Errorf("failed to subscribe to 'order.status'
        subject: %w", err)
    }
    return nil
}
```

8.6 Infrastructure

This section focuses on the messaging adapters that allow the Order Processor to communicate with other services over NATS. We've seen the theory and practice of this in Chapters 5, "Anatomy of a Service," and 6, "(DDD) Domain-Driven Design." This aligns with the broader concept of "infrastructure," separating external communication concerns through the architecture. These adapters are concrete implementations of the interfaces defined in the application layer, acting as outbound adapters. As noted in the previous chapter, adapters are responsible for handling the translation between the internal system and the outside world, converting requests, responses, or data formats as needed. Bear in mind that we separated this paragraph from the database-related paragraph, as we wanted to focus on data storage separately, but in reality, the persistence is part of the infrastructure layer too.

Implementation of OrderStatusPublisher (Outbound Adapter)

This adapter uses the NATS Go SDK to publish updates on order status to the **"order.status"** subject, following the communication model established earlier in Chapter 4, "Working System." It takes the relevant domain-level **OrderStatus** and **Order** data, serializes it into JSON, and sends it as a NATS message. We use the **"nats.PublishMsg"** function, which also allows for custom headers and supports clearer error signaling when necessary.

```
// infrastructure/messaging/nats_order_status_publisher.go
package messaging

import (
    "encoding/json"
    "fmt"
    "myapp/domain" // Depends on domain layer
    "github.com/nats-io/nats.go"
)

// NATSOrderStatusPublisher implements the application.OrderStatusPublisher
interface.
type NATSOrderStatusPublisher struct {
    nc *nats.Conn
}
```

```go
func NewNATSOrderStatusPublisher(nc *nats.Conn) *NATSOrderStatusPublisher {
    return &NATSOrderStatusPublisher{nc: nc}
}

func (p *NATSOrderStatusPublisher) PublishOrderStatus(orderID string,
status domain.OrderStatus, itemName string) error {
    // Define a DTO for external communication, ensuring we only expose
       what's necessary.
    // This DTO mirrors the structure from Chapter 4's OrderStatus for
       consistency.
    statusUpdateDTO := struct {
        OrderID string `json:"order_id"`
        Status  string `json:"status"`
        Item    string `json:"item"` // Added for context in tracking by
                                        other services
    }{
        OrderID: orderID,
        Status:  string(status),
        Item:    itemName,
    }
    statusData, err := json.Marshal(statusUpdateDTO)
    if err != nil {
        return fmt.Errorf("failed to marshal order status update DTO:
        %w", err)
    }
    // Create a NATS message. Use PublishMsg to allow adding headers.
    msg := &nats.Msg{
        Subject: "order.status", // The subject for order status updates
        Data:    statusData,
    }
    // Example of adding a custom header for error context.
    if status == domain.OrderStatusInvalid {
        msg.Header = nats.Header{} //Initialise header if not already
        msg.Header.Add("ErrorType", "InvalidOrder")
```

CHAPTER 8   SAMPLE SERVICE

```
        msg.Header.Add("Reason", "Item Not On Menu") // More specific
        error detail
    }
    return p.nc.PublishMsg(msg)
}
```

The **NATSOrderStatusPublisher** is a clear example of the adapter principle in practice. It hides all NATS-specific details, such as the "**nats.Conn**" connection and the "**nats.Msg**" structure, and handles the translation between the internal "**domain.OrderStatus**" and order data, and the raw byte payloads expected by NATS. This means the application layer does not need to know anything about how the messages are sent, only that they are being sent. It stays completely unaware of the messaging technology underneath, which is exactly how it should be.

Back in Chapter 4, "Working System," NATS Publish calls were made directly from the main function of the service. That was a simple approach, but not scalable. In the reworked architecture, all messaging concerns are cleanly moved into the infrastructure/messaging package. This is more than just tidying up the code. It shows a proper separation of concerns, where the core logic in the application and domain layers no longer knows or cares that NATS is being used. It just calls the OrderStatusPublisher interface.

This separation is a core promise of Hexagonal Architecture. If in the future we want to replace NATS with something else, like Kafka or RabbitMQ, we would only need to implement a new adapter. The core business logic would stay exactly the same. This kind of flexibility is not just nice to have—it protects the system from being tightly coupled to specific technologies, making it far easier to evolve over time.

Although Chapter 6, "(DDD) Domain-Driven Design," focused on DTOs for inbound requests, the **statusUpdateDTO** in **NATSOrderStatusPublisher** plays just as important a role in outbound communication. It acts as a boundary object, ensuring that only the necessary, agreed-upon data is sent to other services. This stops internal domain objects from leaking their full structure and protects the internal model from accidental exposure. It also reduces coupling with other systems, since changes made internally won't break other services. This demonstrates how DTOs are equally relevant for service-to-service messaging as they are for APIs or UIs, and how they help maintain stable and predictable distributed systems.

8.7 Running Everything

We've seen in the previous paragraphs all the layers needed to build the order processor as a microservice; we now need to create the actual microservice, putting everything together.

For the purpose of making everything simple to try out manually, as the order processor is the main piece of the system, with higher interaction, we will build it as a command-line application, which then sends and receives messages from and to other microservices.

We will follow the command pattern and create a **cmd** folder with the main script inside:

```go
//cmd/main.go
package main

import (
    "bufio"
    "encoding/json"
    "fmt"
    "os"
    "strings"
    "time"

    "myApp/application"
    "myApp/domain"
    "myApp/infrastructure/messaging"
    "myApp/infrastructure/persistence"
    "myApp/presentation"

    "github.com/nats-io/nats.go"
)

// Main application entry point
func main() {
    fmt.Println("Starting Restaurant Order Processing Application...")

    // 1. Initialize NATS Connection
    // Check for NATS_URL environment variable, otherwise use nats.
       DefaultURL
```

CHAPTER 8   SAMPLE SERVICE

```go
natsURL := os.Getenv("NATS_URL")
if natsURL == "" {
    natsURL = nats.DefaultURL // Default to "nats://127.0.0.1:4222" if
    env var is not set
    fmt.Printf("NATS_URL environment variable not set. Using default
    NATS URL: %s\n", natsURL)
} else {
    fmt.Printf("Using NATS URL from environment variable: %s\n",
    natsURL)
}

nc, err := nats.Connect(natsURL, nats.Name("OrderProcessorService"))
if err != nil {
    fmt.Printf("Error connecting to NATS: %v\n", err)
    os.Exit(1)
}
defer nc.Close()
fmt.Printf("Connected to NATS server: %s\n", natsURL)

// 2. Setup Domain Layer Components
// Define initial menu items
pizza, _ := domain.NewMenuItem("Pizza", 12.50)
burger, _ := domain.NewMenuItem("Burger", 8.00)
salad, _ := domain.NewMenuItem("Salad", 7.00)
drinks, _ := domain.NewMenuItem("Coke", 2.00)

initialMenuItems := []domain.MenuItem{pizza, burger, salad, drinks}

// MenuService manages the menu items within the domain
menuService := domain.NewMenuService(initialMenuItems)
// OrderFactory is responsible for creating new Order entities
orderFactory := domain.NewOrderFactory(menuService)

// 3. Setup Infrastructure Layer Components
// In-memory repository for orders (simulating a database)
orderRepo := persistence.NewInMemoryOrderRepository()
// NATS publisher for order status updates
statusPublisher := messaging.NewNATSOrderStatusPublisher(nc)
```

```go
// 4. Setup Application Layer
// OrderProcessingService orchestrates the core business logic/
   use cases
orderProcessingSvc := application.NewOrderProcessingService(
    orderRepo,
    orderFactory,
    menuService,
    statusPublisher,
)

// 5. Setup Presentation Layer (NATS Receivers)
// NATSOrderReceiver listens for incoming new order requests and
   status updates
natsReceiver := presentation.NewNATSOrderReceiver(nc,
orderProcessingSvc)

// Start listening for new order requests
if err := natsReceiver.Start(); err != nil {
    fmt.Printf("Error starting NATS order receiver: %v\n", err)
    os.Exit(1)
}
fmt.Println("Subscribed to 'restaurant.orders' for new order
requests.")

// Start listening for order status updates (e.g., from a simulated
   delivery service)
if err := natsReceiver.StartOrderStatusUpdater(); err != nil {
    fmt.Printf("Error starting NATS order status updater: %v\n", err)
    os.Exit(1)
}
fmt.Println("Subscribed to 'order.status' for internal status
updates.")

fmt.Println("\nApplication is running. Send NATS messages to
'restaurant.orders' to create orders.")
fmt.Println("Or send NATS messages to 'order.status' to update existing
order statuses.")
```

CHAPTER 8   SAMPLE SERVICE

```go
        fmt.Println("Type 'exit' or 'quit' to stop the application.")
        fmt.Println("---")

        // Start a simple NATS publisher client for testing
        go startTestPublisher(nc)

        // Keep the main goroutine alive
        select {}
}

// startTestPublisher provides a CLI to send test NATS messages
func startTestPublisher(nc *nats.Conn) {
        reader := bufio.NewReader(os.Stdin)
        fmt.Println("Type 'new <item> <quantity>' to send a new order request (e.g., new Pizza 2)")
        fmt.Println("Type 'update <orderID> <status>' to send a status update (e.g., update 12345 Preparing)")
        fmt.Println("Available statuses: Pending, Preparing, Ready for Delivery, Out For Delivery, Delivered, Invalid")
        fmt.Println("---")

        for {
                fmt.Print("Enter command: ")
                input, _ := reader.ReadString('\n')
                input = strings.TrimSpace(input)

                if input == "exit" || input == "quit" {
                        fmt.Println("Exiting test publisher.")
                        return
                }

                parts := strings.Fields(input)
                if len(parts) == 0 {
                        continue
                }

                command := strings.ToLower(parts[0])
```

```go
switch command {
case "new":
    if len(parts) == 3 {
        item := parts[1]
        quantityStr := parts[2]
        var quantity int
        _, err := fmt.Sscanf(quantityStr, "%d", &quantity)
        if err != nil {
            fmt.Printf("Invalid quantity: %v\n", err)
            continue
        }

        dto := presentation.OrderRequestDTO{Item: item, Quantity: quantity}
        data, err := json.Marshal(dto)
        if err != nil {
            fmt.Printf("Error marshalling new order DTO: %v\n", err)
            continue
        }

        err = nc.Publish("restaurant.orders", data)
        if err != nil {
            fmt.Printf("Error publishing new order: %v\n", err)
        } else {
            fmt.Printf("Published new order request: %s\n",
                string(data))
        }
    } else {
        fmt.Println("Usage: new <item> <quantity>")
    }
case "update":
    if len(parts) >= 3 {
        orderID := parts[1]
        statusStr := strings.Join(parts[2], " ")

        // Basic validation for status string
        validStatus := false
```

```go
        for _, s := range []domain.OrderStatus{
            domain.OrderStatusPending, domain.OrderStatusPreparing,
            domain.OrderStatusReadyForDelivery, domain.
            OrderStatusOutForDelivery,
            domain.OrderStatusDelivered, domain.OrderStatusInvalid,
        } {
            if strings.EqualFold(string(s), statusStr) {
                validStatus = true
                break
            }
        }
        if !validStatus {
            fmt.Printf("Invalid status: %s. Please use one of:
            Pending, Preparing, Ready for Delivery, Out For
            Delivery, Delivered, Invalid\n", statusStr)
            continue
        }

        dto := presentation.OrderStatusUpdateDTO{
            OrderID: orderID,
            Status:  statusStr,
            // Item field is optional for status updates from
                external systems, but often good for context.
            // For this simple client, we'll leave it empty.
            Item: "",
        }
        data, err := json.Marshal(dto)
        if err != nil {
            fmt.Printf("Error marshalling status update DTO:
            %v\n", err)
            continue
        }

        err = nc.Publish("order.status", data)
        if err != nil {
            fmt.Printf("Error publishing status update: %v\n", err)
```

```
            } else {
                fmt.Printf("Published status update for order %s:
                %s\n", orderID, string(data))
            }
        } else {
            fmt.Println("Usage: update <orderID> <status>")
        }
    default:
        fmt.Println("Unknown command. Use 'new' or 'update'.")
    }
    time.Sleep(100 * time.Millisecond) // Small delay to avoid
    busy loop
    }
}
```

This was a lot of code, and it will be easier to read in an editor from the associated files provided; we just pasted it here in full, however, for reference. We will now, however, point out a few key things in the code:

```
natsURL := os.Getenv("NATS_URL")
    if natsURL == "" {
        natsURL = nats.DefaultURL // Default to "nats://127.0.0.1:4222" if
        env var is not set
        fmt.Printf("NATS_URL environment variable not set. Using default
        NATS URL: %s\n", natsURL)
    } else {
        fmt.Printf("Using NATS URL from environment variable: %s\n",
        natsURL)
    }

    nc, err := nats.Connect(natsURL, nats.Name("OrderProcessorService"))
    if err != nil {
        fmt.Printf("Error connecting to NATS: %v\n", err)
        os.Exit(1)
    }
    defer nc.Close()
    fmt.Printf("Connected to NATS server: %s\n", natsURL)
```

Chapter 8 Sample Service

```
    // 2. Setup Domain Layer Components
    // Define initial menu items
    pizza, _ := domain.NewMenuItem("Pizza", 12.50)
```
....

We are here simply instantiating all the things we need, from every layer. We need a NATS connection, so we create it, and then we pass it to the messaging services inside the infrastructure layer. All the services are instantiated here.

The last initialization we perform initializes the NATS message receiver in the presentation layer:

```
// 5. Setup Presentation Layer (NATS Receivers)
    // NATSOrderReceiver listens for incoming new order requests and
       status updates
    natsReceiver := presentation.NewNATSOrderReceiver
    (nc, orderProcessingSvc)
```

This is, in fact, the entry point to the microservice. We then need to start listening to the messages; hence, run the receiver:

```
// Start listening for new order requests
    if err := natsReceiver.Start(); err != nil {
        fmt.Printf("Error starting NATS order receiver: %v\n", err)
        os.Exit(1)
    }
    fmt.Println("Subscribed to 'restaurant.orders' for new order
    requests.")
```

With what we've just seen, we can start accepting messages with new order requests. Our microservice is almost ready, so we can finally accept orders. What is left is being notified of order updates:

```
    // Start listening for order status updates (e.g., from a simulated
       delivery service)
    if err := natsReceiver.StartOrderStatusUpdater(); err != nil {
        fmt.Printf("Error starting NATS order status updater: %v\n", err)
        os.Exit(1)
    }
    fmt.Println("Subscribed to 'order.status' for internal status updates.")
```

CHAPTER 8   SAMPLE SERVICE

At this point, we have everything we need. The status updater is listening for new messages from other services, which we developed in Chapter 4, "Working System."

We now need a way to test the system, so we need a user-facing application to contact the microservice. To make your manual testing of the application easier, we've added the user-facing application (the command-line app) as a separate Go routine inside this microservice's codebase, within the main package's script.

This still sends messages through NATS but is lying inside the same program so that you do not need to run two applications. You can see this application called in this line:

```
go startTestPublisher(nc)
```

And afterwords, you see the actual implementation of this function.

If you wish, you can remove this part and put it inside another script and run the two scripts separately, but the effect won't change.

In order to manually test the microservice, first you need to have a NATS server running, possibly on the default port 4222, and then you can run the **cmd** script, and you will see something like in Figure 8-1.

```
Starting Restaurant Order Processing Application...
NATS_URL environment variable not set. Using default NATS URL: nats://127.0.0.1:4222
Connected to NATS server: nats://127.0.0.1:4222
Subscribed to 'restaurant.orders' for new order requests.
Subscribed to 'order.status' for internal status updates.

Application is running. Send NATS messages to 'restaurant.orders' to create orders.
Or send NATS messages to 'order.status' to update existing order statuses.
Type 'exit' or 'quit' to stop the application.
---
Type 'new <item> <quantity>' to send a new order request (e.g., new Pizza 2)
Type 'update <orderID> <status>' to send a status update (e.g., update 12345 Preparing)
Available statuses: Pending, Preparing, Ready for Delivery, Out For Delivery, Delivered, Invalid
---
Enter command: new Pizza 2
```

Figure 8-1. *Running the application*

Entering the command **new Pizza 2,** you are ordering two pizzas, and an order is created.

If you do that, you will then see something like in Figure 8-2, where the order gets initiated and sent to another microservice.

CHAPTER 8 SAMPLE SERVICE

```
Published new order request: {"item":"Pizza","quantity":2}
Presentation Layer: Received new order request for item: 'Pizza', quantity: 2
Presentation Layer: Order for 'Pizza' (ID: 8d47bd7f-b353-4624-85f1-d35bff99cde5) successfully initiated.
Presentation Layer: Received status update for Order ID '8d47bd7f-b353-4624-85f1-d35bff99cde5': Pending
Application Layer: Order 8d47bd7f-b353-4624-85f1-d35bff99cde5 is already in status 'Pending'. No transition needed.
```

Figure 8-2. *Initiated order*

The order, at this point, will rely on another service to get the updates, and we can simulate that via a direct NATS call. You can use the command-line NATS client and run:

```
nats pub order.status '{"order_id": "8d47bd7f-b353-4624-85f1-d35bff99cde5", "status": "Preparing", "item": "Pizza"}'
```

And you shall see an update in the app command line interface with the order status set to **preparing**. Alternatively, the command-line application running as a subprocess also allows you to send those messages, so you could just write, inside the running application:

```
update 8d47bd7f-b353-4624-85f1-d35bff99cde5 Preparing
```

We've finally concluded the whole microservice. You can understand that the process we went through is very lengthy, and for a small application like this one, it might be overkill. In reality, however, this application will likely grow; you will need a better database, you will need more services and more functionalities, and business requirements will never stop. It might seem that doing all this process at this stage is exaggerated, and it might be, but if you however start with a simpler setup, like the one seen in Chapter 4, "Working System," and then the requirements increase, and you keep the original design, you will find yourself in a highly unmanageable codebase, where there are no clear boundaries between layers and changing external data sources or plugging in new tools will be very complicated.

As always, the decision of when to use DDD and hexagonal architecture and at what level is up to you; you must make a sound decision about that. What we can do in this book is simply provide you with the knowledge and encourage you to consider these design and architectural decisions as you think they might apply to your specific case.

One important consideration, to give more context, is that in a fast-paced environment, like in a startup, starting with all this and even with a distributed system might be counterproductive. We still stress the importance of a domain language and connection with the business, but you might start lower on DD and distributed systems; you can improve the design along the way and go distributed when finally necessary.

The key is to find the right moment to do that so that you have the right balance between urgency, flexibility, and scalability. Even when you have a monolithic application, the first step will be to start applying DDD and hexagonal design to better separate the different concerns. Once you have a properly designed monolithic application, following the DDD and HA principles, you will find that it's very easy to split the monolith into a series of distributed services.

8.8 Summary

In this chapter, we've redesigned the Order Processor to change the basic structure from Chapter 4, "Working System," where the order processor was a simple component of a few lines of code, with a design based on Domain-Driven Design and Hexagonal principles. We essentially turned the Order Processor into a proper microservice. The new version is clearer, more maintainable, and easier to adapt. The initial setup worked for basic service-to-service messaging, but it lacked the structure needed for anything beyond that. This change makes the system suitable for real use.

The DDD model introduces proper types for domain concepts like **Order** and **MenuItem** using a consistent language across the service. This improves alignment between developers and stakeholders. Shifting Order ID generation into the domain layer is one example of services taking full responsibility for their data and logic.

Hexagonal Architecture makes the system more flexible. The application layer defines interfaces, not implementations. Infrastructure handles the actual technologies, such as storage and messaging. Repositories are implemented using in-memory stores for now but can be replaced by production-ready databases without touching application logic. The same applies to NATS. All messaging code is kept inside a dedicated adapter, separate from core logic.

This approach avoids tight coupling with specific tools and keeps the domain isolated. It also makes testing easier, since mocks or in-memory versions can be swapped in without changes elsewhere. The messaging adapter proves this: the service doesn't know it's using NATS, only that it can publish order status.

Low-level messaging like NATS is important in a distributed system, but it's not enough. The internal design of each service matters. Applying DDD and Hexagonal Architecture gives the Order Processor a clear boundary, stable behavior, and room to grow. It's no longer just working; it's maintainable.

PART III

Macroscopic View: Designing Distributed Systems

CHAPTER 9

A Whole System vs. a Bunch of Services

9.1 Foreword to Part 3

With this chapter, we start the final part of this book, where we can finally apply all the knowledge we gained about communication patterns in distributed systems, together with the knowledge on building a scalable and well-crafted service, to create complete, fully distributed systems.

With this part, we are now shifting the focus to the macroscopic view of a complete distributed system, learning how to integrate, manage, and optimize the whole system for production readiness.

In the previous parts, we first analyzed the core elements of distributed systems, starting with the complexities of low-level communication and exploring the underlying mechanisms that enable different components to interact. This provided a good understanding of messaging paradigms and communication topologies, culminating in the construction of a working yet rudimentary distributed setup that showcased inter-service communication. After that, we moved our focus inwards, concentrating on the specifics of designing an individual service. We emphasized the importance of adopting a business-first approach, implemented through Domain-Driven Design, which ensures that technical implementations are closely aligned with the core business needs. Furthermore, we explored the principles of Hexagonal Architecture, which guided the crafting of services with clear boundaries, separating core business logic from external dependencies to ensure their maintainability, testability, and adaptability.

And now in this last part, there's a significant shift in perspective. With the assurance that we can design resilient, well-bounded single services and organize components to communicate in simple or complex topologies for intra-service communication, we arrive at our final goal: integrating our independent service designs into a single, production-ready distributed system. We are now ready to tackle the macroscopic engineering challenges involved in orchestration, management, and optimization in the presence of multiple services operating collectively as a single product in real-world deployment. We will explore how to combine all the knowledge gained so far to create a cohesive and well-performing distributed system, from the inner workings of a single service, through the communication between services, to the orchestration of all components into a new, distributed system.

9.2 One Level Up

The working system that we built in Chapter 4, "Working System," provided a practical example of how services can communicate with each other. It featured distinct components interacting via a messaging system, demonstrating the basic flow of information inside a distributed environment. However, this initial system, by design, was a simplified model. It assumed single instances, often relied on in-memory state, and did not feature complex architectures for each component. These components were neither microservices nor production-ready services, but mere small scripts.

Moving "one level up" marks a crucial transition. In the previous parts, we explored the basic elements required to build a system. We first learned how individual components can communicate effectively in a distributed setting, disregarding their internal architectures. Then, we explored the design principles for building a single, robust component, ready for integration into a larger, distributed environment. Now, we are bringing all these pieces together. This part combines all the previous knowledge, including communication patterns and the principles of well-architected services, to learn how we can construct a complete, resilient distributed system composed of properly designed and communicating services. At this point, we also need to explore how to run multiple instances of the same service, scale their number and resources, and ensure data integrity throughout the system. At this point, then, a new set of challenges emerges:

- **System Coherence:** It ensures a consistent and unified understanding of the overall system state across all components, even with asynchronously updated and distributed data. For example, if multiple services rely on a specific business process's status, a consistent, real-time view must be maintained without introducing undesirable coupling. This often requires complex algorithms for data partitioning and combination, along with careful coordination protocols for node agreement on decisions. It's important to note that this doesn't imply every service must have complete knowledge of all other services, but rather a common, shared contextual understanding of ongoing events.

- **Operational Efficiency:** As the number of services, instances, and their communication pathways grows, optimizing message flows, minimizing network latency, and ensuring efficient resource utilization become critical for operational efficiency. This includes handling high traffic, large data volumes, managing system failures, and controlling costs. While horizontal scaling may seem simple for individual services, it introduces new problems not present in single-instance setups. Adding more instances becomes a complex challenge involving increased network communication, potential data fragmentation, and the need for better synchronization. Proper scalability in distributed systems requires re-evaluating and optimizing communication patterns, data management strategies, and infrastructure to mitigate the complexities introduced by distribution itself.

- **Managing Cross-service State:** When a user interaction or a long-running business process spans multiple services, the accurate maintenance, propagation, and recovery of the overall state of that interaction across the entire distributed system becomes a big concern. This often requires complex algorithms for efficient partitioning and later combining data, as well as coordination protocols for nodes to agree on decisions.

These challenges show that a production-ready distributed system is far more than a bunch of well-designed individual services. It requires a holistic architectural approach, where the interactions, dependencies, and operational characteristics of the entire ecosystem are carefully considered from the beginning of its creation. This perspective is the central theme of this part of the book, giving the reader all the instruments to construct systems that are not merely functional but robust, scalable, and resilient in the face of real-world demands.

9.3 Is This the End?

This book aims to provide a thorough understanding of distributed systems, taking a practical approach by using NATS and selecting Go as the programming language for your system. In this part, we will also see more details on the DevOps aspect, but essentially, we will leverage NATS to ease our need for scalability, and a significant portion of the burden will be alleviated.

Apart from this, however, you must understand that building a production-ready enterprise distributed system is not a matter for a single person, and several people with various roles will be involved. Some of the things needed to productionize the system won't be your direct concern, but, as the content of this book will allow you to both build your own system for your personal projects and design the system with your role of software architect in a bigger context in mind, you need to be aware of a few things that are needed but not exposed in this book. We will now analyze the critical system-wide considerations that demand profound attention and strategic foresight.

First of all, let's focus on network dynamics and latency. In a distributed environment, services communicate over networks, introducing inherent and unpredictable latency, bandwidth constraints, and the constant possibility of network partitions. An operation that is instantaneous within a single process can become a significant performance bottleneck when it requires multiple network traversals. Latency is defined as the time delay between a request and a response, and it is affected by factors such as propagation delay, transmission delay, and processing delay. Network congestion, hardware performance, and protocol inefficiencies also play significant roles in increasing latency. Designing for minimal network chatter, tolerating unavoidable delays, and gracefully handling network unreliability are crucial. High latency can lead to slower response times, increased timeouts, resource underutilization, and data consistency issues.

Another important consideration is that, unlike monolithic applications, where a single component failure often leads to a complete system outage, distributed systems must be designed to be resilient to partial failures. This means one service can fail while others continue to operate, or a network segment might become unavailable. The challenge lies in detecting these localized failures, isolating their impact, and ensuring the system as a whole remains functional or degrades gracefully. This necessitates sophisticated strategies such as asynchronous communication, which helps avoid long chains of synchronous HTTP calls that can cause severe outages and ripple effects. Other crucial strategies include retries with exponential backoff, circuit breakers, and robust timeouts. Fallbacks can provide cached or default values when requests fail, a suitable approach for queries. Limiting queued requests prevents overwhelming a failing service and can proactively shed excess load. While partial failure is often presented as a benefit, it simultaneously introduces a more insidious and harder-to-diagnose class of failure.

The system might appear to be running, but critical business processes could be stalled or producing incorrect results due to subtle inter-service communication issues, resource exhaustion from retries, or cascading timeouts. This presents a far more complex debugging scenario than a simple monolithic crash. Therefore, designing for resilience in distributed systems is not merely about preventing total outages but about actively managing and mitigating the amplification of small, localized issues into widespread, silent failures that degrade user experience and data integrity without immediately bringing the whole system down. This necessitates a proactive approach to resilience patterns and deep observability.

Together, the previous considerations bring to the clear consequence that a distributed system needs complex deployment and release management. Deploying a singular service is often straightforward. The complexity escalates dramatically when deploying dozens or hundreds of interconnected services, each potentially having its own independent release cadence, intricate dependencies, and distinct configuration. The formidable task involves automating this entire process, ensuring absolute consistency across environments, and enabling rapid, reliable rollbacks in case of issues.

Differently from monolithic applications, distributed systems also require ubiquitous monitoring and observability. This is because when a user request or a business transaction spans numerous services, pinpointing the precise source of an error or a performance degradation becomes exceedingly challenging without comprehensive visibility. Centralized logging solutions, aggregated metrics, and sophisticated distributed tracing tools are no longer optional luxuries but indispensable instruments for understanding the system's runtime behavior, diagnosing issues, and ensuring operational excellence.

As many services will need their own data, which, following DDD practices, must be segregated and not directly shared between services and storage solutions, a distributed system will require careful design to support distributed data management and data consistency. While individual services adhere to the principle of data ownership, business processes frequently necessitate a consistent and unified view of data across multiple services. This leads to the profound challenges of managing distributed transactions, navigating various consistency models (from strong to eventual consistency), and implementing sophisticated data synchronization strategies that transcend simple CRUD operations within a single database.

Finally, we cannot forget security and the challenges a distributed system brings up. Securing a monolithic application presents its own set of challenges; however, securing a distributed system with multiple ingress points, complex inter-service communication flows, and diverse data stores demands a multi-layered, end-to-end approach to authentication, authorization, data encryption in transit and at rest, and vulnerability management. Depending on the specific infrastructure, securing communication between services might become a must, especially when regulations are in place, like GDPR. This all translates to the need of what can be called a holistic security posture.

These challenges show you that constructing a distributed system is fundamentally an exercise in managing complexity at a higher order of magnitude than monolithic systems. It mandates a paradigm shift in thinking—from optimizing isolated components to carefully and thoroughly optimizing the interactions, operational characteristics, and emergent behavior of the entire interconnected system.

In the following paragraphs, we will explore some of the strategies used to address the problems stated above. However, as mentioned earlier, we will focus on this and the subsequent chapters on the architectural aspects of distributed systems, leveraging NATS to overcome some of these issues.

9.4 Service-Oriented and Other Experiments

During the history of software architecture, Service-Oriented Architecture (SOA) emerged as an early and influential pattern to decompose monolithic applications into a collection of discrete, reusable services. These services communicated via well-defined interfaces, often mediated by a centralized Enterprise Service Bus (ESB). SOA represented a significant leap towards modularity and distribution, laying essential groundwork for the following architectural evolutions.

However, the practical implementation of SOA frequently encountered substantial drawbacks. The pervasive reliance on a centralized ESB or orchestration engine for mediating nearly all inter-service interactions inadvertently introduced a new form of tight coupling. To explain more precisely, some components were dedicated to providing the communication system between other components, which was their only purpose. Component A needed to send a message to Component B, and a specific third service was used to allow this communication. Such services were spread throughout the system, and each one focused on communication between specific services. The set of communication services formed the layer called Service Bus. Figure 9-1 shows how the ESB works and how this type of communication differs from the way microservices communicate; the ESB is a whole different layer only managing communication between services.

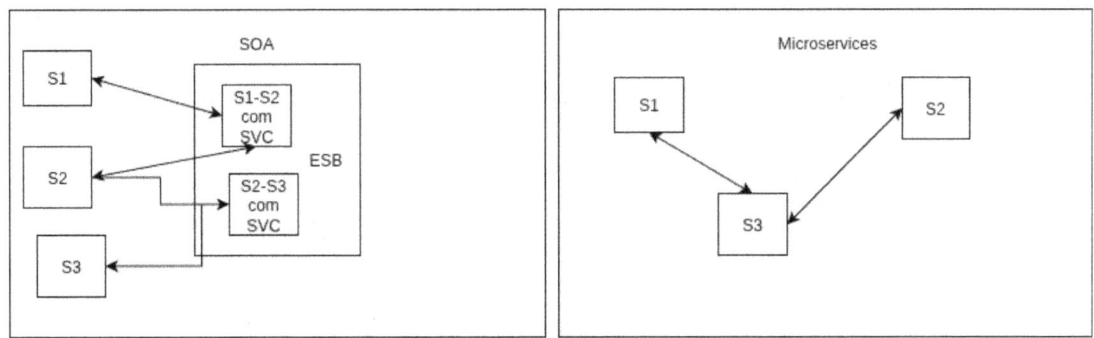

Figure 9-1. *SOA vs. microservices communication*

This communication layer often evolved into a single point of failure and a considerable performance bottleneck, thereby hindering the system's scalability and maintainability. Changes within a single service can trigger a cascade of dependencies throughout the ESB, necessitating complex, coordinated deployments and extensive

CHAPTER 9   A WHOLE SYSTEM VS. A BUNCH OF SERVICES

system-wide testing. ESBs were seen as a new tier in the architecture, leading to "noisy neighbor" problems due to excessive shared functionality, and could cause latency due to extra hops. They also suffered from a lack of a single accepted standard for service models.

Bear in mind that an ESB is different from a message broker like the one provided by NATS, because a message broker is totally agnostic to the contract that each service provides and only offers a way to interact, like a motorway allowing several cars to reach their destinations. An ESB, instead, is like offering a new road for each car and destination.

This unintended outcome often resulted in what is colloquially termed a "distributed monolith"—a system that, despite being technically distributed, exhibited the behavioral characteristics of a tightly coupled, inflexible monolithic application due to its strong interdependencies and centralized control. This anti-pattern fundamentally undermined many of SOA's intended benefits.

The subsequent evolution towards microservices, a concept explored in the previous part of this book, was a direct response to these identified shortcomings. Microservices advocate for extreme decentralization: each service is deliberately kept small, operates independently, is focused on a specific business capability (bounded context), and typically runs in its own process. Crucially, microservices forsake centralized communication intermediaries, preferring lightweight communication mechanisms such as direct HTTP-based APIs or asynchronous messaging (like NATS, Kafka, etc.). The core objective is to enable true independent development, deployment, and scaling of each service, pushing for unparalleled agility and resilience within the overall system.

The lessons derived from SOA are invaluable for anyone embarking on a microservices journey. The vital warning remains the imperative to avoid inadvertently creating a "distributed monolith." This detrimental outcome typically manifests when:

- **Persistent Tight Coupling**: Services remain deeply dependent on each other's internal implementation details, data schemas, or specific deployment order, leading to cascading failures or necessitating synchronized deployments. This violates the core benefit of microservices: independent evolution.

- **Shared Data Stores**: Multiple services directly access and modify the same underlying database, violating the critical principle of data ownership and fostering implicit coupling that undermines service independence. This makes Data Transfer Object (DTO) versioning difficult and can lead to data consistency challenges.

- **Over-reliance on Synchronous Communication**: An excessive use of synchronous calls between services creates elongated dependency chains, significantly increasing latency, reducing fault tolerance, and making the system brittle in the face of partial failures. Asynchronous communication via events is preferred to reduce direct dependencies and improve scalability, ensuring eventual consistency.

- **Impaired Independent Deployment**: Services cannot be deployed, updated, or rolled back independently without affecting other services, thereby negating a core, fundamental benefit of the microservices paradigm.

- **Over-Microservices/Excessive Fragmentation**: Dividing the system into too many fine-grained microservices, where each encapsulates only a small portion of functionality, can lead to low cohesion, scattered business logic, and increased operational overhead and communication costs.

- **Violating Single Responsibility Principle (SRP)**: Lumping multiple responsibilities into a single service leads to tight coupling and reduced maintainability.

- **Spaghetti Architecture**: This refers to a microservices architecture where dependencies between services become tangled and complex, lacking clear structure and organization.

The historical shift from SOA to microservices represents a fundamental architectural philosophy change: from attempting to control complexity through centralization (ESB) to managing complexity through decentralization and autonomy (individual services). The failures of ESBs highlighted that centralizing communication and integration logic often creates more problems than it solves in highly dynamic, large-scale systems. The "distributed monolith" anti-pattern is a critical lesson that simply breaking down a monolith into services without addressing the underlying coupling mechanisms (especially shared data and centralized communication) will not hold the benefits of true distributed architecture. True agility and scalability stem from empowering individual services with autonomy, even if it means increased complexity in other areas, such as observability and distributed data management.

Effective interaction and prudent management of services in a distributed system demand a conscious, continuous effort to cultivate loose coupling, enforce strict data isolation, and strategically favor asynchronous communication where appropriate. While SOA was an instrumental "experiment" that illuminated many of the inherent challenges of distributed systems, microservices offer a more refined and robust approach by championing genuine independence and decentralized governance, principles that will be thoroughly explored and applied throughout this part of the book.

One final note is that, even with microservices, issues may still arise, including extreme fragmentation, poor decomposition, and overengineering. Not every coupling must be necessarily removed, but a good compromise must be made. Also, asynchronous communication should be preferred, but a system fully asynchronous up to the presentation, or interaction with the user, might be either an unnecessary burden or even impractical to the user when implemented.

9.5 Like Russian Dolls

Consider a perfectly crafted set of Russian nesting dolls—each doll is a complete, self-contained entity, yet it fits perfectly within a slightly larger doll, which in turn nests within an even grander one. This elegant metaphor powerfully illustrates the nested complexity and hierarchical structure inherent in a well-architected distributed system.

CHAPTER 9   A WHOLE SYSTEM VS. A BUNCH OF SERVICES

Figure 9-2. *Russian dolls view*

Figure 9-2 shows a high-level overview of this analogy; at the outermost layer there is the entire distributed system—the largest Russian doll. This represents the complete, production-ready product or platform that users interact with, including all its functionalities, underlying services, and supporting infrastructure. It is the comprehensive solution delivered to the end-user.

285

CHAPTER 9   A WHOLE SYSTEM VS. A BUNCH OF SERVICES

Figure 9-3. *Russian dolls expanded*

A different, more expanded view of the Russian dolls metaphor is depicted in Figure 9-3, where the whole system is still the outer doll, but we used several small dolls to represent each single service, and inside each service, its layers are several smaller dolls.

Peeling back this outer layer, the individual services, often microservices, that constitute the system appear. These represent the medium-sized dolls. As thoroughly explored in the previous part of this book, each of these services is a highly cohesive and independent unit, meticulously designed and implemented using principles such as domain-driven design and Hexagonal Architecture.

- **Domain-Driven Design (DDD)**: Within each service, DDD ensures that the general business logic takes precedence. The Ubiquitous Language defines the core entities, value objects, and domain services that directly mirror the specific business domain. This rigorous approach renders each service a self-contained, business-aligned entity, singularly focused on a well-defined bounded context. A domain language exists for the overall system, and then each service or area of the system will have a specific domain language, in addition to the general one.

- **Hexagonal Architecture**: This architectural style further refines the internal structure of each service. It robustly ensures that the core business and application logic (the innermost part of the service-doll) remain entirely decoupled from their external dependencies, whether they be databases, messaging systems, or user interfaces. All communication occurs via well-defined "ports" and "adapters," empowering the service to be developed, tested, and evolved independently of its external environment.

Now, consider the smallest Russian dolls nested within each individual service. These represent the internal components, layers, and modules of the service itself—the domain layer, the application layer, and the specific implementations within the infrastructure layer. Even at this granular level, the foundational principles of separation of concerns, clear interface definitions, and dependency inversion are diligently applied.

CHAPTER 9   A WHOLE SYSTEM VS. A BUNCH OF SERVICES

The "Russian dolls" metaphor illustrates several critical facets of distributed system design:

- **Cohesive Autonomy**: Each service, much like a perfectly formed doll, stands as a complete and functional unit in its own right. It possesses its distinct responsibilities, manages its own data, and encapsulates its internal logic.

- **Hierarchical Principle Application**: The deep design principles learned in earlier parts—particularly Domain-Driven Design and Hexagonal Architecture—are not confined solely to individual services. They apply hierarchically. The entire distributed system can conceptually be viewed as a larger "domain" possessing its own "ubiquitous language" (e.g., "Order Fulfillment System" vs. "Order Processor Service"). The meticulously defined boundaries between individual services effectively become the "ports" and "adapters" at the overarching system level, precisely governing how these larger dolls interact.

- **Encapsulation and Decoupling**: Just as each Russian doll expertly conceals its inner workings from external view, each service meticulously encapsulates its internal complexity. This rigorous encapsulation fosters independent development, deployment, and scaling, thereby minimizing ripple effects throughout the system when modifications are introduced.

- **Emergent System Behavior**: While each service is an expertly designed unit, the true power, intricate complexity, and emergent properties of the system manifest when these services are intelligently connected, synchronized, and orchestrated to form the complete product. The precise interactions between these "dolls," their communication protocols, and the collective management of their distributed state ultimately define the overall system's behavior and performance.

There is a subtle but critical paradox: the very autonomy that makes microservices powerful (independent evolution, fault isolation) also creates the greatest challenge in ensuring they function as a coherent, unified system. The "Russian Dolls" are self-contained, but their nesting implies a dependency and a larger purpose. This means the boundaries and interfaces between services become as critical as the internal design of each service. Achieving a "whole system" from a "bunch of services" requires a constant tension between promoting service independence and designing robust, efficient integration patterns. Overemphasizing independence without considering the system-level interactions can lead to a fragmented, unmanageable system, while overemphasizing integration can lead back to a distributed monolith. The art lies in balancing these forces.

A thorough understanding of this nested complexity is necessary. It means that while the objective is to cultivate independent, well-bounded services, the overarching system architecture must be simultaneously considered, ensuring that the interactions between these "dolls" are efficient, resilient, and unequivocally aligned with the product's macroscopic business objectives.

9.6 Infrastructure

In the previous section, we introduced the Infrastructure Layer as the component within a single service responsible for interacting with external resources such as databases, messaging systems, and other third-party services. As we move to a macroscopic view of the entire distributed system, the concept of infrastructure can be mirrored at this level too. It goes beyond the individual service's external connections to include the shared, foundational services that underpin the entire ecosystem of interconnected components.

System-wide infrastructure components are absolutely critical for the efficient operation, solid reliability, and comprehensive observability of a distributed system. They offer common platform-level features on which microservices are built and operated and on which they rely, abstracting away much of the underlying complexity and enabling consistent functionality across the entire architecture.

Key aspects of system-wide infrastructure include

- Distributed Data Management
- Message Brokers
- Comprehensive Observability
- Security Infrastructure

We will now see them in detail in the following paragraphs.

9.6.1 Distributed Data Management

While the principle of "each service owning its data" is a fundamental characteristic of microservices architecture, the reality is that business processes often necessitate data sharing or synchronization across services. This necessitates careful consideration of

- **Consistency Models**: Beyond traditional ACID transactions within a single service, distributed systems frequently employ various consistency models, ranging from strong consistency (e.g., synchronous replication, ensuring all operations appear in a total order, used in leader election, configuration management) to eventual consistency (e.g., asynchronous replication, where data might be temporarily inconsistent but eventually converges, prioritizing availability and partition tolerance, used in global-scale applications, social media feeds, e-commerce). Other models include causal consistency (operations causally related are seen in the same order), read-your-writes (a process always sees its own writes), and monotonic reads/writes (processes do not see older data versions later).

- **Data Replication**: Strategies like master-slave (one primary server accepts writes, one or more secondary servers replicate for reads, suitable for read-heavy workloads), multi-master (multiple servers accept writes, data replicated across all, improves write availability but can lead to conflicts), and leaderless (any node can accept writes, uses a quorum of nodes to confirm, high availability, tunable consistency) ensure data availability and fault tolerance. Synchronous replication guarantees strong consistency but impacts write performance, while asynchronous replication offers better performance but weaker consistency.

- **Data Partitioning (Sharding)**: Distributing data across multiple database instances to achieve horizontal scalability and improve query performance. Common architectures include range-based (splits by value range, but can lead to data overloading on a single node), hashed (uses a hash function for even distribution, but reassigning hash values when adding new shards can be difficult), and directory sharding (uses a lookup table for flexibility, but is susceptible to lookup table failure). Sharding, also known as horizontal partitioning, distributes data across multiple servers, while partitioning, instead, splits tables within one server.

- **Avoiding Shared Databases**: A critical anti-pattern in microservices is allowing multiple services to access and modify the same transactional database directly. This introduces tight coupling, reduces service autonomy, complicates schema evolution, and creates a single point of failure. Instead, services should expose data via well-defined APIs or asynchronous events.

9.6.2 Message Brokers

As demonstrated with NATS, message brokers serve as the central nervous system for asynchronous communication across the system. They enable:

- **Event-Driven Architectures**: Services publish events (e.g., "Order Placed," "Payment Processed") to the broker, and other interested services subscribe to these events, reacting autonomously. This promotes loose coupling.

- **Load Balancing and Queuing**: Features like NATS Queue Groups distribute messages efficiently among multiple instances of the same service, ensuring parallel processing and preventing duplicate work.

- **NATS JetStream**: This persistence engine for NATS transforms it into a robust streaming platform, enabling messages to be stored and replayed. It offers features such as configurable retention policies (limits-based, work-queue, interest-based), message replay capabilities (from a specific sequence number or time), and stream consumers for guaranteed delivery. It supports an "at least once" quality of service and includes a Key-Value Store (a map with atomic operations) and an Object Store (for file transfer, replication, and storage API) for distributed state management. JetStream uses a NATS-optimized RAFT distributed quorum algorithm to maintain immediate consistency.

9.6.3 Comprehensive Observability

In a distributed system, system health and performance insights are crucial. Designing and managing observability involves taking care of

- **Centralized Logging**: Aggregating logs from all service instances into a single, searchable repository enables system-wide debugging and auditing. This can be enhanced via structured logging, which means to log messages as key-value pairs or in structured data formats such as JSON or XML. This is essential for machine readability, which then gives improved human readability via integration with external tools, which provide the ability of searching and filtering. Best practices include using a consistent log format, adhering to standard data formats, including all necessary context and metadata, ensuring the data is useful for all stakeholders, avoiding excessive verbosity, and following established security practices.

- **Aggregated Metrics**: Collecting performance metrics (CPU, memory, network I/O, request rates, error rates, latency) from all services and infrastructure components. Tools like Prometheus provide real-time dashboards and alerting.

- **Distributed Tracing**: When a request traverses multiple services, distributed tracing tools (e.g., Jaeger, Zipkin, OpenTelemetry) visualize the entire flow, identifying latency bottlenecks and pinpointing the exact service responsible for an issue. This is crucial for understanding complex interactions and the "RED" metrics (Request, Error, Duration). Instrumentation is vital for collecting telemetry data.

9.6.4 Security Infrastructure

Designing and ensuring system-wide security is necessary for any system, independently of the architectural style. There are several techniques that come into place when handling this; they include

- **API Gateways**: Acting as a single, centralized entry point for external clients, API Gateways handle common concerns such as authentication, authorization, rate limiting, caching, request aggregation, and protocol translation (e.g., converting REST to gRPC). They also offer fault tolerance features like circuit breakers and retries.

- **Service Meshes**: An infrastructure layer that enables managed, observable, and secure communication between services. Tools like Istio and Linkerd provide traffic management (routing, load balancing, fault injection, traffic shifting), security (mutual TLS, access policies), and observability (metrics, logs, traces) without requiring changes to service code. They enforce policies uniformly across the mesh. Service meshes, however, add complexity and resource overhead. Table 9-1 gives an overview of the features of service meshes in a more schematic way.

Table 9-1. *Service meshes*

Feature/Aspect	Istio	Linkerd
Traffic Management	Extensive, with advanced routing rules, traffic splitting, fault injection, and request manipulation.	Basic, with load balancing, retries, and timeouts, but fewer complex routing rules.
Security	Comprehensive, including mutual TLS (mTLS) for service-to-service encryption, JWT validation, and fine-grained access policies.	mTLS is enabled by default for automatic encryption between services, with a simpler policy setup.
Observability	Deep integration with telemetry and logging tools like Prometheus, Grafana, and Jaeger, providing detailed metrics, logs, and traces.	Built-in metrics and tracing, offering a lighter but still comprehensive view of service communication.

(*continued*)

Table 9-1. (*continued*)

Feature/Aspect	Istio	Linkerd
Resource Usage	Higher resource consumption due to its extensive feature set and complexity.	Lightweight and optimized for Kubernetes, resulting in lower resource usage.
Complexity/Learning Curve	Higher complexity, suitable for complex Kubernetes environments with extensive networking requirements.	Simpler to learn and manage, suitable for most Kubernetes users and smaller deployments.
Target Use Case/Philosophy	Designed for enterprises seeking advanced control and a comprehensive set of features for complex microservices.	Focuses on simplicity and ease of use, ideal for those looking for a less resource-intensive solution.

9.6.5 Configuration Management

Externalizing and centralizing application configurations (e.g., database connection strings, API keys, service endpoints, feature flags) allows for dynamic updates without service redeployments, fostering agility. Centralized management offers easier maintenance and improved consistency but can be a single point of failure and have scalability limitations. Distributed configuration management, while more complex to manage, offers improved scalability and fault tolerance. Version control and auditing are critical for tracking changes and enabling rollbacks.

The independence and autonomy of microservices are not inherent properties but are enabled and enforced by a sophisticated, shared infrastructure. Without robust message brokers, comprehensive observability, and intelligent gateways or meshes, microservices would quickly devolve into an unmanageable, insecure, and unreliable spaghetti architecture. The success of microservices shifts complexity from within the service to the surrounding infrastructure. This implies a significant investment in DevOps, Site Reliability Engineering (SRE), and platform engineering capabilities.

The robust and carefully managed infrastructure layer forms the bedrock upon which the entire distributed system operates. A well-designed infrastructure is fundamental to achieving the scalability, reliability, maintainability, and security essential for any production-ready system.

9.7 Orchestration

While individual, well-designed services and a robust infrastructure provide the necessary components, the true challenge of a production-ready distributed system lies in its orchestration—the automated management, dynamic coordination, and intelligent scaling of these numerous, interconnected services. Orchestration platforms abstract away the profound complexities of deploying, running, and maintaining applications in a distributed environment, enabling development teams to concentrate predominantly on business logic rather than operational intricacies. A quick overview of deployment orchestration can be seen in Figure 9-4, with two different strategies, canary releases and blue-green deployments, which we will introduce later in this paragraph.

As introduced in earlier practical examples, container orchestration platforms, notably Kubernetes, have become the de facto industry standard for managing distributed systems. They furnish the comprehensive capabilities required to transform a mere "bunch of services" into a coherent, self-healing, immensely scalable, and resilient system.

CHAPTER 9 A WHOLE SYSTEM VS. A BUNCH OF SERVICES

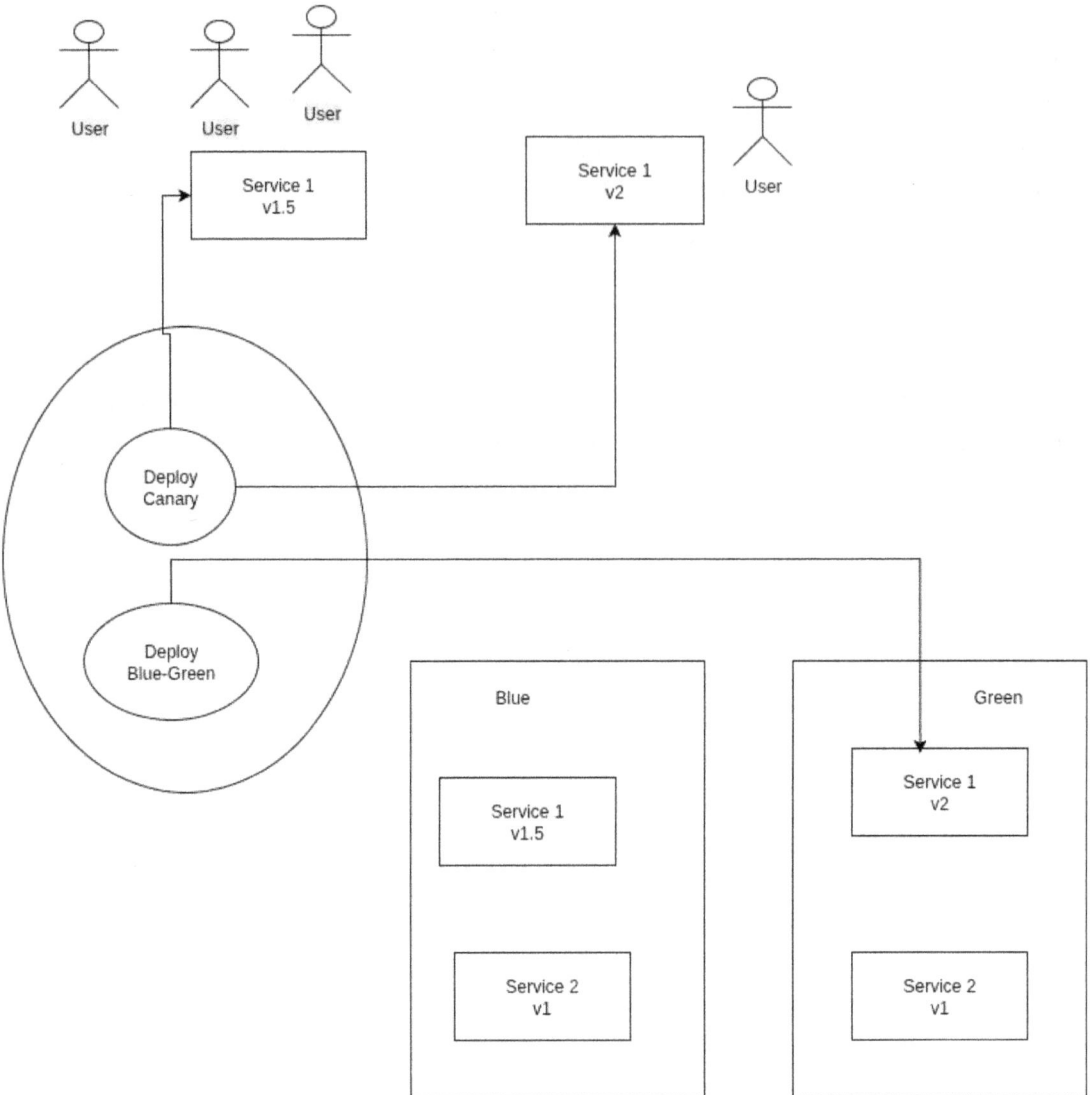

Figure 9-4. *Orchestration strategies*

Key aspects of orchestration include

- **Advanced Deployment Strategies**: Orchestrators enable sophisticated deployment techniques crucial for continuous delivery and minimal downtime.
    - **Blue-Green Deployments**: This Involves running two identical production environments ("Blue" and "Green"). New versions of the application, or parts of it, like one single service, are deployed

to the inactive environment ("Green"), thoroughly tested, and then all traffic is instantly switched from "Blue" to "Green." This allows for immediate rollback by switching traffic back to "Blue" if issues arise. It is similar to a QA or pre-production environment, keeping the specularity between what is active and inactive even closer.

- **Canary Releases**: A new version of a service is deployed to a small subset of users or servers (the "canary"). If no issues are detected, the new version is gradually rolled out to more users. This minimizes risk by limiting the blast radius of potential problems. This is similar, in a way, to AB testing.

- **Automated Rollbacks**: Orchestration platforms inherently support automated rollbacks. If a new deployment introduces errors or violates health checks, the system can automatically revert to the last stable version, ensuring rapid recovery.

- **GitOps**: A paradigm that uses Git as the single source of truth for declarative infrastructure and application configurations. Changes to the desired state are made in Git, and an automated process ensures the actual state of the cluster converges with the declared state in the repository. This promotes auditability, versioning, and collaborative operations. Benefits include improved security, collaboration, productivity, and faster, more reliable deployments.

Table 9-2. Deployment strategies

Strategy Name	Mechanism	Primary Goal	How It Reduces Downtime	Potential Pitfalls	Rollback Mechanism
Blue-Green Deployment	Two identical production environments ("Blue" and "Green") are maintained. New versions are deployed to the inactive environment ("Green"), then traffic is switched.	Zero downtime, immediate rollback capability.	A stable environment is always available to serve traffic during deployment and development.	Higher infrastructure costs (duplicate environments), potential for microservice version mismatch, constant monitoring required.	Instantaneous switch of traffic back to the "Blue" (previous stable) environment.
Canary Release	A new version of a service is deployed to a small, controlled subset of users or servers (the "canary") before a full rollout.	Risk minimization, early problem detection, gradual rollout.	Problems are detected early, before the new version is exposed to the entire system, limiting the blast radius of potential issues.	Risk of releasing microservices too early, frequent issues can slow down development, complexity in traffic routing and monitoring.	Traffic can be quickly routed back to the stable (old) version if issues are detected in the canary.

- Dynamic Scaling: One of the most significant advantages of distributed systems is their ability to adapt to varying workloads. Orchestrators enable:

  - Horizontal Scaling: Automatically adding or removing instances of a service based on demand (e.g., CPU utilization, memory usage, message queue depth, custom metrics). This is typically handled by the Horizontal Pod Autoscaler (HPA) in Kubernetes.

  - Vertical Scaling: Adjusting the allocated resources (CPU, memory) to individual service instances, managed by the Vertical Pod Autoscaler (VPA).

  - Cluster Autoscaler: Automatically adjusts the number of nodes in the cluster based on the pending pods.

  - Event-Driven Autoscaling (KEDA): Monitors external event sources and scales pods dynamically when predefined conditions are met, allowing fine-grained, real-time scaling beyond just CPU/memory.

  - Advanced techniques include predictive scaling with machine learning to proactively anticipate demand.

Table 9-3. Scaling resources

Mechanism	What it Scales	Trigger Metrics	Primary Benefit	Considerations/ Trade-offs
Horizontal Pod Autoscaler (HPA)	Number of running pods in a deployment, ReplicaSet, or StatefulSet.	Observed CPU utilization, memory usage, or custom application metrics.	Automatically adapts to fluctuating workloads, improving responsiveness and resource efficiency.	Requires a metrics server or external monitoring system; tuning polling intervals and thresholds is crucial.
Vertical Pod Autoscaler (VPA)	Resource requests and limits (CPU and memory) for individual pods.	Historical resource usage analysis.	Optimizes resource allocation for individual pods, reducing waste and improving performance.	Can cause pod restarts for resource adjustments; may conflict with HPA if both adjust CPU/memory.
Cluster Autoscaler	Number of worker nodes in the Kubernetes cluster.	Pending pods that cannot be scheduled due to insufficient resources.	Ensures the cluster has sufficient capacity to run all workloads; scales infrastructure up and down.	May introduce delays as new nodes are provisioned; requires integration with cloud provider APIs.
Event-Driven Autoscaling (KEDA)	Number of pods based on external event sources.	Message queue depth, custom events (e.g., Kafka topics, cron jobs, external HTTP requests).	Enables fine-grained, real-time scaling based on actual demand signals beyond CPU/memory.	Requires external event sources to be integrated; adds another layer of complexity.

- Service Discovery and Load Balancing: In dynamic environments where service instances are frequently created, destroyed, or moved, services require a reliable mechanism to locate and communicate with each other. Orchestrators provide built-in service discovery (e.g., DNS-based lookup in Kubernetes) that allows services to refer to each other by logical names rather than ephemeral IP addresses. Intelligent load balancing automatically distributes incoming requests across multiple healthy instances of a service, ensuring even workload distribution and preventing bottlenecks. Kubernetes offers various service types (ClusterIP, NodePort, LoadBalancer, ExternalName, Headless) to expose applications internally and externally.

- Health Checks and Self-Healing Capabilities: Orchestrators continuously monitor the health and responsiveness of deployed service instances.

    - Liveness Probes: Determine if a container is running correctly. If a liveness probe fails, Kubernetes assumes the container is broken and restarts it, ensuring automated self-healing from deadlocks or unresponsiveness.

    - Readiness Probes: Determine if a container is ready to receive traffic. If a readiness probe fails, the container is temporarily removed from service load balancers but is not restarted. This is crucial for applications needing time to initialize or connect to dependencies.

    - These probes ensure reliability and availability, especially during scaling events.

- Resilience Patterns: Orchestration platforms, often in conjunction with service meshes, facilitate the implementation of critical resilience patterns:

    - Circuit Breakers: Prevent a service from continuously trying to connect to a failing downstream service, allowing the failing service to recover and preventing cascading failures.

    - Retries and Retry Budgets: Automatically re-attempt failed requests, but with careful exponential backoff and limits to avoid overwhelming the system.

- Bulkheads: Isolate failures by partitioning resources (e.g., thread pools, connection pools) for different services or requests, preventing one failing component from consuming all resources and affecting others.

- Chaos Engineering: The practice of intentionally injecting faults into a system in a controlled manner to identify weaknesses and build resilience before they cause real outages. It involves defining a steady state, creating hypotheses about failure scenarios, and experimenting under real-world conditions. Tools like Chaos Monkey randomly disable instances to test resilience.

- Operational Excellence and SRE Principles: Orchestration aligns closely with Site Reliability Engineering (SRE) principles, fostering a culture of automation, measurement, and continuous improvement. Key operational considerations include capacity planning, disaster recovery (e.g., multi-region deployments, robust backup/restore), automation of repetitive tasks, and defining error budgets and Service Level Objectives (SLOs).

Orchestration is the crucial layer that transforms a collection of independent, potentially chaotic services into a coherent, self-managing, and resilient system. It acts as the "conductor" that ensures the individual "musicians" (services) play in harmony, adapt to changing tempos (load), recover from mistakes (failures), and deploy new "scores" (versions) seamlessly. Without it, the benefits of microservices (agility, scalability) would be negated by operational complexity and instability. The operational burden of distributed systems is immense, and manual management is unsustainable. Orchestration is not merely a tool but a fundamental shift towards automated, declarative system management. This necessitates a strong investment in automation, SRE principles, and a cultural embrace of "infrastructure as code" (GitOps) to truly unlock the potential of distributed architectures.

By leveraging sophisticated orchestration platforms and embracing these advanced operational principles, organizations can achieve unprecedented levels of availability, scalability, and operational efficiency for their distributed systems. These tools and practices provide the necessary control plane to manage the entire lifecycle of services, ensuring that the complete system operates reliably, adapts dynamically to changing demands, and remains truly "production-ready."

9.8 Summary

This chapter marks an important and pivotal transition in the comprehensive exploration of distributed systems, shifting the focus from the internal, granular design of individual services to the overall, macroscopic view of integrating, managing, and optimizing an entire system for production readiness. The chapter began by acknowledging the strong foundational knowledge meticulously built in the initial part of this book, covering low-level communication and robust messaging systems. It then seamlessly integrated the principles of well-crafted, independent service design, informed by domain-driven design and Hexagonal Architecture, which were the core tenets of the second part.

The discussion ascends "one level up," recognizing that a fully operational distributed system transcends a mere assembly of services. This elevated perspective compels us to confront new, intricate challenges: ensuring system-wide coherence, optimizing efficiency across a multitude of interactions, maintaining stringent data consistency amidst distribution, and mastering the inherent complexities of inter-service communication. The discussion highlights how simple horizontal scaling introduces emergent complexities, transforming the perception of scalability from merely adding resources to a fundamental architectural reevaluation.

The chapter poses the critical question, "Is this the end?"—only to reveal the persistent and often formidable challenges that emerge at the system level, including network dynamics and latency, the inevitability of partial failures, the complexities of coordinated deployment, the absolute necessity of comprehensive observability, and end-to-end security. We observe that while partial failure is a feature, it introduces insidious failure modes that can amplify localized issues into widespread, silent system degradation.

We revisit the historical context of Service-Oriented Architecture, discerning its inherent limitations, particularly its tendency to manifest as a "distributed monolith." This retrospective analysis underscores the fundamental tenets of truly independent microservices, cautioning against the anti-patterns that can undermine their promised benefits, such as tight coupling, shared data stores, and over-reliance on synchronous communication. We present the evolution from SOA to microservices as a shift from centralized control to decentralized governance, with the failures of ESBs demonstrating that centralization often creates more problems than it solves in dynamic systems.

CHAPTER 9   A WHOLE SYSTEM VS. A BUNCH OF SERVICES

The evocative "Like Russian Dolls" metaphor beautifully illustrates the nested layers of complexity, demonstrating how well-designed services, engineered with domain-driven design and Hexagonal Architecture, form cohesive units within the expansive, integrated system. Core principles apply hierarchically from the grand system down to its most minute components. This highlights the paradox that service autonomy, while beneficial, necessitates sophisticated integration and orchestration to ensure overall system coherence.

We subsequently broaden the understanding of the critical roles of system-wide infrastructure and advanced orchestration. We explore the infrastructure layer, evolving from a single service's external connections, as a shared foundation including sophisticated distributed data management strategies (consistency models, replication, avoiding shared databases), powerful message brokers like NATS JetStream (offering persistence, retention, and advanced messaging patterns), comprehensive observability solutions (structured logs, aggregated metrics, distributed tracing), robust security mechanisms (API Gateways, Service Meshes), and centralized configuration management. This underscores that the independence of microservices relies on and is reinforced by this robust external infrastructure, implying significant investment in platform engineering.

Finally, we explored the intricacies of orchestration, the automated control plane for managing the lifecycle of numerous services. This includes a detailed examination of advanced deployment strategies (Blue-Green, Canary, Automated Rollbacks, GitOps), dynamic scaling capabilities (HPA, VPA, Cluster Autoscaler, KEDA), intelligent service discovery and load balancing, proactive health checks and self-healing mechanisms (Liveness and Readiness probes), and critical resilience patterns (Circuit Breakers, Retries, Bulkheads, Chaos Engineering). We integrate key operational principles, including those from Site Reliability Engineering (SRE) and strategic disaster recovery planning, all of which are crucial for achieving a truly robust and resilient production system. We identify orchestration as the crucial layer that transforms a collection of independent services into a coherent, self-managing, and resilient system, necessitating a shift towards automated, declarative system management.

This chapter meticulously lays the conceptual and practical groundwork for the remainder of this part. It comprehensively equips the reader to explore specific architectural patterns, advanced technologies, and real-world implementation strategies for connecting services, managing distributed data, and ensuring the unparalleled resilience, scalability, and operational excellence of complex distributed architectures.

CHAPTER 9   A WHOLE SYSTEM VS. A BUNCH OF SERVICES

The journey from a collection of discrete services to a seamlessly integrated, high-performing, and production-grade system is both challenging and immensely rewarding. The reader is now poised to navigate it with confidence and expertise.

9.9 Questions

1) **What is the primary focus shift in this chapter compared to preceding parts of the book?**

    a) From the internal, granular design of individual services to the macroscopic view of integrating, managing, and optimizing an entire system for production readiness.

    b) From microscopic design of individual services to low-level communication protocols.

    c) From system-wide challenges to the intricacies of internal service design.

2) **What is one of the critical challenges that emerges when deploying multiple instances of services in a production-scale distributed setting?**

    a) The increased simplicity of a basic setup.

    b) Ensuring system coherence, operational efficiency, and distributed data consistency.

    c) Reduced inter-service communication and simpler data management.

3) **What was a significant drawback of Service-Oriented Architecture (SOA) that led to the concept of a "distributed monolith"?**

    a) Each service operating independently and focusing on a specific business capability.

    b) Pervasive reliance on a centralized Enterprise Service Bus (ESB), which introduced tight coupling and a single point of failure.

    c) Extreme decentralization and lightweight communication mechanisms.

CHAPTER 9 A WHOLE SYSTEM VS. A BUNCH OF SERVICES

4) **How does the "Russian Dolls" metaphor illustrate distributed system design?**

   a) It suggests that the entire system is a single, undifferentiated block.

   b) It shows that each service is completely isolated and has no interaction with others.

   c) It represents the nested complexity and hierarchical structure where each service is a cohesive, autonomous unit that fits within a larger integrated system.

5) **Which of the following is NOT a key aspect of system-wide infrastructure discussed in the chapter?**

   a) Centralized team communication platforms.

   b) Distributed Data Management.

   c) Comprehensive Observability.

6) **What is the primary goal of canary releases as a deployment strategy?**

   a) To maintain two identical production environments simultaneously.

   b) To minimize risk by gradually rolling out a new version to a small subset of users or servers to detect problems early.

   c) To instantly switch all traffic to a new environment for immediate rollback.

CHAPTER 10

DDD for Systems

10.1 DDD Refresher

In Part 2 of this book, we took a careful tour through Domain-Driven Design (DDD), showing that it is a powerful methodology for building a single service that's deeply in sync with the company's goals. This approach, as we defined it, goes beyond the technical patterns themselves: It's a philosophy that starts with "business-minded" thinking, promotes "cohesion across crafts," and manifests through a Ubiquitous Language.

This language defines a shared vocabulary, which is mirrored in the programming code so that everybody (from businesspeople to developers) will understand and use it. We're modeling exactly what everyone is talking about and what should happen in the business. In the context of distributed systems, where different parts of the whole can change independently, this Ubiquitous Language becomes an essential tool for enforcing consistency. Each service, ideally, operates within its distinct conceptual area, known as a Bounded Context, and possesses its specific domain model, as well as a unique "dialect" and extension of the Ubiquitous Language. Nevertheless, the entire structure of the knowledge system needs to be managed; without any kind of control or tracking process, inconsistencies can arise in how shared concepts will be understood and implemented across services. This can easily lead to miscommunication, data integrity issues, and sudden system failures that are challenging to diagnose.

Thus, the Ubiquitous Language, which was initially defined for a single context, evolves into a meta-language or a set of inter-context contracts in a distributed system, which is fundamental for ensuring logical coherence and preventing "distributed monoliths" stemming from conceptual misalignment. It effectively acts as a "canary in a coal mine" for detecting such inconsistencies.

Within the boundaries of a single service, we dug into the core components of the Domain Layer: Entities, which are objects defined by their unique identity rather than by their attributes only (such as our order in Chapter 8, "Sample Service," or a Patient in a health system, each with a unique ID, encapsulating behavior like a Patient having a BookAppointment() method); Value Objects, which represent descriptive aspects of the domain that lack of a conceptual identity and are typically immutable (like a MenuItem in an order system or an Appointment without its unique ID, simply signifying a specific time and reason for a patient to be examined); and Domain Services, which encapsulate operations or processes that do not naturally fit within an Entity or Value Object (such as a MenuService or OrderFactory in the Order Processor, or an AppointmentBookingService coordinating logic for booking appointments by manipulating entities and value objects). These elements collectively form the pure, untainted core of the business logic, intentionally decoupled from external concerns. This purity and isolation are not simply aesthetic design choices; they represent a fundamental strategy for building resilient systems. In a distributed system, external dependencies are inherently volatile and prone to changes, failures, or evolution. By isolating the core business logic within the domain layer, a service becomes significantly more resilient and adaptable to these external shifts, ensuring that changes in external technologies do not necessitate modifications to core business rules. This drastically reduces the "blast radius" of changes, allowing for faster, more independent evolution and deployment of services. The internal DDD layering, particularly the strict isolation and purity of the domain layer, is a prerequisite for achieving the external loose coupling that is the main aim of successful microservices.

The overarching "Business First" philosophy of DDD fundamentally reverses traditional software development by prioritizing business goals and the problems being solved over initial technical considerations. This philosophical shift ensures that the software system becomes a direct reflection of real-world business processes and operations. By engaging with domain experts early in the development cycle, engineers gain a deep understanding of the business, leading to systems designed around actual needs rather than assumptions. This fosters a collaborative environment among developers, product teams, and stakeholders, breaking down silos and ensuring that all parties contribute to shaping a system that truly aligns with its intended purpose. This business-first approach is crucial for creating adaptable systems that can evolve seamlessly with changes in business strategy.

Beyond the Domain Layer, we introduced the Application Layer, which orchestrates the service's use cases, acting as a thin coordination layer between the domain and external dependencies. This layer defines the "ports" in Hexagonal Architecture, specifying what the application needs to achieve (e.g., OrderRepository interface). Finally, the Infrastructure Layer provides the concrete "adapters" that implement these ports, handling interactions with databases, messaging systems (like NATS), and other external services, thereby isolating the core logic from technological specifics. The presentation layer serves as the entry point for inbound communication, translating external requests into a format understandable by the application layer. The re-architecture of the Order Processor in Chapter 8, "Sample Service," served as a practical demonstration of these principles, transforming a "minimalistic" system into a robust, maintainable, and testable service. This foundational understanding of DDD within a single service is determinant as we now elevate our perspective to apply these very same principles to the macroscopic design of an entire distributed system.

10.2 At a System Level

Having carefully designed individual services, we now face the challenging task of integrating them into a cohesive, production-ready distributed system. This transition, as highlighted in the previous chapter, moves us "one level up" from isolated service design to a holistic system view. The current landscape of software engineering has been and remains increasingly dominated by distributed systems, a trend that introduces both immense potential and significant complexity, demanding a broader perspective on system coherence, operational efficiency, distributed data consistency, and mastery of inter-service communication. Domain-driven design, initially applied to the internal structure of a single service, proves equally indispensable when addressing the complexities that emerge at this higher architectural stratum. Distributed systems inherently introduce a significantly higher order of complexity, making manual management unsustainable. In this intricate environment, DDD emerges as a determinant methodology, providing a robust framework for managing this complexity by ensuring that technical implementations are deeply aligned with core business needs and processes, thereby transcending mere code elegance to deliver tangible business value.

CHAPTER 10   DDD FOR SYSTEMS

The big increase in complexity associated with distributed systems is not simply an incremental rise but a qualitative transformation. For example, in a monolithic system, a payment timeout would typically just throw an exception in a single codebase and roll back the transaction in one place. In a distributed system, the same timeout may leave the payment service and the order service in conflicting states—the customer charged, but the order not confirmed. This "complexity multiplier" introduces emergent properties such as partial failures, unpredictable network latency, and the intricate challenges of maintaining distributed data consistency, all of which are either absent or negligible in monolithic or single-service contexts. The complexity scales non-linearly with the number of interconnected services, making manual system management infeasible. This exponential increase demands that organizations adopt rigorous, strategic, and often automated design approaches. The ultimate success of distributed systems, therefore, hinges less on the individual perfection of each service and more on the effective management of their interdependencies and the emergent behavior of the system as a whole. DDD provides the conceptual tools required to model and control this intricate interplay.

10.2.1 Business

At the system level, the "business-first" approach of DDD becomes even more critical. A distributed system, by its very nature, is a complex tapestry of interconnected services, each potentially serving a distinct business capability. Without a clear, overarching understanding of the business domain, these services risk becoming fragmented and misaligned rather than forming a unified product. DDD at the system level catalyzes a deeper alignment between the entire software landscape and the enterprise's strategic business objectives. It necessitates a continuous dialogue with business stakeholders to define the enterprise-wide "Ubiquitous Language" and to identify the core business processes that span multiple services. This ensures that the boundaries between services, their communication patterns, and their data ownership strategies are not merely technical decisions but direct reflections of the business's operational model. For instance, the Order Processor in Chapter 8, "Sample Service," had the central role of managing the order lifecycle, and this naturally positions it as a core business capability, influencing how other services (like the Restaurant Gateway or Delivery Tracker) interact with it. By prioritizing the business, we ensure that the distributed system is not just technically sound but also strategically valuable, capable of evolving in lockstep with changing market demands.

Furthermore, DDD functions as a "strategic compass" for distributed systems. In a distributed system, particularly one developed by multiple, often independent, teams, there is a significant risk that individual services, when introduced into the system, might become a mere "bunch of services" rather than a unified product. Each team might optimize its service in isolation, leading to a fragmented system that fails to meet overarching business objectives. Without a robust strategic framework like DDD, technical decisions regarding service boundaries, communication protocols, and data ownership might be made in isolation or based purely on technical convenience. This can lead to conceptual misalignment throughout the entire system, making it difficult for the system to evolve in response to changing business needs. Through its emphasis on a Ubiquitous Language and Bounded Contexts, DDD provides the necessary framework to maintain business alignment across the entire distributed landscape. This strategic application ensures that the distributed system is not just a collection of technically sound microservices but a coherent, unified product capable of adapting and evolving in lockstep with the enterprise's strategic goals and market demands. It elevates architecture from a purely technical exercise to a fundamental business enabler.

You can think of the whole system as a swarm of ants; each ant acts locally, but higher-level patterns emerge only when every ant's behavior aligns with the overall goal—much like services in bounded contexts operating under a shared domain language.

From a DDD perspective, there will be a domain language that will span over the whole product, hence the entire system, and each area of the system (logging, user facing, etc.) might have a second domain language to handle its specific needs, and then each single service might have to develop yet another language.

Looking at the business, what most likely will happen is that services providing features needed by the marketing teams will have their specific sub-language, but you will hardly have to generate a language for a specific service if you think at the business level.

10.2.2 Layers vs. Components

Within a single service, DDD guides us in structuring code into four distinct layers: domain, application, infrastructure, and presentation. These layers enforce a clear separation of concerns, with dependencies flowing inwards, ensuring the purity of the core business logic. At the system level, these well-defined services become the "components" of a larger distributed architecture.

Domain Layer: The innermost core, where the fundamental business rules, entities, and value objects reside. It remains intentionally isolated from technical concerns to preserve the purity and longevity of the core model.

Application Layer: A thin orchestration layer that coordinates use cases and business processes. It defines service interfaces and handlers, delegating real work to the domain rather than embedding business rules itself.

Infrastructure Layer: The bridge to the external world—databases, messaging systems, and external APIs. It implements the abstractions defined by the upper layers, hiding real-world complexity (such as network failures or storage peculiarities) without polluting the core logic.

Presentation Layer: The entry point, whether via HTTP, NATS, or CLI. It validates input, transforms it into structures the application layer understands, delegates processing, and formats outputs into responses.

Hexagonal Architecture (Ports and Adapters): It complements this by enforcing clear boundaries between a service's core logic (domain and application) and its external dependencies. Ports define how the core expects to interact with the outside world; adapters provide the actual implementations. This makes the core "adapter-agnostic"—able to switch databases or external services without rewriting the business rules. Without such a structure, a so-called "microservice" often becomes a brittle, tightly coupled block, negating the promise of independent deployment and resilience.

The "Russian Dolls" metaphor from the previous chapter illustrates this hierarchy elegantly. Each service, designed with DDD and hexagonal principles, is a self-contained "doll." The system as a whole is the largest doll; each service is a medium-sized one, and its internal layers are the smallest. At this higher level, the same principles apply: services expose well-defined interfaces ("ports"), which others consume as "adapters." This layered thinking, carried through from code to architecture, helps avoid the infamous "distributed monolith."

It is worth clarifying a common misconception: not every microservice will be directly exposed to the client, nor will they all operate in total independence. In a large-scale product—consider a global e-commerce platform, where one click on "checkout" triggers inventory checks, payment authorizations, shipping calculations, and notification flows—services form chains and orchestrations far more intricate than the naïve picture of isolated, user-facing endpoints. Microservices started as a way to simplify service orientation, but the systems we now build often exceed that early simplicity.

In short, the promise of microservices lies not in isolation for its own sake, but in well-bounded, loosely coupled collaboration. DDD, paired with Hexagonal Architecture, provides the discipline to achieve that balance.

10.2.3 Do We Always Need It?

The comprehensive application of DDD, with its emphasis on rich domain models and layered architectures, is undeniably beneficial for complex, business-critical services, such as our Order Processor, and for complex systems. However, the question arises: is a full DDD approach always necessary for every service within a large distributed system? Is it always necessary for every single distributed system?

The decision to apply a full DDD approach across all services in a distributed system depends heavily on the complexity of the domain and the strategic importance of each service. DDD is particularly valuable for complex, evolving business domains where deep modeling and clear boundaries are essential. It provides a valuable methodology for building modular, scalable, and maintainable systems, thereby contributing to system availability, reliability, and resilience in cloud-native architectures.

For simpler services, often referred to as CRUD (Create, Read, Update, Delete) services, or those primarily acting as data conduits or specialized infrastructure components, a full-blown DDD implementation is an overkill. Such services may not involve complex business rules or a rich domain to model, and their primary purpose may be to expose data or perform straightforward operations. In these instances, a more lightweight architectural style, perhaps focusing solely on Hexagonal Architecture to ensure clear boundaries and testability, could be a more pragmatic choice.

However, even when individual services adopt a simpler internal design, the principles of DDD remain highly valuable at the system level. The overall distributed system still needs a clear "Ubiquitous Language" to define its various "Bounded Contexts" and the relationships between them. The strategic decisions about which services correspond to which business capabilities, and how they interact, are inherently DDD concerns, regardless of the internal complexity of each component. Therefore, while the depth of DDD application may vary per service, its strategic influence on the entire distributed system's architecture is consistently vital. The key is to align the architectural depth with the inherent complexity and business criticality of the specific service or subdomain.

CHAPTER 10   DDD FOR SYSTEMS

You can think of it this way: many very simple services might still be combined into a system that is complex enough to justify DDD practices. Furthermore, specific ideas from DDD, like ubiquitous language, are always beneficial to align business with development and foster mutual understanding.

10.3 Bounded Context and Segregation

One of the most important concepts in strategic DDD, particularly for distributed systems, is the Bounded Context. As the previous chapter alluded, the Order Processor's designation as "the core of the system" suggests its natural fit as a Bounded Context.

A Bounded Context (BC) defines a logical boundary within which a specific "Ubiquitous Language" is consistent and meaningful. Outside this boundary, terms might have different meanings, or concepts might not exist. A BC also represents an explicit boundary inside which a particular domain model is consistent and valid. It allows us to separate an application into distinct conceptual areas, ensuring that inside each BC, business rules, terminology, and models are consistent and isolated from other contexts. This clear delineation of responsibilities is fundamental for managing complexity in large systems by breaking them into smaller, manageable services.

Bounded Contexts are particularly crucial for microservices architecture. They define clear technical and functional boundaries for each microservice, which in turn enables independent development, deployment, scalability, and maintainability of services.

In a distributed system, each microservice (or a small group of highly related services) should correspond to a Bounded Context. This ensures that each service has a clear, well-defined responsibility and its consistent domain model, preventing the "Ubiquitous Language" from becoming ambiguous or contradictory across the entire system. For example, the concept of an "Order" in the Order Processing Bounded Context might include states such as "Preparing" or "Ready for Delivery," whereas in a separate "Billing" Bounded Context, an "Order" might primarily concern financial attributes and payment status.

The principle of segregation is essential here. Each Bounded Context should own its data and its business logic, communicating with other contexts only through well-defined interfaces or events. This strict segregation prevents the creation of a "distributed monolith," where services are technically separate but remain tightly coupled through shared databases or implicit dependencies. By enforcing clear boundaries and data ownership, Bounded Contexts enable independent development, deployment, and scaling of services, fostering true agility and resilience within the distributed system. The "Database per Service" pattern is a direct, practical implementation of the Bounded Contexts' principle of data isolation. This pattern dictates that each microservice's persistent data should be private to that service and accessible exclusively via its API. This means that transactions are confined to a single service's database. If multiple services directly access and modify the same underlying database, it introduces tight coupling. This implicit coupling undermines service independence, even if services run in separate processes. Such a violation of data ownership leads to what is explicitly termed a "distributed monolith." This anti-pattern negates the core benefits of microservices, such as independent evolution, scalability, and agility, by reintroducing a single point of contention and complex dependencies at the data layer. Therefore, adhering to the "Database per Service" pattern is not merely a technical choice but a fundamental enabler for realizing the strategic benefits promised by Bounded Contexts and microservices architecture.

While Bounded Contexts promote independence, they are not entirely isolated. They must interact to achieve the overarching goals of the larger system. These interactions are governed by clearly defined "contracts."

Context mapping is a valuable technique for visualizing how different Bounded Contexts integrate and relate to each other, often including the relationships between the teams responsible for maintaining them. Several strategic patterns guide the integration of Bounded Contexts:

> **Partnership**: In this model, two teams or contexts share common goals and are interdependent for success. This necessitates coordinated planning and joint management of integration efforts.
>
> **Shared Kernel**: This pattern involves an explicitly shared subset of the domain model, often implemented as a compiled library, which is owned and referenced by multiple Bounded Contexts. While it promotes consistency, it requires high commitment and synchronization between teams, as changes to the shared kernel must trigger integration tests for all affected contexts. Its scope should be kept intentionally small to minimize coupling.

Customer-Supplier: This establishes a clear upstream-downstream relationship. The supplier (upstream team) delivers solutions based on the customer's (downstream team) prioritized needs, with the customer relying on the supplier to fulfill their requirements.

Anti-Corruption Layer (ACL): This is an isolating translation layer created by the downstream context. Its purpose is to protect the downstream's domain model from a problematic, legacy, or frequently changing upstream model. By translating foreign concepts into its own ubiquitous language, the ACL simplifies the consumer's model and language.

Open-Host Service: In this pattern, the supplier (upstream) exposes a well-documented protocol or API, referred to as a "published language," that is convenient for consumers. This approach decouples the supplier's internal implementation from its public interface, allowing independent evolution. It can be seen as a reversal of the anti-corruption layer, with the supplier performing the translation.

Conformist: The downstream context chooses to directly conform to the upstream's model. This often occurs when the downstream team lacks the motivation or resources to create a custom translation layer, or when the upstream provides insufficient support.

Separate Ways: This pattern involves no collaboration between contexts, and functionality might be duplicated if the cost of integration outweighs the benefits of sharing.

Table 10-1. Patterns of segregation

Pattern Name	Team Relationship	Description/Purpose	Key Characteristics	When to Use/Avoid
Partnership	Partnership	Teams share common goals; they succeed or fail together.	High collaboration, joint planning, mutual commitment.	High interdependency, shared fate.
Shared Kernel	Partnership	Explicitly shared subset of domain model (e.g., library).	Small, defined contract; requires high synchronization; changes affect all.	Shared ownership, common core functionality; avoid for large or frequently changing models.
Customer-Supplier	Upstream/Downstream	Supplier delivers based on customer's prioritized needs.	Clear roles; customer influences supplier's roadmap.	Clear dependency, supplier needs to be responsive to customer.
Anti-Corruption Layer	Upstream/Downstream	Downstream translates upstream's model to protect its own.	Isolates consumer from foreign concepts; simplifies consumer's model.	Upstream model is problematic/legacy, or changes frequently; downstream has a core subdomain.
Open-Host Service	Upstream/Downstream	Supplier exposes a well-documented "published language" (API).	Decouples internal implementation from public interface; supplier protects consumers.	Supplier needs to integrate with many consumers; consumer power is high.
Conformist	Upstream/Downstream	Downstream directly adopts upstream's model.	Simplifies integration; downstream has no influence.	Upstream model is stable and suitable; cost of translation is too high.
Separate Ways	Non-related	No collaboration; functionality duplicated.	No integration overhead; potential for redundant work.	Integration costs outweigh benefits; generic subdomains; communication difficulties.

Table 10-1 helps identify the sociotechnical implications of each pattern, not just the technical ones. For instance, "Partnership" implies high team coordination, while "Anti-Corruption Layer" emphasizes protecting a core subdomain. This guidance is practical for architects making design decisions in real-world distributed systems, helping to avoid anti-patterns like the "Big Ball of Mud" and ensuring loose coupling.

10.4 Different Levels of Depth

The "Russian Dolls" metaphor from the previous chapter serves as an excellent framework for understanding how DDD principles apply at various levels of granularity within a distributed system. Here we give you one perspective on how this doll's metaphor can be translated in the architecture of a distributed system, giving each doll a meaning within the overall system:

> **Innermost Doll (Within a Service):** At the deepest level, within each individual service, we implement the core DDD patterns, which involve defining Entities, Value Objects, and Domain Services. This is the level where the fine-grained business rules and behaviors are encapsulated, ensuring the internal consistency and purity of the service's core logic.
>
> **Medium Doll (Between Services/Bounded Contexts):** The next level of depth involves the interactions between different services, each representing a distinct Bounded Context. Here is where we extend DDD patterns to handle relations between services. We define explicit relationships between contexts, such as Customer-Supplier (where one context provides a service to another), Shared Kernel (a small, shared portion of code), or Anti-Corruption Layer (translating between two incompatible models). Communication between these contexts should primarily occur via well-defined APIs or asynchronous events, reinforcing loose coupling and autonomy.
>
> **Outermost Doll (The Entire System/Enterprise):** At the highest level, the entire distributed system can be viewed as a single, overarching domain. While a single "Ubiquitous Language" might be too broad for the entire enterprise, there will be a high-

level business vocabulary that defines the system's purpose and its major capabilities. Strategic DDD at this level involves identifying the core business domains, their interdependencies, and how the various Bounded Contexts contribute to the overall product vision. This holistic perspective ensures that even with decentralized development, the system remains coherent and aligned with enterprise goals.

This multi-layered application of DDD ensures that complexity is managed effectively at every scale, starting from the granular details of a single entity and ending with the intricate interactions of an entire distributed ecosystem.

10.5 What About REST

RESTful APIs are still the prevalent communication mechanism in distributed systems, and although we will focus on a different protocol in our more practical chapters, it is still important to provide some notions of how it works in this book. You might already know what REST is; after all, you might have used it for client-facing APIs. Nevertheless, it is beneficial to refresh and see it in the context of what this book is trying to convey.

When a service exposes a REST API, it typically acts as an inbound adapter within its presentation layer. This adapter receives HTTP requests, translates them from the external wire format (e.g., JSON) into the internal Data Transfer Objects (DTOs) or directly into domain/application commands, and then delegates the processing to the Application Layer.

Crucially, the REST API should expose concepts from its Bounded Context's Ubiquitous Language. For instance, the Order Processor's API might expose endpoints like

/orders or /orders/{id}/status,

directly reflecting the Order entity and its lifecycle. The DTOs used for request and response payloads should be carefully designed to avoid "leaking" internal domain model details. This means that the DTOs might not be identical to the internal Order entity; instead, they represent a simplified or transformed view suitable for external consumption. This practice maintains the encapsulation of the domain model, preventing tight coupling with external consumers and allowing the internal domain to evolve independently.

Furthermore, REST can also be used for outbound communication where one service acts as a client to another service's REST API. In this scenario, the client service's infrastructure layer would contain an outbound adapter (e.g., an HTTP client) that implements an interface (a "port") defined in its application layer. This ensures that the calling service's core logic remains unaware of the specific REST implementation details, adhering to the principles of Hexagonal Architecture.

10.6 Infrastructure and Orchestration

Knowing how to design the logical parts of a system and how to combine them into a cohesive and perfectly functional structure is surely most of the work you will do as an architect; still, even though a DevOps engineer might deploy the actual infrastructure, you need to understand how to deploy a distributed system. This will help you both prepare the system so that it is straightforward for the infrastructure team to do their job and run your system locally. It is all part of what is known as the DevOps mentality, which is now pervasive across the engineering team, regardless of the function. This also extends to the concept that each team is responsible for their developed services, which includes deployment. In the previous chapter, we extensively covered the macroscopic view of infrastructure and orchestration, and here we connect these concepts directly to DDD at the system level. These elements are not simply supportive; they are fundamental enablers of the loose coupling and autonomy that DDD promotes.

Effective communication and integration are essential in distributed systems, where numerous services must interact seamlessly to achieve overarching goals. The choice of communication paradigm has a significant impact on the system's resilience, scalability, and operational characteristics.

Here we present some concepts and tools applicable for orchestrating and managing the infrastructure:

- **Synchronous Communication:** This is a communication pattern that requires the components communicating with each other to be available and actively exchanging messages; in this pattern, the sender must wait for a response before proceeding with the next task. This pattern offers immediate feedback and is often seen implemented with RESTful HTTP interactions. However, in distributed environments, synchronous communication can lead to tight coupling, increased latency due to network traversals, and the potential for cascading failures if a downstream service becomes unresponsive. An operation that is instantaneous within a single process can become a significant performance bottleneck when it requires multiple network hops.

- **Asynchronous Communication:** This is the opposite of synchronous communication, which enables non-blocking message exchange, allowing services to continue processing without waiting for responses. Typically implemented with message queues or middleware, it decouples sender and receiver, enhancing scalability and fault tolerance. In distributed systems, this pattern helps manage partial failures and network issues by avoiding tight coupling and cascading errors. If a service is slow or fails, messages can be queued and processed later, enabling the system to self-heal or degrade gracefully. As a result, asynchronous communication is not just efficient but a fundamental strategy for building resilient, event-driven architectures. Exposing each microservice individually, however, remains a security and complexity concern.

- **API Gateways:** These are special client-facing services that serve as a single, centralized entry point for external clients, abstracting the internal complexity of the microservices architecture. They handle cross-cutting concerns such as authentication, authorization, rate limiting, caching, and request aggregation, and can also provide fault tolerance features like circuit breakers and retries.

  They might, as message brokers, become single points of failure, but in a holistic view of the system, it might not make sense that some parts of the system can still work if, say, authentication is broken. An API Gateway, like a message broker, is a potential single point of failure, and as such, it requires specific replication and other strategies to ensure high availability.

- **Nginx:** This is an HTTP server that can be effectively utilized as a reverse proxy to route incoming requests to the appropriate microservices. It offers capabilities for load balancing across multiple backend services, SSL/TLS termination to offload encryption from individual services, and security features like IP-based access control. Nginx can also perform URL rewrites to modify request paths before forwarding them to backend services.

This allows for encapsulating microservice URLs, enabling access by logical names instead of specific port numbers. API Gateways and Nginx, while distinct tools, collectively serve as the external "presentation layer" for a distributed system, abstracting internal complexities and enforcing system-wide policies that complement internal DDD principles.

The presentation layer in DDD is responsible for receiving external input and mapping it to internal structures. In a distributed system with many microservices, exposing each service directly to clients would be chaotic and insecure. API Gateways and Nginx (as a reverse proxy) provide a unified external interface. They abstract away the internal topology, allowing clients to interact with a single endpoint while requests are routed to the correct backend service. This separation allows the internal architecture to evolve without impacting external clients. This external abstraction layer is crucial for managing the macroscopic complexity of a distributed system, as it complements the internal decoupling achieved by DDD and Hexagonal Architecture by providing a controlled, secure, and performant "front door" to the entire system, ensuring that the benefits of internal modularity are not undermined by chaotic external exposure.

- **NATS:** We've seen the basic usage of NATS in the first part of this book. The messaging backbone of the distributed system, enabling reliable communication between services while we focus on system-level design, DDD, and orchestration. The benefits of using a message broker like NATS in a microservices architecture are many. Such a tool can decouple producers and consumers, protect against data loss by holding messages if a recipient is temporarily unavailable, increase system flexibility when adding or removing services, enable asynchronous communication patterns, and aid in load distribution across services.

NATS JetStream, which we will see later, further transforms NATS into a robust streaming platform with persistence, configurable retention policies, and message replay capabilities.

Table 10-2. *NATS communication patterns*

Topology Name	Core Mechanism	Communication Style (Typical)	Key Use Cases	Load Balancing Behavior	Advantages/ Disadvantages
Pub/Sub	Publishers send messages to subjects; all subscribed clients receive.	Asynchronous	Event broadcasting, real-time updates, notifications, logging.	All subscribers receive all messages.	High fan-out, loose coupling; messages can be lost if no active subscribers.
Req/Rep	Requester sends message with ephemeral reply subject; replier sends response to that subject.	Synchronous (over asynchronous core)	API calls, command execution, querying specific data from a service.	Load-balances requests across available responders (via queue groups).	Immediate feedback, simplifies client logic; can introduce coupling if overused.
Push/Pull (via Queue Groups)	Publishers send messages to a subject; NATS distributes messages to one random subscriber in a defined queue group.	Asynchronous	Work queues, task distribution, processing pipelines.	Distributes messages amongst members of a queue group.	Efficient workload distribution, prevents duplicate processing; requires explicit queue group setup.

Table 10-2 provides a clear, comparative view of NATS's primary communication patterns, which are fundamental to building distributed systems. It helps in selecting the most appropriate pattern for a given inter-service communication need, considering factors like message delivery guarantees, latency requirements, and scalability. By explicitly linking "Push/Pull" to "Queue Groups," it clarifies how NATS achieves this common pattern using its underlying pub/sub mechanism, demonstrating the tool's versatility.

System-wide infrastructure components are critical for the efficient operation, unwavering reliability, and comprehensive observability of a distributed system. They provide the common, shared services upon which individual microservices depend, abstracting away much of the underlying complexity and enabling consistent functionality across the entire architecture.

Key aspects of system-wide infrastructure include

- **Distributed Data Management:** We've seen this in the previous chapter; we will try to give a quick tour of all the techniques that can be utilized for this:
    - **Consistency Models:** Beyond traditional ACID transactions, distributed systems frequently employ various consistency models, ranging from strong consistency (e.g., synchronous replication) to eventual consistency (e.g., asynchronous replication), causal consistency, read-your-writes, and monotonic reads. The CAP theorem highlights the fundamental trade-offs between consistency, availability, and partition tolerance.

Table 10-3. Consistency models

Model Name	Key Guarantee	Primary Focus/ Trade-off	Typical Use Cases	Advantages	Disadvantages	Related Concepts
Strong Consistency	All operations appear to take place in some total order; every read retrieves the latest write.	Consistency over Availability	Leader election, Configuration management, Distributed locks, Transaction coordination.	High data integrity, predictable behavior.	High latency, reduced availability during network failures, difficult to scale.	CAP Theorem, Paxos/Raft
Eventual Consistency	If no new updates are made, all replicas will converge to the same value eventually.	Availability and Partition Tolerance over immediate consistency	Global-scale applications, Social media feeds, E-commerce shopping carts, CDNs, Messaging/ notification systems.	High availability, scalability, low latency.	Potential for stale data, requires conflict resolution mechanisms.	BASE principles, NoSQL
Causal Consistency	Operations that are causally related will be seen in the same order by all processes.	Causality	Distributed queues, collaborative editing.	Preserves causal order without strict total order.	More complex than eventual, weaker than strong consistency.	Logical clocks

(continued)

Table 10-3. (continued)

Model Name	Key Guarantee	Primary Focus/ Trade-off	Typical Use Cases	Advantages	Disadvantages	Related Concepts
Read-Your-Writes	A process that performs a write and then a read will always see the value it previously wrote.	Individual client's view	User profiles, session management.	Ensures a user sees their own updates immediately.	Does not guarantee consistency for other users.	
Monotonic Reads	Processes that perform sequences of reads will not see older versions of data later.	Individual client's view, sequential consistency	News feeds, ordered log consumption.	Prevents "going back in time" for reads.	Weaker than strong consistency.	
ACID	Atomicity, Consistency, Isolation, Durability (transaction treated as single unit).	Strong Consistency	Traditional relational databases, financial transactions.	Highest level of data integrity and reliability.	Limited availability during failures, higher coordination overhead.	
BASE	Basically Available, Soft State, Eventually Consistent (prioritizes availability and partition tolerance).	Availability and Partition Tolerance	Large-scale web services, NoSQL databases.	High availability, scales well during failures.	Temporary inconsistencies, requires conflict resolution.	

Table 10-3 is crucial for understanding the fundamental tradeoffs in distributed data management, particularly relevant when services own their data. It moves beyond simply listing models to explaining their practical implications, such as why eventual consistency is chosen for global-scale applications. This helps architects make informed decisions about data consistency across Bounded Contexts, balancing the need for data integrity with availability and performance in a partitioned environment, directly addressing a key challenge identified in the previous chapter.

- **Data Replication:** Strategies such as master-slave, multi-master, and leaderless replication ensure data availability and fault tolerance. Data partitioning (sharding) distributes data across multiple database instances to achieve horizontal scalability and improve query performance. Avoiding shared databases is a critical anti-pattern in microservices, as it introduces tight coupling, reduces service autonomy, complicates schema evolution, and creates a single point of failure. Instead, services should expose data via well-defined APIs or asynchronous events.

CHAPTER 10 DDD FOR SYSTEMS

Table 10-4. Data replication strategies

Strategy Name	Mechanism	Consistency Type (Typical)	Advantages	Disadvantages	Typical Use Cases	Replication Type
Master-Slave (Single-Leader)	One master node handles all writes and propagates changes to one or more slave nodes, which primarily serve reads.	Strong if reads from master (or after sync)	Simple to implement, good for read-heavy workloads, simplifies data backup and disaster recovery.	Master is a single point of failure (SPOF), can lead to replication lag.	Web applications with high read volumes, reporting and analytics systems.	Synchronous or Asynchronous
Multi-Master (Multi-Leader)	Multiple nodes accept writes and exchange updates with each other.	Eventual, conflicts must be resolved	Improves write availability, increases concurrency, allows writes to multiple servers.	Complex conflict resolution mechanisms are required, higher complexity.	Real-time collaboration tools, distributed systems requiring data consistency across multiple locations.	Synchronous or Asynchronous
Leaderless (Quorum)	Any node can accept writes; a quorum of nodes confirms writes and reads.	Tunable consistency (from strong to eventual)	High availability (no single point of failure), tunable consistency, resilient to node failures.	Possibility of conflicts or reading stale data if quorum sizes are not majority, increased complexity in managing quorums.	Systems like Apache Cassandra, Amazon DynamoDB.	Typically Asynchronous

328

Table 10-4 provides a clear comparison of how data is replicated in distributed systems, a direct consequence of the "database per service" pattern and the need for high availability. It details the mechanisms and consistency implications of each strategy, helping to understand how data durability and fault tolerance are achieved.

- **Message Brokers:** These serve as the central nervous system for asynchronous communication across the system. They work like a postal system; the services only communicate with the broker and never directly with another service. The only thing a service needs to know is what events it wants to subscribe to; the broker will then deliver the messages. When a service needs to send a message, it sends it to the broker, which then delivers it to the interested parties. This way, brokers promote loose coupling. Message brokers also facilitate load balancing and queuing, distributing messages efficiently amongst multiple instances of the same service. NATS JetStream, for instance, transforms NATS into a robust streaming platform with persistence, configurable retention policies, and message replay capabilities.

- **Comprehensive Observability:** In a distributed system, it is crucial to have comprehensive visibility into system health and performance. This involves centralized logging (aggregating logs into a searchable repository, ideally with structured logging for machine-readability), aggregated metrics (collecting performance data like CPU, memory, request rates, and error rates), and distributed tracing tools (visualizing the entire flow of a request across multiple services to identify bottlenecks and pinpoint issues).

- **Security Infrastructure:** Securing a distributed system demands a multi-layered, end-to-end approach. API Gateways act as centralized entry points, handling authentication, authorization, and other security concerns. Service meshes (e.g., Istio, Linkerd) provide an infrastructure layer for managed, observable, and secure communication between services, enforcing policies like mutual TLS and access controls without requiring changes to service code.

CHAPTER 10 DDD FOR SYSTEMS

Table 10-5. *Popular service mesh characteristics*

Feature/Aspect	Istio	Linkerd
Traffic Management	Extensive, with advanced routing rules, traffic splitting, fault injection, and request manipulation.	Basic, with load balancing, retries, and timeouts, but fewer complex routing rules.
Security	Comprehensive, including mutual TLS (mTLS) for service-to-service encryption, JWT validation, and fine-grained access policies.	mTLS is enabled by default for automatic encryption between services, with a simpler policy setup.
Observability	Deep integration with telemetry and logging tools like Prometheus, Grafana, and Jaeger, providing detailed metrics, logs, and traces.	Built-in metrics and tracing, offering a lighter but still comprehensive view of service communication.
Resource Usage	Higher resource consumption due to its extensive feature set and complexity.	Lightweight and optimized for Kubernetes, resulting in lower resource usage.
Complexity/Learning Curve	Higher complexity, suitable for complex Kubernetes environments with extensive networking requirements.	Simpler to learn and manage, suitable for most Kubernetes users and smaller deployments.
Target Use Case/Philosophy	Designed for enterprises seeking advanced control and a comprehensive set of features for complex microservices.	Focuses on simplicity and ease of use, ideal for those looking for a less resource-intensive solution.

Table 10-5 shows how service meshes enhance the operational capabilities of microservices in a distributed environment, particularly in terms of inter-service communication, security, and observability. It provides a direct comparison of two leading tools, aiding in strategic technology choices.

- **Configuration Management**: Externalizing and centralizing application configurations (e.g., database connection strings, API keys) allows for dynamic updates without service redeployments, fostering agility and consistency.

- **Container orchestration platforms**, notably Kubernetes, have become the de facto industry standard for managing distributed systems. They abstract away the profound complexities of deploying, running, and maintaining applications in a distributed environment, enabling development teams to concentrate predominantly on business logic rather than operational intricacies.

Key aspects of orchestration include:

- **Dynamic Scaling:** One of the most significant advantages of distributed systems is their ability to adapt to varying workloads. Orchestrators enable:

    - **Horizontal Scaling (HPA):** Automatically adding or removing instances of a service based on demand (e.g., CPU utilization, memory usage, message queue depth, custom metrics).

    - **Vertical Scaling (VPA):** Adjusting the allocated resources (CPU, memory) to individual service instances.

    - **Cluster Autoscaler:** Automatically adjusts the number of nodes in the cluster based on pending pods.

    - **Event-Driven Autoscaling (KEDA):** Monitors external event sources and scales pods dynamically when predefined conditions are met, allowing fine-grained, real-time scaling beyond just CPU/memory.

Table 10-6. Autoscaling types

Mechanism	What It Scales	Trigger Metrics	Primary Benefit	Considerations/ Trade-Offs
Horizontal Pod Autoscaler (HPA)	Number of running pods in a deployment, ReplicaSet, or StatefulSet.	Observed CPU utilization, memory usage, or custom application metrics.	Automatically adapts to fluctuating workloads, improving responsiveness and resource efficiency.	Requires a metrics server or external monitoring system; tuning polling intervals and thresholds is crucial.
Vertical Pod Autoscaler (VPA)	Resource requests and limits (CPU and memory) for individual pods.	Historical resource usage analysis.	Optimizes resource allocation for individual pods, reducing waste and improving performance.	Can cause pod restarts for resource adjustments; may conflict with HPA if both adjust CPU/memory.
Cluster Autoscaler	Number of worker nodes in the Kubernetes cluster.	Pending pods that cannot be scheduled due to insufficient resources.	Ensures the cluster has sufficient capacity to run all workloads; scales infrastructure up and down.	May introduce delays as new nodes are provisioned; requires integration with cloud provider APIs.
Event-Driven Autoscaling (KEDA)	Number of pods based on external event sources.	Message queue depth, custom events (e.g., Kafka topics, cron jobs, external HTTP requests).	Enables fine-grained, real-time scaling based on actual demand signals beyond CPU/memory.	Requires external event sources to be integrated; adds another layer of complexity.

Table 10-6 should give you a high-level understanding of how modern orchestration platforms like Kubernetes enable the dynamic scalability that is a core benefit of distributed systems. It provides a structured overview of different autoscaling approaches, their triggers, and their specific use cases, moving beyond a generic understanding of "scaling."

- **Advanced Deployment Strategies:** Orchestrators enable sophisticated deployment techniques crucial for continuous delivery and minimal downtime. Examples include

    - **Blue-Green Deployments:** Involves running two identical production environments ("Blue" and "Green"). New versions are deployed to the inactive environment, thoroughly tested, and then all traffic is instantly switched. This allows for immediate rollback if issues arise.

    - **Canary Releases:** A new version of a service is deployed to a small subset of users or servers (the "canary"). If no issues are detected, the new version is gradually rolled out, minimizing the blast radius of potential problems.

    - **Automated Rollbacks:** Orchestration platforms inherently support automated rollbacks, allowing the system to automatically revert to the last stable version if a new deployment introduces errors or violates health checks.

    - **GitOps:** A paradigm that uses Git as the single source of truth for declarative infrastructure and application configurations, promoting auditability, versioning, and collaborative operations.

Table 10-7. Deployment strategies

Strategy Name	Mechanism	Primary Goal	How It Reduces Downtime	Potential Pitfalls	Rollback Mechanism
Blue-Green Deployment	Two identical production environments ("Blue" and "Green") are maintained. New versions deployed to "Green," then traffic switched.	Zero downtime, immediate rollback capability.	A stable environment is always available to serve traffic during deployment and development.	Higher infrastructure costs (duplicate environments), potential for microservice version mismatch, constant monitoring required.	Instantaneous switch of traffic back to the "Blue" (previous stable) environment.
Canary Release	New version deployed to a small, controlled subset of users/servers ("canary") before full rollout.	Risk minimization, early problem detection, gradual rollout.	Problems detected early, limiting blast radius before full exposure.	Risk of releasing microservices too early, frequent issues can slow down development, complexity in traffic routing and monitoring.	Traffic can be quickly routed back to the stable (old) version if issues are detected in the canary.

- **Service Discovery and Load Balancing:** In dynamic environments where service instances are frequently created, destroyed, or moved, services require a reliable mechanism to locate and communicate with each other. Orchestrators provide built-in service discovery (e.g., DNS-based lookup in Kubernetes) and intelligent load balancing to distribute incoming requests amongst multiple healthy instances.

- **Health Checks and Self-Healing Capabilities:** Orchestrators continuously monitor the health and responsiveness of deployed service instances through liveness probes (determining if a container is running correctly, restarting if not) and readiness probes (determining if a container is ready to receive traffic, temporarily removing it from load balancers if not). These ensure reliability and availability, especially during scaling events.

- **Resilience Patterns:** Orchestration platforms, often in conjunction with service meshes, facilitate the implementation of critical resilience patterns such as circuit breakers (preventing continuous attempts to connect to failing services), retries with exponential backoff (re-attempting failed requests with increasing delays), bulkheads (isolating failures by partitioning resources), and Chaos Engineering (intentionally injecting faults to identify weaknesses).

Table 10-7 gives a schema of all these deployment strategies.

By now, it should be obvious that good service design is just one piece of the puzzle. You've seen it throughout this chapter—infrastructure isn't merely a background concern; it's absolutely central to making distributed systems function properly. All those tools and practices we've explored—message brokers, orchestration, observability, automation—they're not optional extras. They are what make true service autonomy possible. Without a solid infrastructure layer, even the cleanest, most carefully designed services can end up tangled together in fragile, hard-to-manage "spaghetti architecture."

So, when applying domain-driven design in a distributed environment, you must think beyond the code and the boundaries of your services. The platform beneath needs to carry much of the complexity that distribution inevitably brings: network issues, partial failures, scaling challenges, and operational overhead. It's the infrastructure that ensures services can be deployed, observed, and managed reliably, so your teams can stay focused on their bounded contexts and business logic without being overwhelmed by the system's complexity.

In short, infrastructure is the foundation that transforms good design into a maintainable, scalable, and resilient system. Design points you in the right direction; infrastructure is what keeps you there—steady, sustainable, and ready for whatever the real world throws at you. In practice, infrastructure is what makes the system work reliably every day.

10.7 Summary

This chapter applies the principles of Domain-Driven Design (DDD) from within individual services to encompass the broader picture—the entire distributed system. We kicked off by going back over the basics—the "business-first" mindset, the "Ubiquitous Language," and those core building blocks like entities, value objects, and domain services—and showed how they still hold up, even when you zoom way out.

Then we dug into how doing DDD at the system level really means lining things up with the business goals. The distributed system shouldn't just be a random collection of services; it needs to work as one product. The "Russian Dolls" metaphor helped explain this layered approach, starting with the fine details inside each service, moving out to how services talk to each other, and finally looking at the big enterprise-wide picture. We also touched on when going full DDD might be overkill for smaller services but stressed it's crucial for the overall system architecture.

A big focus in this chapter was on Bounded Contexts—the secret sauce for setting clear, consistent boundaries around business capabilities in a distributed setup. Ideally, each service (or group of services that fit well together) maps to a Bounded Context. This keeps concerns cleanly separated, data owned properly, and stops the dreaded "distributed monolith" from creeping in.

We didn't skip how RESTful APIs fit into all this either. They act as the presentation layer adapters, exposing domain concepts but still carefully managing data transfer objects so the domain stays encapsulated and clean.

And then there's infrastructure and orchestration—the unsung heroes that make a DDD-driven distributed system tick. Message brokers like NATS are what keep things loosely coupled and event-driven between Bounded Contexts, while distributed data management strategies make sure data ownership and consistency don't fall apart. Orchestration platforms like Kubernetes handle the heavy lifting on the operations side—managing, scaling, and deploying services, turning the whole design from theory into a real, resilient, production-ready system.

Moving from a bunch of separate services to a smoothly integrated, high-performing distributed system is no walk in the park—but it's hugely rewarding. It takes a big-picture architectural mindset that goes beyond just designing individual components. DDD gives you the framework to align software and business through Ubiquitous Language and Bounded Contexts, making sure things make sense and that services can evolve independently, which is vital in a distributed world. Inside each service, architectural patterns like Hexagonal Architecture keep things strong and maintainable, making sure they're not tangled up with outside concerns. This internal strength is a must-have if you want true loose coupling on the outside.

When it comes to services talking to each other, asynchronous communication via message brokers like NATS acts like the system's nervous system. It makes sure services stay loosely connected and can handle failures and unpredictable networks without falling over. Meanwhile, infrastructure and orchestration platforms like Kubernetes provide the operational backbone—automating deployment, scaling, healing, turning what would be a nightmare of manual operations into smooth, manageable workflows. This investment in shared infrastructure shifts complexity away from individual developers and onto a specialized platform layer, which is absolutely key to making a DDD-driven distributed system work well.

But success here isn't just about tech—it's a socio-technical challenge. It requires real teamwork across different roles and a product-first mindset so that every technical choice actually drives business value. Because complexity moves out of the services and into the shared platform, you need strong platform engineering and Site Reliability Engineering (SRE) practices. Achieving real agility and scale requires continually working to keep things loosely coupled, enforcing strict data boundaries, and making informed choices about asynchronous communication.

In short, it's the mix of DDD, solid architectural patterns, and smart infrastructure plus orchestration that turns a mere collection of services into a production-ready, resilient, and high-performing distributed system, ready to handle whatever the real world throws at it.

10.8 Questions

1. **What is the primary purpose of a Bounded Context in domain-driven design for distributed systems?**

    a) To define a shared database schema for all services.

    b) To establish a logical boundary where a specific Ubiquitous Language is consistent.

    c) To centralize all business logic into a single service.

    d) To eliminate the need for inter-service communication.

CHAPTER 10 DDD FOR SYSTEMS

2. **How does the "Russian Dolls" metaphor relate to DDD in distributed systems?**

   a) It suggests that all services should be identical in size and complexity.

   b) It illustrates the nested application of DDD principles at various levels of granularity.

   c) It implies that services should be tightly coupled and managed centrally.

   d) It describes a system where only the outermost layer is designed with DDD.

3. **Which of the following is a key benefit of applying DDD at the system level in a distributed architecture?**

   a) It simplifies the deployment of monolithic applications.

   b) It ensures that technical decisions are made independently of business goals.

   c) It fosters a deeper alignment between the entire software landscape and strategic business objectives.

   d) It eliminates the need for any infrastructure components.

4. **When might a full DDD approach be considered "overkill" for an individual service within a larger distributed system?**

   a) When the service is highly complex and business-critical.

   b) When the service primarily performs simple CRUD operations or acts as a data conduit.

   c) When the service needs to communicate with many other services.

   d) When the service is developed by a large team.

CHAPTER 10 DDD FOR SYSTEMS

5. **How do message brokers like NATS support DDD principles in a distributed system?**

    a) By enforcing synchronous communication between all services.

    b) By centralizing all data storage for multiple Bounded Contexts.

    c) By enabling loose coupling and event-driven communication between Bounded Contexts.

    d) By eliminating the need for any form of data consistency.

CHAPTER 11

Fully Synchronous Systems

11.1 Introduction

Still today, synchronous communication is a common pattern of communication used in software design to handle the communication between different components in distributed systems. Synchronous communication means that all the parts involved in the communication, be they processes, services, or entire systems, need to be always ready and available at the same time to send and receive messages with each other. When one component sends a message, it must wait and stop whatever it was doing until it gets a reply back. As a real-life example, consider a live conversation where you expect an immediate answer to your question and you cannot continue talking or doing other things till the other person has replied.

In software, this is similar to a payment service waiting for a bank's API to authorize a transaction before completing a checkout. Until the bank replies, the whole process is stalled, even if everything else in the system is ready to continue.

This kind of communication usually assumes that there are some limits on how long it takes for each part to process things and how long messages take to travel across the network. This assumption is often important for systems where things need to happen quickly or for services that have to behave consistently.

Even if synchronous communication seems natural and straightforward, it is not free of problems when architecting a fully distributed system, as there are many considerations to make. One of the most significant issues with this type of communication is latency, which is the waiting time to get a response. In reality, latency is always present when two distributed services are communicating, but with synchronous communication, it is a bigger problem. When one service calls another synchronously, as explained above, it has to stop and wait for the answer before it can continue its work. This waiting time can really pile up when a lot of services are calling each other or when one service is slow or unresponsive. Even though there are modern programming tools that try to deal with concurrency, most network protocols we use, like HTTP, are synchronous at the core level. This means the client has to wait for the entire response before it can do anything else. This can cause overhead and slow things down, especially when many requests or things need to happen very quickly.

Another significant issue with synchronous communication, still related to the waiting time, is the one called "cascading failures." Because synchronous communication connects services tightly, if one service fails or is slow, it can cause other services to fail or hang too. This can cause a domino effect where many parts of the system stop working, making outages far worse than if the components were independent. This problem is not just a simple sum of failures, because the waiting time and the missed replies can multiply their effect, and the overall system outage can get much worse than expected. That's why system architects have to use patterns like circuit breakers and retries to protect the system and avoid a total collapse. It's not really optional; it's a must-have in engineering.

Another issue that can arise is not specifically about communication, but any system needs to be prepared for peak loads. Now, this means that more resources have to be available all the time, which can be excessive during quiet times. With synchronous communication, scaling is harder because if one service depends on another synchronously, most likely both need to be scaled at the same time because the number of requests to one service will match the number of requests to the second service. This is more complicated than asynchronous systems, where each part can be scaled separately. Error handling is tricky as well, since every service in the chain must handle failures properly, or the problems spread further.

There is a real tension, however, in how modern distributed systems are built. While asynchronous communication is generally preferred inside the system for scalability and resilience, the way users interact with systems, like making real-time requests or API calls, is often intrinsically synchronous. The goal isn't to get rid of synchronous communication completely but to manage it carefully inside a system that is mostly asynchronous.

When people talk about "fully synchronous systems," they usually mean that the main external interfaces are synchronous, but inside the system, things need to be handled carefully. Often, this means turning synchronous external calls into asynchronous internal workflows where possible, or using tools like API Gateways and Service Meshes to contain and isolate synchronous parts so their downsides don't affect the whole system. Handling this well is key to making distributed systems robust.

In this chapter, we will look at how to design and build systems that mostly rely on synchronous communication. We will see how RESTful APIs provide direct access to services, how tools like Nginx help route and transform requests, and how service meshes can manage communication between services. We'll also examine NATS, which is basically asynchronous but can be used to support synchronous request/reply with REST proxies and its microservices package. Important topics like authorization and how API Gateways secure and control synchronous traffic will be covered too. Finally, we'll revisit Space-Based Architecture, which was designed for high-performance synchronous interactions, and explore what that means in real life.

11.2 REST and Direct Service Access

RESTful APIs are the most common way to handle communication between services and between a server and a client. They've been around for so long, and they are pretty much a standard everybody must know, and this is why we start with them now that we talk about synchronous communication in distributed systems. Furthermore, especially with microservices, it's just what people use the most, although as we shall see, it should not be the favorite choice internally for inter-service communication. REST provides a client-server model where everything is stateless, and you can use HTTP to expose resources or actions through endpoints. Because it's stateless, it simplifies how the client and server communicate, which is one of the reasons people like it so much, particularly in web apps. So what ends up happening is that every service has its little REST API, and that becomes the way it exposes what it can do.

That said, exposing every microservice with its REST API directly to the outside world is not always such a great idea. It might seem reasonable at first, but then you will quickly realize that it brings a lot of problems. First of all, security must be handled for every single endpoint, and if you have many services, that becomes very hard to manage properly. For example, many companies that start with a small set of services later struggle when their ecosystem grows to dozens or even hundreds of REST endpoints. Managing security rules, routing logic, and versioning across all of them becomes a full-time job for entire teams. Then you have to deal with routing, which involves deciding which request goes where and ensuring it ends up in the right place. Additionally, you have to handle API versioning, which is often underestimated but can cause significant headaches if not handled from the beginning. So the more services you have, the more complicated it gets. Someone has to take care of all of that, make it work smoothly, and make sure it doesn't fall apart, which is not something you can just ignore or leave for later.

It shall be now clear that even though people think HTTP is simple, it still comes with its share of complexities, which are simply pushed somewhere else rather than at the communication level. Now, what this synchronous communication also brings is that when two services talk over HTTP, the connection stays open until the whole thing, the request and the reply, is done. That might not seem like a big deal at first, but when you have a lot of services making a lot of requests all the time, the overhead from keeping those connections open really adds up. This means that apart from the latency and the services hanging on, the whole communication itself indirectly can take a big chunk of the system's resources while everything is just waiting around.

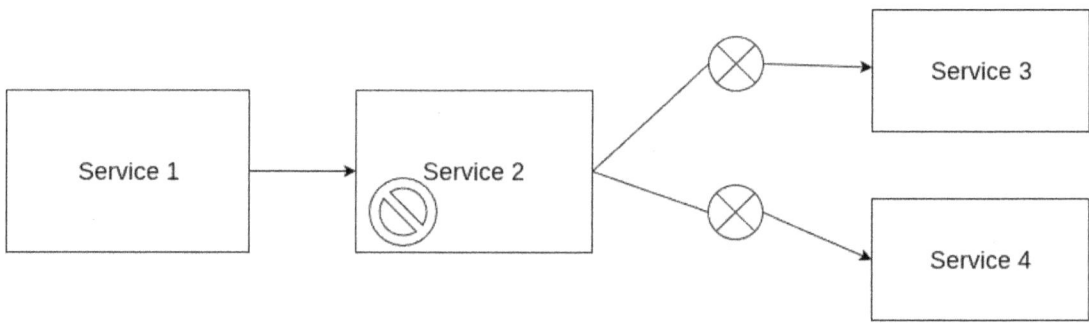

Figure 11-1. *REST communication chain failure*

Another thing that's kind of tricky is error handling. When you've got a bunch of services calling each other one after the other, as in a typical call chain, any failure in that chain can cause a whole set of troubles. This is clearly depicted in Figure 11-1, where If one link in the chain fails and the others don't know how to deal with it properly, then the failure spreads, and that's why we use the term cascading failures: One thing breaks, and if the next thing doesn't handle it well, it breaks too, and it keeps going. In Figure 11-1, there is a failure in Service 2, which prevents Services 3 and 4 from operating. To help this situation, every service in that chain has to know how to deal with upstream and downstream failures, and that adds complexity.

11.2.1 A Dummy Example

Consider a simple scenario where a customer service representative needs to retrieve user profile information from a user profile service. In a direct REST access model, the customer service would make an HTTP GET request to a specific endpoint exposed by the user profile service:

```go
// customer_service/main.go

package main

import (
    "fmt"
    "net/http"
    "io/ioutil"
)

func main() {
    resp, err := http.Get("http://localhost:8080/users/123")
    if err!= nil {
        fmt.Println("Error fetching user profile:", err)
        return
    }
    defer resp.Body.Close()
    body, err := ioutil.ReadAll(resp.Body)
    if err!= nil {
        fmt.Println("Error reading response body:", err)
        return
    }
    fmt.Printf("Received user profile: %s\n", string(body))
}

// user_profile_service/main.go

package main

import (
    "fmt"
    "net/http"
)
```

```
func main() {
    http.HandleFunc("/users/{id}", func(w http.ResponseWriter, r *http.
    Request) {
        userID := r.URL.Path[len("/users/"):]
        fmt.Fprintf(w, "User profile for ID: %s", userID)
    })
    http.ListenAndServe(":8080", nil)
}
```

In this basic example, the customer service directly calls the user profile service. The example is a dummy example, as it exchanges simple text rather than a structured document like a JSON string. However, it demonstrates how synchronous communication between services is achieved via REST, utilizing basic Go packages.

While straightforward for simple interactions, this direct coupling can lead to challenges in a large-scale distributed system, such as managing service discovery and load balancing, plus all the issues explained in the introduction.

11.2.2 Managing Traffic with Nginx

As applications grow into collections of microservices, each running on its host or container, there's an essential need to expose these services to the outside world in a controlled, manageable way. It would be bad practice, very impractical, and dangerous to just hardcode IPs and ports everywhere like we did in the previous paragraph or expect clients to know how to reach every service instance of a service directly. This is where Nginx comes in.

Introducing a reverse proxy, such as Nginx allows teams to centralize control of inbound traffic while improving system resilience and flexibility. Operating both as a high-performance web server and a reverse proxy, Nginx intercepts incoming client requests and forwards them to the appropriate backend services based on rules defined in its configuration. This design establishes a single external entry point, simplifying external communication and shielding clients from the internal structure of the microservices architecture. It becomes the front line of traffic management and the first decision point in the routing process. For instance, when the User Profile service resides at 192.168.1.100:8081 and the Order service at 192.168.1.101:8082, Nginx can route requests with the path /users/ to the former and /orders/ to the latter using a configuration like the following:

nginx.conf

```
http {
    upstream user_profile_service {
        server 192.168.1.100:8081;
    }
    upstream order_service {
        server 192.168.1.101:8082;
    }
    server {
        listen 80;
        server_name example.com;

        location /users/ {
            proxy_pass http://user_profile_service/;
        }
        location /orders/ {
            proxy_pass http://order_service/;
        }
    }
}
```

We will not cover how to install Nginx here, as the installation process depends on your setup. It may be in your VM on a cloud provider, your local machine, or within a Kubernetes cluster, which is what we will assume. We simply provided a config file for Nginx to show how it works in relation to the dummy example we've given you in the previous paragraph. Beyond basic routing, Nginx can transform URLs before forwarding them, which is particularly useful when services undergo internal restructuring without changes to the public API surface. For example, a request to /oldpath/resource can be redirected permanently to /newpath/resource using rewrite ^/oldpath/ (.*)$ /newpath/$1 permanent. These rewrites can be unconditional or dynamically determined by inspecting headers such as the User-Agent, enabling context-aware routing decisions. This flexibility allows Nginx to adapt traffic flow without modifying service code or redeploying infrastructure. The same mechanisms enable intricate request rewriting logic for complex APIs, where Nginx directives such as rewrite, return, and proxy_pass can be composed to remap paths, redirect clients, or modify upstream destinations. Requests can also be routed by inspecting HTTP headers or methods.

While if conditions provide basic branching, the map directive is more performant and better suited for advanced routing logic. This level of control over URL parsing and transformation allows services to evolve independently while maintaining compatibility at the system boundary.

To support high availability and resilience, Nginx provides multiple load balancing strategies through the upstream directive. These include Round Robin, which distributes traffic evenly across instances; Least Connections, which favors the least-loaded backend; and IP Hash, which ensures session stickiness by routing requests from the same client IP to the same backend. These approaches allow Nginx to distribute load intelligently and recover gracefully from individual instance failures, which is essential in environments with fluctuating demand or rapid scaling. Routing can also be tied to API versioning strategies. The most explicit approach is URI path versioning, where the version is embedded directly in the request path (e.g., /v1/resource, /v2/resource). This method is highly visible, easy to test, and compatible with caching strategies. Nginx can route versioned paths to different backend services, allowing multiple API versions to coexist. In contrast, header-based versioning moves version information into custom request headers such as X-API-Version or Accept-Version. This decouples the API surface from the URI structure and enables cleaner, more RESTful designs. Nginx can inspect these headers and dispatch requests accordingly, enabling fine-grained control without polluting endpoint URLs.

As services evolve, Feature Flags become instrumental in rolling out new functionality without deploying new service versions. Flags allow teams to expose features to targeted users, conduct A/B experiments, or quickly disable unstable components in production. While Nginx does not evaluate feature flags natively, it can route traffic based on headers or other request metadata if the flag state is injected upstream or exposed by an identity service. This enables Nginx to participate in flag-driven control flows and influence routing logic dynamically, making it a powerful part of the release pipeline. When these advanced capabilities are brought together, Nginx becomes more than just a gateway. It acts as a programmable traffic control plane that enables advanced delivery strategies like blue/green deployments, canary releases, or phased rollouts without touching backend code or triggering full redeployments. By moving traffic-shaping logic to the system edge, Nginx decouples release coordination from internal service logic and reduces the risk of cascading failures or tight coupling. Its role shifts from basic request forwarding to that of an orchestrator of synchronous

CHAPTER 11 FULLY SYNCHRONOUS SYSTEMS

service interactions. This evolution reflects a deeper architectural insight: infrastructure tools, when strategically configured, can shoulder critical delivery responsibilities and become central to operational resilience and continuous delivery.

Table 11-1. *Nginx routing strategies for microservices (URL rewriting, API versioning)*

Strategy	Nginx Directive/Concept	Description/Use Case
URL Path Routing	location, proxy_pass	Routes requests based on a specific URL path segment (e.g., /v1/users to users-v1-service). Useful for explicit API versioning.
Header-Based Routing	if/map, proxy_set_header	Routes requests based on the value of a custom HTTP header (e.g., X-API-Version: 2 to users-v2-service). Promotes cleaner URIs.
URL Rewriting/Redirects	rewrite, return	Modifies the URL of a client request or redirects clients to a new location (e.g., /old-path to /new-path). Used for canonical URLs or correcting misspellings.
Load Balancing	upstream, proxy_pass	Distributes incoming requests across multiple healthy backend instances using algorithms like Round Robin, Least Connections, or IP Hash.
Feature Flag-Based Routing (Conceptual)	if/map (with external data), proxy_pass	Dynamically routes traffic to different service versions or functionalities based on feature flag states, enabling A/B testing or gradual rollouts.

Table 11-1 summarizes Nginx's routing capabilities for microservices, and it is very important because it provides a concise, at-a-glance summary of Nginx's advanced capabilities. It allows developers and architects to rapidly remember the different routing strategies, their associated Nginx directives, and their specific use cases, such as when to use URI path routing versus header-based routing for API versioning, or which load balancing algorithm is suitable for a given scenario. By consolidating this information, the table significantly enhances the practical utility of the chapter, making the complex topic of Nginx configuration more accessible and actionable for real-world applications.

11.2.3 Service Mesh

We've seen how Nginx helps configure service URLs and endpoints, but what about inter-service communication? As systems grow, the direct coupling of services through point-to-point communication becomes increasingly complex to manage and inherently fragile. What we did in the earlier paragraph with the dummy example was to hardcode the user service's URL inside the caller's code. If multiple instances of the same user service exist, the customer service will need to know all of the user service's instances and somehow choose one to call. We've spoken about this both in the previous chapter and earlier in this chapter. It is all about load balancing and service discovery: we need a system that decouples services at an infrastructure level, allowing for minimal knowledge exchange between services and their infrastructure, while ensuring they communicate effectively without overloading any instance.

While Nginx handles traffic at the edge, a service mesh works inside the cluster, providing a whole infrastructure layer dedicated to managing, observing, and securing communication between services. This layer takes complex networking concerns out of the application code itself, adding essential reliability, security, and observability features at scale, without forcing changes to the actual service logic. The magic happens by injecting a proxy, called a sidecar, alongside each service instance. This sidecar intercepts every bit of inbound and outbound network traffic. This sidecar proxy is the core mechanism. It handles all those tricky, cross-cutting concerns transparently, so the app code doesn't have to care. Developers get to focus on business logic only, speeding up development cycles, lowering mental load, and making the system easier to maintain. It's a paradigm shift, moving operational complexity into this invisible infrastructure layer.

The benefits of a service mesh are huge:

- **Traffic Management:** You get fine-grained control over inter-service traffic. Load balancing algorithms like round-robin, least connections, weighted distribution, and all three. Add advanced routing rules, traffic splitting for canary deployments or A/B testing, plus fault injection to simulate failures and build resilience.

- **Security:** Robust security built in. Automatic mutual TLS encryption and authentication between services, JWT validation, and fine-grained access policies, all protecting communication like a vault.

- **Observability:** Full observability baked in. Metrics (latency, error rates, request counts) collected automatically. Logs aggregated centrally, structured logging for easy parsing. Distributed tracing that maps every hop and timing of requests across services.

- **Resilience:** Resilience patterns built right in, circuit breakers, retries with exponential backoff, and timeouts. These protect the system from cascading failures and network hiccups, dramatically improving fault tolerance.

But service meshes are not just about stability or safety. They're strategic tools for innovation, experimentation, and proactive risk reduction. They enable controlled rollouts of new features or service versions to subsets of users (canaries, A/B tests), so real feedback can be gathered while minimizing blast radius. Fault injection allows "chaos engineering," breaking stuff on purpose to find weaknesses and improve before the real disaster hits. This directly tackles the risks of synchronous changes by providing sophisticated, controlled dynamic adjustments and validations, making the system way more adaptable and robust.

Among the biggest service mesh players, Istio and Linkerd stand out with very different philosophies and feature sets. Istio is heavyweight, comprehensive, and powerful. It offers extensive routing capabilities, deep observability integrations with tools like Kiali, Prometheus, and Grafana, and very robust security with mutual TLS and fine-grained access control policies. The trade-off: higher resource usage and a steep learning curve due to its vast configuration options. Istio uses the Envoy proxy, which is implemented in C++. Linkerd goes minimalist. It's designed for performance, simplicity, and ease of use. Lightweight and highly optimized, it covers essential service mesh features with automatic mutual TLS enabled by default for all TCP traffic. It generally uses fewer resources and is simpler to operate. Linkerd employs its own Rust-based proxy. Choosing between them depends on whether you want granular control and a rich feature set (Istio) or operational simplicity and efficiency (Linkerd). Either way, service meshes add complexity and resource overhead, so that's a factor to keep in mind.

11.3 NATS Services

As we've seen in the first part of this book, NATS, primarily known for its asynchronous Pub/Sub capabilities, also provides robust mechanisms for synchronous Req/Rep communication, making it a versatile tool for building services that require immediate responses.

11.3.1 Direct Access

As demonstrated in Chapter 3, NATS supports a Req/Rep pattern where a client sends a request to a subject and waits for a reply from a responder. NATS automatically load-balances requests across multiple responders for the same subject, effectively creating a push/pull-like distribution for synchronous messages.

// **nats_requester/main.go (simplified)**

```
package main

import (
    "fmt"
    "log"
    "time"
    "github.com/nats-io/nats.go"
)
func main() {
    nc, err := nats.Connect(nats.DefaultURL)
    if err!= nil {
        log.Fatal(err)
    }
    defer nc.Close()
    msg, err := nc.Request("service.sum",byte("1,2,3"), 1*time.Second)
    if err!= nil {
        log.Fatal(err)
    }
    fmt.Printf("Received response: %s\n", string(msg.Data))
}
```

// **nats_replier/main.go (simplified)**

```go
package main

import (
    "fmt"
    "log"
    "strconv"
    "strings"
    "time"
    "github.com/nats-io/nats.go"
)

func main() {
    nc, err := nats.Connect(nats.DefaultURL)
    if err!= nil {
        log.Fatal(err)
    }
    defer nc.Close()
    nc.Subscribe("service.sum", func(m *nats.Msg) {
        data := string(m.Data)
        parts := strings.Split(data, ",")
        sum := 0.0
        for _, p := range parts {
            num, err := strconv.ParseFloat(p, 64)
            if err!= nil {
                m.Respond(byte("Error: Invalid number"))
                return
            }
            sum += num
        }
        m.Respond(byte(fmt.Sprintf("%f", sum)))
    })
    for {
        time.Sleep(time.Second) // Keep the replier alive
    }
}
```

This direct NATS Req/Rep approach is efficient and leverages NATS's built-in load balancing and ephemeral reply subjects to ensure that responses are routed back to the correct requester, regardless of the responder's location.

11.3.2 REST Proxy

For systems that need to expose NATS-based services via a traditional HTTP/REST interface, a REST-to-NATS proxy can act as a bridge. This proxy receives HTTP requests, translates them into NATS messages, sends them to the appropriate NATS subject, waits for a NATS reply, and then translates that reply back into an HTTP response. Projects like sohlich/nats-proxy provide a micro-framework for this purpose, mapping HTTP methods and URLs to NATS subjects (e.g., /user/info GET maps to GET.user.info NATS subject). This allows existing REST-based architectures to migrate to a NATS messaging platform or for NATS services to be consumed by traditional HTTP clients without direct NATS client integration.

```go
// Example of a NATS-to-REST proxy setup (conceptual, using sohlich/nats-proxy)

package main

import (
    "gopkg.in/sohlich/nats-proxy.v1"
    "net/http"
    "github.com/nats-io/nats"
)

func main() {
    proxyConn, _ := nats.Connect(nats.DefaultURL)
    proxy, _ := natsproxy.NewNatsProxy(proxyConn)
    defer proxyConn.Close()
    // HTTP server listening for requests
    http.ListenAndServe(":8080", proxy)
}
```

```go
// Example of a NATS client acting as a REST endpoint (conceptual)
package main

import (
    "gopkg.in/sohlich/nats-proxy.v1"
    "github.com/nats-io/nats"
    "fmt"
    "os"
    "syscall"
    "os/signal"
)

func main(){
    clientConn, _ := nats.Connect(nats.DefaultURL)
    natsClient, _ := natsproxy.NewNatsClient(clientConn)
    defer clientConn.Close()
    natsClient.Get("/user/info", func(c *natsproxy.Context) {
        user := struct { Name string }{"Alan"}
        c.JSON(200, user)
    })
    // Keep client alive
    sig := make(chan os.Signal, 1)
    signal.Notify(sig, syscall.SIGINT, syscall.SIGTERM)
    fmt.Println("Press Ctrl+C to exit.")
    <-sig
}
```

This pattern is particularly useful for exposing internal NATS services to external clients or integrating with legacy systems that only understand HTTP. This highlights NATS's strategic value in enabling hybrid communication architectures. It allows organizations to incrementally adopt new messaging paradigms without a "big bang" rewrite, facilitating a gradual transition from purely synchronous REST to more asynchronous, event-driven models, or conversely, exposing internal asynchronous services synchronously to external consumers. This flexibility is crucial for managing the architectural tension between synchronous and asynchronous communication discussed in the introduction, providing a pragmatic path for modernization and integration with legacy systems, thereby reducing the risk and complexity of large-scale architectural shifts.

11.3.3 NATS Microservices Package

The NATS Go client library includes a dedicated package called "micro," aimed at simplifying the creation of microservices that leverage NATS as a communication means so that they can benefit from its scalability, load management, and observability. This package provides a higher-level abstraction over raw NATS Req/Rep, allowing developers to define services, endpoints, and groups. A service in the micro package aggregates endpoints for handling application logic, and the services are named and versioned, and endpoints can be registered under specific subjects or grouped with common subject prefixes.

// **nats_microservice/main.go (using nats.go/micro)**

```go
package main

import (
    "fmt"
    "log"
    "github.com/nats-io/nats.go"
    "github.com/nats-io/nats.go/micro" // Import the micro package
)

func main() {
    nc, err := nats.Connect(nats.DefaultURL)
    if err!= nil {
        log.Fatal(err)
    }
    defer nc.Close()

    // Define a request handler
    echoHandler := func(req micro.Request) {
        fmt.Printf("Received request on subject '%s': %s\n", req.Subject(),
        string(req.Data()))
        req.Respond(req.Data()) // Respond with the received data
    }

    // Create a new NATS microservice
    srv, err := micro.AddService(nc, micro.Config{
        Name:    "EchoService",
        Version: "1.0.0",
```

```
        // Define a base endpoint for the service
        Endpoint: &micro.EndpointConfig{
            Subject: "svc.echo", // The subject this endpoint listens to
            Handler: micro.HandlerFunc(echoHandler),
        },
    })
    if err!= nil {
        log.Fatal(err)
    }
    defer srv.Stop() // Ensure graceful shutdown
    log.Printf("NATS Microservice '%s' (v%s) started on subject '%s'\n",
    srv.Name(), srv.Version(), "svc.echo")

    // Keep the service running
    select {}
}
```

Clients can then send requests to svc.echo (e.g., nats req svc.echo "hello!") and receive responses directly. This package simplifies common microservice patterns, providing built-in features for load management and observability, making it an excellent choice for building synchronous NATS-native services.

Let's analyze the core parts of this code:

```
srv, err := micro.AddService(nc, micro.Config{
        Name:    "EchoService",
        Version: "1.0.0",
        // Define a base endpoint for the service
        Endpoint: &micro.EndpointConfig{
            Subject: "svc.echo", // The subject this endpoint listens to
            Handler: micro.HandlerFunc(echoHandler),
        },
    })
```

This creates a NATS microservice and adds it to the NATS store so that it is discoverable by whoever wants to use it. The config also adds an endpoint:

```
Endpoint: &micro.EndpointConfig{
        Subject: "svc.echo", // The subject this endpoint listens to
        Handler: micro.HandlerFunc(echoHandler),         },
```

using the function **echoHandler,** which was previously defined. Essentially, in order to define an endpoint for a service, we can use any function with this signature:

```
func(req micro.Request) {}
```

And, as we have access to the request object from inside the function, we can use the **Respond** method to send the answer back to the requester.

We need to see, however, how to do this programmatically inside a service so that a service can call another one and how to add several "endpoints" to this service.

Here is an example where we create a NATS microservice and we add an endpoint afterwards:

```go
package main

import (
    "context"
    "log"

    "github.com/nats-io/nats.go"
    "github.com/nats-io/nats.go/micro"
)

// Define the handler function for the endpoint
func handleCustomerCreate( req micro.Request) {
    // In a real app, decode and validate the payload here
    data := string(req.Data())
    log.Printf("Received customer.create request: %s", data)

    // Respond back to the caller
    err := req.Respond([]byte("Customer created: " + data))
    if err != nil {
        log.Printf("Error responding: %v", err)
    }
}

func main() {
    // Connect to NATS
    nc, err := nats.Connect(nats.DefaultURL)
    if err != nil {
```

CHAPTER 11   FULLY SYNCHRONOUS SYSTEMS

```go
        log.Fatal(err)
    }
    defer nc.Drain()

    // Define service metadata
    config := micro.Config{
        Name:        "CustomerService",
        Version:     "1.0.0",
        Description: "Handles customer-related operations",
    }

    // Register the service with NATS Micro
    service, err := micro.AddService(nc, config)
    if err != nil {
        log.Fatal(err)
    }
    defer service.Stop()

    log.Printf("Microservice registered: %s", service.Info().Name)

    // Create a group under the service
    customerGroup := service.AddGroup("customer")

    log.Printf("Group created: %s", customerGroup.Subject())

    // Register the "create" endpoint under the group
    err = customerGroup.AddEndpoint("create", micro.HandlerFunc(handleCustomerCreate))
    if err != nil {
        log.Fatal(err)
    }
    log.Println("Endpoint 'customer.create' registered")

    // Block forever
    select {}
}
```

As you can see, we create a service without endpoints, and then we use

```
err = customerGroup.AddEndpoint("create", micro.HandlerFunc
(handleCustomerCreate))
```

which again accepts a micro.HandlerFunc, which is a function with the expected signature.

Till now, however, we have simply used a microservice package, but we haven't really used DDD, but the aim of this chapter is to show how to combine distributed communication patterns, NATS as a broker, and DDD to design a service. We will give here an example of how this works.

Let's start with the domain layer:

```
package domain

type Customer struct {
    Name  string
    Email string
}
```

This defines a value object that can be used across layers.

We now need a function to actually create the customer, most likely using a database or adding it to the memory:

```
package app

import (
    "errors"
    "fmt"
    "myservice/domain"
)

func CreateCustomer(c domain.Customer) (string, error) {
    if c.Name == "" {
        return "", errors.New("name required")
    }
    if c.Email == "" {
        return "", errors.New("email required")
    }
    // Business logic here (e.g. DB save)
```

```go
fmt.Printf("Customer %s (%s) created", c.Name, c.Email)
return c, nil
}
```

In this example, we simply print the created user and return it as it is, but in a real application, we would use a persistence layer to add the user to the database, and the newly created user would then be returned.

We have our domain and application layer, but now we need, somehow, to expose our function. We will do it with the presentation layer, which is built with NATS micro in mind, as it will include a micro **HandlerFunc**:

```go
package presentation

import (
    "encoding/json"
    "log"
    "myservice/app"
    "myservice/domain"
    "github.com/nats-io/nats.go/micro"
)

func HandleCustomerCreate(req micro.Request) {
    var c domain.Customer
    if err := json.Unmarshal(req.Data(), &c); err != nil {
        log.Printf("Invalid data: %v", err)
        _ = req.Respond([]byte("Invalid customer data"))
        return
    }

    log.Printf("Creating customer: %+v", c)

    result, err := app.CreateCustomer(c)
    if err != nil {
        log.Printf("Create error: %v", err)
        _ = req.Respond([]byte("Failed: " + err.Error()))
        return
    }

    _ = req.RespondJSON(result)
}
```

CHAPTER 11   FULLY SYNCHRONOUS SYSTEMS

This function receives a request object and unmarshals the content into a domain object, then passes it to the app layer's function. When it gets the result back, it sends it to the client. The last part is the actual main package of our application, where things will be initialized:

```go
package main

import (
    "log"
    "myservice/presentation"

    "github.com/nats-io/nats.go"
    "github.com/nats-io/nats.go/micro"
)

func main() {
    nc, err := nats.Connect(nats.DefaultURL)
    if err != nil {
        log.Fatal(err)
    }
    defer nc.Drain()

    config := micro.Config{
        Name:        "CustomerService",
        Version:     "1.0.0",
        Description: "Customer operations",
    }

    svc, err := micro.AddService(nc, config)
    if err != nil {
        log.Fatal(err)
    }
    defer svc.Stop()

    group := svc.AddGroup("customer")
```

```
    err = group.AddEndpoint("create", micro.HandlerFunc(presentation.
    HandleCustomerCreate))
    if err != nil {
        log.Fatal(err)
    }

    log.Println("Customer service running...")
    select {} // block
}
```

This is all just setting up the system and instantiating connections and services. This setup is already somewhat valid, but it can be improved. For instance, the domain object is used to directly unmarshal a micro request. This could work, but you should understand that the domain structs are not necessarily what will reach the client, nor what will be received by the service, nor what will reach an eventual database.

There is no problem with this small example, but let's see a small change:

```
package domain

type Customer struct {
    Name  string `json:"name"`
    Email string `json:"email"`
}
```

We simply added JSON tags for a better serialization so that the JSON expected and sent back will be

`{"name":" John", "email":"john.smith@myemail.com"}`

This is all good, but in reality, you might start adding specific JSON tags, or BSON tags if you are using MongoDB, or any other specific tag that is not meant for a domain layer. Serialization is not really needed when handling domain structs, so a more appropriate solution would be to have a presentation struct:

```
package presentation

import (
    "encoding/json"
    "log"
    "myservice/app"
```

```go
    "myservice/domain"
    "github.com/nats-io/nats.go/micro"
)
type Customer struct {
    Name  string `json: "name"`
    Email string `json: "email"`
}
func HandleCustomerCreate(req micro.Request) {
var c Customer
    if err := json.Unmarshal(req.Data(), &c); err != nil {
.......................................
dc:= domain.Customer {Name: c.Name, Email = c.Email}
.......................................
result, err := app.CreateCustomer(dc)
```

Which seems like overkill. In this instance, it is actually overkill, but in general, it is not in real apps. We leave you to judge when to use domain structs directly and when to use specific layer-dependent structs, but we stress that any layer-specific tag or property should not be included within the domain. A little more verbosity helps in big projects to keep layers clean and not entangled. To explain further the issue, there is no problem in adding JSON tags to a struct, wherever it is, but these tags are only needed when serializing the structs. When we use domain structs in our business logic, we do not need to serialize them; we use them as they are. If the serialization is used to then store the struct or to share it, it's not a problem that these tags are in the domain, because we can see them as simply a way to serialize our domain structs. If, however, the tags are solving a specific problem, such as maintaining data structures with a specific shape within the database, where you have a convention of snake case attributes, camel case, or fully uppercase, etc., then an issue starts to emerge: you are injecting specific infrastructure needs inside the domain, and that defies the whole point of DDD. This same issue happens when you shape your JSON tags inside your domain to suit a preexisting API or any API convention that is a matter only of your presentation layer.

Is that the case that every serialization tag is a wrong choice in the domain layer? That is a valid argument, and yes, we are supposed to avoid it. In this instance, however, what we want to stress is that we need the right tool for the right job, and if you think that something like a serialization tag can be decided at the domain level, it is coming from the domain and not from other layers into the domain, and it helps reduce verbosity and help clarity. It is up to you how you decide to act.

In a nutshell, we are providing you with the tools to build a complex, distributed system. How you decide to make use of them after considering all the tradeoffs is up to you. This does not mean that you should be free to do everything you want; there are still good and bad practices, but the decision of which tradeoffs you will make is ultimately up to you.

11.4 Authorization

Authorization is one of the features that are absolutely critical in any distributed system; it ensures that users and services only get access to what they're actually allowed to access. As you might imagine, authorization brings complexity, because every action performed, every data accessed, and every interaction with the system needs to be aware of what each single user or service can actually access or not. Authorization is also linked to authentication, although they are two different concepts. Authentication is what identifies a user, be it human or synthetic; it's what tells the resource receiving the request who is contacting it. Once and only after the requester has a known identity, it will be possible to then check for the requester's permissions on the specific resource or interaction requested.

We will not focus on authentication here, because there are numerous ways you may already know to handle it, whether through external tools or a simple credential check in the database. This approach will not change significantly in a distributed system compared to a non-distributed one.

Going back to the actual authorization, there are several models in distributed systems to handle that, and they typically fall into two main categories:

- **Centralized Authorization:** In this model, there is a single point, such as an API Gateway or a dedicated service, that handles all authorization decisions across the system. It means you manage policies in one spot, which can be really handy, with less duplication, easier-to-update rules, and fewer chances of services doing things in their own slightly different ways. Tools like Cerbos or built-in features in your gateway are typical examples of this.

- **Decentralized Authorization:** Here, each service takes care of its own authorization logic. It provides more independence to services, which can be beneficial, but it also means you need to exercise caution. Policies can drift, things can get inconsistent, and keeping everything aligned across a growing system becomes its own kind of problem. It's more flexible, but it needs discipline.

To decide whether to grant or deny a specific authorization to perform an action/retrieve a resource, or to request that permission be granted, clients and servers generally share a token that is somehow connected to a specific user. A token, essentially, shares the user information and guarantees that the request comes from the asserted user.

We will now see two different types of token-based authorization mechanisms:

- **JWT (JSON Web Tokens):** JWTs are compact and self-contained tokens used to carry information between parties. In most systems, they're used to share identity, in other words, to say who the user is, and maybe include a few stable facts that don't change often. What they're not good for is carrying fine-grained permissions or real-time context. Doing that tends to increase the token size, introduces security risks, and generally goes against the idea of keeping things small and focused. A good rule here is similar to the principle of least privilege: only put into the token what absolutely needs to be there.

  Fine-grained and context-aware decisions are better handled by external policy engines, which can make those checks at runtime. This type of separation enhances both security and flexibility, particularly in complex synchronous systems. JWTs should be short-lived, ideally lasting only minutes or a few hours, and you should use refresh tokens to manage longer user sessions. What goes into the JWT should be minimal: user ID, maybe an email, or a stable, high-level role. But definitely avoid sticking specific permissions or resource lists inside.

  And of course, always transmit JWTs over a secure connection like HTTPS or NATS with TLS, make sure they're signed and verified using strong cryptographic algorithms, and rotate keys regularly. One limitation to keep in mind is that once a JWT is issued, it's static. You can't revoke it easily unless you add some external tracking, and that starts to cancel out the benefit of being stateless. So JWTs are useful, but they're not a full access control system, and trying to cram too much into them usually backfires.

- **OAuth2:** OAuth 2.0 is a widely adopted standard for delegated authorization. It allows a system to access protected resources on behalf of a user, without requiring the user to share or store their actual credentials. It's often used together with JWTs, where the Authorization Server issues a JWT as the access token.

When using OAuth2, a few practices are essential. You need proper client authentication, ideally with multi-factor authentication, and you should implement refresh token rotation to avoid long-lived tokens becoming a weak spot. It's also important to monitor token usage, detect suspicious patterns early, and revoke any compromised tokens immediately. And don't forget secure storage of client secrets, as that's a non-negotiable action.

Authorization models also define how permissions are structured and applied, and here we present two mechanisms for that:

- **Role-Based Access Control (RBAC):** RBAC is based on assigning permissions to users through predefined roles, such as Sales, Support, or Admin, in a typical organization. It's usually easier to set up and manage, especially for small or medium-sized setups, because the mapping between roles and their associated capabilities is clear and fairly stable. Once a role is defined, you assign it to users, and that's it; there's no need to rethink the logic for every single user.

- **Attribute-Based Access Control (ABAC):** ABAC, on the other hand, adopts a more dynamic approach. Access decisions are made by evaluating a set of attributes, not just about the user but also about the resource being accessed and even the environment (like time of day, location, device type, etc.). This allows for much more fine-grained and contextual policies. It gives you more control but also comes with more complexity. Compared to RBAC, ABAC can handle more advanced scenarios; however, you'll need a proper policy engine to support it and a good understanding of which attributes actually matter in your system.

In order to practically implement your access control, there are many choices, and it all comes down to how you manage your data access. In many cases, depending on how difficult your rules are, you might simply check for ownership of a resource, check the roles of the person, etc. You might even just go down to the query to retrieve the data and perform the check down there. As an example, let's say you are looking for a document, and in the database it is stored as

```
{
  "id": "987",
  "name": "My Awesome Policy",
  "content": "This policy...........",
  "user_id": "12345"
}
```

You might run a query in your database to select a document with an **id** equal to **987** and a **user_id** equal to **12345**. This is a relatively simple scenario, and in some applications, it will be sufficient; however, let's examine it again in the context of DDD. We need to be independent of the data source, and we can still push this check to the infrastructure layer, but things can get messy for more complicated checks. In many cases, it is better to defer this to a dedicated part of the application, an application or domain service, for example, that handles access permissions. You can implement that by yourself, but if you want something very robust, you can look at a policy engine.

Policy engines are dedicated tools that help move authorization logic out of your core application code. The idea is to make decisions about whether something is allowed or not elsewhere, outside of your service, and away from your business logic. This separation allows you to define policies in one place and have them evaluated externally, resulting in cleaner, more consistent, and easier-to-manage processes.

One of the most well-known examples here is **Open Policy Agent (OPA)**. OPA uses its own declarative language, Rego, and exposes a REST API you can call to ask, "Is this action allowed?" You can run it as a sidecar right next to your services, which means policy decisions happen fast and locally, without adding latency to every request. And because policies live outside the application, you can change them on the fly without redeploying anything. That's a big win.

What policy engines like OPA provide is a way to define access logic once and then apply it consistently across all your services, regardless of the language in which they're written. You get a unified model, dynamic updates, and support for very granular rules based on user attributes, resource types, or even request context.

CHAPTER 11   FULLY SYNCHRONOUS SYSTEMS

As we are stressing the use of NATS and Go in this book, OPA has a Go client and can even be loaded as a library. Furthermore, OPA is generally deployed as a sidecar to a microservice, and we are inside the Kubernetes realm here, so you will have one pod with your main microservice and a small OPA agent running inside the same pod, which can communicate via REST or client library with the microservice itself.

```
The way OPA works, as you can see in the main website:
default allow := false
allow if {
    input.method == "GET"
    input.path = ["documents", document_id]
    input.id == input.user_id
}
```

In this setup, your code will simply have to retrieve the needed information, generally into a domain model, and use the domain model to define the input that will be sent to the OPA, something like

```
{
  "role": "staff",
  "id": "12345",
  "path": [
    "documents",
    "987"
  ],
  "method": "GET",
  "user_id": "12345"
}
```

Of course, if you are using NATS, you will not have the HTTP method, and you won't put it inside your rule definition. You can learn more about **OPA** at

`https://www.openpolicyagent.org/`

OPAL (Open Policy Administration Layer) builds on top of OPA and is designed specifically to handle even more fine-grained access models, particularly when it comes to relationship-based access control (ReBAC). It ensures that your policies and data remain consistent across all instances, even in large-scale environments. OPAL introduces sharding for performance, built with low latency in mind, essentially aiming to make fine-grained decisions without sacrificing speed.

The rise of tools like OPA and OPAL shows a clear shift in how we think about authorization in distributed systems. It's no longer just a feature hidden inside services; it's becoming a dedicated layer of the architecture. Moving the logic out means services get simpler, policies get more consistent, and updates become easier to manage.

In synchronous systems, this tends to lead to a hybrid model. Gateways at the edge handle coarse-grained checks, and internal services rely on dedicated engines for the more fine-grained, contextual stuff. JWTs still handle identity, but the actual permission checks are handled where they make the most sense.

The following table provides a comparison of various authorization mechanisms in synchronous distributed systems:

Table 11-2. Authorization mechanisms in synchronous distributed systems

Mechanism	Primary Role	Key Features/Benefits	Considerations/Limitations
API Gateway Authorization	External access control for incoming client requests.	Request routing, aggregation, rate limiting, protocol translation. Centralized policy enforcement for external clients.	Can become a single point of failure if not properly scaled. Adds some latency for all requests.
Service Mesh Authorization	Internal service-to-service communication security.	Mutual TLS (mTLS) for encryption and authentication, fine-grained access policies, traffic management, observability.	Adds complexity and resource overhead to the infrastructure.

(*continued*)

Table 11-2. (*continued*)

Mechanism	Primary Role	Key Features/Benefits	Considerations/Limitations
JWT (JSON Web Tokens)	Identity carrier and stateless authentication.	Compact, self-contained, scalable, interoperable across platforms. Eliminates server-side session management.	Difficult to revoke in real-time without external mechanisms. Not suitable for storing fine-grained, dynamic permissions due to static nature.
RBAC (Role-Based Access Control)	Coarse-grained permissions based on user roles.	Simple to implement and understand. Good for small to medium organizations with clear role definitions.	Can become rigid and complex for highly dynamic or granular permission requirements.
ABAC (Attribute-Based Access Control)	Fine-grained permissions based on attributes (user, resource, environment).	Highly flexible and granular control. Adapts to complex, dynamic authorization scenarios.	More complex to design and implement. Policies can become difficult to manage if not well-structured.
Policy Engines (OPA/OPAL)	Centralized policy management with distributed enforcement for fine-grained authorization.	Decouples authorization logic from services. Dynamic policy updates without redeployment. Unified policy model. Supports ReBAC.	Introduces an external dependency for authorization decisions. Requires expertise in policy language (e.g., Rego).

Table 11-2 provides a quick, side-by-side view of the main authorization approaches we've discussed so far, including API Gateway checks, Service Mesh controls, JWTs, RBAC, ABAC, and Policy Engines. It highlights what each is best at, what to watch out for, and how they fit into the bigger picture. The goal here isn't to pick one over the others but to understand how they work together as part of a layered security setup. That way, you can design systems that are secure, flexible, and better prepared to deal with the shifting complexity of synchronous interactions.

11.5 The API Gateway
11.5.1 The Pattern

The API Gateway pattern is a core part of many modern distributed systems, especially when dealing with a lot of synchronous communication. It sits at the edge of your system, acting as the single entry point for all external traffic coming into your microservices. Without it, you'd be exposing every individual service directly to the outside world, and that quickly turns into a mess.

By using an API Gateway, you centralize a number of concerns that you'd otherwise have to implement repeatedly in each service. Things like authentication, authorization, rate limiting, caching, aggregating requests, or even protocol translation are all handled in one spot. That simplifies both your services and your clients, providing a single, clean API to interact with without tying them directly to internal service details.

So the API Gateway becomes a smart front door: it keeps complexity contained, improves manageability, and helps you stay in control of all those synchronous calls.

On top of that, we'll focus on API Gateways in particular because of the role they play in security; they act as a first line of defense, a filter that stands between the outside world and your internal system. Everything goes through it, and that gives you a chance to block, validate, or shape traffic before it ever hits a backend service.

Its main roles are the following:

- **Request Routing:** The API Gateway sits between clients and your services, so it's in the perfect position to decide where requests should go. It uses routing rules based on things like the URL path, HTTP method, or headers to figure out which backend service should handle what. This means clients don't need to know where services live or how they're organized; they just send requests to the gateway, and it takes care of the rest.

- **Request Aggregation:** Sometimes a single client request actually needs data from more than one service. Rather than having the client make multiple round trips, the gateway can call those services in parallel, collect the responses, and stitch them together into a single response. That reduces latency and makes the client's life easier; there's no need to juggle multiple service calls or responses.

- **Authentication and Authorization:** The gateway is also the ideal place to handle authentication and authorization. It can validate tokens, talk to identity providers (like OAuth2 or any JWT-based system), and enforce access policies before anything reaches your backend. That way, you're not duplicating the same security logic across every service; it's centralized, consistent, and right at the edge.

- **Rate Limiting and Throttling:** To prevent abuse, whether from accidental client overloads or actual attacks, the gateway can apply rate limits to incoming traffic. That helps protect your services from being flooded and ensures that resources are shared fairly between users. It also gives you a safety net if a bug or misconfigured client starts hammering the system.

- **Protocol Translation:** Gateways don't just route and filter; they can also translate. That means clients can use one protocol (like REST), while services inside your system might use something different (like gRPC or messaging). The gateway bridges the two, keeping things decoupled and giving you the freedom to choose the right tool for the job inside your system without exposing that complexity externally.

The value of an API Gateway isn't just in routing traffic or blocking bad requests; it's also about managing complexity for everyone involved. From the outside, it gives consumers a clean, unified interface that hides the messiness of your internal service landscape. For example, Netflix uses an API Gateway to expose a single entry point for all its streaming services, so clients don't need to know how many microservices are involved or how they communicate internally; they just get a seamless experience; they just see one consistent entry point.

At the same time, this abstraction buys freedom for your internal teams. They can change, version, or replace services without worrying about breaking anything upstream. That separation is what keeps the system agile; it means you can keep evolving your backend without constantly renegotiating with whoever's using your APIs. In large synchronous systems, where every client expects predictable behavior and a stable contract, that's a big deal.

Let's now see how to implement this with Go and NATS. Let's start with our domain. We need a value object for a customer:

```go
// customer.go
package main

// Customer represents the core domain entity for our application.
// It contains attributes directly relevant to the business concept of a
customer.
type Customer struct {
    Name   string
    Email  string
}
```

This defines a struct that we can share around our layers, representing a customer. As you can see, it does not have an ID because we assume, in this context, that we do not need it, but of course, depending on your application, you might need an Entity or a Value Object or even both.

Let's now see the service used to contact the external NATS-based microservice:

```go
package application

import (
    "api_gateway/domain" // Import the domain package for the Customer type
)

// CustomerCreator is a "driven port" interface.
type CustomerCreator interface {
    CreateCustomerRemote(customer domain.Customer) (string, error)
}

// CustomerApplicationService implements the application's use case for
customer creation.
// It depends on the CustomerCreator port.
type CustomerApplicationService struct {
    creator CustomerCreator // This is the 'port'
}
```

```
// NewCustomerApplicationService creates an instance of the application
service.
func NewCustomerApplicationService(creator CustomerCreator)
*CustomerApplicationService {
    return &CustomerApplicationService{creator: creator}
}

func (s *CustomerApplicationService) CreateCustomer(customer domain.
Customer) (string, error) {
    return s.creator.CreateCustomerRemote(customer)
}
```

In this code, we define an interface called **CustomerCreator,** which is used to share a contract about how a customer is created, and its implementation is used within **CustomerApplicationService**. At this point, we need to see the actual implementation for the interface used by our application service, and this will lie in the infrastructure layer. As a reminder, infrastructure is about concretely connecting with third-party applications, so it will have specific code for database connections and, in this case, NATS communication. Here is our sample infrastructure:

```
package infrastructure

import (
    "encoding/json"
    "errors"
    "time"

    "api_gateway/domain" // Import domain for the Customer type
    "github.com/nats-io/nats.go"
)

// NATSRequest represents the JSON structure sent to the external NATS
microservice.
type NATSRequest struct {
    Name  string `json:"name"`
    Email string `json:"email"`
}
```

```go
// NATSResponse represents the JSON structure received from the external
NATS microservice.
type NATSResponse struct {
    ID    string `json:"id,omitempty"`
    Name  string `json:"name"`
    Email string `json:"email"`
}

// NATSCustomerAdapter is a "driven adapter" for NATS communication.
type NATSCustomerAdapter struct {
    natsConn *nats.Conn
}

// NewNATSCustomerAdapter creates a new NATS adapter.
func NewNATSCustomerAdapter(nc *nats.Conn) *NATSCustomerAdapter {
    return &NATSCustomerAdapter{natsConn: nc}
}

// CreateCustomerRemote sends a customer creation request to a NATS microservice
// and expects a domain.Customer object in return upon success.
func (a *NATSCustomerAdapter) CreateCustomerRemote(customer domain.Customer) (domain.Customer, error) {
    natsReq := NATSRequest{
        Name:  customer.Name,
        Email: customer.Email,
    }

    reqData, err := json.Marshal(natsReq)
    if err != nil {
        return domain.Customer{}, errors.New("internal
        serialization error")
    }

    msg, err := a.natsConn.Request("customer.create", reqData,
    5*time.Second)
    if err != nil {
```

```
        return domain.Customer{}, errors.New("external service unavailable
            or unresponsive")
    }

    var natsResp NATSResponse
    // Expect the microservice to respond directly with the customer JSON.
    if err := json.Unmarshal(msg.Data, &natsResp); err != nil {
        // If unmarshaling fails, it implies the response was not a valid
            customer,
        // which we treat as an error from the service.
        return domain.Customer{}, errors.New("external service returned
            invalid customer data")
    }

    // If unmarshaling succeeded, we assume it's a valid customer.
    return domain.Customer{ID: natsResp.ID, Name: natsResp.Name,
        Email: natsResp.Email}, nil
}
```

We define infrastructure-specific structs:

```
type NATSRequest struct {
    Name  string `json:"name"`
    Email string `json:"email"`
}
type NATSResponse struct {
    ID    string `json:"id,omitempty"`
    Name  string `json:"name"`
    Email string `json:"email"`
}
```

In our application, for now, we do not care about ID, so in our function, even if we receive it, we will just convert the response to a domain Customer:

```
return domain.Customer{ID: natsResp.ID, Name: natsResp.Name, Email:
natsResp.Email}, nil
```

CHAPTER 11　FULLY SYNCHRONOUS SYSTEMS

In order to get the actual customer, we need to ask the external microservice to create it:

```
msg, err := a.natsConn.Request("customer.create", reqData, 5*time.Second)
```

Where **reqData** is the JSON marshaled version of the infrastructure-specific struct created upon the domain.Customer parameter passed to the function:

```
natsReq := NATSRequest{
      Name:  customer.Name,
      Email: customer.Email,
   }

   reqData, err := json.Marshal(natsReq)
```

At this point, we have our domain, we have our NATS infrastructure, and we have our application service. We need two more things: a port to the external world to accept requests, HTTP requests, and some kind of glue to initialize everything.

Let's start with the presentation:

```go
package http_handler
import (
    "encoding/json"
    "errors"
    "net/http"

    "api_gateway/application" // Import application for Customer type and
    service port
    "api_gateway/domain"     // Import domain for Customer type
)

// CustomerHTTPPayload represents the JSON structure for both incoming HTTP requests
// and outgoing HTTP responses, containing only Name and Email.
type CustomerHTTPPayload struct {
    Name  string `json:"name"`
    Email string `json:"email"`
}
```

```go
// CustomerServicePort is a "driving port" interface.
// It defines what the presentation layer needs from the application layer.
// It still expects a domain.Customer back from the application layer,
// as the application/infrastructure layers might handle the ID internally.
type CustomerServicePort interface {
    CreateCustomer(customer domain.Customer) (domain.Customer, error) //
    Expects domain.Customer back
}

// CustomerHandler is a "driving adapter" that handles incoming HTTP requests.
type CustomerHandler struct {
    service CustomerServicePort // This is the 'port'
}

// NewCustomerHandler creates an instance of the HTTP handler.
func NewCustomerHandler(svc CustomerServicePort) *CustomerHandler {
    return &CustomerHandler{service: svc}
}

// CreateCustomer handles the POST /customers HTTP endpoint.
func (h *CustomerHandler) CreateCustomer(w http.ResponseWriter, r *http.Request) {
    if r.Method != http.MethodPost {
        http.Error(w, "Method Not Allowed", http.StatusMethodNotAllowed)
        return
    }

    var reqPayload CustomerHTTPPayload
    if err := json.NewDecoder(r.Body).Decode(&reqPayload); err != nil {
        http.Error(w, "Invalid request payload", http.StatusBadRequest)
        return
    }

    // Create domain.Customer from the HTTP request payload.
    // We pass an empty ID here, as the external microservice is assumed to
        generate it.
```

```go
    // Create domain.Customer directly from the HTTP request payload.
    customer := domain.Customer{Name: reqPayload.Name, Email: reqPayload.Email}

    // Call the application service (through the driving port).
    createdCustomer, err := h.service.CreateCustomer(customer)
    if err != nil {
        status := http.StatusInternalServerError // Default error
        // Map generic errors to HTTP status codes
        if errors.Is(err, errors.New("external service unavailable or
        unresponsive")) {
            status = http.StatusBadGateway
        } else if errors.Is(err, errors.New("internal serialization
        error")) || errors.Is(err, errors.New("internal deserialization
        error from service")) {
            status = http.StatusInternalServerError
        } else if errors.Is(err, errors.New("external service returned
        invalid customer data")) {
            status = http.StatusServiceUnavailable // Treat invalid data
            from service as service error
        } else if errors.Is(err, errors.New("customer ID cannot be empty"))
{ // If domain.NewCustomer fails due to ID
            status = http.StatusInternalServerError // This would be an
            internal gateway issue if NewCustomer validates ID
        }
        http.Error(w, err.Error(), status)
        return
    }

    // Respond with the Name and Email from the *returned domain.Customer*.
    respPayload := CustomerHTTPPayload{
        Name: createdCustomer.Name,
        Email: createdCustomer.Email,
}

    w.Header().Set("Content-Type", "application/json")
    json.NewEncoder(w).Encode(respPayload) // nolint: errcheck
}
```

In here, again, we create a layer-specific strut:

```go
type CustomerHTTPPayload struct {
    Name  string `json:"name"`
    Email string `json:"email"`
}
```

This struct, in this case, is actually called a DTO, which means a Data Transfer Object. These are generally aggregates, but in substance, they are simply handling data transfer between services or any external source. We use the same struct as input and output, as this is a sample application. However, in reality, we would want a response with an ID, which would then necessitate a domain entity with an ID. We can assume that the email is unique; hence, the email will be some sort of ID for our simple scenario.

Let's now glue all together:

```go
package main

import (
    "log"
    "net/http"

    "api_gateway/application"
    "api_gateway/infrastructure"
    "api_gateway/presentation/http_handler"
    "github.com/nats-io/nats.go" // Necessary for NATS connection
)

func main() {
    // Infrastructure: Connect to NATS (driven adapter dependency)
    nc, err := nats.Connect(nats.DefaultURL)
    if err != nil {
        log.Fatalf("API Gateway: Failed to connect to NATS: %v", err)
    }
    defer nc.Close() // Ensure NATS connection is closed on exit
    log.Println("API Gateway connected to NATS server.")

    // Infrastructure Layer Adapter (Driven Adapter): Implements the port
    customerNATSAdapter := infrastructure.NewNATSCustomerAdapter(nc)
```

```
// Application Layer Service: Uses the port defined in
    Application layer
customerAppService := application.NewCustomerApplicationService
(customerNATSAdapter)

// Presentation Layer Handler (Driving Adapter): Uses the
    Application Service
httpHandler := http_handler.NewCustomerHandler(customerAppService)

// HTTP Server: Exposes the REST endpoint
http.HandleFunc("/customers", httpHandler.CreateCustomer)
log.Println("API Gateway HTTP server listening on :8080")
log.Fatal(http.ListenAndServe(":8080", nil))
}
```

In this code, we first create a NATS connection:

```
nc, err := nats.Connect(nats.DefaultURL)
```

We then create our services and structs:

```
customerNATSAdapter := infrastructure.NewNATSCustomerAdapter(nc)
customerAppService := application.NewCustomerApplicationService(customer
NATSAdapter)
```

And finally, we create the struct for our presentation layer:

```
httpHandler := http_handler.NewCustomerHandler(customerAppService)
```

The only thing that remains is to use our HTTP handler in our HTTP server:

```
http.HandleFunc("/customers", httpHandler.CreateCustomer)      log.
Println("API Gateway HTTP server listening on :8080")
```

We now have a very simple but working API gateway contacting an external service written using the NATS micro package. The API gateway simply forwards the request to the service and returns, via a REST endpoint, the result.

11.5.2 Authentication

Authentication is a well-defined step: it's where a client proves who they are by presenting some credentials, an API key, a username and password, or an OAuth2 code, for example, and the system checks whether those credentials are valid. Where this check happens can vary depending on the architecture.

Sometimes, authentication occurs before the request even reaches your system, such as when the user logs in through an identity provider (IdP) and receives a signed JWT. In that case, the API Gateway just validates the token: checks the signature, ensures it hasn't expired, and confirms it was issued by someone you trust. While this is often called authentication, it's really more about authorization, because you're not verifying credentials anymore; you're checking whether a previously issued token is still valid.

However, authentication can also occur within the system, directly at the API Gateway. In this case, the gateway receives the raw credentials directly, maybe via headers, a login request, or a basic auth flow, and forwards them to a dedicated authentication service that knows how to validate them. Once the user is authenticated, the gateway can either mint its own token or just inject useful identity info (like user ID, roles, or tenant ID) into the request before passing it along to internal services.

Either way, the key idea is this: **authentication is the act of verifying identity**. Everything else, like checking whether the user is allowed to do something (authorization) or adding identity headers to the request (propagation), comes later.

This separation is critical. It keeps responsibilities clean, avoids duplicating authentication logic across services, and ensures that by the time a request reaches your backend, you already know who it's from, and that trust is based on a single, consistent process.

In order to implement this, we will provide some sample but incomplete code that will give you an idea of how authentication could be handled.

We will extend the main package of the previous paragraph:

```
import (
    "log"
    "net/http"
    ........................................................
    // --- New imports for Login functionality---
    loginApplication "api_gateway/application/login"
    loginInfrastructure "api_gateway/infrastructure/login"
```

```
    loginHTTPHandler "api_gateway/presentation/http/login_handler"
    // ----------------------------------------------------------------
)
func main() {
    // Infrastructure: Connect to NATS (driven adapter dependency)
    nc, err := nats.Connect(nats.DefaultURL)
 ----------
customerHTTPHandler :=   http_handler.NewCustomerHandler(customerAppService)
http.HandleFunc("/customers", customerHTTPHandler.CreateCustomer)
-----------------------------

    // --- New Login Service Setup (assuming these components exist
        elsewhere) ---
    loginNATSAdapter := loginInfrastructure.NewLoginNATSAdapter(nc)

    loginAppService := loginApplication.NewLoginApplicationService(loginNATSAdapter)
    loginHTTPHandler := loginHTTPHandler.NewLoginHandler(loginAppService)

    // Register the new HTTP endpoint for Login
    http.HandleFunc("/login", loginHTTPHandler.Login)
```

We assume that the layers mirror what happened for the customer creation, but we will not give the code here as it is essentially the same but contacting a different service. You should be able to build the remaining layers by yourself, which is a good exercise indeed.

11.5.3 Authorization

Once a user's identity has been established, the API Gateway moves on to authorization. This is where it determines whether the user is actually allowed to perform the action they're attempting, such as accessing a resource, triggering an operation, or calling a specific service. The decision is usually based on the identity data obtained during authentication, such as roles, tenant context, or other claims, and it's checked against either a simple set of rules defined in the gateway itself or by calling out to a dedicated policy engine or external authorization service.

If the request doesn't pass the authorization checks, the gateway can immediately block it before it ever reaches your internal services. That's a big deal because it means you're filtering out bad or unauthorized traffic at the edge, rather than forcing every microservice to defend itself individually. It also helps you enforce a consistent security posture across your system; services don't have to guess what "allowed" means, and they're not responsible for keeping policies in sync. You define access rules once, and the gateway applies them uniformly, right where the request enters your system.

We need, at this point, to reflect on what authorization really means and what role it should play in a distributed system. Having a centralized entry point that handles authorization, like an API Gateway, is incredibly useful. However, if every single rule about who can do what resides only within the gateway, we encounter a significant problem: the gateway must be aware of *everything* about *every* possible request that could potentially reach a microservice.

In other words, first of all, the gateway needs to be fully aware of all endpoints, whether REST, NATS, or any other type, for every service it's routing to. That is expected, unless we decide to rely on naming conventions or other strategies to dynamically discover things. However, in addition to routing, we are now also requiring the gateway to handle all the permission logic. That means pulling access rules out of the services themselves and centralizing them at the edge, and that can easily become a bottleneck, both in terms of complexity and system maintainability.

The most common way to handle authorization in the API gateway is actually performing the token check, where the token holds everything needed to first identify (authenticate) the user and then add any information needed for further rule-based access to deeper resources. What the API gateway will do, possibly relying on a third dedicated microservice (authorization microservice), is verify the identity provided via the token and then add any meaningful characteristic to it (user id, role, level, organization, and any other thing that will be required to be checked when contacting internal microservices). This way, when the request is forwarded to the internal microservice, it will include all the necessary information for determining, via OPA or any other method, the access rights to the requested resource or action by the caller.

We will not give code for the OPA and microservice-level authorization, but we will see, roughly, how to implement a middleware that validates a token. We assume that in order to create a customer, the user is logged in, so it will have a token. The token will be passed via the HTTP request's header section as a header with key **Authorization**. This is a standard header, and its content will be: **Bearer the_actual_token**. Somehow the code will need to strip the **Bearer** part and check the token. We will extend the code of the previous paragraph, adding the middleware inside the presentation layer. The following code will handle the retrieval of the token:

```go
// AuthMiddleware creates an HTTP middleware that validates a Bearer token.
func AuthMiddleware(next http.Handler, validator TokenValidator) http.Handler {
    return http.HandlerFunc(func(w http.ResponseWriter, r *http.Request) {
        authHeader := r.Header.Get("Authorization")
        if authHeader == "" {
            http.Error(w, "Authorization header required", http.StatusUnauthorized)
            return
        }

        if !strings.HasPrefix(authHeader, "Bearer ") {
            http.Error(w, "Invalid Authorization header format", http.StatusUnauthorized)
            return
        }

        token := strings.TrimPrefix(authHeader, "Bearer ")

        userID, err := validator.ValidateToken(token)
        if err != nil {
            http.Error(w, err.Error(), http.StatusUnauthorized)
            // Return specific error from validator
            return
        }

        // Add user_id to the request context
        ctx := context.WithValue(r.Context(), userIDKey, userID)
        next.ServeHTTP(w, r.WithContext(ctx)) // Pass request with new context to next handler
    })
}
```

This code exposes a handler function that will run before the actual customer create function; it will use

```
authHeader := r.Header.Get("Authorization")
```

to get the header and will strip the value from the prefix Bearer:

```
token := strings.TrimPrefix(authHeader, "Bearer ")
```

and finally it will use a validator to validate the token:

```
userID, err := validator.ValidateToken(token)
```

If the token is valid, it will then add it to the context:

```
ctx := context.WithValue(r.Context(), userIDKey, userID)
```

And as the last action, it will call the next handler (the customer create in our application, as it is the only handler needing the validation):

```
next.ServeHTTP(w, r.WithContext(ctx))
```

Now we need to see how the validation happens, and it is similar to how we handle the login or the customer creation:

```go
// NATSAuthAdapter is the "driven adapter" implementation for
TokenValidator using NATS.
type NATSAuthAdapter struct {
    natsConn *nats.Conn
}

// NewNATSAuthAdapter creates a new NATSAuthAdapter.
func NewNATSAuthAdapter(nc *nats.Conn) *NATSAuthAdapter {
    return &NATSAuthAdapter{natsConn: nc}
}

// ValidateToken sends the token to a NATS microservice for validation.
func (a *NATSAuthAdapter) ValidateToken(token string) (string, error) {
    reqData, err := json.Marshal(TokenValidationRequest{Token: token})
    if err != nil {
        return "", errors.New("middleware: internal serialization error")
    }
```

```go
    msg, err := a.natsConn.Request("auth.validate_token", reqData, 3*time.
    Second) // Assuming "auth.validate_token" subject
    if err != nil {
        return "", errors.New("middleware: auth service unavailable or
        unresponsive")
    }

    var resp TokenValidationResponse
    if err := json.Unmarshal(msg.Data, &resp); err != nil {
        return "", errors.New("middleware: auth service returned invalid
        response")
    }

    if !resp.Valid {
        return "", errors.New("middleware: invalid or expired token: " +
        resp.Error)
    }

    return resp.UserID, nil
}
```

The key is that we call an external microservice built with NATS micro:

```go
msg, err := a.natsConn.Request("auth.validate_token", reqData,
3*time.Second)
```

which returns a:

```go
// TokenValidationResponse is the DTO for the NATS token validation
service's response.
type TokenValidationResponse struct {
    UserID string `json:"user_id"`
    Valid  bool   `json:"valid"`
    Error  string `json:"error,omitempty"`
}
```

From this, what will be finally returned by the **ValidateToken** function is the actual user id:

```
return resp.UserID, nil
```

We are now technically all set for being able to validate a request for the presence of a valid token, but we need to attach it to our flow, so let's see again the main package. We used to have a customer HTTP handler like this:

```
customerHTTPHandler :=   http_handler.NewCustomerHandler(customerAppService)
```

But now we need to wrap it with the authHandler:

```
rawCustomerHandler := http_handler.NewCustomerHandler(customerAppService)
http.Handle("/customers", authenticatedCustomerHandler)
```

The AuthMIddleware it's actually compliant with the signature for an HTTP handler, but it acts as middleware because it takes the original request, does something with it, and then calls the next handler, as seen earlier:

```
next.ServeHTTP(w, r.WithContext(ctx))
```

We are now all set, but we are not actually using the user id. We will not go into how to perform the microservice-level authorization, but we will show how to use the user id in the handler. Here is the beginning of the function seen earlier, with a user id check:

```
// CreateCustomer handles the POST /customers HTTP endpoint.
func (h *CustomerHandler) CreateCustomer(w http.ResponseWriter, r *http.
Request) {
    // Retrieve user_id from context (added by middleware)
    userID, ok := GetUserIDFromContext(r.Context())
    if !ok {
        // This should ideally not happen if middleware is correctly
            applied,
        // but it's a safeguard.
        http.Error(w, "User ID not found in context", http.
        StatusInternalServerError)
        return
    }
```

We can now send the user id to the external microservice, if it accepts it, and the microservice might use an OPA to validate the request.

We've shown a partial but hopefully exhaustive example of how to handle an authorization check inside an API Gateway, and earlier, a whole skeleton for a plausible API Gateway. We leave to the reader the challenge to apply their newly acquired knowledge to build a full API Gateway, maybe using GraphQL or something else they wish rather than REST.

11.5.4 First-Level Communication

The API Gateway is the very first point of contact between external clients and your system. Whether it's a frontend web app, a mobile client, or some external third-party service, all inbound traffic typically goes through the gateway. This is the first level of communication in a distributed system: the outer edge, where client calls hit your infrastructure.

At this stage, the gateway acts as a central, programmable entry point. It receives the incoming request, usually over HTTP or HTTPS, and performs the initial logic required to get that request routed, validated, transformed, or combined as needed. Most API Gateways behave like smart reverse proxies here: they don't just forward traffic blindly; they apply logic on top of it.

This first level of communication includes several key behaviors:

- **Request Routing:** The gateway uses rules based on things like URL paths, headers, HTTP methods, or even user identity claims to determine where a request should be directed. This is how it knows which microservice (or group of services) to forward the call to. Without this, you'd have to expose each internal service directly, which is usually a bad idea.

- **Protocol Translation:** The gateway can act as a bridge between the client world and the service world. For example, a client might make an HTTP request, but your internal services speak gRPC, AMQP, or, obviously, NATS. The gateway handles the translation, decoupling clients from backend protocol details.

- **Request Aggregation:** Sometimes a single client request needs data from multiple backend services. Rather than forcing the client to orchestrate multiple calls (which adds complexity and latency), the gateway can do that work: fan out requests to several services, collect the responses, and stitch them together into a single payload. A very simple example of this is the actual authorization. If it is handled via an authorization microservice, the gateway will forward the token each time to that service before contacting the one that will perform the action.

This entire first layer is about creating a clean boundary. You don't want clients talking directly to your microservices. You want a gate, a filter, and a translation layer, and that's exactly what the API Gateway provides here. It's not just about routing traffic; it's about controlling what gets into your system, how, and in what shape.

11.5.5 Deeper Level Communication

Once a request passes through the first layer, the external-facing API Gateway, it moves deeper into the system, toward the actual services that perform the work. From this point onward, the gateway becomes responsible for managing how the request travels within the system, ensuring it reaches the correct destination and that all downstream components behave predictably, even under stress or failure.

This deeper level of communication is not just about moving data around; it's about maintaining resilience, stability, and smart routing across all the services behind the edge. The API Gateway plays a big role here, and it does that in a few key ways:

- **Load Balancing:** At its core, the gateway knows how to spread traffic across multiple instances of a service. This isn't just about performance; it's about making sure the system doesn't collapse when one instance gets overloaded. Whether round-robin, least-connections, or something more dynamic, load balancing is a core function that ensures high availability and keeps your services breathing under pressure.

- **Resilience Patterns:** This is where things get serious. The gateway becomes a safety net. If a service starts failing, you don't want to keep sending it requests; that's how cascading failures occur. Instead, the gateway can implement Circuit Breakers, temporarily cutting off traffic to a broken service and giving it room to recover. It can also handle retries, re-attempting failed calls after a short delay, ideally using exponential backoff with jitter. This means that each retry is delayed by an increasing amount of time, and a small amount of randomness is added to each delay. The purpose of the jitter is to avoid a situation where many clients retry at the exact same moment, which could overwhelm a recovering service. Together, these resilience mechanisms help absorb shocks and reduce system-wide fallout.

- **Service Discovery:** In more dynamic environments, like Kubernetes, services come and go all the time. Hardcoding service addresses don't cut it. The API Gateway is usually plugged into a service registry, constantly aware of which instances are live, healthy, and ready to receive traffic. It routes requests accordingly, without you having to manage anything manually. That flexibility is essential for scalability and resilience.

Now, this is the point where people often confuse API Gateways with Service Meshes. It is true that they both handle routing, security, retries, and observability, but that doesn't mean they're interchangeable; they solve different problems at different layers of your architecture.

The API Gateway resides at the edge of your system, serving as the gatekeeper to manage traffic from the outside world, enforce external-facing policies, and simplify interactions for clients. It understands the shape of external requests and translates them into something your backend can handle.

A Service Mesh, on the other hand, lives inside the system. It manages service-to-service communication, transparently handling retries, load balancing, mutual TLS, and metrics, without touching application code. You don't use it to expose your system to the world; you use it to maintain reliable, secure, and observable internal communication.

It's not about choosing one or the other; it's about using both where they make sense. The gateway is your front door, responsible for filtering, authenticating, validating, and routing client requests. The Service Mesh is your internal logistics layer, making sure that once a request is inside, it's handled with care.

When used together, they form a powerful architectural stack: clean boundaries, robust security, and deep-layered resilience. The gateway handles external contracts, while the Mesh manages internal protocols. This kind of separation of concerns is what keeps distributed systems maintainable at scale. It allows each service to stay focused on its own logic, while cross-cutting concerns like traffic management, security, and observability are handled by infrastructure, not by every team, in every service, over and over again.

This isn't just about good design; it's about survivability. In large, synchronous systems, having clearly defined layers that deal with communication, failure, and complexity at the right level can be the difference between systems that recover under pressure and systems that fall apart.

Table 11-3. API gateway vs. service mesh: Key features and responsibilities

Feature/Aspect	API Gateway	Service Mesh
Primary Scope	External client-to-service communication	Internal service-to-service communication
Entry Point	Edge of the microservices architecture	Internal to the cluster
Communication Type	Primarily external (e.g., HTTP/REST)	Primarily internal (e.g., HTTP, gRPC, TCP)
Key Functionalities: Routing	Routes external requests to appropriate microservices based on URI patterns and headers.	Advanced traffic management: intelligent load balancing, traffic splitting (canary, A/B testing), fault injection, granular routing rules.
Key Functionalities: Auth/Auth	Centralized authentication and coarse-grained authorization for external clients (JWT, OAuth 2.0).	Mutual TLS (mTLS) for inter-service encryption and authentication; fine-grained access policies.
Key Functionalities: Rate Limiting	Protects backend services from excessive load by enforcing rate limits and throttling.	Can enforce rate-limiting policies as part of traffic management.
Key Functionalities: Aggregation	Aggregates responses from multiple services into a single response for the client.	Not typically an aggregation point; focuses on individual service communication.

(*continued*)

Table 11-3. (*continued*)

Feature/Aspect	API Gateway	Service Mesh
Key Functionalities: Observability	Provides basic logging and metrics for external API calls.	Comprehensive built-in observability: detailed metrics, distributed tracing, aggregated logs.
Key Functionalities: Resilience	Implements circuit breakers, retries (with exponential backoff), and timeouts for external calls.	Inherently supports circuit breakers, retries, and timeouts for internal calls.
Deployment Model	Centralized component, often deployed as a set of highly available instances.	Distributed sidecar proxies are deployed alongside each service instance, managed by a control plane.
Impact on Service Code	Minimal to no changes required in individual service code for gateway-level concerns.	Minimal to no changes are required in the individual service code due to sidecar injection.

Table 11-3 lays things out in a way that's easy to digest but also quite powerful. It puts API Gateways and Service Meshes side by side, showing exactly where they overlap, where they differ, and why they actually work better together than apart. It compares their main responsibilities, like whether they focus on external or internal traffic, how they handle communication, where they sit in the system, and which concerns they're designed to own (routing, auth, rate limiting, observability, and so on).

By organizing all this in one place, it gives you a solid foundation to reason about your architecture. It helps you avoid duplicating effort, applying the wrong tool to the wrong layer, or missing out on key benefits just because the roles weren't clearly defined. This kind of clarity is critical when building systems that are meant to scale, stay secure, and recover under pressure.

11.6 Space-Based Architecture

11.6.1 Refresher

Space-Based Architecture (SBA) is an architectural style built for extreme scalability and concurrency, particularly effective in systems with highly variable or unpredictable loads. As introduced back in Chapter 1, "Overview of Distributed Systems," SBA moves away from the traditional reliance on a single, central database. Instead, it organizes the system around "spaces," distributed, replicated in-memory data grids that hold and synchronize data across multiple Processing Units (PUs). Each PU is independent and stateless, containing its own business logic and local data. This setup allows for horizontal scaling by simply adding more PUs. When a PU updates data, those changes are asynchronously propagated to persistent storage, typically through messaging queues, keeping the system responsive, loosely coupled, and resilient.

The core components of SBA include

- **Processing Units (PUs):** Autonomous instances that run business logic and handle requests independently.

- **Space (In-Memory Data Grid):** A distributed memory grid shared across PUs, providing fast, low-latency access to data and enabling high availability.

- **Router:** Directs incoming requests to the appropriate PU, balancing the load and distributing traffic intelligently.

- **Messaging Grid:** An event-driven communication layer that connects PUs and other parts of the system, often used for pushing updates or propagating state changes asynchronously.

This architecture promotes resilience and loose coupling by design. Since each PU operates independently and can replicate both data and tasks, the system continues to function even when individual nodes fail. SBA fits naturally in high-demand environments where scalability is critical, and it shines when the goal is to maintain responsiveness under unpredictable or spiky traffic.

Figure 11-2 shows a schematic representation of space-based architecture, with the Data Grid and the Database clearly positioned for their role.

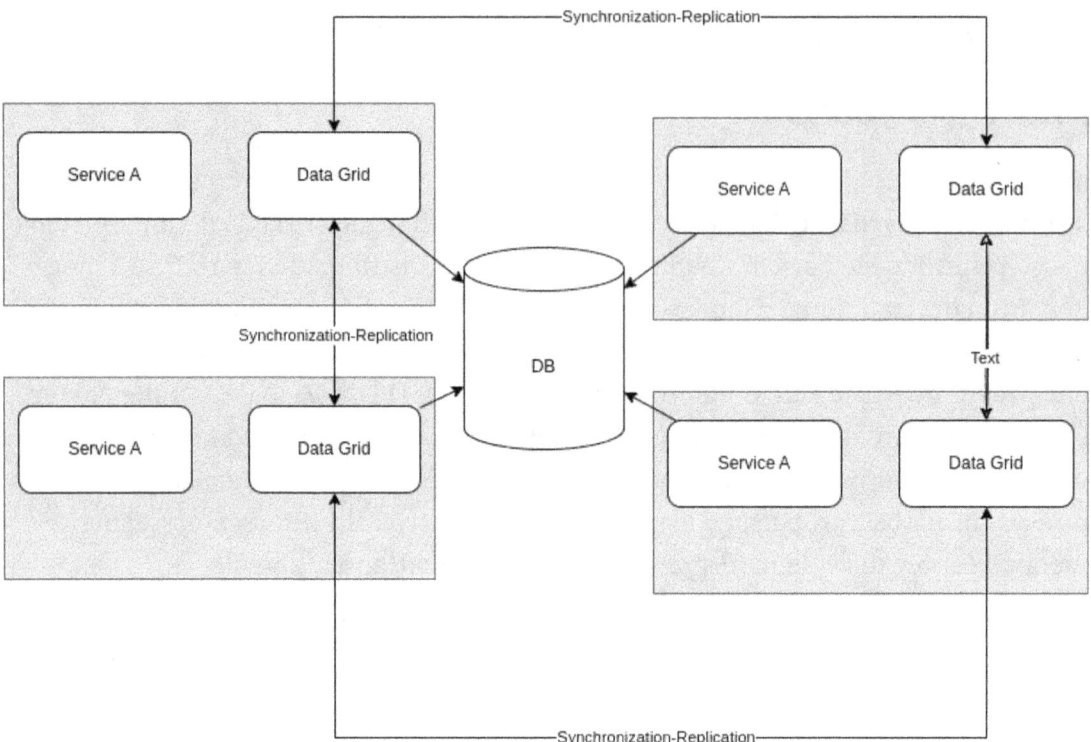

Figure 11-2. *Space-based architecture*

11.6.2 Tools

Putting space-based architecture into practice typically requires specialized tools to manage the distributed memory grid, coordinate parallel processing, and enable event-driven communication across nodes. These tools are not just caching layers; they're the operational backbone that makes SBA feasible at scale, ensuring that data and logic are efficiently distributed, replicated, and processed in real time.

- **Apache Ignite:** One of the most feature-rich open-source in-memory data grids available. Ignite goes far beyond basic caching; it supports read-through/write-through integration with existing databases, co-locates data and logic to minimize network overhead, and allows distributed SQL queries to be executed across the grid. It also includes native persistence, eliminating the need for manual warm-up or data reloads after restarts, and supporting smooth recovery in the face of failures.

- **Hazelcast:** Another major player in the IMDG space, Hazelcast offers distributed caching, fine-grained data partitioning, and native support for event-driven computation. It's often favored in Java-heavy environments for its smooth integration and predictable performance under high-throughput, low-latency scenarios.

- **Redis (with clustering):** Although Redis isn't a traditional IMDG, it can still be used in SBA contexts for specific use cases. When deployed in clustered mode, Redis supports partitioned, in-memory data storage that is fast and fault-tolerant. For simple key-value patterns, caching layers, or ephemeral states where co-located logic and complex querying aren't required, Redis provides a lightweight and pragmatic solution.

- **NATS (with JetStream):** While not an in-memory data grid, NATS plays a critical supporting role in many SBA-style architectures. Acting as a high-performance, cloud-native messaging system, NATS enables ultra-fast, low-overhead communication between distributed nodes. With built-in support for publish/subscribe, request/reply, and JetStream for persistence and key-value storage, it helps coordinate distributed components, handle transient state, and decouple services cleanly, all of which are essential in dynamic, event-driven environments.

These tools together form the infrastructure layer that makes SBA viable in production. Whether it's real-time analytics, fraud detection pipelines, IoT telemetry platforms, financial trading engines, or high-scale e-commerce systems, SBA systems rely on these components to keep data in-memory, keep coordination fast, and keep performance consistent, even under unpredictable or extreme load.

11.6.3 Implementation Example

To see how space-based architecture plays out in practice, imagine a high-traffic e-commerce platform handling bookings, say, for travel, events, or product reservations. In a traditional setup, every order might hit the central database directly. But with SBA, the flow looks very different, faster, more scalable, and far more resilient under pressure.

- **Client Request:** A customer places an order through the app. That request hits the booking service as a typical synchronous call.

- **Processing Unit (PU):** Instead of being one monolithic backend, the booking service is made up of multiple stateless processing units. The request gets routed to one of these available PUs, ready to handle it independently.

- **In-Memory Data Grid (Space):** The PU immediately writes the order data to its local copy of the in-memory data grid. That data is then replicated across other PUs, with no central bottleneck; instead, it utilizes fast, distributed memory that keeps everyone in sync.

- **Synchronous Response:** Because the data is already in memory and synchronized, the PU can confirm the order back to the user almost instantly. There's no waiting on a database write.

- **Asynchronous Persistence:** Behind the scenes, the in-memory grid takes care of writing that order to a persistent store, such as PostgreSQL or MongoDB, through a messaging queue. The user doesn't have to wait for this step, and it keeps the system decoupled and responsive.

- **Event-Driven Communication:** At the same time, the PU might publish an OrderPlaced event to a broker like NATS, so other services, Inventory, Payment, and Notifications, can pick it up and act on it asynchronously, without blocking the booking flow.

This setup is what gives SBA its edge: fast responses for users, decoupled persistence, and the ability to absorb huge spikes in load by just spinning up more PUs. Since each PU has its own data and logic, and coordination happens through shared memory and messaging, the system scales horizontally without putting pressure on any single database. It's low-latency on the outside, eventually consistent underneath, and built to keep going, even when individual parts fail.

11.7 Summary

This chapter focused on fully synchronous distributed systems, architectures where services interact directly and synchronously, often over HTTP, or in our case NATS Req/Rep, and responses are expected in real time. While many systems today blend both synchronous and asynchronous patterns depending on the use case, here we explored what it means to go all-in on the synchronous side. This design is commonly used in the user-facing parts of a system, where users click a button and expect a result immediately. That kind of immediacy, while straightforward for the end user, introduces a unique set of challenges beneath the surface. Many systems are still, however, fully synchronous today, and every system will still have some synchronous parts; that's why we spent so much time on this type of system and communication.

We started with the basics: REST, HTTP calls, and direct service-to-service interactions. From there, we zoomed out to look at how systems manage that traffic at scale, starting with Nginx. Far more than just a reverse proxy, Nginx acts as a powerful control layer, handling routing, headers, versioning, feature flags, and dynamic traffic shaping. It's what makes things like canary releases, blue/green deployments, and A/B testing possible in a world where changes can't break live services.

Then we looked at infrastructure layers built specifically to handle the complexities of modern sync systems. The API Gateway sits at the edge, taking care of request routing, rate limiting, auth, and response shaping, offloading those concerns from individual services and centralizing control. Behind the scenes, the Service Mesh takes over, dealing with internal service-to-service communication. It adds mutual TLS, fine-grained traffic policies, observability, retries, and circuit breakers, all without touching application code.

One common mistake is assuming the gateway and the Mesh are interchangeable. They're not. The gateway manages what comes in from the outside world; the Mesh handles what happens once requests are inside. Used together, they create a layered architecture that separates concerns cleanly: external vs. internal, coarse-grained vs. fine-grained, and public contract vs. internal protocol.

We also explored how modern systems deal with authorization. Rather than baking permissions into every service, many teams externalize this logic. Gateways can handle the first round of access control, but for anything beyond that, policy engines like OPA and OPAL take over, providing consistent, fine-grained decisions across services. Tokens like JWTs carry identity, not permissions, avoiding duplication and keeping things clean.

Finally, we closed the chapter with a different approach to scaling synchronous systems: **Space-Based Architecture (SBA)**. Instead of routing traffic through layers of proxies and meshes, SBA uses in-memory data grids and autonomous processing units to achieve massive scalability and low-latency response times. It sidesteps central databases by replicating data across nodes and decouples persistence using asynchronous messaging. SBA isn't for every system, but for those facing unpredictable, high-volume traffic patterns, such as e-commerce, trading, and real-time analytics, it offers an elegant alternative to traditional synchronous designs.

When you put all these pieces together—Nginx at the edge, API gateways for traffic control, Service Meshes for internal reliability, and externalized policy engines for authorization—you get a system that can handle the pressure. One that's secure, scalable, and ready for real-time demand without falling over when things get messy.

This isn't just a pattern, but it's how teams make synchronous systems resilient and survivable at scale. And it's not about adding complexity for its own sake. It's about assigning the right responsibilities to the right layers, so every service can stay focused on its job without worrying about traffic management, failure recovery, or access rules.

11.8 Questions

1. **What is the primary purpose of Nginx in a microservices architecture when dealing with synchronous communication?**

    a) To manage asynchronous message queues.

    b) To act as a reverse proxy for routing and load balancing requests.

    c) To provide persistent storage for microservices.

    d) To perform real-time data analytics.

2. **Which of the following is a key benefit of using a service mesh (e.g., Istio, Linkerd) in a synchronous distributed system?**

    a) It eliminates the need for any form of authentication.

    b) It centralizes all business logic into a single service.

    c) It provides advanced traffic management, security, and observability for inter-service communication.

    d) It forces all communication to be asynchronous.

CHAPTER 11   FULLY SYNCHRONOUS SYSTEMS

3. **How does the NATS micro package simplify building synchronous microservices?**

    a) By providing a low-level API for direct socket programming.

    b) By offering a declarative way to define services, endpoints, and groups over NATS Req/Rep.

    c) By converting all synchronous requests into asynchronous events.

    d) By integrating directly with traditional SQL databases.

4. **What is the main advantage of space-based architecture (SBA) for synchronous systems?**

    a) It relies on a single, centralized database for all data.

    b) It enables extreme scalability and low-latency responses through in-memory data grids.

    c) It strictly enforces asynchronous communication between all components.

    d) It simplifies deployment by packaging all services into a single executable.

5. **In the context of an API Gateway, what is the primary function of "request aggregation"?**

    a) To combine multiple incoming client requests into a single batch.

    b) To collect performance metrics from all backend services.

    c) To gather data from multiple backend services and combine it into a single response for the client.

    d) To authenticate multiple users simultaneously.

CHAPTER 12

Asynchronous Systems

12.1 Introduction

In the previous chapter, we've seen how services communicate with each other using synchronous communication, which is still the most common setup in distributed systems. Synchronous communication is simple to understand and easy to implement; hence, it's a common way to start. Furthermore, some parts of any system will have a synchronous flow, especially the interaction with the user. Once things scale up, however, problems start appearing and might escalate quickly. Latency during communication between services accumulates, and if one link in the chain is slow or fails, the entire system can start to slow down and ultimately fall apart. You will end up needing things like retries and circuit breakers just to keep things from crashing, and although these techniques are valid for achieving their goal, there are ways to avoid these issues and the need for such artifacts altogether.

Another big issue related to synchronous communication is that maintaining connections while waiting for a response consumes resources, and, under heavy load, this becomes a very serious problem for the health of the system, increasing resource consumption for idle tasks. Furthermore, when your services are tightly coupled, as in this case, you might often have to scale them together, which is significantly harder than scaling them independently. Of course, you can reduce this issue if you did not create a distributed monolith, but having a perfect architecture and codebase is idealistic; in practice, we must manage imperfections. Reducing the possible issues by leveraging known techniques is our only weapon.

This is where asynchronous communication comes to help. Instead of waiting around for a response, a service just sends a message and moves on. That decoupling means services aren't blocked by each other, so the system becomes more resilient, and if one part of the system can be slow or even go down, that won't drag the rest of the system with it. The idea is simple: the work still gets done, but not by holding up the service that asked for it. To make a comparison or a metaphor, this whole process, within an asynchronous-based architecture, is similar to what you might see when programming in Go: you use go routines and queues.

This can work even with intrinsically synchronous flows, like UI or client interaction: even though users often expect real-time responses in their UI, behind the scenes, it's usually better to handle things asynchronously. It helps with performance, scalability, and overall system stability.

To manage all that, we have several techniques, but here we will use NATS again. Not only is it, as we've seen already, a lightweight, high-performance messaging system built around publish/subscribe patterns, which are perfect for event-driven setups, but also, since it's written in Go, it's a natural fit for Go-based services, making testing and development much easier.

Switching from synchronous to asynchronous communication isn't just a fancy architectural idea, but it's a practical solution to address real-world problems such as latency, downtime, and scaling challenges. By using a message broker to push the waiting away from the services doing the actual work, your services remain neat, light, and free up resources, making your system much easier to manage as it grows.

12.2 Fully Asynchronous

12.2.1 Introduction

Let's start by defining what a fully asynchronous system is, which is a system that operates in a way that we can describe as "fire-and-forget." This means that when a publisher sends a message, it does not expect an immediate reply or even explicit confirmation that it has received the message from the consumers. This approach allows for extreme decoupling, as publishers and subscribers are unaware of each other's existence, availability, or internal state, and their only shared understanding is the message's subject. For a system to be fully asynchronous, we expect it to operate at every level like we described. Fully asynchronous systems might not exist, but even synchronous parts can be built on top of a base that is intrinsically asynchronous.

This asynchronous approach has many other benefits too, like high throughput for message producers, minimal latency for the sender, and intrinsic resilience to individual component failures. Since senders are not blocked while waiting for the receivers to

CHAPTER 12   ASYNCHRONOUS SYSTEMS

acknowledge the message, the system can continue to operate smoothly even if some consuming services are temporarily unavailable or slow. This pattern is particularly well-suited for scenarios such as event streaming, logging, system notifications, and other use cases where temporal coupling between components is undesirable, allowing for maximum flexibility and responsiveness.

12.2.2 An Example

The core of NATS's functionalities is its publish/subscribe (Pub/Sub) model, which is by default asynchronous. Even the req/rep functionality is built on top of that, proving that we can leverage asynchronous communication for any use case scenario. In this model (Pub/Sub), messages are dispatched to designated "subjects" (NATS's terminology for topics), and all active subscribers who have expressed an interest in that subject will receive a copy of the message.

Subjects are dynamic, which means that they do not require pre-definition or schema; you are free to put anything you want as the content of a message, be it JSON, YAML, or even images or any other binary content, as long as it does not exceed the maximum allowed size in bytes. To have a message delivered, it's simply enough to express an interest by notifying NATS, and it will recognize and route messages for your consumer. In fact, producers can just produce messages and send them to any subject; it will be up to the consumer to register an interest in the topic (subject).

To group subjects' interests and diversify the actions triggered by the message revival, NATS also supports wildcards for more flexible subscription patterns:

- The single-level wildcard (*) matches a single token in a subject hierarchy (e.g., events.*.created). *In* this case, the (*) symbol gets replaced by one string and matches: *events.user.created*, or *events. order.created* but not *events.order.new.created*. If the subject was *events.** it would catch *events.created* and *events.deleted* but not *events.user.created* as it only works on one single string token.

- In order to achieve what we couldn't with the single-level wildcard, we have the multi-level wildcard (>), which matches one or more tokens at the end of a subject hierarchy. In this case, e.g., *events.>*, will match *events.user.created* and *events.user.deleted*.

CHAPTER 12   ASYNCHRONOUS SYSTEMS

It is important to note that core NATS Pub/Sub does not persist messages by default. If no subscriber is active when a message is published, that message is lost. This characteristic is part of its "fire-and-forget" nature and distinguishes it from persistent messaging systems. The typical message size in core NATS is limited to a few megabytes, making it ideal for concise notifications and small data payloads rather than large file transfers.

Of course, you might need persistence at some point, as even if a producer can forget after firing, we might want to have extra resilience, and consumers need to catch up with messages they otherwise would have lost when down. This and when to use it will be the subject of one of the next paragraphs; for now, we will focus on non-persisting messages.

The following Go code examples illustrate a pure NATS Pub/Sub scenario, demonstrating the fire-and-forget mechanism. We've seen it in Chapter 3, "NATS Fundamentals," but we will refresh it here so that we can build upon it and extend it with our newly acquired knowledge of microservices and hexagonal architecture. So here we have a simple publisher and subscriber to start with

Publisher

This program connects to NATS and publishes five messages to the *events.user. created* subject at half-second intervals.

```go
package main

import (
    "fmt"
    "log"
    "time"
    "github.com/nats-io/nats.go"
)

func main() {
    nc, err := nats.Connect(nats.DefaultURL)
    if err!= nil {
        log.Fatal(err)
    }
    defer nc.Close() // Ensure connection is closed on exit
    defer nc.Drain() // Ensure graceful shutdown
```

```go
    subject := "events.user.created"
    for i := 0; i < 5; i++ {
        msg := fmt.Sprintf("User %d created at %s", i+1, time.Now().
        Format(time.RFC3339))
        err := nc.Publish(subject,byte(msg))
        if err!= nil {
            log.Printf("Error publishing message: %v", err)
        } else {
            fmt.Printf("Published: %s on subject '%s'\n", msg, subject)
        }
        time.Sleep(500 * time.Millisecond) // Simulate some work
    }
    fmt.Println("Publisher finished sending messages.")
}
```

Subscriber (Asynchronous)

This program connects to NATS and subscribes asynchronously to the *events.user.created* subject. It uses a callback function to handle incoming messages.

```go
package main

import (
    "fmt"
    "log"
    "os"
    "os/signal"
    "syscall"
    "time"
    "github.com/nats-io/nats.go"
)

func main() {
    nc, err := nats.Connect(nats.DefaultURL)
    if err!= nil {
        log.Fatal(err)
    }
```

```
    defer nc.Close()
    defer nc.Drain()

    subject := "events.user.created"

    // Asynchronous Subscriber with callback
    _, err = nc.Subscribe(subject, func(m *nats.Msg) {
        fmt.Printf("Subscriber 1 received: %s on subject '%s'\n",
        string(m.Data), m.Subject)
    })
    if err!= nil {
        log.Fatal(err)
    }
    fmt.Printf("Subscriber 1 listening on subject '%s'\n", subject)

    // Keep the subscriber running
    sigChan := make(chan os.Signal, 1)
    signal.Notify(sigChan, syscall.SIGINT, syscall.SIGTERM)
    <-sigChan
    fmt.Println("Subscriber 1 shutting down.")
}
```

In the subscriber, the key part is

```
_, err = nc.Subscribe(subject, func(m *nats.Msg) {.............}
```

where we pass a function with signature **func(m *nats.Msg)** to handle the received message, the NATS Go SDK internally uses the **Subscribe** function go routines in order to work concurrently on all the received messages. On top of that, you can see that there is more code after that line, and the system won't block waiting for the messages to come but will carry on with its flow.

We can now compare what we've just done with a synchronous subscriber and then analyze what it all means from the perspective of asynchronous systems. We will not provide the full code but only the critical parts.

The subscriber itself will be called with:

```
sub, err := nc.SubscribeSync(subject)
    if err!= nil {
        log.Fatal(err)
```

```
    }
    defer sub.Unsubscribe()
    defer sub.Drain()
```

In this case, the function will not expect a function but only the subject, and it will actually return a subscriber, and we can then use it in the following way:

```
for {
    msg, err := sub.NextMsg(1 * time.Second)
    if err!= nil {
        if!errors.Is(err, nats.ErrTimeout) {
            log.Printf("Error receiving message: %v", err)
        }
        continue
    }
    fmt.Printf("Subscriber 2 received: %s on subject '%s'\n", string(msg.
    Data), msg.Subject)
}
```

As you can see, we have a for loop, and we process one message at a time.

This seems to defy the purpose of pub/sub, but in reality, pub/sub does not necessarily mean the processing will be asynchronous; it is simply a topology that expresses its best when used asynchronously, but at times, you might need a synchronous subscriber. One such case is when you want to limit the number of requests to be fulfilled, as it takes a long time to process. In such a case, however, remember that NATS core is fire and forget, which also means it does not store messages, and this means that although there is an in-memory buffer to handle the sending of a certain amount of messages before they get processed, if the process is too slow, the messages will be dropped and you will lose them. We will see how to handle long-running processes in the next few paragraphs, as you might understand that this will involve message persistence, so for now, we will still focus on fully asynchronous communication without persistence.

Suppose we now want to test our asynchronous pub/sub system and observe the "fire-and-forget" nature. In that case, we can run the publisher program first, let it complete, and then start the subscriber, and we will see that it will not receive any of the messages published before it became active. This behavior clearly shows that the subscribers must be actively connected to receive messages as they are published. This important characteristic of NATS' core Pub/Sub, while excellent for achieving high throughput and promoting decoupling, forces the responsibility of message durability and guaranteed delivery totally on the application layer, if such assurances are required.

The difference NATS has from traditional queuing systems or persistent messaging implies that for applications that need to ensure every message is processed, relying solely on core NATS Pub/Sub is insufficient. Such applications would need to implement their retry mechanisms, dead-letter queues, or, more practically, leverage a persistent layer within the messaging system itself, which naturally leads to the discussion of NATS JetStream.

To test how to receive the messages, you could run the subscriber first and then the publisher. In this case, the subscriber will be idle but already available when the publisher starts sending messages.

12.3 Internally Asynchronous

12.3.1 Introduction

As we already said, many contemporary distributed systems are designed with a dual communication strategy: they present a synchronous interface to external clients, such as web applications responding to user requests via RESTful APIs, while internally leveraging asynchronous communication for their core processing workflows. This hybrid approach allows systems to reap the benefits of asynchronous processing, including enhanced scalability, improved resilience, and greater decoupling, while still meeting user expectations for immediate feedback.

This immediate feedback might simply be an acknowledgement that a long-running task has been successfully initiated, rather than a confirmation of completion. The core objective of this design pattern is to transform synchronous external calls into efficient, non-blocking asynchronous internal workflows wherever possible.

12.3.2 API Gateway

We've seen what an API gateway is in the previous chapter, when analyzing fully synchronous systems; now we will see how they serve as a glueing component in this hybrid architectural model, acting as the primary entry point for all external synchronous requests into the asynchronous distributed system. Their role extends beyond the simple request routing, as an API gateway can receive an incoming HTTP request, interpret it, and then translate it into an internal NATS message. This message is subsequently published to a designated subject for asynchronous processing by backend services. Very importantly, the API Gateway can then immediately return a lightweight HTTP response, such as a 202 Accepted status, to the originating client. This response signifies that the request has been received and processing has been initiated, without waiting for the actual completion of the potentially long-running backend task. This pattern isolates the synchronous, client-facing part of the system from the internal asynchronous workflow. This isolation is vital for preventing cascading failures, as a slow or failing backend service will not directly block the API Gateway or the client. Furthermore, it allows internal services to scale independently based on their processing load, rather than being constrained by the synchronous demands of the external interface.

Let's see a quick example of how this works. We will now create a small server accepting an HTTP request and publishing a meaningful message to NATS:

```go
package main

import (
    "fmt"
    "log"
    "net/http"
    "github.com/nats-io/nats.go"
)

func main() {
    nc, err := nats.Connect(nats.DefaultURL)
    if err != nil {
        log.Fatal(err)
    }
    defer nc.Close()
    defer nc.Drain()

    http.HandleFunc("/process_order", func(w http.ResponseWriter, r *http.Request) {
        if r.Method != http.MethodPost {
            http.Error(w, "Only POST method is supported", http.
```

CHAPTER 12   ASYNCHRONOUS SYSTEMS

```
StatusMethodNotAllowed)
            return
        }

        orderID := r.URL.Query().Get("orderId")
        if orderID == "" {
            http.Error(w, "Order ID is required", http.StatusBadRequest)
            return
        }

        orderData := fmt.Sprintf("Order %s received for processing.", orderID)
        subject := "orders.new"

        // Publish message to NATS for asynchronous processing
        err := nc.Publish(subject,byte(orderData))
        if err!= nil {
            log.Printf("Failed to publish order message: %v", err)
            http.Error(w, "Internal server error", http.StatusInternalServerError)
            return
        }

        fmt.Printf("API Gateway: Published '%s' to '%s'\n", orderData, subject)
        w.WriteHeader(http.StatusAccepted) // 202 Accepted - processing initiated
        fmt.Fprintf(w, "Order %s accepted for asynchronous processing.\n", orderID)
    })

    fmt.Println("API Gateway listening on :8080")
    log.Fatal(http.ListenAndServe(":8080", nil))
}
```

The key points from this code are

```
http.HandleFunc("/process_order", func(w http.ResponseWriter, r *http.
Request) {
```

This code handles the REST endpoint, and then, inside the callback:

```
err := nc.Publish(subject,byte(orderData))
```

Where we publish the message with the data to the order service, we will not show you the service here; as you can imagine, it can be a service reading the messages via an asynchronous or synchronous client and won't acknowledge the publisher that it has started processing.

This flow works very well in some cases, but in other cases, you might still want to notify the client about when the processing is complete. If a client is sending an order and there is an error, it needs to know that it has failed or, in case it went through, when it has been completed.

There are several ways to do this, and we will show you the code of the API gateway again, but in this case, we will wait for a response back. As always, after giving you the whole code, we will analyze the important parts:

```go
package main

import (
    "encoding/json"
    "fmt"
    "log"
    "net/http"
    "time"

    "github.com/google/uuid"
    "github.com/nats-io/nats.go"
)

// NATSMessage defines the structure for messages sent to and received
from NATS.
type NATSMessage struct {
    ID      string `json:"id"`
    Content string `json:"content"`
```

```go
        Error    string `json:"error,omitempty"` // Used for backend-
        reported errors
}

func main() {
    // Connect to NATS server
    nc, err := nats.Connect(nats.DefaultURL)
    if err!= nil {
        log.Fatalf("Failed to connect to NATS: %v", err)
    }
    defer nc.Close()
    defer nc.Drain() // Ensure graceful shutdown of NATS connection

    log.Println("API Gateway connected to NATS server.")

    // Define the HTTP handler for processing requests
    http.HandleFunc("/sync_process", func(w http.ResponseWriter, r *http.Request) {
        if r.Method!= http.MethodPost {
            http.Error(w, "Only POST method is supported", http.StatusMethodNotAllowed)
            return
        }

        // Decode the incoming HTTP request payload
        var reqPayload struct {
            Input string `json:"input"`
        }
        if err := json.NewDecoder(r.Body).Decode(&reqPayload); err!= nil {
            http.Error(w, "Invalid request payload", http.StatusBadRequest)
            return
        }

        // Generate a unique ID for this request to correlate the NATS
            response
        requestID := uuid.New().String()
        log.Printf("Received HTTP request for '%s', assigned ID: %s\n",
        reqPayload.Input, requestID)
```

CHAPTER 12   ASYNCHRONOUS SYSTEMS

```go
// Create a buffered channel to receive the NATS response for this
   specific request
responseChan := make(chan *nats.Msg, 1)

// Define the unique NATS subject this API Gateway instance will
   listen on for this response
replySubject := fmt.Sprintf("responses.gateway.%s", requestID)

// Subscribe to the unique reply subject. This subscription is
   ephemeral.
sub, err := nc.Subscribe(replySubject, func(m *nats.Msg) {
   // When a message arrives on this subject, send it to
      the channel
   select {
   case responseChan <- m:
      log.Printf("Correlated NATS response received for ID %s\n",
      requestID)
   default:
      // This case handles if the channel is already full (e.g.,
         a duplicate message or late delivery)
      log.Printf("Dropping late NATS response for ID %s, channel
      full or closed\n", requestID)
   }
})
if err != nil {
   log.Printf("Error subscribing to reply subject %s: %v\n",
   replySubject, err)
   http.Error(w, "Internal server error: could not set up NATS
   listener", http.StatusInternalServerError)
   return
}
// Ensure the subscription is unsubscribed and drained when the
   HTTP handler exits
defer func() {
   sub.Unsubscribe()
   sub.Drain() // Ensures no pending messages are delivered after
   unsubscribe
```

```go
        log.Printf("Unsubscribed from %s\n", replySubject)
    }()

    // Construct and publish the NATS message to the backend
    //   processing subject
    natsReq := NATSMessage{
        ID:      requestID,
        Content: reqPayload.Input,
    }
    natsReqBytes, err := json.Marshal(natsReq)
    if err != nil {
        log.Printf("Error marshalling NATS request: %v\n", err)
        http.Error(w, "Internal server error: marshalling NATS
        request", http.StatusInternalServerError)
        return
    }

    publishSubject := "requests.backend"
    if err := nc.Publish(publishSubject, natsReqBytes); err != nil {
        log.Printf("Error publishing NATS message to %s: %v\n",
        publishSubject, err)
        http.Error(w, "Internal server error: publishing NATS message",
        http.StatusInternalServerError)
        return
    }
    log.Printf("Published NATS request for ID %s to subject '%s'\n",
    requestID, publishSubject)

    // Block and wait for the NATS response on the channel with
    //   a timeout
    select {
    case natsRespMsg := <-responseChan:
        // A NATS response was received
        var resp NATSMessage
        if err := json.Unmarshal(natsRespMsg.Data, &resp); err != nil {
            log.Printf("Error unmarshalling NATS response for ID
            %s: %v\n", requestID, err)
```

```go
            http.Error(w, "Internal server error: unmarshalling NATS 
            response", http.StatusInternalServerError)
            return
        }

        if resp.Error!= "" {
            // Backend reported an error
            log.Printf("Backend error for ID %s: %s\n", requestID, 
            resp.Error)
            w.WriteHeader(http.StatusInternalServerError)
            json.NewEncoder(w).Encode(map[string]string{
                "status":  "error",
                "message": fmt.Sprintf("Backend processing failed: %s", 
                resp.Error),
                "id":      requestID,
            })
            return
        }

        // Successful response from backend
        log.Printf("Received successful response for ID %s: %s\n", 
        requestID, resp.Content)
        w.Header().Set("Content-Type", "application/json")
        json.NewEncoder(w).Encode(map[string]string{
            "status":  "success",
            "message": resp.Content,
            "id":      requestID,
        })
    case <-time.After(5 * time.Second): // Configurable timeout for the 
synchronous wait
        // Timeout occurred
        log.Printf("Timeout waiting for NATS response for ID %s\n", 
        requestID)
        w.WriteHeader(http.StatusRequestTimeout)
        json.NewEncoder(w).Encode(map[string]string{
            "status":  "timeout",
```

CHAPTER 12 ASYNCHRONOUS SYSTEMS

```
                "message": "Backend processing timed out",
                "id":      requestID,
            })
        }
    })

    fmt.Println("API Gateway HTTP server listening on :8080")
    log.Fatal(http.ListenAndServe(":8080", nil))
}
```

After the usual boilerplate imports, we first create a structure that we need for the message:

```
type NATSMessage struct {
    ID      string `json:"id"`
    Content string `json:"content"`
    Error   string `json:"error,omitempty"` // Used for backend-
    reported errors
}
```

In this example, we need some more structure, as we will need an ID and an error message.

The next step will be to create, as before, the HTTP handler:

```
http.HandleFunc("/sync_process", func(w http.ResponseWriter,
r *http.Request) {
```

And inside it, we validate the request, and then we create a new universal ID:

```
requestID := uuid.New().String()
```

This ID will be used to identify and retrieve the request across all the asynchronous requests inside the system. In order to practically do so, we leverage the NATS subject system:

```
replySubject := fmt.Sprintf("responses.gateway.%s", requestID)
```

As you can see, the subject consists of a fixed part, *"responses.gateway,"* and a random part that is the unique identifier. We've seen earlier how the wildcards work, but in this case, we will simply subscribe to the specific subject:

```
sub, err := nc.Subscribe(replySubject, func(m *nats.Msg) {
```

This code creates a subscriber for the specific subject, and when a message is received, it just sends the message to a go channel. It works as a forwarding function and is there simply to ensure smooth concurrency. The code might be complicated, but we wanted to provide a code that is as complete as possible for a production scenario. Inside the subscriber's callback, we use a select to handle any possible channel blockage.

We now need to understand what channel we are talking about, and you can see it in this part of the code:

```
responseChan := make(chan *nats.Msg, 1)
```

In this code, we create a simple channel with pointers to NATS messages of buffer size 1. As you might imagine, or if you went through the full code provided, we use this channel to communicate between the subscriber and the HTTP handler's callback, which will be blocked until the message from the channel, which was pushed there by the subscriber that received it from NATS, arrives:

```
select {
        case natsRespMsg := <-responseChan:
```

We use a select because we want a timeout so that if the response does not come quickly enough, the client, which might be a browser making an HTTP request, won't timeout while waiting for our system to send a response. We will fail earlier than that so that we can manage the failure ourselves:

```
 case <-time.After(5 * time.Second):
```

In this whole example, we kept the internal system fully asynchronous, but we managed to keep our front synchronous. This puts quite a lot of stress on the API gateway, which will have to keep more open connections and idle processes than the internal system and will most likely require a lot more resources. It might not be ideal, but a browser and the person behind it are surely expecting a synchronous interface, so this is one of the best solutions, as the increased resources will be only needed in one component, the API gateway, while in a synchronous system we might need all the touched components to be scaled at the same time, which is a waste of resources. We did not speak about how the internal services will handle the request, but essentially, they will simply need to expect a struct like we've seen before:

```
type NATSMessage struct {
    ID       string `json:"id"`
```

```
    Content string `json:"content"`
    Error   string `json:"error,omitempty"` // Used for backend-
reported errors
}
```

And all they have to do is to include this UUID in the response and/or use it to publish to the correct subject, depending on how the contract is expecting the response back. This means that if the flow includes a transaction between several services, by sending this UUID id over, we can track, log, and trace the full path of the request and its process across all the services, which is very powerful in distributed systems. Even in synchronous systems, it is a good approach to use universal unique identifiers.

We will not dig into different ways to handle the synchronizations of the API gateway, but we could optimize things by using a single subscriber and a set of channels for the REST handler; however, this is not in the scope of this book, and we leave it to the reader.

12.3.3 Actor Model

The actor model is a conceptual framework specifically designed for helping with the design of robust and scalable concurrent systems. In this model, the basic unit of computation is called an "actor," and everything gravitates around it. This model provides a robust and scalable approach to the design of distributed systems, which defines clear rules for how components behave and interact. The key principles of the actor model are

- **Actors**: These are self-contained, independent units, each maintaining its own private state and defining specific behaviors to process incoming messages. Actors do not share memory directly; their only means of interaction is through message passing. This design inherently prevents race conditions and simplifies concurrent programming. In terms of implementation, these could be, for example, functions or structs with a **run** method.

- **Actor References and Addresses**: Every actor within a system possesses a unique address or reference, which means that two actors, even performing the same duties, are different actors. Other actors utilize these references to send messages, abstracting away the physical location of the recipient. These references can be shared by passing them via messages, which allows for dynamic communication patterns and creates flexible system topologies.

- **Message Passing**: Communication between actors is exclusively achieved by sending immutable messages asynchronously. Since no shared state exists, this asynchronous message transmission is the sole mechanism for interaction, enabling non-blocking, distributed, and highly scalable computation.

- **Mailboxes**: When an actor receives a message, that message is not necessarily processed immediately, as an actor won't block incoming messages. What happens instead is that the messages are placed inside the actor's "mailbox," which is essentially a message queue. This mailbox buffers communication, allowing senders to continue their work without waiting, preserving message order (typically FIFO), and assisting in load management during periods of high traffic.

- **Sequential Processing**: One of the key characteristics of the actor model is that actors process only one message at a time. This sequential processing within an actor eliminates the need for locks or other synchronization primitives in the actor's internal logic, highly simplifying concurrent programming and allowing safe modification of internal state without concern for race conditions.

- **Location Transparency**: This characteristic of the actor model means that the physical location of an actor, be it the same process, a different CPU core, a separate machine across a network, or a different Kubernetes pod, is abstracted away. Actors communicate uniformly regardless of their physical deployment, which enables flexible scaling and migration strategies as system requirements evolve.

The actor model has many benefits, as it is intrinsically concurrent and asynchronous, which promotes scalability and high availability; hence, it is a perfect fit for systems where there is a need for complex workflows with data streaming and a lot of concurrent communication and concurrent processes.

You might wonder how NATS fits in all this or how it can be used, and while NATS is not a full-fledged actor framework like Akka or Erlang/Elixir's OTP—in fact, it is not a framework at all but a message broker, its core features, Pub/Sub, Queue Groups, and Request/Reply, can still be used to provide powerful primitives that can be leveraged to implement actor-like patterns effectively. There are

- **Message Passing**: NATS subjects directly facilitate asynchronous message passing between services, acting as the communication channels for "actors."

- **Location Transparency**: NATS abstracts away the physical location of services; clients only need to know the subject to which they wish to send or subscribe, simplifying discovery and routing.

- **Isolation**: Services built on NATS naturally gravitate towards isolation, as they react to incoming messages rather than being invoked through direct, tightly coupled method calls.

- **Mailboxes (via Queue Groups)**: NATS Queue Groups can effectively mimic an actor's mailbox. By having multiple instances of a service subscribe to the same subject within a common queue group, NATS ensures that only one instance in that group receives and processes each message. This mechanism efficiently load-balances work across "actor instances," ensuring that tasks are distributed without redundant processing.

Conceptual Go Code (Actor-Like Service Using NATS Queue Groups):

We will now see a small code example where we can create small actors that process tasks. Each actor is a task processor, and we will leverage NATS queue groups to load balance the tasks across the actors. As this is an example, we will publish messages to NATS from inside the same script:

```go
package main

import (
    "fmt"
    "log"
    "os"
    "os/signal"
    "syscall"
```

```go
    "time"
    "github.com/nats-io/nats.go"
)

// An "Actor" that processes tasks
type TaskProcessorActor struct {
    ID string
    nc *nats.Conn
}

func NewTaskProcessorActor(id string, nc *nats.Conn) *TaskProcessorActor {
    return &TaskProcessorActor{ID: id, nc: nc}
}

func (a *TaskProcessorActor) Start() {
    subject := "tasks.process"
    queueGroup := "task_processors" // This acts like a shared mailbox for
    actor instances

    _, err := a.nc.QueueSubscribe(subject, queueGroup, func(m *nats.Msg) {
        fmt.Printf("Actor %s: Processing task '%s' from subject '%s'\n",
        a.ID, string(m.Data), m.Subject)
        time.Sleep(1 * time.Second) // Simulate task processing
        fmt.Printf("Actor %s: Finished task '%s'\n", a.ID, string(m.Data))
    })
    if err!= nil {
        log.Fatalf("Actor %s failed to subscribe: %v", a.ID, err)
    }
    fmt.Printf("Actor %s listening on subject '%s' in queue group '%s'\n",
    a.ID, subject, queueGroup)
}

func main() {
    nc, err := nats.Connect(nats.DefaultURL)
    if err!= nil {
        log.Fatal(err)
    }
```

```go
    defer nc.Close()
    defer nc.Drain()

    // Create multiple "actor" instances
    actor1 := NewTaskProcessorActor("A", nc)
    actor2 := NewTaskProcessorActor("B", nc)
    actor3 := NewTaskProcessorActor("C", nc)

    actor1.Start()
    actor2.Start()
    actor3.Start()

    // Publisher sending tasks
    go func() {
        for i := 0; i < 10; i++ {
            task := fmt.Sprintf("Task-%d", i+1)
            err := nc.Publish("tasks.process",byte(task))
            if err!= nil {
                log.Printf("Publisher: Error publishing task: %v", err)
            } else {
                fmt.Printf("Publisher: Sent task '%s'\n", task)
            }
            time.Sleep(500 * time.Millisecond)
        }
    }()

    sigChan := make(chan os.Signal, 1)
    signal.Notify(sigChan, syscall.SIGINT, syscall.SIGTERM)
    <-sigChan
    fmt.Println("System shutting down.")
}
```

The publisher is simply a go routine:

```go
go func() {
    for i := 0; i < 10; i++ {
        task := fmt.Sprintf("Task-%d", i+1)
        err := nc.Publish("tasks.process",byte(task))
```

```
        if err!= nil {
            log.Printf("Publisher: Error publishing task: %v", err)
        } else {
            fmt.Printf("Publisher: Sent task '%s'\n", task)
        }
        time.Sleep(500 * time.Millisecond)
    }
}()
```

Which publishes 10 messages. The actor is defined by a simple struct:

```
// An "Actor" that processes tasks
type TaskProcessorActor struct {
    ID string
    nc *nats.Conn
}
```

It contains the NATS connection and a unique identifier. We also define a constructor function for the actor, and we add a method to run the actor:

```
func (a *TaskProcessorActor) Start() {
    subject := "tasks.process"
    queueGroup := "task_processors" // This acts like a shared mailbox for
    actor instances

    _, err := a.nc.QueueSubscribe(subject, queueGroup, func(m *nats.Msg) {
        fmt.Printf("Actor %s: Processing task '%s' from subject '%s'\n",
        a.ID, string(m.Data), m.Subject)
        time.Sleep(1 * time.Second) // Simulate task processing
        fmt.Printf("Actor %s: Finished task '%s'\n", a.ID, string(m.Data))
    })
    if err!= nil {
        log.Fatalf("Actor %s failed to subscribe: %v", a.ID, err)
    }
    fmt.Printf("Actor %s listening on subject '%s' in queue group '%s'\n",
    a.ID, subject, queueGroup)
}
```

The important thing used here is the queue group, which, as you shall remember from Chapter 3, "NATS Fundamentals," is a way to tell NATS that all the subscribers belonging to the same group do not want to receive the same messages, as they are inside the same group. The messages will be load-balanced across the subscribers inside the same queue group. **QueueSubscribe** is the method used to achieve that, and, as you can see, all the actors (3 in this case) are created and run; each one subscribes to the same subject inside the same queue group.

12.3.4 Asynchronous Services

In the previous chapter, we explored how to build synchronous services and applied our DDD and hexagonal architecture knowledge to build such services. In this chapter, we've seen quite a few techniques to build asynchronous components, and we now need to wrap it all up to create asynchronous services.

It should be clear that we need to create services able to receive messages but also to send a reply back. Although some services may be just ingesting data and processing it without sending a response, many services will eventually have to send a response. We've seen this when talking about the API gateway, but we focused on the gateway rather than the services. We will analyze here what is needed to create proper asynchronous services and how they should interact.

We will start now with the way a service should receive messages, and we will begin from where we left off in the previous paragraph: the queue groups. We've seen that the queue groups could be used to load-balance messages across actors inside the same service; however, we will now reflect on how services are actually deployed. When you deploy a service, it will have some limited resources. You can surely increase these resources, but we've seen in the previous chapters that in order to provide an efficient, reliable, and robust system, we can scale our services. As a reminder, this means that we can deploy several instances of the same service, exactly the same service, and have these instances split the work. This will ensure, again, that even if one instance fails, the other can keep working and process the remaining messages, plus we can create more and more instances if we have more resource needs, achieving virtually an infinite processing capability. As we are using NATS for our services, our asynchronous services, we will subscribe, inside each service, to one or more subjects; however, if we just subscribe with a simple subscriber, be it synchronous or asynchronous, NATS will send all the messages to each instance of the same services, as, for NATS, they all are different subscribers. That's where the queue groups come to help: when several instances of a service subscribe to the same NATS subject and specify an identical queue group name, NATS automatically ensures that only one instance within that designated group receives and processes each message. This effectively load-balances messages across the service instances, preventing the redundant and most likely damaging processing of the same message and enabling seamless horizontal scaling.

We will list here some benefits and characteristics of queue groups:

- **Scalability**: Services can easily scale horizontally by adding more instances to a queue group. This increases processing capacity to handle elevated loads without requiring any modifications to the message producers.

- **Resilience**: If an individual service instance within a queue group fails, NATS automatically reroutes messages to other available, healthy instances in the same group. This ensures continuous message processing and enhances overall system fault tolerance.

- **Efficiency**: By guaranteeing that only one instance processes a given message within the group, queue groups prevent redundant work. This contributes to efficiency and helps to achieve "exactly-once" processing semantics for tasks that should not be duplicated.

The combination of API Gateways and NATS Queue Groups enables a robust "request-response-acknowledgement" pattern for long-running tasks, effectively decoupling the user experience from the complexities of backend processing. The API Gateway's immediate synchronous response, an acknowledgement that the request has been received, frees the client from waiting for the task to complete. The actual work is then offloaded to an asynchronous NATS message, which is reliably picked up by a single available service instance via a queue group. This design prevents the client from directly experiencing backend latency or failures.

This pattern is especially important for user-facing applications that need to initiate complex, time-consuming operations without blocking the user interface or risking timeouts. It provides a perception of responsiveness while ensuring that the backend work is reliably distributed and processed.

```
order_service/
├── main.go
├── domain/
│   └── order.go
├── application/
│   └── order_service.go
├── infrastructure/
│   └── nats_order_adapter.go
└── presentation/
    └── nats_handler.go
```

Figure 12-1. Project structure for asynchronous order processor

We will now see how to build an order processor again, using DDD and NATS, but as an asynchronous service. We will not provide the complete code here, which will be available in full in the extra content instead. Let's start with the project structure, which is available in Figure 12-1. It contains a main file, acting as a scaffolding piece, gluing everything together, and several folders with the packages for the domain, application, infrastructure, and presentation layers.

The domain layer will include simply the order definition:

```
package domain

// Order represents the core domain entity for an order.
// It contains attributes directly relevant to the business concept of
an order.
type Order struct {
    ID        string // This will serve as the correlation ID (UUID)
    ProductID string
    Quantity  int
    Status    string // e.g., "Pending", "Processed", "Failed"
}
```

We keep an order ID, which means this is an entity and not a value object, and this ID is also used to share the order updates via NATS messages. Of course, at the domain level, we do not care about NATS, and we don't even have to know that NATS exists, but in this implementation, we assume that the ID is needed to identify and manipulate or share an order; hence, it is here, and, in different layers, this will also match the NATAS subject, unbeknown to the domain layer.

CHAPTER 12 ASYNCHRONOUS SYSTEMS

An order will then reach the service via the presentation layer, which is made of just one handler, using NATS messages to communicate:

```
package presentation

import (
    "encoding/json"
    "fmt"
    "log"

    "chapter-12/application"      // Import application for
                                  OrderApplicationService
    "chapter-12/domain"           // Import domain for Order type
    "chapter-12/infrastructure"   // Import infrastructure for
                                  NATSOrderRequest and NATSOrderAdapter
    "github.com/nats-io/nats.go"
)
// NATSOrderHandler is a "driving adapter" that handles incoming NATS messages.
// It orchestrates the flow from NATS message reception to application logic and back to NATS reply.
type NATSOrderHandler struct {
    appService  application.OrderServicePort     // Port to the
                                                 application layer
    natsAdapter *infrastructure.NATSOrderAdapter // Adapter to send the
                                                 reply back via NATS
}

// NewNATSOrderHandler creates an instance of the NATS handler.
func NewNATSOrderHandler(appSvc application.OrderServicePort, natsAdpt *infrastructure.NATSOrderAdapter) *NATSOrderHandler {
    return &NATSOrderHandler{appService: appSvc, natsAdapter: natsAdpt}
}

// HandleNATSOrder is the NATS callback function that processes incoming order messages.
// This function will be passed to nc.QueueSubscribe in main.
func (h *NATSOrderHandler) HandleNATSOrder(m *nats.Msg) {
```

429

```go
    log.Printf("Presentation Layer: Received NATS message on subject '%s' 
    from NATS Queue Group.\n", m.Subject)

    var req infrastructure.NATSOrderRequest
    if err := json.Unmarshal(m.Data, &req); err!= nil {
        log.Printf("Presentation Layer: Invalid NATS request payload: 
        %v\n", err)
        // Attempt to send a generic error reply if reply subject is 
            available
        if req.ReplySubject!= "" {
            h.natsAdapter.SendOrderReply(req.ReplySubject, domain.Order{ID: 
            "unknown"}, fmt.Errorf("invalid request format"))
        }
        return
    }

    // Map NATS request DTO to domain entity
    order := domain.Order{
        ID:        req.OrderID,
        ProductID: req.ProductID,
        Quantity:  req.Quantity,
        Status:    "Pending", // Initial status before processing
    }

    // Call the application service (through the driving port) to handle 
        the order
    processedOrder, appErr := h.appService.HandleOrder(order)

    // Send the reply back to the API Gateway using the 
        infrastructure adapter
    // The replySubject is carried from the incoming NATS request.
    h.natsAdapter.SendOrderReply(req.ReplySubject, processedOrder, appErr)
}
```

CHAPTER 12   ASYNCHRONOUS SYSTEMS

The key points to notice are that the handler will use a "port" as defined in the Hexagonal Architecture, which looks like this:

```
type OrderServicePort interface {
    HandleOrder(order domain.Order) (domain.Order, error)
}
```

It is an interface implemented inside the application layer and used here in the presentation. It is a port, which is an interface defining a contract, and its implementation is still inside the application layer. This is an inward port, used to accept requests, and used by the presentation. The presentation, then, when receiving a NATS message, will try to transform the incoming message into a sharable structure:

```
var req infrastructure.NATSOrderRequest
    if err := json.Unmarshal(m.Data, &req); err!= nil {
```

By unmarshaling and then converting it into a domain entity:

```
order := domain.Order{
        ID:        req.OrderID,
        ProductID: req.ProductID,
        Quantity:  req.Quantity,
        Status:    "Pending", // Initial status before processing
    }
```

The application service will be used to process the order:

```
// Call the application service (through the driving port) to handle the order
    processedOrder, appErr := h.appService.HandleOrder(order)
```

and finally, when the order has been processed, it will send the reply:

```
h.natsAdapter.SendOrderReply(req.ReplySubject, processedOrder, appErr)
```

The **processedOrder** value will include the order ID again. Notice that, when sending the response, we use **req.ReplySubject**. The NATS message is defined, in the infrastructure layer, as

```
type NATSOrderRequest struct {
    OrderID      string `json:"order_id"`    // This is the correlation ID
    ProductID    string `json:"product_id"`
    Quantity     int    `json:"quantity"`
    ReplySubject string `json:"reply_subject"` // The subject the API
    Gateway is listening on for this specific request.
}
```

If you recall the API Gateway implementation, the subject was

```
replySubject := fmt.Sprintf("responses.gateway.%s", requestID)
```

And we could construct this without passing it via the message, but in this case, if we wanted to change any logic inside the API gateway, we would have to change the code of the processor too. This would be a dependency that is not even clearly written and difficult to spot, defining the reply subject inside the requester (the API gateway) and passing it through, helping us with decoupling.

As earlier mentioned, you can find the full code inside the extra content, but what we've shown here should be sufficient for you to understand how it all should work. If you wish, you could also try to use actors for your order service or any other service.

12.4 Long-Running Processes

12.4.1 Introduction

Long-running processes are operations that require a considerable amount of time to complete, frequently exceeding the typical timeouts associated with synchronous request-response interactions. HTTP requests, in fact, have their own timeouts, and even if a synthetic client can increase this timeout, an application that is expected to be consumed via a browser won't have this option, and a long-running process will fail the interface interaction. Examples of long-running processes include complex data analysis, video encoding, large file transfers, and extensive batch processing tasks. Handling these operations synchronously in a distributed system poses significant challenges, primarily due to the issues of latency, resource contention, and cascading failures previously discussed in Chapter 11, "Fully Synchronous Systems." Consequently, employing asynchronous patterns is not just an option but an essential requirement for ensuring that the execution of such processes is reliable and scalable.

12.4.2 REST

If we think again about traditional RESTful APIs, they are, by their very nature, synchronous and therefore ill-suited for initiating and managing long-running processes. Clients making synchronous REST calls for such operations would either face prolonged waiting times, encounter timeouts, or be compelled to implement intricate polling mechanisms to repeatedly check for task completion. This polling approach introduces considerable overhead, complexity, and inefficiency into both the client and server components. While webhooks can offer a push-based notification system for task completion, they still necessitate a separate initial request mechanism and a means for clients to track the status of their initiated tasks. The API Gateway pattern, as discussed in Section 12.3.2, provides a common and effective solution for initiating long-running processes via REST by immediately acknowledging the receipt of the request and subsequently offloading the actual, time-consuming work to an asynchronous backend. The way to receive an update in the front end will vary, be it some recurring polling, notifications, push messages, or even websockets; that is dependent on the situation, but still, that is one thing to think of that is separated by the actual processing of a request, which can progress without the need of caring when the result will be given back, if ever.

12.4.3 Scaling Up

We shall stress again that asynchronous messaging inherently provides robust support for scaling long-running processes. When a service is designed to process tasks asynchronously, for instance, by consuming messages from a NATS queue, its processing capacity can be dynamically increased by simply adding new instances to the relevant queue group (as detailed in Section 12.3.4). This horizontal scaling can be performed without any modifications to the message producers, as NATS transparently distributes new messages to the available service instances. This flexibility allows for dynamic scaling based on the current workload, thereby optimizing resource utilization and ensuring that the system can adapt to fluctuating demands.

12.4.4 Piling Up

Asynchronous queues, such as those leveraging NATS, are then a very powerful instrument for managing message backlogs and preventing system overload. In scenarios where a sudden surge of long-running tasks occurs, messages can "pile up" within the queue without overwhelming the processing services. This queuing mechanism acts as a vital buffer, allowing services to consume these messages at their own pace or enabling new instances to be spun up dynamically to drain the queue very quickly.

This buffering capability is determinant for ensuring system stability and facilitating graceful degradation under peak loads, hence effectively preventing the cascading failures that are common in synchronously coupled systems. This handling of backlogs in asynchronous systems with NATS Queue Groups transforms what would otherwise be a potential system collapse under heavy load into a manageable scaling problem. The ability for messages to accumulate without blocking producers means that this "piling up" is not a sign of failure but a deliberate and beneficial feature. It functions as a resilient buffer, fundamentally changing the operational paradigm from one focused on "preventing failure" to one centered on "managing load." This allows asynchronous systems to queue work gracefully and enables operators to react by scaling out consumers, rather than contending with system-wide outages.

12.5 JetStream

12.5.1 Persistence

We've already seen how queue groups are helpful for long-lasting processes, on top of being essential for scaling up services, but there is a catch: if processing is too long and messages keep coming, the internal buffer will time out, and messages will be lost. We could automatically scale our services, but if one service can only handle a handful of requests, which was not the case before AI, ETL, and real-time data analytics, but now it is, then the only solution we have would be to continuously scale our services, which can lead to thousands of instances of our services running.

It is fair to assume that many long-lasting processes might be queued and processed when it is time. This might happen when generating AI images or any other long process. We need, then, a way to store these messages for later use, and if we were using tools like

RabbitMQ or any other proper message queue, we would be fine, but we are using NATS, which is a message broker built on top of a pub/sub mechanism and not a queuing system. Hopefully, for us, the NATS team thought of that.

While the core mechanism NATS operates on is based on a "fire-and-forget" model, which means messages are discarded if no active subscribers are present, NATS JetStream introduces a built-in persistence engine that changes this dynamic. JetStream enables messages to be stored and replayed, effectively overcoming the temporal coupling inherent in core NATS. This means that consumers can receive messages that were published even when they were offline or disconnected, ensuring no data is lost. JetStream achieves its high reliability and fault tolerance in a clustered environment by utilizing a NATS-optimized RAFT distributed quorum algorithm, which provides immediate consistency across the cluster even in the face of server failures.

JetStream allows for the creation of "streams," which act as dedicated message stores. Each stream can be configured to define precisely how messages are stored and what retention policies apply to them. Any message published on subjects that are bound to a particular stream will be automatically captured and persisted within that stream's configured storage system. This capability is foundational for building reliable event-driven architectures, enabling event sourcing, persistent queues, and robust data pipelines.

There are several ways to create a stream and define how and where the messages will be stored, and for how long. We will see now how to do it via code by using a script that creates the stream utilizing the SDK:

```go
package main

import (
    "context"
    "fmt"
    "log"
    "time"

    "github.com/nats-io/nats.go"
    "github.com/nats-io/nats.go/jetstream"
)
```

CHAPTER 12   ASYNCHRONOUS SYSTEMS

```go
func main() {
    nc, err := nats.Connect(nats.DefaultURL)
    if err != nil {
        log.Fatal(err)
    }
    defer nc.Close()
    defer nc.Drain()

    // Create a JetStream Context
    js, err := jetstream.New(nc)
    if err != nil {
        log.Fatal(err)
    }

    ctx, cancel := context.WithTimeout(context.Background(),
    10*time.Second)
    defer cancel()

    // Use a stream name and subject pattern suitable for an
        ordering system
    streamName := "ORDER_EVENTS"
    subject := "order.>" // Capture all subjects starting with "order."

    // Define stream configuration
    _, err = js.CreateStream(ctx, jetstream.StreamConfig{
        Name:     streamName,
        Subjects: []string{subject},
        Storage:  jetstream.FileStorage, // Persist messages to disk
    })
    if err != nil {
        log.Fatalf("Error creating stream: %v", err)
    }
    fmt.Printf("Stream '%s' created, capturing subjects '%s'\n",
    streamName, subject)

    // Publish messages representing different order events
    for i := 0; i < 3; i++ {
        // Example: Publish a new order event
```

```go
        newOrderMsg := fmt.Sprintf("Order %d placed by user 123", i+1)
        _, err = js.Publish(ctx, fmt.Sprintf("order.new.%d", i+1),
        []byte(newOrderMsg))
        if err != nil {
            log.Printf("Error publishing new order message: %v", err)
        } else {
            fmt.Printf("Published: '%s' to 'order.new.%d'\n",
            newOrderMsg, i+1)
        }
        time.Sleep(100 * time.Millisecond)

        // Example: Publish an order update (e.g., payment received)
        paymentReceivedMsg := fmt.Sprintf("Payment received for order %d",
        i+1)
        _, err = js.Publish(ctx, fmt.Sprintf("order.payment_received.%d",
        i+1), []byte(paymentReceivedMsg))
        if err != nil {
            log.Printf("Error publishing payment received message:
            %v", err)
        } else {
            fmt.Printf("Published: '%s' to 'order.payment_received.%d'\n",
            paymentReceivedMsg, i+1)
        }
        time.Sleep(100 * time.Millisecond)
    }
    fmt.Println("Order events published to stream.")
}
```

In this code, we firstly connect to NATS normally:

```go
nc, err := nats.Connect(nats.DefaultURL)
```

And after that, we create a JetStream object:

```go
js, err := jetstream.New(nc)
```

After that we can finally create a stream:

```
_, err = js.CreateStream(ctx, jetstream.StreamConfig{
    Name:     streamName,
    Subjects:string{subject},
    Storage:  jetstream.FileStorage, // Persist messages to disk
})
```

Bear in mind that this will create a stream inside the NATS server, so it will be available to be used by other services, consumers, and command-line NATS client instances. We are essentially telling our NATS server to create this stream, and we pass some clear instructions like the name of the stream, which will identify it for later use, the available subjects, and the type of storage. We choose here to store the stream on a filesystem, but we could choose memory instead. Memory storage will still allow for new service or client instances to get past messages, but if NATS fails or gets restarted, we will lose the messages. Of course, the choice between memory and filesystem is a choice that is up to the architect and needs to be cautiously pondered.

The subjects part is interesting, because while a simple NATS subscriber subscribes to a subject, here a stream can have multiple subjects. The way you should think of it is that when a message gets published, it will reach the subscribers who expressed an interest in the subject, and that's what a JetStream stream actually is: a subscriber to a set of subjects. The NATS server will effectively push all the messages to a stream that has expressed interest in the subjects. A stream is effectively like an intermediate subscriber handled by NATS.

One last thing, apart from creating a stream, we also need to publish messages to it:

```
js.Publish(ctx, fmt.Sprintf("order.new.%d", i+1), []byte(newOrderMsg))
```

In reality, you do not need the **js** object to publish a message to the stream; you can do it, but for simple messages, from the publisher side, you could just publish a message from your **nc** connection, and it will work exactly the same. As we've already mentioned, it is the NATS server that pushes messages to the stream, but for a publisher, there is not much of a difference; it is the consumer that has to be tied explicitly to a stream.

12.5.2 Retention

Apart from deciding where to store the messages and which subjects to register an interest in, we also need to provide a retention policy. It would be silly to think that this wasn't an option, because the whole point of JesStream is to provide storage for later use, and a retention policy is needed so the system knows when to drop messages and how to deliver them. It comes as no surprise that we also need to tell JetStream from where to start when a new subscriber comes in, because some subscribers will be inside a queue group and will just need the newest messages, while other subscribers might need messages from the beginning.

For this, JetStream streams offer a comprehensive set of retention policies and limits, allowing fine-grained control over how messages are managed and when they are automatically deleted to conserve storage resources.

Retention Policies:

- **LimitsPolicy (default):** This policy retains messages based on various configurable limits such as MaxMsgs (maximum number of messages), MaxBytes (maximum total size of messages), MaxAge (maximum age of any message), and MaxMsgsPerSubject (maximum messages per subject). Messages are automatically deleted when any of these limits are met, ensuring the stream adheres to its defined boundaries. It is clearly up to the architect, in this case, to decide what limit to use for a specific stream.

- **WorkQueuePolicy:** Designed to function like a traditional FIFO queue, this policy ensures that each message can be consumed only once. Once a message is successfully acknowledged by a consumer, it is automatically deleted from the stream. Any configured limits (like MaxMsgs or MaxAge) will still apply, potentially discarding messages even if they haven't been consumed yet.

- **InterestPolicy:** Messages are retained under this policy only for as long as there are active consumers interested in them. Once all consumers who were filtering on a message's subject have acknowledged it, the message is deleted. Similar to WorkQueuePolicy, configured limits will still be enforced.

Discard Policies (when limits are hit): These policies dictate what happens when a stream reaches one of its defined limits and a new message is published.

- **DiscardOld (default):** When a limit is reached, the oldest messages in the stream are automatically removed to make room for new incoming messages. This is common for continuous data streams where the latest information is most critical.

- **DiscardNew:** Under this policy, if a new message would cause the stream to exceed one of its limits, the new message is rejected, and the publisher receives an error. This is useful for critical, bounded streams where preserving older data is more important than accepting new data during overload. A variation, DiscardNewPerSubject, applies this rejection policy on a per-subject basis within the stream.

We now provide another example where we create two streams with these limit policies set:

```go
package main

import (
    "context"
    "fmt"
    "log"
    "time"
    "github.com/nats-io/nats.go"
    "github.com/nats-io/nats.go/jetstream"
)

func main() {
    nc, err := nats.Connect(nats.DefaultURL)
    if err != nil {
        log.Fatal(err)
    }
    defer nc.Close()
    defer nc.Drain()
```

```go
js, err := jetstream.New(nc)
if err != nil {
    log.Fatal(err)
}

ctx, cancel := context.WithTimeout(context.Background(),
10*time.Second)
defer cancel()

// Stream for restaurant logs, with a retention policy
logStreamName := "RESTAURANT_LOGS"
logSubject := "restaurant.logs.>" // Captures logs for all restaurant services

_, err = js.CreateStream(ctx, jetstream.StreamConfig{
    Name:      logStreamName,
    Subjects:  []string{logSubject},
    MaxAge:    24 * time.Hour, // Keep logs for 24 hours
    Retention: jetstream.LimitsPolicy,
    Discard:   jetstream.DiscardOld,
    Storage:   jetstream.FileStorage,
})
if err != nil {
    log.Fatalf("Error creating logs stream: %v", err)
}
fmt.Printf("Stream '%s' created with MaxAge: 24h for restaurant logs.\n", logStreamName)

// Stream as a WorkQueue for kitchen tasks
workQueueStreamName := "KITCHEN_TASKS"
workQueueSubject := "kitchen.orders.new" // Specifically for new orders

_, err = js.CreateStream(ctx, jetstream.StreamConfig{
    Name: workQueueStreamName,
    Subjects: []string{workQueueSubject},
    Retention: jetstream.WorkQueuePolicy, // A message is deleted after a single consumer acknowledges it
    Storage: jetstream.MemoryStorage, // Use memory for high-speed
```

kitchen task processing
```
    })
    if err != nil {
        log.Fatalf("Error creating work queue stream: %v", err)
    }
    fmt.Printf("Stream '%s' created with WorkQueuePolicy for new kitchen orders.\n", workQueueStreamName)

    fmt.Println("NATS JetStream streams for restaurant system configured successfully.")
}
```

The first stream has these policies:

```
MaxAge:    24 * time.Hour, // Keep logs for 24 hours
Retention: jetstream.LimitsPolicy,
Discard:   jetstream.DiscardOld,
```

This means we retain messages until the maximum age of 24 hours is reached, and then we start discarding the older messages. The stream in question has been used for logs.

The second stream has this retention configuration:

```
Retention: jetstream.WorkQueuePolicy,
```

This means that as soon as one of the subscribers has acknowledged the message, it will be discarded and removed from the stream. We ensure that the message is received, but then we do not need it any more.

12.5.3 Consumers

We've seen how to create streams and how to publish messages to JetStream, but we haven't seen yet how a subscriber captures these messages. In fact, while we can simply publish a message with a subject, and it will reach a stream if it has been set to capture that subject, a subscriber won't automatically receive messages from a stream; in fact, it will not. Subscribers are still bound to the fire-and-forget mechanism, so we need something else called a consumer. Consumers are responsible for reading messages from streams and can be configured in two primary modes: "Push" or "Pull." The choice between these modes depends on the application's specific requirements for message flow control, backpressure handling, and reliability.

Push Consumers: With push consumers, the NATS server proactively pushes messages to the subscriber's active subscription, up to a configured MaxAckPending limit. This model is generally simpler to set up for basic "fire-and-forget" scenarios where the subscriber is expected to keep pace with the incoming message rate consistently. However, push consumers can become "unwieldy" and difficult to manage if the subscriber falls behind, leading to potential message redelivery and interleaving of new and redelivered messages. Push consumers can be either ephemeral (automatically removed after inactivity or client unsubscribe) or durable (their state, including the last acknowledged message, is tracked on the server, allowing them to resume processing after disconnection).

Pull Consumers: In contrast, pull consumers empower the application to explicitly "fetch" messages on demand, giving it precise control over the message flow. This approach is ideal for scenarios that demand controlled processing, batching of messages, and explicit acknowledgement of message processing. Pull consumers intrinsically provide support for scaling out consumption, as multiple pull consumers can concurrently fetch messages from the same stream, distributing the workload. Like push consumers, pull consumers can also be configured as ephemeral or durable, with durable pull consumers being particularly recommended for reliable, fault-tolerant processing.

Go Code Example: JetStream Push Consumer

This program sets up a JetStream stream and then creates a durable push consumer to receive messages.

```go
package main

import (
    "context"
    "fmt"
    "log"
    "time"
    "github.com/nats-io/nats.go"
    "github.com/nats-io/nats.go/jetstream"
)
```

```go
func main() {
    // Connect to a NATS server
    nc, err := nats.Connect(nats.DefaultURL)
    if err != nil {
        log.Fatal(err)
    }
    defer nc.Close()
    defer nc.Drain()

    // Create a JetStream Context
    js, err := jetstream.New(nc)
    if err != nil {
        log.Fatal(err)
    }

    ctx, cancel := context.WithTimeout(context.Background(),
    10*time.Second)
    defer cancel()

    // --- Stream Setup (from previous code) ---

    // Stream for restaurant logs, with a retention policy
    logStreamName := "RESTAURANT_LOGS"
    logSubject := "restaurant.logs.>" // Captures logs for all restaurant
    services

    _, err = js.CreateStream(ctx, jetstream.StreamConfig{
        Name:      logStreamName,
        Subjects:  []string{logSubject},
        MaxAge:    24 * time.Hour, // Keep logs for 24 hours
        Retention: jetstream.LimitsPolicy,
        Discard:   jetstream.DiscardOld,
        Storage:   jetstream.FileStorage,
    })
    if err != nil {
        log.Fatalf("Error creating logs stream: %v", err)
    }
    fmt.Printf("Stream '%s' created with MaxAge: 24h for restaurant
    logs.\n", logStreamName)
```

```go
// Stream as a WorkQueue for kitchen tasks
workQueueStreamName := "KITCHEN_TASKS"
workQueueSubject := "kitchen.orders.new" // Specifically for new orders

_, err = js.CreateStream(ctx, jetstream.StreamConfig{
    Name: workQueueStreamName,
    Subjects: []string{workQueueSubject},
    Retention: jetstream.WorkQueuePolicy, // A message is deleted after
    a single consumer acknowledges it
    Storage: jetstream.MemoryStorage, // Use memory for high-speed
    kitchen task processing
})
if err != nil {
    log.Fatalf("Error creating work queue stream: %v", err)
}
fmt.Printf("Stream '%s' created with WorkQueuePolicy for new kitchen orders.\n", workQueueStreamName)
fmt.Println("NATS JetStream streams for restaurant system configured successfully.")

// --- Push Consumer Setup ---

// Create a new push consumer on the KITCHEN_TASKS stream
// This consumer will receive a copy of each new message pushed to
   the queue.
consumer, err := js.CreateOrUpdateConsumer(ctx, workQueueStreamName,
jetstream.ConsumerConfig{
    Durable: "kitchen_worker_1", // A durable name so the server
    remembers this consumer
    // The queue group "kitchen" ensures only one consumer in this
       group receives a message.
    DeliverGroup: "kitchen",
})
if err != nil {
    log.Fatalf("Error creating consumer: %v", err)
}
```

```go
fmt.Printf("Consumer 'kitchen_worker_1' created for stream '%s' with
    DeliverGroup 'kitchen'.\n", workQueueStreamName)

// Start a subscription to listen for messages
sub, err := consumer.Consume(func(msg jetstream.Msg) {
    // This function is executed for every message received.
    fmt.Printf("Kitchen received a new order: %s\n", string(msg.Data()))

    // Simulate order processing time.
    time.Sleep(1 * time.Second)

    // Send a message to show the order is being prepared
    // This is a great example of an event-driven system!
    processedMsg := fmt.Sprintf("Order %s is now being prepared.",
        string(msg.Data()))
    _, publishErr := js.Publish(ctx, "kitchen.orders.processing",
        []byte(processedMsg))
    if publishErr != nil {
        log.Printf("Error publishing 'processing' message: %v",
            publishErr)
    } else {
        fmt.Println("Published: 'order processing' update.")
    }

    // Acknowledge the message to JetStream. This is crucial for
        WorkQueuePolicy
    // because it tells the server to remove the message from
        the stream.
    if err := msg.Ack(); err != nil {
        log.Printf("Error acknowledging message: %v", err)
    } else {
        fmt.Println("Order acknowledged and removed from queue.")
    }
})
if err != nil {
    log.Fatalf("Error starting consumer: %v", err)
}
defer sub.Stop()
```

```
// --- Publisher for new orders ---

// Publish some sample orders to the stream to see the consumer
    in action
for i := 1; i <= 3; i++ {
    orderMsg := fmt.Sprintf("Order %d: 1x Cheeseburger, 1x Fries", i)
    _, publishErr := js.Publish(ctx, workQueueSubject,
    []byte(orderMsg))
    if publishErr != nil {
        log.Printf("Error publishing message: %v", publishErr)
    } else {
        fmt.Printf("Published a new order: '%s' to subject '%s'\n",
        orderMsg, workQueueSubject)
    }
    time.Sleep(500 * time.Millisecond)
}
fmt.Println("\nFinished publishing all orders. Waiting for the kitchen
to finish...\n")

// Keep the main function running so the consumer can process messages
select {}
}
```

The first key part here is

```
js.CreateOrUpdateConsumer(ctx, workQueueStreamName, jetstream.
ConsumerConfig{
    Durable: "kitchen_worker_1", // A durable name so the server
    remembers this consumer
    // The queue group "kitchen" ensures only one consumer in this
        group receives a message.
    DeliverGroup: "kitchen",
})
```

CHAPTER 12   ASYNCHRONOUS SYSTEMS

Where the consumer is created, attached to the stream called **workQueueStreamName,** set as durable (it will be registered inside the NATS server and can be used later if the service goes down) "kicthen_worker_1," and finally it is part of the JetStream equivalent of a "queuegroup," called **DeliverGroup**, which here is called "kicthen."

We now need to actually process the messages, and we can see it here:

```
sub, err := consumer.Consume(func(msg jetstream.Msg) {
..................................................................
 processedMsg := fmt.Sprintf("Order %s is now being prepared.", string(msg.Data()))
..................................................................
 if err := msg.Ack(); err != nil {
         log.Printf("Error acknowledging message: %v", err)
     } else {
..................................................................
```

The **Consume** function expects a callback receiving a JetStream Message, and you will put the processing logic inside that callback. At the end of the process, you shall never forget to acknowledge that the message has been received. We did not need that with the core NATS functionalities, as the pub/sub system is not built for explicit acknowledgement of messages, which is by design. In the case of queues, which have a retention policy, it is extremely important to acknowledge the messages, which will otherwise be sent again and again, and that's hardly what you want.

A push consumer is easy to implement, but, as we've already said, might not be very performant and may result in problems under heavy load. A pull consumer is leaner from the NATS server side, as it will push the logic into the consumer, which means in your code. Let's see how the consumer creation and usage changes for a pull consumer:

```
// --- Pull Consumer Setup ---
// Create a new pull consumer on the KITCHEN_TASKS stream.
consumer, err := js.CreateOrUpdateConsumer(ctx, workQueueStreamName,
jetstream.ConsumerConfig{
    Durable: "kitchen_worker_pull", // A durable name for the consumer
    // Pull consumers don't need a DeliverGroup.
})
```

448

```go
if err != nil {
    log.Fatalf("Error creating pull consumer: %v", err)
}
fmt.Printf("Pull consumer 'kitchen_worker_pull' created for stream '%s'.\n", workQueueStreamName)

// --- Consumer Message Loop ---

// Loop to continuously pull for new messages.
for {
    // Fetch a batch of up to 10 messages with a 1-second timeout.
    msgs, err := consumer.Fetch(10, jetstream.FetchMaxWait(1*time.Second))
    if err != nil {
        if err == context.DeadlineExceeded {
            fmt.Println("No new orders in the last second. Waiting...")
            continue // Try fetching again
        }
        log.Fatalf("Error fetching messages: %v", err)
    }

    // Process each message in the batch.
    for msg := range msgs.Messages() {
        fmt.Printf("Kitchen worker received and is pulling a new order: %s\n", string(msg.Data()))

        // --- Message Processing Logic ---
        // (Same as push consumer: simulate work, publish updates, and
        //    acknowledge)
        time.Sleep(500 * time.Millisecond)
        processedMsg := fmt.Sprintf("Order %s is now being prepared.", string(msg.Data()))
        _, publishErr := js.Publish(ctx, "kitchen.orders.processing", []byte(processedMsg))
        if publishErr != nil {
            log.Printf("Error publishing 'processing' message: %v", publishErr)
```

```
        } else {
            fmt.Println("Published: 'order processing' update.")
        }

        if err := msg.Ack(); err != nil {
            log.Printf("Error acknowledging message: %v", err)
        } else {
            fmt.Println("Order acknowledged and removed from queue.")
        }
    }
}
```

The creation of the consumer does not change, as we still use the function **CreateOrUpdateConsumer**, but what changes is the way we receive the messages. Instead of relying on a callback inside the **Consume** function, we use a **Fetch** function:

```
msgs, err := consumer.Fetch(10, jetstream.FetchMaxWait(1*time.Second))
```

This function allows you to pull a specific number of messages of your choice. You could set it to one, so you would only receive one message at a time, but, as we are using Go and it has good concurrency features, it is generally more performant if you fetch a batch of messages and you process them as you wish, synchronously or concurrently.

In our previous code snippet, we do not process them concurrently, but one by one. Bear in mind that even though you might ask for 10 messages, you are not sure of how many you will receive. You won't receive more than 10, but you might receive, at a specific iteration, less than that. The number is, effectively, an upper bound limit and not a hard limit. If that wasn't the case, your system might find itself in a situation where it has to wait indefinitely until the specific number of messages has been reached. If that were happening after ten days, your users would have to wait ten days for their messages to be processed.

As soon as a message is processed, notice again the line:

```
  if err := msg.Ack(); err != nil {
```

Which shows how the message is acknowledged.

An important thing to notice here is that even with the streams, NATS has some timeouts. If your message takes one hour to be processed, it is likely that the message will be considered not acknowledged and put back in the queue. This means that when you finally acknowledge the message, you will receive an error. You can surely increase the timeout in the consumer definition, but that is not the most efficient way and still might not work properly at the server side. For very long-running processes, as is the case with AI applications, you might want to give a quick acknowledgement and then pause message retrieval until you have completed your processing. You can consider this scenario as something like: Yes, I acknowledge that I received the message, but I haven't processed it yet. This is perfectly fine, but then you need to manage the situation where an error occurs by yourself, and you have to manually put the original message back into the queue, without relying on the NATS internal functionalities.

We've created all these consumers and streams via code, but in the first part of this book, you've also played with the NATS CLI. In reality, you can do all these things via the command line interactively:

```
$ nats stream add
```

And you will be prompted with some questions about storage, subjects, and retention policies. This is fine for prototyping, but if you want to keep your streams somewhere under version control and use the CLI to recreate them, instead of using a Go code snippet, you can save your streams and consumers' configurations as JSON files. Here is a stream example:

```
{
  "name": "user_subjects",
  "subjects": [
    "user.>"
  ],
  "retention": "limits",
  "max_consumers": -1,
  "max_msgs_per_subject": -1,
  "max_msgs": -1,
  "max_bytes": -1,
  "max_age": 604800000000000,
  "max_msg_size": -1,
  "storage": "file",
  "discard": "old",
  "num_replicas": 1,
  "duplicate_window": 120000000000,
  "sealed": false,
```

```
  "deny_delete": false,
  "deny_purge": false,
  "allow_rollup_hdrs": false
}
```

In order to create this stream via command line, and assuming the JSON is stored in a file called user_subjects, you can do:

```
$ nats stream add user_subjects --config user_subjects.json
```

In the same way, you can create consumers. Consider this configuration:

```
{
  "ack_policy": "explicit",
  "ack_wait": 30000000000,
  "deliver_policy": "all",
  "durable_name": "user_consumer",
  "max_ack_pending": 20000,
  "max_deliver": -1,
  "max_waiting": 512,
  "replay_policy": "instant",
  "num_replicas": 0
}
```

To create this consumer and attach it to the previous stream, you can do so via the command line:

```
$ nats consumer add user_subjects --config user_consumer.json
```

We add a consumer to the **user_subjects** stream with the configuration available inside the **user_consumer.json** file.

12.5.4 Asynchronous Services (JetStream)

As we've seen, JetStream, by extending NATS capabilities, also provides a simple, scalable, and robust way to build microservices and to glue them into powerful, resilient, and reliable distributed systems.

At the heart of this technique lie Durable JetStream consumers, which allow for the realization of reliable, fault-tolerant asynchronous services, particularly good for handling long-running tasks. In other words, the persistence capabilities of JetStream, combined with the explicit control offered by durable consumers, elevate NATS from a transient messaging system to a robust event streaming platform, which in turn can be used as an excellent platform for building great distributed systems.

Looking at microservices specifically, JetStream provides several key advantages:

> **Reliability**: Messages are persisted within the stream. This ensures that even if a service instance crashes or goes offline, the message is not lost. When the service recovers—or when another instance becomes available—processing can resume from where it left off. It is important to choose the appropriate storage type: in-memory storage is fast but volatile, whereas persistent storage safeguards messages against NATS/JetStream failures.

> **At-Least-Once Delivery**: JetStream guarantees that messages are delivered at least once. Combined with explicit acknowledgements (ACKs) from consumers, this allows developers to implement idempotent logic within services, meaning that even if the same message is delivered multiple times, processing it repeatedly does not change the result beyond the first execution, achieving "exactly-once" semantics for critical operations. While JetStream handles delivery, avoiding duplicate effects relies on the service's implementation.

> **Replay Policies**: Consumers can be configured to start consuming messages from the beginning of a stream, the last acknowledged message, or a specific sequence number or timestamp. This capability is essential for disaster recovery, debugging, and historical reprocessing of events.

The addition of persistence and sophisticated consumer models, particularly durable pull consumers, transforms NATS into the robust event streaming platform needed for distributed systems.

For example, a consumer can be configured as follows:

```
cons, err := js.CreateOrUpdateConsumer(ctx, streamName, jetstream.
ConsumerConfig{
        Durable:       consumerName,
        DeliverPolicy: jetstream.DeliverAllPolicy, // Start from beginning
        if new, or last acked
        AckPolicy:     jetstream.AckExplicitPolicy,
        MaxDeliver:    5, // Max redelivery attempts
    })
```

In the above code, we used the attribute **DeliveryPolicy** to tell NATS that the consumer will need the messages from the beginning; however, this still does not guarantee that each message can be delivered at least once. NATS is programmed to try to deliver the messages as requested, but there might still be issues preventing it from happening. In order to control this even more, we can tell NATS how many times we want it to try to redeliver a failed attempt for any message. In the code above, we see:

```
MaxDeliver:    5, // Max redelivery attempts
```

This configuration means that NATS will try up to five times to deliver a message and stop and remove it from the specific queue for that consumer after that.

Table 12-1. *NATS Asynchronous Communication Patterns*

Pattern/Feature	NATS Mechanism	Characteristics	Ideal Use Cases
Pub/Sub (Core NATS)	nc.Publish, nc.Subscribe	Fire-and-forget; messages not persisted; temporal coupling (subscriber must be active).	Real-time notifications, logging, and simple event broadcasting (where message loss is acceptable).
Queue Groups (Core NATS)	nc.QueueSubscribe	Load-balances messages across multiple subscribers in a group; messages are not persisted; one consumer in the group receives the message.	Horizontal scaling of stateless services, task distribution, and work queues (where message loss on consumer failure is acceptable).

(*continued*)

Table 12-1. (*continued*)

Pattern/Feature	NATS Mechanism	Characteristics	Ideal Use Cases
JetStream Streams	js.CreateStream, js.Publish	Messages are persisted, overcoming temporal coupling; configurable retention policies.	Event sourcing, persistent queues, reliable data pipelines, and command logging.
JetStream Push Consumers	js.Subscribe, js.SubscribeSync (with jetstream. ConsumerConfig)	Server pushes messages; simpler setup; can be unwieldy if consumer lags; ephemeral or durable.	Simple, high-throughput processing where backpressure is handled externally or for non-critical, one-off consumption.
JetStream Pull Consumers	cons.Fetch, cons. Consume	Application pulls messages on demand; explicit control over flow; durable state on server.	Controlled processing, batch jobs, reliable long-running tasks, and idempotent processing.

As a conclusion to our JetStream exploration, we want to offer a summary of all the characteristics and features of NATS and JetStreams applicable to the design of asynchronous services and, ultimately, distributed systems. Table 12-1 shows all the possible communication patterns and what features can be used to implement them, and it also provides an ideal use case/scenario where that specific feature is best suited. Table 12-2 instead groups all the retention and discard policies that you can use to configure NATS streams, with a description of the behavior and again a sample use case suited for that specific policy.

CHAPTER 12   ASYNCHRONOUS SYSTEMS

Table 12-2. NATS JetStream Retention and Discard Policies

Policy Type	Configuration Options	Description	Discard Behavior	Use Case Example
Retention Policies				
LimitsPolicy (Default)	MaxMsgs, MaxBytes, MaxAge, MaxMsgsPerSubject	Messages are retained based on configured limits. Whichever limit is hit first triggers deletion.	DiscardOld (default): Oldest messages removed. DiscardNew: New messages rejected.	Auditing logs (retain for X days/size), bounded event streams.
WorkQueuePolicy	(Optional: MaxMsgs, MaxBytes, MaxAge)	FIFO queue behavior. Each message is consumed once. Deleted after successful acknowledgement by any consumer.	DiscardOld/DiscardNew still apply if limits are hit.	Distributed task queues, processing pipelines where each task needs single processing.
InterestPolicy	(Optional: MaxMsgs, MaxBytes, MaxAge)	Messages are retained only if there are active consumers interested in the subject. Deleted after acknowledgement by all interested consumers.	DiscardOld/DiscardNew still apply if limits are hit.	Fan-out processing, where all downstream services must consume a message before it's gone.

Discard Policies

DiscardOld (Default)	When a stream limit is reached, the oldest messages are removed to make space for new ones.	Removes the oldest messages.	Continuous data streams where the latest data is most important, e.g., real-time sensor data.
DiscardNew	When a stream limit is reached, new messages are rejected (the publisher receives an error).	Rejects new messages.	Preventing data loss on critical, bounded streams where older data is more valuable than new data during overload.

Finally, Table 12-3 summarizes again the two consumer types provided by JetStream and how and when to use them.

Table 12-3. *NATS JetStream Consumer Types*

Consumer Type	Control Mechanism	Durability	Message Delivery	Use Cases	Advantages	Disadvantages
Push Consumer	Server pushes messages to client subscription.	Ephemeral (default) or Durable (explicitly configured).	Proactive pushing up to MaxAckPending.	Real-time dashboards, simple event listeners, one-off consumption.	Easy to set up, low latency for simple cases.	Can become unwieldy with backpressure, messages interleaving, less control over flow.
Pull Consumer	Client explicitly fetches messages on-demand.	Ephemeral (default) or Durable (explicitly configured).	On-demand fetching in batches.	Controlled processing, batch jobs, reliable long-running tasks, idempotent processing.	Full control over message flow, robust backpressure handling, scales well.	Requires explicit polling/fetching logic, potentially higher latency if not tuned well.

12.6 NATS KV Store

We enter here into one of the two extensions to NATS that set it apart from other systems and that seem at first even out of scope: NATS also includes a key-value store for you to use. This NATS key-value (KV) store is a high-performance, distributed key-value store built as an abstraction layer on top of NATS JetStream, which provides persistence functionalities. The store uses message subjects as keys, providing a familiar key-value interface while leveraging JetStream's underlying replication capabilities. This design optimizes the KV store for typical key-value workloads and incorporates advanced features such as revision tracking, which is essential for implementing optimistic concurrency control.

CHAPTER 12   ASYNCHRONOUS SYSTEMS

We will now explore the concepts exposed by the store. First of all, you would not expect the values to be just stored in a big pot without any organization, and in fact, like any store, it provides something called buckets. While you might be familiar with tables or collections in a common database management system, the NATS KV store provides buckets, which are what the name says: buckets where you can put your keys and values. You can create as many buckets as you want and decide how the content will be persisted. Internally, each bucket is mapped to a dedicated JetStream stream, configured with specific settings optimized for KV access patterns. This abstraction simplifies the user experience while benefiting from JetStream's robust infrastructure.

Now, what we store are values, and to retrieve these values, we obviously use keys. The store operates on standard key-value pairs, where keys are strings (derived from NATS subjects) and values are byte slices, which allows for flexible data storage; hence, you are not restricted by text-based values.

A handy feature of the NATS KV store is its tracking of a revision number for each entry. This revision number is used for implementing an optimistic concurrency control, preventing "last writer wins" scenarios where concurrent updates could lead to non-deterministic outcomes, in other words, race conditions. By specifying an expected revision number during an update, conflicts can be detected and managed.

In order to operate on the store, it provides an interface that provides standard operations: Put (to store or update a value), Get (to retrieve a value), Update (which allows for optimistic concurrency by requiring an expected revision), and Delete (to remove a key-value pair). It is not different from what you will find in Redis, Consul, or Vault.

Like the last tool mentioned (Consul), the KV store offers the ability to "watch" for changes to specific keys or entire buckets. This is exposed via watchers, which can allow you to receive updates on the values stored as messages, enabling services to react to configuration or state changes in real-time without the need for polling.

In summary, the NATS KV store, by abstracting JetStream's persistence, provides a highly available and eventually consistent (with watch capabilities for immediate updates) solution for shared configuration and state management in distributed services. This capability significantly reduces the reliance on external databases for simple state management. The underlying JetStream infrastructure ensures data durability and availability across the NATS cluster. The Watch feature, in particular, allows services to react to configuration or state changes in real-time, enabling dynamic updates without the overhead of polling. This positions NATS KV as a powerful alternative or complement to traditional configuration services (such as Consul, etcd, or ZooKeeper) or simple key-value databases for managing dynamic, shared state within a distributed system, especially within the integrated NATS ecosystem. It simplifies the overall architecture by consolidating messaging and state management onto a single, cohesive platform.

Let's now see how the KV store can be used via the Go SDK. We will revisit our ordering system for the restaurant we've worked through this book. We assume we want to get items from the menu, and we will store the menu inside the KV store.

First of all, we need to get access to the KV store:

```go
// Connect to the NATS server
nc, err := nats.Connect(nats.DefaultURL)
if err != nil {
    log.Fatal(err)
}
defer nc.Close()
defer nc.Drain()

// Create a JetStream Context
js, err := jetstream.New(nc)
if err != nil {
    log.Fatal(err)
}

// Access the Key-Value store
bucketName := "my_kv_store"
kv, err := js.CreateKeyValue(ctx, jetstream.KeyValueConfig{
    Bucket: bucketName,
})
if err != nil {
    log.Fatal(err)
}
```

As you will have noticed, we still need a NATS connection first, then we need to access a JetStream object, and finally we use

```
bucketName := "my_kv_store"
kv, err := js.CreateKeyValue(ctx, jetstream.KeyValueConfig{
    Bucket: bucketName,
})
```

To get the **kv** reference, which is tied to a bucket called "my_kv_store." If the bucket does not exist, it will be created; otherwise, **kv** will simply grant access to the existing bucket.

Now that we know how to access a store, let's get an item from the menu:

```
// Put a new menu item
_, err = kv.Put(ctx, "burgers.cheeseburger", []byte(`{"price": 9.99, "description": "Classic cheeseburger with fries"}`))
if err != nil {
    log.Fatal(err)
}
fmt.Println("Put: burgers.cheeseburger")

// Get the menu item's details
entry, err := kv.Get(ctx, "burgers.cheeseburger")
if err != nil {
    log.Fatal(err)
}
fmt.Printf("Get: %s @ %d -> %s\n", entry.Key(), entry.Revision(), string(entry.Value()))
```

In this code, we first put an item via the **kv.Put** function, and then we used **kv.Get** to retrieve it. The key we used to store our menu item is "burgers.cheeseburger."

Let's now say we want to update that entry:

```
// Get the current entry to find its revision
entry, err := kv.Get(ctx, "burgers.cheeseburger")
if err != nil {
    log.Fatal(err)
}
currentRevision := entry.Revision()
```

```
// Update the menu item with the correct revision
_, err = kv.Update(ctx, "burgers.cheeseburger", []byte(`{"price": 10.50,
"description": "Classic cheeseburger with fries"}`), currentRevision)
if err != nil {
    log.Fatal(err)
}
fmt.Printf("Updated burgers.cheeseburger to new price with revision %d.\n",
currentRevision)
```

We used the **kv.Update** method, which also includes the current revision of the value associated with that key. To get the current revision, we used

```
currentRevision := entry.Revision()
```

where **entry** is the value just retrieved via the **kv.Get** method.

At this point, we want to watch for any change; we will use a small script to simulate a change and capture it:

```
fmt.Println("\nWatching for menu changes...")
w, err := kv.Watch(ctx, "burgers.>") // Watch all keys in the 'burgers'
category
if err != nil {
    log.Fatal(err)
}
go func() {
    for {
        select {
        case kve := <-w.Updates():
            if kve == nil { // Watcher closed
                fmt.Println("KV Watcher closed.")
                return
            }
            op := "PUT"
            if kve.Operation() == jetstream.KeyValueDelete {
                op = "DEL"
            }
```

```
                fmt.Printf("KV Watch: %s %s @ %d -> %s\n", op, kve.Key(), kve.
                    Revision(), string(kve.Value()))
            case <-ctx.Done():
                return
            }
        }
    }()

    // Simulate a change
    kv.Put(ctx, "burgers.veggie", []byte(`{"price": 11.99, "description":
    "Veggie burger"}`))
    time.Sleep(1 * time.Second)
```

The key part of this snippet is

```
w, err := kv.Watch(ctx, "burgers.>")
```

which returns a watcher object **w**. This object provides a method called **Updates**, which returns a channel, and it is used, in the snippet, like this:

```
select {
        case kve := <-w.Updates():
```

One thing to notice is that the watcher was defined to watch on "burgers.>", which means on all the keys starting with "burgers.", in fact, as the KV store is built on top of JetStream and it uses the message subjects as keys, we have all the power of wildcards from NATS.

If you, however, need to get all the items inside a store, you do not have a method that does that; however, you can achieve that with

```
keys, err := kv.Keys(ctx)
for _, key := range keys {
        entry, err := kv.Get(ctx, key)
        if err != nil {
            log.Printf("Error getting value for key '%s': %v", key, err)
            continue
        }
        fmt.Printf("Key: %s, Value: %s\n", entry.Key(), string(entry.
        Value()))
    }
```

If you want to get all the values inside the bucket that have keys "users.>" instead, you are out of luck. You can surely achieve it, but NATS KV store is not built for being a complete database management system, so it does not yet expose a functionality to query for multiple queries inside the store. You will have, if you want to do that, to retrieve al the keys and manually select the ones you need and then call the **Get** method to retrieve each value.

12.7 NATS Object Store

NATS provides yet another store, very similar to the KV store, which is the NATS Object Store. You might wonder why this extra store has been built and why the KV store wasn't enough, as this is again based on a Key/Value paradigm. In reality, the Object Store (OS) has been specifically engineered for the storage of large binary data, commonly referred to as files or "objects." This capability is achieved through an intelligent chunking mechanism that transparently breaks down large files into smaller, manageable segments ready for efficient storage and retrieval.

The Object Store allows developers to associate large data blobs with a logical path and filename, effectively serving as a distributed file or blob storage solution within the NATS ecosystem. In this case, the keys will actually be the file names, although the concept does not change in practice. These file names, however, can be used by some convenience functions to store the retrieved object into the current filesystem automatically or to store it into the store files from their name on the filesystem, without having to manually read them and get their byte content.

The OS concepts and functionalities are pretty similar to the ones of the KV store: Similarly to the KV store, objects are organized into named "object stores" called buckets, which provide logical containers for related binary data.

A concept specific to the OS is chunking, which is OS's core innovation and essentially refers to its automatic chunking mechanism, which handles large files by dividing them into smaller data chunks, which are then stored and managed by NATS. This process is entirely transparent to the user, who interacts with the object as a single entity, regardless of its underlying fragmented storage.

The Object Store provides a comprehensive set of operations for managing objects, like the KV store for values. In order to add objects, we use the **Put** operation, which puts the content of an **io.Reader** into a new object. If the object already exists, it is overwritten. The **Get** operation is used to retrieve an object's content into an **io.Writer**.

The store also provides a **GetInfo** operation to retrieve metadata about an object without fetching its entire content, which can otherwise be a resource-intensive request. **UpdateMeta** can be used to modify an object's metadata.

One operation specific to the OS not present in the KV store is **AddLink.** This operation is used to create links to other objects or object stores. It can be used to give a second name to a file. Let's say you have a file called release-1.2 and that's the latest release; you can create a link called "latest" and make it point to the same object.

The oS also includes the **Watch** operation, like the KV store, to monitor for updates or changes within a store.

Unlike the KV store, the OS store has a **List**, which can be used to retrieve information about all objects within a store.

Another operation specific to the OS is **Status**, used to obtain the configuration and current status of an object store.

This OS makes NATS a more comprehensive platform for building event-driven microservices that also need to handle large binary assets. In fact, by integrating object storage directly into the NATS ecosystem, developers can avoid the complexity and operational overhead of introducing separate, external blob storage solutions (such as AWS S3 or MinIO) for certain use cases. This approach simplifies deployment and keeps large data assets closer to the messaging layer, which is particularly useful for event-driven architectures where large files might be part of an event payload or a broader workflow. It positions NATS as a more "all-in-one" solution for a wider range of distributed system requirements.

Let's now see how to use some of the operations provided by the store:

```go
// Connect to the NATS server
nc, err := nats.Connect(nats.DefaultURL)
if err != nil {
    log.Fatal(err)
}
defer nc.Close()
defer nc.Drain()

// Create a JetStream Context
js, err := jetstream.New(nc)
if err != nil {
    log.Fatal(err)
}
```

```
// Access the Object Store
bucketName := "menu_images"
os, err := js.CreateObjectStore(ctx, jetstream.ObjectStoreConfig{
    Bucket: bucketName,
})
if err != nil {
    log.Fatalf("Error accessing Object Store bucket: %v", err)
}
```

This code is very similar to the one used to retrieve a KV store instance object; we just use **CreateObjectStore** instead of **CreateKeyValue**.

In this example, we want to get the images for our menu items, and while menu items might be lightweight JSON strings, their images might be big, and an item might have several big images. At this point we want to add and retrieve an image, exactly like we did for the menu item:

```
// --- Put an object from a file ---
objectName := "cheeseburger.jpg"
filePath := "./cheeseburger.jpg" // The path to your file

// Open the file to get an io.Reader
file, err := os.Open(filePath)
if err != nil {
    log.Fatalf("Error opening file '%s': %v", filePath, err)
}
// This is necessary to ensure the file handle is released
defer file.Close()

// Put the content of the file directly into the object store
info, err := os.Put(ctx, jetstream.ObjectMeta{
    Name: objectName,
}, file) // The file handle is passed here
if err != nil {
    log.Fatal(err)
}
fmt.Printf("Put object '%s' (size: %d bytes, digest: %s)\n", info.Name, info.Size, info.Digest)
```

```
// --- Get the object's content ---
var buf bytes.Buffer
reader, err := os.Get(ctx, objectName)
if err != nil {
    log.Fatal(err)
}
defer reader.Close()

_, err = io.Copy(&buf, reader)
if err != nil {
    log.Fatal(err)
}
fmt.Printf("Got object '%s' with content size: %d bytes\n", objectName,
buf.Len())
```

We assumed in this snippet that a file called cheeseburger.jpg exists in the specific folder where the script will run. At this point we've also retrieved the image via the **Get** method; however, when working with the OS, you might need to get details about the object (or file) before downloading it, as it might be slow and you might not need it. We can achieve that like this:

```
// Get object info without retrieving content
info, err := os.GetInfo(ctx, "cheeseburger_image.jpg")
if err != nil {
    log.Fatal(err)
}
fmt.Printf("Object Info for 'cheeseburger_image.jpg': Size=%d, ModTime=%s,
Digest=%s\n", info.Size, info.ModTime, info.Digest)
```

We used the operation to get the image size, the modification time, and the digest. What we still need to see is how to delete and object:

```
err = os.Delete(ctx, "cheeseburger_image.jpg")
if err != nil {
    log.Fatal(err)
}
fmt.Printf("Deleted object 'cheeseburger_image.jpg'.\n")
```

CHAPTER 12   ASYNCHRONOUS SYSTEMS

```go
// And confirm it's gone
_, err = os.Get(ctx, "cheeseburger_image.jpg")
fmt.Printf("Get after delete (expected error): %v\n", err)
```

For what concerns watchers, the API works exactly like for the KV store; the interface is exactly the same.

As one feature specific to the OS is the linking, here is a small snippet of code regarding how to add links:

```go
// 1. First, you get the ObjectInfo for the target object.
// You can get this from a 'Put' or 'GetInfo' call.
targetInfo, err := os.GetInfo(ctx, "financial_report_v2.pdf")
if err != nil {
    log.Fatal(err)
}

// 2. Then, you use os.AddLink with the new link name and the ObjectInfo.
// This is the correct way to link to an object within the same bucket.
_, err = os.AddLink(ctx, "latest_report.pdf", targetInfo)
if err != nil {
    log.Fatal(err)
}
fmt.Println("Link 'latest_report.pdf' created, pointing to 'financial_report_v2.pdf'.")
```

To remove the link, you just need to remove its key, and that won't affect the original file. If you need to update the link to point to a new file, you can just use the **Update** method.

As you can see, NATS is way more than a pub/sub streaming server; it can be used for communication and for storing and sharing big chunks of data. In the current situation where AI, ETL, and data analytics are increasingly becoming the focus of many software systems, sending small messages with requests is not enough anymore. You might have pipelines and workflows requiring the handling and processing of images, audio files, or other big chunks of data. In order to do so, people generally make use of tools like Airflow, Apache Arrow, Spark, and whatever new tool comes out. These tools have specific use cases and strengths, and NATS is not there to replace them; however, in a big and complex distributed system, having something like NATS that can be used to handle several different scenarios is a good way to simplify your infrastructure and architecture.

Let's imagine you have a system that needs to upload and analyze images via an AI inference tool; your system will have to get the image, process its metadata, then analyze the image and from the details generate a report. When the user uploads the image, your system can store it inside the Object Storage and then send a message via core NATS or most likely JetStream, as persistency might be needed due to the lengthy nature of processing and analyzing an image. The next service in line will receive the message with the request to work on the image and a reference to the file name and bucket. This service will only work on the metadata and do its work and then send a message to the next service, which will instead pull the full object and perform an analysis, all ending up with some data, which will be shared again either via an object or a value in the KV store or just a JetStream message if not too big. The last service will generate a report.

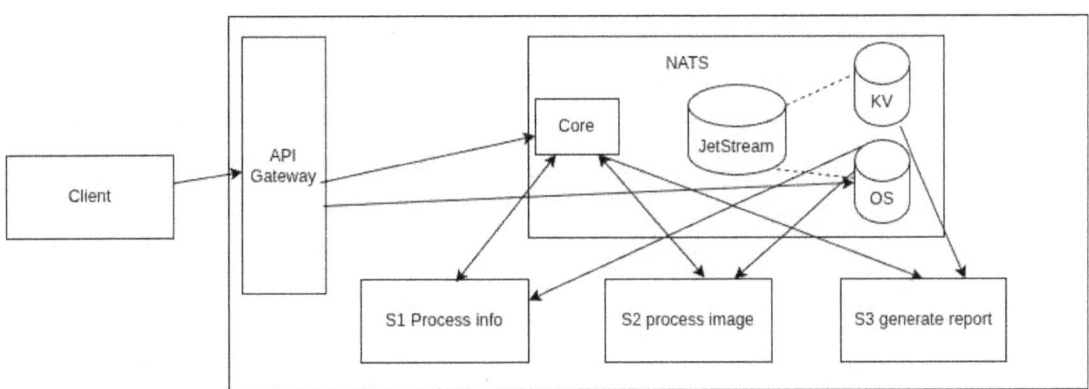

Figure 12-2. *Complex flow including Core NATS and Stores*

The full process is shown in Figure 12-2, with all the services in line and connected with NATS, specifically its underlying extensions.

We've used the expression "will send to the next service" earlier, but you need to be careful with what this means. NATS is not a queuing system, and although it is a messaging system, a publisher (by extension, a service) will not send a message to another service but will simply publish to a subject, and the subscriber will express interest in the subject. It is via a specific configuration of subjects, publishers, and consumers that we can create a flow like in Figure 12-2. It is also very important to notice that, thanks to this intrinsic characteristic of NATS, the system does not necessarily need to be linear; in fact, if services 1 and 2 in Figure 12-2 can act in parallel, they can simply both subscribe to the same subject and pull data from the same store. Of course, you will need to be careful with what is needed by service 3 in terms of completion from both services 1 and 2, as you might need a system to ensure both parallel processes have been completed before passing to step 3 (service 3).

We just remind you that all this is different from the req/rep pattern, still provided by NATS core, because in that case, there is a one-to-one relationship between requester and replier, although it is all handled by NATS behind the scenes on top of the same pub/sub pattern.

We've now concluded with all the features that NATS provides for the creation of asynchronous services, which, together with what we've seen in the previous chapter, should give you an extensive idea and all the necessary tools to build robust and resilient distributed systems.

12.8 Summary

In this chapter, we explored in depth what asynchronous distributed systems and services are how to implement them in general and specifically with NATS as the central messaging platform. We showed how to use every basic and more advanced feature of NATS to build robust, resilient, and reliable distributed systems. We started our analysis by contrasting the inherent challenges offered by synchronous systems, such as accumulating latency and cascading failures, with the robust solutions provided by NATS's asynchronous design, emphasizing its natural ability to foster decoupling, scalability, and resilience.

The chapter first dug into fully asynchronous patterns using core NATS Pub/Sub, showing its "fire-and-forget" nature and how and when to use it. This characteristic enables high-throughput, decoupled event broadcasting, particularly suitable for scenarios where message loss under a transient subscriber unavailability is acceptable.

Afterwards, we shifted the focus to what we called internally asynchronous systems, illustrating how external synchronous interfaces can be easily bridged to internal asynchronous workflows via API Gateways. This architectural approach effectively insulates the system's core processing from external latency and potential failures, enhancing overall stability.

We then introduced the Actor Model as a conceptual framework for concurrent computation, highlighting its principles of isolation, message passing, and location transparency. We did not go in-depth into the actor model but gave the instruments to start thinking in actors and provided the fundamental ideas for you to start introducing actors inside your projects. In reality, to go all in with actors, you'd need a dedicated framework or build your actor system by yourself. We've shown, however, how NATS can be leveraged to do that, especially when we then illustrated how NATS's Pub/Sub and Queue Group features can be used to implement actor-like patterns, promoting efficient load balancing and isolation across service instances.

We then moved to the next big topic, which took a significant portion of the chapter, which is NATS JetStream, exploring its persistence capabilities and its diverse array of retention and discard policies.

JetStream transforms NATS into a powerful event streaming platform, enabling reliable, fault-tolerant message delivery and replay, even when consumers are offline.

We also explained the differences between Push and Pull consumers via practical examples, emphasizing particularly the control and reliability offered by durable pull consumers for managing long-running processes.

Finally, we concluded the chapter by exploring NATS's built-in data storage abstractions: the Key-Value (KV) store and the Object Store. The KV store, built atop JetStream, provides a robust solution for managing distributed, versioned configuration and shared state, complete with optimistic concurrency control and real-time watch capabilities. The Object Store, also leveraging JetStream, extends NATS's utility to include the handling of large binary data through transparent chunking.

We've also seen how core NATS and its extension can be used for modern systems, including AI or ETL workflows.

Through numerous practical Go code examples, this chapter has equipped you with the basic and advanced knowledge required to design and implement highly scalable, resilient, and decoupled asynchronous distributed systems utilizing the comprehensive capabilities of NATS.

12.9 Questions

1) **What is the primary benefit of using asynchronous communication in distributed systems, as opposed to synchronous communication?**

    a) Reduced development complexity.

    b) Increased direct coupling between services.

CHAPTER 12   ASYNCHRONOUS SYSTEMS

   c) Enhanced scalability and resilience.

   d) Guaranteed immediate response for all operations.

2) **In core NATS Pub/Sub, what happens to a message if no subscriber is active when it is published?**

   a) The message is stored by NATS indefinitely.

   b) The message is immediately sent to a dead-letter queue.

   c) The message is lost.

   d) The publisher receives an error and retries automatically.

3) **Which NATS JetStream feature allows messages to be stored and replayed, overcoming the temporal coupling of core NATS?**

   a) Queue Groups

   b) Request/Reply

   c) Streams

   d) Wildcards

4) **When designing an internally asynchronous system, what is the primary role of an API Gateway in relation to NATS?**

   a) To directly process all long-running tasks.

   b) To translate synchronous external requests into asynchronous NATS messages.

   c) To manage database connections for internal services.

   d) To provide direct synchronous access to all microservices.

5) **Which NATS JetStream consumer type provides the application with explicit control over message flow and is recommended for reliable, batch-oriented processing?**

   a) Ephemeral Push Consumer

   b) Durable Push Consumer

   c) Ephemeral Pull Consumer

   d) Durable Pull Consumer

6) **What is the main purpose of NATS Key-Value (KV) store?**

   a) To store large binary files.

   b) To manage distributed, versioned configuration and shared state.

   c) To provide real-time chat functionality.

   d) To execute long-running computational tasks.

CHAPTER 13

Reactive Systems

13.1 Reactivity

13.1.1 Introduction

As we've seen till now, building distributed systems is not a mere act of splitting our code into components and letting them sit in different locations. If that were so, we could have stopped at the first part of this book. We've seen, of course, that communication patterns, building up topologies, form the first and most basic part of a distributed system, because when components are spread across different locations, it is crucial to let them communicate in the most efficient way possible.

Brute communication patterns are not enough, and that's why we introduced, in Part 2, all the principles behind the design of a proper (micro)service, making use of DDD and Hexagonal Architecture. In this third part of the book, we've built upon the previous two and seen how to create robust and scalable systems, focusing on how to let fully fledged microservices interact with each other in various scenarios. When systems grow, however, communication patterns raise even more issues, and although an asynchronous system might be much more optimized when thinking about resource usage, that still can lead to problems if not used properly. In this chapter, we will introduce a paradigm that has become central to modern distributed systems: Reactive Systems. This is actually an architectural style, with roots in patterns that have existed for some time, which was formally articulated in the Reactive Manifesto. This chapter provides a lightweight guiding manual for building systems that are not simply functional but that are designed to perform very well under high pressure, respond gracefully to failure, and adapt dynamically to their environment.

13.1.2 The Reactive Manifesto

Let's start, then, with talking about the Reactive Manifesto, which was initially published in 2013, and it defined a set of principles that systems should incorporate to be considered "Reactive." The reason behind the creation of this manifesto was the need to address the core challenges encountered when building software that is both interconnected and highly distributed, and that's why these specific principles were chosen. By providing a common framework to achieve a high level of robustness, flexibility, and scalability in such a complicated scenario, the manifesto aimed to give a go-to guide to solve most distributed systems pitfalls by using proper architectural design. The manifesto's four core principles are interconnected, with each one building upon the others to create a cohesive and powerful architectural philosophy. We will now see and analyze all four principles one by one.

The first principle of reactive systems is **responsiveness**, which is the key to building a system with high usability. A responsive system provides responses that are rapid and consistent and aims to establish predictable upper bounds on its performance. From a user's perspective, a system that fails to respond on time is functionally the same as a system that has failed. This principle is not just about speed but also about consistency, because a system that delivers a reliable quality of service simplifies error handling and builds user confidence, encouraging further interaction. For a system to be considered truly responsive, problems must be detectable quickly and addressed effectively, and this detectability must be intrinsic to the system.

The next principle of reactive systems is **resilience**, which means that a system must remain responsive even in the face of failure. A resilient system is designed with the assumption that failures are not a rare exception to handle in the unlucky case they happen but an inevitable occurrence that must be designed for from the beginning. Resilience is achieved through a combination of replication, containment, isolation, and delegation. Components are designed to be isolated from one another so that a failure in one part of the system is contained and does not affect the rest of the system. There should also be a recovery mechanism for when a component fails, a mechanism that must be delegated to external components, ensuring that a component's client is not burdened with handling its failures. This approach allows a system to "treat itself" and recover automatically from faults. To implement this, there could be watchers, detecting failures and redirecting workload to a different instance of the same component, with retries.

The third principle is elasticity. An elastic system maintains its responsiveness under varying workloads by dynamically increasing or decreasing the resources allocated to service incoming requests. This scalability must be achieved without introducing central bottlenecks or points of contention. Elasticity enables a system to manage its resources efficiently and operate cost-effectively on any hardware, including that provided by cloud platforms. Reactive systems can support both predictive and reactive scaling algorithms, providing the necessary live performance metrics to make informed decisions about resource allocation. Predictive algorithms, as the name suggests, try to predict a future problem before it happens, increasing the resources upfront when limits are approached. Reactive scaling algorithms instead scale resources when the issue arises. In general, both algorithms should be used to design a very resilient system.

The last principle of reactive systems, the one allowing for the other three, is that of being message-driven. Reactive Systems must use asynchronous message-passing to share information between components. This mechanism ensures loose coupling, isolation, and location transparency, which happens because asynchronous messages are non-blocking and do not require the sender and the receiver to depend on each other to keep running.

Non-blocking communication, which is a core feature of a message-driven approach, also leads to less system overhead by allowing recipients to consume resources only when they are active. It is this principle that fundamentally reverses the traditional synchronous, blocking model, enabling the other three tenets of the manifesto. It shall be clear that NATS fits perfectly in this, and the features involved are those related to asynchronous systems. In other words, not all asynchronous systems are reactive, but all reactive systems are asynchronous, and we can leverage NATS for that.

All these four properties together do not just represent a simple checklist but a deep architectural philosophy. The central idea is to build systems that actively react to their environment, whether that environment is characterized by user input, system load, or failures, rather than passively waiting for commands. This big mindset shift from assuming stability to actively planning for instability is what distinguishes a Reactive System and makes it intrinsically more robust in the real world. We summarized the four principles in Table 13-1, which also gives a schematic, quick view of why these principles matter and what enables their implementation inside a real system.

Table 13-1. The four key principles of reactive systems

Principle	Definition	Key Enablers	Why It Matters
Responsive	The system provides rapid and consistent response times to ensure a predictable quality of service.	Non-blocking I/O, event loops, low-latency communication.	Delivers a predictable and reliable user experience; problems are detected quickly.
Resilient	The system remains responsive in the face of failure by containing and delegating recovery.	Isolation, containment, replication, automatic recovery.	The system can self-heal, preventing small failures from becoming major outages.
Elastic	The system stays responsive under varying workloads by dynamically scaling resources.	Horizontal scaling, sharding, distributed load balancing, back-pressure mechanisms.	Efficient use of resources, cost-effectiveness, and the ability to handle unpredictable load spikes.
Message-Driven	Components communicate asynchronously through messages, ensuring loose coupling and isolation.	Asynchronous messaging, subjects/topics, message queues, location transparency.	Enables the other three principles; allows for independent evolution and fault isolation.

13.1.3 Reactive Systems vs. Reactive Programming

The terms "Reactive Systems" and "Reactive Programming" are often used interchangeably, but it is important to understand the distinction between them, because although they are related and similar in principle and to a higher level, they differ in the scope of where they are applied.

Reactive Programming refers to a programming paradigm for managing asynchronous and non-blocking data flow, typically within a single component or host. It focuses on the internal mechanics of a service, such as handling a continuous stream of data without blocking a thread. It is a powerful tool that enables non-blocking execution, which is crucial for maximizing the utilization of computing resources on modern multicore hardware. You would implement something like this by using Go functionalities like Go routines and channels, for example.

In contrast, Reactive Systems describe the architectural style of a full, distributed system. The focus here is on the interaction between individual parts, specifically how multiple independent services communicate and coordinate to achieve system-level properties like resilience and elasticity. A system can implement Reactive Programming within its components, but if the overall architecture is not designed for resilience and elasticity, it will not be a Reactive System. For example, consider a ride-hailing app where the driver location service continuously streams GPS updates from thousands of drivers. Using reactive programming techniques (e.g., channels or event streams), this service can handle all updates in real time without blocking threads. If another service, such as payments, fails, a non-reactive system might experience cascading failures across ride requests, live maps, or messaging. In contrast, a Reactive System is designed so that such failures do not disrupt other services because components are loosely coupled and communicate asynchronously. This distinction highlights that the architectural style of Reactive Systems is a higher-level concern that surely builds upon the techniques of Reactive Programming but does not stop there and reaches a different scope of action.

13.1.4 The Other Reactive Principles

Apart from the four core principles included in the manifesto, there is a wider set of principles that provides more detailed guidance for implementing Reactive Systems, which derive directly from the four original principles and can be seen as an extension to them or a way to see them from another angle. These principles collectively form a guide for addressing the intrinsic unreliability of distributed computing and show the fundamental shift mentioned earlier in how a system is thought from the beginning, which is: rather than assuming stability, we must actively plan for instability.

A key principle is the one of **decouple time**, which is a direct extension of the message-driven principle. It advocates for the use of asynchronous communication to avoid blocking and waiting for responses, hence increasing responsiveness and resilience. This approach is essential for preventing the cascading failures and resource exhaustion that are common in tightly coupled, synchronous systems. We've spoken about this in the previous two chapters, about synchronous and asynchronous communication, and how tight coupling consumes more resources by keeping idle connections and routines on hold.

Another important principle is the one of **decouple space**, which emphasizes that components should not be tied to a specific physical location. This is achieved through location-transparent messaging, a core feature of many modern messaging systems. This location transparency allows for flexible scaling, dynamic service discovery, and fault tolerance, as a service's physical location can change without affecting its consumers. Again, as you might understand, NATS provides both decouple space and decouple time by default. To understand what we are referring to, just think about the fact that your services only need to care about the NATS location (server address) and the subjects they handle (publish or subscribe to), but they have no idea who or where the receiver or the publisher of the messages for such topics is.

The principle of embracing failure is an architectural mindset that assumes things will go wrong and designs for resilience from the start. This involves delegating failure handling and isolating components so that a localized failure does not spread. It is an active approach to building survivable systems.

Finally, the principle of asserting autonomy states that components should be designed to be independent and self-contained, yet still capable of collaborating effectively. This is a fundamental concept for building systems composed of smaller, loosely coupled services, and it aligns directly with the principles of domain-driven design that have been explored in previous chapters. The synthesis of these principles provides a robust framework for building systems that are not only capable of withstanding the challenges of a distributed environment but also of thriving within it.

13.2 Relation with DDD

13.2.1 Introduction

Domain-Driven Design (DDD), as introduced in Part 2 of this book, provides the foundational principles for building resilient and decoupled systems. DDD, as we've seen earlier, focuses on building one component, but in reality, its principles are not tied to one small component inside a bigger system; it gives us the instruments for building any system of any type, be it monolithic or distributed. If you think about it, the ubiquitous language and the domain are concepts that can be applied to different levels of software. Surely, the domain layer in one application will be particular to that specific component, but the domain of the full application is still something that can be tracked across code bases, and it's still understandable as a whole. On top of that, DDD gives some concepts that are crucial for distributed systems and connect well with reactivity. Let's consider, for example, the concepts of bounded context and domain events; they are not just good practices for a single service; they are the ideal intellectual model for designing any large, architecturally solid Reactive System. In some way, DDD gives form and meaning to the abstract principles of reactivity.

13.2.2 Bounded Contexts as Autonomous Units

A core concept from DDD is the Bounded Context, which defines a logical boundary where a specific domain model and a Ubiquitous Language are consistent and unambiguous. This concept is a perfect match for the Reactive Principle of "Assert Autonomy," which calls for the design of independent and self-contained components. In a reactive architecture, each microservice can correspond to a single Bounded Context. This alignment ensures that the logical boundaries of the business domain directly inform the physical and operational boundaries of the deployed services.

To understand practically what a bounded context is, let's say you have an application with user management, bookings, and articles. Although these things might make sense in the final application, they are all about three different things. One or more services in your application will have to take care of bookings, but not necessarily articles. Both articles and bookings will have some relation with users, who will write or read articles and make bookings, but the relation is somewhat superficial.

Each one of these three aspects of the application will have a different bounded context, which means they will have their own vision of entities and values and events and anything else that matters. If we have a component or two managing users and accounts, they won't hold any concept of an article or booking.

On the other hand, a booking needs to be linked to a user and somehow must record the booking against the user. We will not tell you here if storing the link between a user and a booking is a matter of either of the two contexts; we leave it to you as an exercise. What we will say, though, is that although a user is a concept that will be placed inside the user management bounded context, hence implemented in their related services, the booking context, made of one or more services, will need to hold somehow the concept of a user. The result is that while a user in the bounded context of user management will have details like **name, birth date, location,** and so on, in the bounded context of bookings, the concept of user might just need an ID and possibly a name or a group

ID. This means that although the concept of a **user** is a concept that we see in multiple contexts, in each context, the same word might represent different concepts, with distinct details and properties.

By treating each Bounded Context as an autonomous unit, a system can achieve a dual form of autonomy. The first is the logical autonomy of the domain, where the business rules and language are consistent within a defined boundary. The second is the physical autonomy of the service, where each service owns its data and logic and can be developed, deployed, and scaled independently. This tight coupling between business logic and system architecture is a central tenet of DDD and is a prerequisite for building a truly resilient, elastic, and message-driven system. Without this intellectual rigor in defining service boundaries, a system risks becoming a "distributed monolith," a collection of services that are technically separate but remain tightly coupled by shared data or implicit dependencies.

13.2.3 Domain Events and the Ubiquitous Language

Reactive Systems are fundamentally message-driven, and a key challenge is defining the content and structure of these messages. This is where DDD's concept of a Domain Event provides a powerful solution. A Domain Event is a fact about something that happened in the business domain, described in the past tense (e.g., OrderPlaced, PaymentReceived). These immutable facts are the ideal form of message for a Reactive System. By publishing these events, a service broadcasts a change of state without being concerned with who consumes the message or what they do with it. This creates an elegant "publish-and-react" model that is far more loosely coupled than a traditional "cause-and-effect" model.

We did not actually see domain events in Chapter 5, "Anatomy of a Service"; it was one of the concepts we cut from the DDD discussion because we would speak about it here. We are not giving a full manual for DDD or reactive systems, but we are essentially giving you the maximum amount of concepts and practical techniques to build distributed systems the right way. We kept domain events for this chapter because, although they make sense even inside a microservice, and in fact they were formalized for any type of application, the place where they shine and their benefits are more clearly visible is in inter-service communication.

Going back to what we said earlier, the domain layer does not need to be defined for a single component or microservice but spans the whole application, and it will have several bounded contexts, which might also span over a few components, although most likely one. It is clear, then, that events might be beneficial to define what happens in an application, following the pattern facilitated by NATS. A component does something and notifies via a message with a subject that has occurred: booking-done, user-logged-in, order-shipped, etc. These events, in a reactive system, are not just mere event logs; the system can act upon them **reactively**. This is where everything comes together: messaging, DDD, and reactivity, so that we can start to see how all the pieces of the puzzle can cohesively be connected to build something highly functional, robust, and resilient.

Furthermore, DDD's Ubiquitous Language amplifies the value of this approach. This shared, unambiguous vocabulary, agreed upon by all stakeholders, ensures that the terms used in the code (e.g., Order, Customer, Product) are the same terms used to describe the business. In a reactive architecture, this language is extended to the events themselves. An OrderPlaced event means the same thing to the Billing Service, the Delivery Service, and the Notification Service, preventing miscommunication and conceptual misalignment across service boundaries. This shift from using imperative commands (MarkOrderAsReady) to publishing immutable facts (OrderMarkedAsReady) moves the entire system away from tight coupling and toward a highly decoupled, reactive paradigm.

13.2.4 Aggregates and Consistency Boundaries

In DDD, an aggregate acts as a transactional consistency boundary, encapsulating a cluster of domain objects that are treated as a single unit. In a Reactive System, this concept can be extended to use Event Sourcing, where the state of an aggregate is not mutated directly but is instead determined by a sequence of events. Each state change is appended to an event stream, creating an immutable, append-only log of all events that have occurred within that aggregate.

This approach has significant benefits for a Reactive System. First, it makes the aggregate a single source of truth, as its entire history is preserved. Second, it allows other services to consume these events directly from the stream, ensuring they are always in sync with the latest state changes. Finally, it aligns perfectly with the reality of distributed systems. The research material suggests that in these environments, a deep understanding of Eventual Consistency and Compensating Transactions is required, as a traditional distributed transaction is not feasible. NATS JetStream, with its guarantee of at-least-once delivery, reinforces this need for services to be idempotent, or capable of processing the same message multiple times without causing unintended side effects. This pragmatic approach to consistency is a critical characteristic of a well-designed Reactive System.

13.3 Relation with Hexagonality

13.3.1 Introduction

Hexagonal Architecture, or Ports and Adapters, is not an alternative to building a Reactive System but rather another basic pattern for structuring its individual services. The principles of this architecture ensure that a service's internal design is conducive to operating as an autonomous, decoupled component within a larger reactive ecosystem.

13.3.2 The Inner Core and the Reactive System

A core principle of Hexagonal Architecture is the strict separation of a service's business logic from its external dependencies. This "inner core," which contains the domain and application layers, is completely insulated from the details of the outside world, such as the type of database, web framework, or messaging system being used. This isolation is not merely an aesthetic design choice; it is a prerequisite for achieving the core tenets of a Reactive System.

The internal architectural strength provided by this separation directly enables a service to be truly resilient and elastic. Because the core logic is independent of its infrastructure, the service can be easily scaled, deployed, and tested on its own. This decoupling of concerns means that a change in an external dependency (e.g., switching from one database to another) does not necessitate a change to the core business rules. This drastically reduces the "blast radius" of changes and allows services to evolve independently, which is a hallmark of a robust, Reactive System. Without this internal decoupling, a so-called "microservice" would remain a brittle, tightly coupled unit, negating the benefits of a distributed architecture.

13.3.3 Ports and Adapters as Communication Boundaries

The conceptual model of Ports and Adapters provides the perfect vocabulary and structure for a message-driven architecture. A port is an interface that defines the contract for how the application's core logic communicates with the outside world, without specifying the implementation details. An adapter is the concrete implementation that connects a port to a real-world external system, such as a database, a web client, or a message broker.

In a Reactive System, these concepts are realized as follows:

- **Driving Ports and Adapters**: A driving port represents an incoming request to the application's core (e.g., an OrderProcessor interface). The driving adapter provides the entry point, translating an external request (e.g., a NATS message from the orders.created subject) into a format that the core application can understand. This adapter encapsulates the specific details of the message broker, so the core logic remains blissfully unaware of NATS.

- **Driven Ports and Adapters**: A driven port represents a dependency of the application's core on an external system (e.g., a NATSMessagePublisher interface). The driven adapter is the implementation that handles the concrete interaction (e.g., calling NATS.Publish). This allows the core logic to rely on an abstraction for communicating with the outside world, and an adapter can be easily swapped to change the communication mechanism without touching the core logic.

This clear separation of concerns ensures that the internal business logic of a service is completely insulated from the communication protocol. It allows for the easy adoption of a message-driven approach, directly enabling the principles of "Decouple Space" and "Decouple Time." By depending on abstractions rather than concrete implementations, the architecture allows for unparalleled flexibility, enabling services to be truly independent, testable, and adaptable within a dynamic distributed system.

13.4 Checking the Tools We Have

After seeing what reactivity is and what its principles are, we now need to see what tools we can use to do so, if we need to introduce something else, or if what we've used till now is good enough. We know that we've used NATS as our main tool for messaging and for all communication things, and so far, it's been a key enabler of what we needed. We will examine now if its core features and extensions provide a cohesive tool set that embodies the principles of the Reactive Manifesto.

We said that one of the core principles of reactive systems is to be message-driven, and it is obvious that NATS, as a message broker, fulfills this need. Messaging also has to be asynchronous, and NATS's native Publish/Subscribe (Pub/Sub), with its "fire-and-forget" mechanism that is inherently asynchronous and non-blocking, directly enables the principles of **Decouple Time** and **Decouple Space**. By processing messages asynchronously, NATS avoids coordination and waiting, while the pub/sub model ensures location transparency and loose coupling, as a sender does not need to know the location or even the existence of a receiver. This message-passing approach creates an essential boundary between components, ensuring loose coupling, isolation, and location transparency, which is a prerequisite for achieving other reactive principles. NATS also provides a sophisticated Request/Reply pattern that still maintains asynchronous boundaries; a unique "inbox" is created for the requester, allowing the responder to send a reply without any direct, synchronous connection, preserving the decoupled nature of the system.

Building on this message-driven foundation, NATS enables **Elasticity** through its use of Queue Groups. This mechanism, as we've seen in Chapter 12, "Asynchronous Systems," allows multiple service instances to subscribe to the same subject, with NATS automatically load-balancing incoming messages across them. Queue Groups are dynamic, meaning subscribers can join or leave at any time without pre-configuration, making them ideal for scaling stateless services horizontally in response to real-time demand fluctuations. This stateless and simple design, with its focus on ultra-low latency, is in stark contrast to traditional systems that often require complex partitioning and manual tuning. Here, we can add and remove resources when needed, and there is nothing to know other than NATS's server location.

For **Resilience**, NATS is extended with the JetStream persistence engine, which provides a robust, multi-layered architecture for fault tolerance and graceful recovery. This directly addresses the reactive principle to embrace failure and to "design with failure in mind," which assumes that things will go wrong and plans for them. JetStream uses a NATS-optimized RAFT distributed quorum algorithm to maintain immediate consistency across a cluster of servers, even during failures. In this algorithm, the quorum refers to the minimum number of nodes in a cluster that must be available and responsive for the cluster to operate correctly and make progress on tasks like electing a leader and committing data. To give more details, we've always spoken about NATS as a single entity, and you might have in mind a specific NATS server running, as we've run it locally for our examples. In practice, if a server storing order messages goes down, the cluster automatically elects a new leader and preserves unprocessed messages, so no data is lost and users experience no downtime. In order to avoid that, in production, we would set up a NATS cluster, made of several servers, and when one goes down, the RAFT algorithm will make sure that another instance takes the lead. The quorum, hence, ensures fault tolerance and consistency by requiring a majority of nodes to agree on decisions. The resilience of the message store can be precisely configured via a replication factor (e.g., R=3), allowing the system to tolerate the loss of one server without data loss, a clear example of planning for hardware or network uncertainty. Features like durable subscriptions and message retention are essential for gracefully handling consumer failures, as JetStream stores messages in a stream, enabling a restarted consumer to resume processing exactly from where it left off, which prevents data loss and ensures service continuity. JetStream's extensions, such as the Key-Value (KV) and Object stores, are also built on this resilient foundation.

Both stores are abstractions over a stream, and their watch functionality allows for real-time tracking of changes, which also aligns with the message-driven principle.

While NATS's core patterns and the underlying Request/Reply mechanism are asynchronous, the use of toolkits like the micro package, which is built on NATS's Request/Reply to provide synchronous RPC, can introduce a more tightly coupled, blocking paradigm that runs counter to the reactive principle of Decouple Time.

Ultimately, **Responsiveness** is the emergent characteristic of a system that is message-driven, elastic, and resilient. Thanks to NATS's ultra-low latency and high-throughput design, combined with dynamic scaling provided by Queue Groups and JetStream's fault tolerance, a user checking live order status sees updates within milliseconds, even under high traffic. In essence, NATS intrinsically pushes for these reactive patterns, as it was designed with them in mind. The synthesis of NATS's low-latency core with JetStream's persistence and replication capabilities creates a system where responsiveness is a predictable, holistic, and durable property.

CHAPTER 13   REACTIVE SYSTEMS

As you've seen, we haven't introduced new concepts or tools here, but we've proved that we indeed have all the tools we need to implement reactivity and build a reactive system. In reality, also just following DDD, you shall see that we partially cover aspects of reactivity, the same if we use hexagonality, as we've seen in the previous paragraph. By using all these techniques and NATS as a facilitator, we can then create rock-solid systems that are easy to maintain and difficult to make fail. In fact, it is ideally impossible to make a system fail that has been built with failure in mind. Parts will fail, but the user will never see it.

13.5   In-Depth Examples

To fully grasp the principles of Reactive Systems, you need to see them in action. This paragraph presents a series of examples using the restaurant system from previous chapters. The goal is to demonstrate how the tools provided by NATS and the architectural patterns of DDD and Hexagonal Architecture work in concert to create a robust and resilient system that is also reactive.

This example will move beyond simple messaging concepts to showcase how to build for responsiveness, resilience, and elasticity by designing for failure from the outset. We will use an order processing workflow as our case study, where an internal service handles new orders by publishing an immutable domain event to a persistent stream, and a pool of workers processes these events asynchronously, ensuring the system remains fast, fault-tolerant, and scalable under any load. The key is to leverage NATS JetStream's advanced capabilities, which are essential for building a production-ready system. The core of our example is an OrderService that acts as an internal, responsive handler. It demonstrates that the internal components of a reactive system communicate exclusively via asynchronous, "fire-and-forget" messages. In this model, an external API gateway (simulated here for clarity) sends a command to our OrderService. The OrderService receives this command, processes it, and then publishes an OrderCreated domain event to a stream. This design ensures that the system as a whole is responsive, as the OrderService's publishing of the event is a non-blocking operation, and no service is forced to wait for a reply. The time-consuming tasks like payment processing are delegated to separate services that consume this event, allowing for independent scaling and failure handling. To ensure a professional and type-safe approach, we will define specific structs for both the incoming command and the outgoing event.

CHAPTER 13   REACTIVE SYSTEMS

We will now break down the high-level overview of the event-driven workflow demonstrated in the code examples, illustrating the flow of a command from a client through the internal system to its final processing and state update.

1. **Command Arrival**: A command to create a new order, originating from an external source like an API gateway, is sent to the OrderService on a command subject. This is a non-blocking, asynchronous message.

2. **Order Service Receives Command**: The OrderService subscribes to the order.command subject. It receives the command and, after validation, creates a new OrderCreated domain event.

3. **Event Publishing**: The OrderService publishes the OrderCreated event as an immutable fact to the orders.created subject, which is captured by the NATS JetStream ORDERS stream. This is a non-blocking operation, which is the key to maintaining a responsive system.

4. **No Direct Response**: The OrderService's task is complete after successfully publishing the event. It does not reply directly to the sender. This completely breaks the synchronous coupling of a traditional request-reply pattern, embodying the principle of decouple time.

5. **Payment Processor Reacts**: One of the instances of the PaymentProcessor service, which is part of a NATS queue group, receives the OrderCreated event. The use of a queue group ensures that only one worker processes each event, providing elasticity and load balancing.

6. **State Update**: The PaymentProcessor updates the status of the order to "Processing" in a key-value store, which is a durable, stream-backed abstraction for managing state.

7. **Processing and Final Update**: After simulating a long-running task, such as payment processing, the worker updates the order's status to "Completed" in the key-value store. It then publishes a new OrderCompleted event to signal the end of its work.

CHAPTER 13   REACTIVE SYSTEMS

8. **Resilient Acknowledgement**: The worker sends an explicit acknowledgement to JetStream, confirming that the message was successfully processed. If the worker were to fail before sending this acknowledgement, JetStream would re-deliver the message to another available worker, ensuring resilience and at-least-once processing.

We will now see the actual code of the **order service**:

```go
// order_service/main.go
package main

import (
    "context"
    "encoding/json"
    "log"
    "os"
    "os/signal"
    "syscall"
    "time"

    "github.com/nats-io/nats.go"
    "github.com/nats-io/nats.go/jetstream"
)

// OrderRequest represents the incoming request payload from the API gateway.
type OrderRequest struct {
    UserID string  `json:"user_id"`
    Amount float64 `json:"amount"`
}

// OrderCreated is a Domain Event, an immutable fact about a business change.
type OrderCreated struct {
    ID     string  `json:"id"`
    UserID string  `json:"user_id"`
    Amount float64 `json:"amount"`
```

```go
        Created time.Time `json:"created"`
}
func main() {
    nc, err := nats.Connect(nats.DefaultURL)
    if err!= nil {
        log.Fatal(err)
    }
    defer nc.Close()

    js, err := jetstream.New(nc)
    if err!= nil {
        log.Fatal(err)
    }

    // Create or update a durable stream for our orders.
    // We configure a replication factor of 3 for high availability,
    // ensuring the stream can tolerate the loss of a single server.
    ctx, cancel := context.WithTimeout(context.Background(), 10*time.Second)
    defer cancel()

    stream, err := js.CreateOrUpdateStream(ctx, jetstream.StreamConfig{
        Name:     "ORDERS",
        Subjects: string{"orders.created", "orders.completed"},
        Replicas: 3, // Planning for failure: data is replicated.
        Storage:  jetstream.FileStorage,
    })
    if err!= nil {
        log.Fatal(err)
    }
    log.Printf("Stream '%s' configured with %d replicas.", stream.CachedInfo().Config.Name, stream.CachedInfo().Config.Replicas)

    // The OrderService acts as a consumer for an order command.
    _, err = nc.QueueSubscribe("order.command", "order-service", func(msg *nats.Msg) {
        var request OrderRequest
        if err := json.Unmarshal(msg.Data, &request); err!= nil {
```

```go
            log.Printf("Failed to unmarshal request: %v", err)
            return
        }

        // Create the domain event from the request data.
        order := OrderCreated{
            ID:      nats.NewInbox(),
            UserID:  request.UserID,
            Amount:  request.Amount,
            Created: time.Now(),
        }
        eventPayload, _ := json.Marshal(order)

        // Publish the event to the JetStream stream.
        // This is a synchronous publish to ensure the message is
            persisted.
        _, err := js.Publish(ctx, "orders.created", eventPayload)
        if err!= nil {
            log.Printf("Failed to publish order event: %v", err)
            return
        }
        log.Printf("Order %s event published.", order.ID)

        // The OrderService's job is done. It does not respond to
            the sender.
    })
    if err!= nil {
        log.Fatal(err)
    }

    log.Println("OrderService is listening for commands on 'order.command'...")

    sigChan := make(chan os.Signal, 1)
    signal.Notify(sigChan, syscall.SIGINT, syscall.SIGTERM)
    <-sigChan
}
```

Notice that we use a message for the order request, but also the order created event is represented by a struct sent as a message. In DDD, a domain event is a concept which can be implemented via a method but also a message, and in this case, a Go struct used as message content. The two structs are these:

```go
// OrderRequest represents the incoming request payload from the API
gateway.
type OrderRequest struct {
    UserID string  `json:"user_id"`
    Amount float64 `json:"amount"`
}

// OrderCreated is a Domain Event, an immutable fact about a
business change.
type OrderCreated struct {
    ID      string    `json:"id"`
    UserID  string    `json:"user_id"`
    Amount  float64   `json:"amount"`
    Created time.Time `json:"created"`
}
```

And to create the order, the code acts like this:

```go
    // Create the domain event from the request data.
    order := OrderCreated{
        ID:      nats.NewInbox(),
        UserID:  request.UserID,
        Amount:  request.Amount,
        Created: time.Now(),
    }
    eventPayload, _ := json.Marshal(order)
```

The event is then published via JetStream for persistence, as you can see from the stream definition:

```go
    stream, err := js.CreateOrUpdateStream(ctx, jetstream.StreamConfig{
        Name:     "ORDERS",
        Subjects: string{"orders.created", "orders.completed"},
```

CHAPTER 13   REACTIVE SYSTEMS

```
        Replicas:  3, // Planning for failure: data is replicated.
        Storage:   jetstream.FileStorage,
})
```

The system's **Elasticity** and **Resilience** are provided by the PaymentProcessor workers. This service demonstrates how to build a self-scaling, fault-tolerant consumer using a durable queue consumer, which is the powerful JetStream feature that combines the load-balancing of NATS queue groups with the persistence and redelivery guarantees of a durable consumer, and that we've also seen in Chapter 12, "Asynchronous Systems." When multiple instances of this PaymentProcessor are started, they automatically form a load-balanced group, with each message being delivered to only one worker. This queue group functionality is the direct implementation of elasticity, allowing the system to scale its processing power horizontally by simply adding more worker instances as the order volume increases. At the same time, the consumer is resilient because its state (its position in the stream) is tracked by NATS, and it uses explicit acknowledgements **(msg.Ack())** to confirm successful message processing. If a worker fails or crashes mid-task, the unacknowledged message is not lost; it remains in the stream and will be re-delivered to another active worker in the queue group, ensuring that no orders are ever lost or missed. This design is a direct and elegant implementation of the "Embrace Failure" principle.

A key aspect of a reactive system is how it responds to events by updating its internal state without relying on a centralized database. JetStream's Key-Value (KV) store is a natural fit for this, as it is a durable abstraction built on top of a stream that allows for simple state management. A service can "react" to an event by reading from the stream and then atomically updating a value in the KV store, providing a simple way to maintain a consistent state.

```go
// payment_processor/main.go
package main

import (
    "context"
    "encoding/json"
    "log"
    "os"
```

```go
        "os/signal"
        "syscall"
        "time"

        "github.com/nats-io/nats.go"
        "github.com/nats-io/nats.go/jetstream"
)

// OrderCreated is a Domain Event, an immutable fact about a
   business change.
type OrderCreated struct {
    ID      string    `json:"id"`
    UserID  string    `json:"user_id"`
    Amount  float64   `json:"amount"`
    Created time.Time `json:"created"`
}

// OrderCompleted is the final event of this workflow.
type OrderCompleted struct {
    ID        string    `json:"id"`
    UserID    string    `json:"user_id"`
    Amount    float64   `json:"amount"`
    Completed time.Time `json:"completed"`
}

func main() {
    nc, err := nats.Connect(nats.DefaultURL)
    if err!= nil {
        log.Fatal(err)
    }
    defer nc.Close()

    js, err := jetstream.New(nc)
    if err!= nil {
        log.Fatal(err)
    }
```

```go
    ctx, cancel := context.WithTimeout(context.Background(),
    10*time.Second)
    defer cancel()

    streamName := "ORDERS"
    consumerName := "payment-processor"
    queueGroup := "payment-workers"

    // Create a durable queue consumer which combines resilience and
        elasticity.
    consumer, err := js.CreateOrUpdateConsumer(ctx, streamName, jetstream.
    ConsumerConfig{
        Durable:       consumerName,
        DeliverGroup: queueGroup,
        AckPolicy:     jetstream.AckExplicitPolicy, // We must explicitly
        Ack to confirm processing.
        FilterSubjects:string{"orders.created"}, // Only consume
        'created' events.
    })
    if err!= nil {
        log.Fatal(err)
    }

    // Create or get the Key-Value store for maintaining state.
    kv, err := js.CreateOrUpdateKeyValue(ctx, jetstream.KeyValueConfig{
        Bucket:      "order-status-kv",
        Description: "Stores the status of each order.",
        Replicas:    3,
    })
    if err!= nil {
        log.Fatal(err)
    }
    log.Printf("Durable queue consumer '%s' is listening for events.",
    consumer.CachedInfo().Name)

    // Use a push consumer to receive messages via a callback.
    _, err = consumer.Consume(func(msg jetstream.Msg) {
        var order OrderCreated
```

```go
        if err := json.Unmarshal(msg.Data(), &order); err!= nil {
            log.Printf("Worker %s failed to unmarshal message: %v",
            os.Getenv("WORKER_ID"), err)
            msg.Nak() // Negative Acknowledge - message will be
            redelivered.
            return
        }

        // Respond to the event by updating the state in the KV store.
        log.Printf("Worker %s received order %s. Processing payment...",
        os.Getenv("WORKER_ID"), order.ID)

        // Update a key to show the order is being processed.
        kv.Put(ctx, order.ID,byte("Processing"))

        // Simulate payment processing.
        time.Sleep(3 * time.Second)

        // Upon success, update the state again.
        kv.Put(ctx, order.ID,byte("Completed"))

        // Publish a new domain event to signal completion.
        completedEvent := OrderCompleted{
            ID:        order.ID,
            UserID:    order.UserID,
            Amount:    order.Amount,
            Completed: time.Now(),
        }
        eventPayload, _ := json.Marshal(completedEvent)
        js.Publish(ctx, "orders.completed", eventPayload)

        // Acknowledge the message upon successful processing.
        // If this is not called, the message will be redelivered.
        msg.Ack()
        log.Printf("Worker %s successfully processed and acknowledged
        message for order %s. Status updated in KV store and OrderCompleted
        event published.", os.Getenv("WORKER_ID"), order.ID)
    })
```

CHAPTER 13   REACTIVE SYSTEMS

```
    if err!= nil {
        log.Fatal(err)
    }

    log.Printf("Payment processor worker %s is running. Press CTRL+C to
    stop.", os.Getenv("WORKER_ID"))

    // Keep the application running indefinitely.
    sigChan := make(chan os.Signal, 1)
    signal.Notify(sigChan, syscall.SIGINT, syscall.SIGTERM)
    <-sigChan
}
```

    Notice that in this example we've used the KV store to persist the state of the order. We could have simply passed the message with changes over different streams or via different subjects to the same stream. This would, for example, move messages where most of the content is the same, except for the "status." This is a good approach, but at times a stat might either be too big, or you want to handle the status better from your side, and the KV store is simpler. In reality, avoiding the store when possible makes a flow that is generally more difficult to grasp or to track from a human perspective, yet reduces problems when multiple consumers are modifying the same value inside the KV store.

    You shall have noted how this single, comprehensive example demonstrates the power of combining NATS's core patterns with its advanced persistence features to build a complete reactive system. The OrderService is responsive because it handles requests and publishes messages without blocking, enabling the system to scale its throughput independently of the consumer's processing speed. The PaymentProcessor workers are elastic because they automatically scale via the queue group to handle varying loads. The entire system is resilient because the JetStream stream stores events durably, and the durable consumer with explicit acknowledgements guarantees that every message is processed, even if a worker fails. Furthermore, the system demonstrates how a consumer can react to a domain event by updating a separate, persistent state store (KV store), which in itself is a reactive primitive that allows other services to watch for state changes in real-time. The ultimate response to the original order is a new event (OrderCompleted), which fully decouples the entire workflow. All of this is built on top of NATS's message-driven architecture, which establishes the necessary boundaries for isolation and loose coupling.

13.6 Summary

This chapter has provided a quick but functional overview of Reactive Systems, building upon the acquired knowledge of DDD, Hexagonal Architecture, and NATS. The discussion began with the core principles of the Reactive Manifesto, which posits that a system must be responsive, resilient, elastic, and message-driven to be genuinely effective in a distributed environment. It was emphasized that these principles are not a simple checklist but a holistic architectural philosophy that guides a system's design at every level.

The deep and synergistic relationship between Reactive Systems and established architectural patterns was also explored. Domain-Driven Design provides the ideal framework, with Bounded Contexts serving as the key enabler for autonomous, isolated services, and Domain Events providing the unambiguous, immutable messages that drive the entire system. Similarly, Hexagonal Architecture provides the internal structure for these services, ensuring that their core business logic is decoupled from external concerns. This internal strength is a necessary prerequisite for a service to operate with true autonomy and resilience in a larger Reactive System.

A significant portion of the chapter was dedicated to demonstrating how the NATS ecosystem serves as the ideal technical foundation for a reactive architecture. From the core Pub/Sub model that enables a message-driven approach to the advanced JetStream platform that provides resilience and elasticity through message persistence and back-pressure management, NATS provides the technical fabric for every reactive principle. The chapter further highlighted how NATS's extensions—the key-value store and Object Store—reduce operational complexity by consolidating messaging, state management, and large data storage into a single, cohesive platform.

The ultimate takeaway from this analysis is the importance of a fundamental shift in mindset. A Reactive System is not a synchronous, command-and-control hierarchy. It is an asynchronous, event-driven ecosystem of autonomous services that react to their environment and to each other's actions. This paradigm shift, when supported by a robust platform like NATS and guided by principles like DDD and Hexagonal Architecture, is what enables the creation of truly scalable, resilient, and adaptive systems that can meet the unpredictable demands of the modern world.

This chapter also essentially concludes this book, as we've given all the information and examples, starting from the low-level communication patterns and topologies to more high-level patterns, passing through DDD and hexagonal architecture, then analyzing how it all comes together when building a full system.

13.7 Questions

1. **What is the primary purpose of asynchronous message-passing in a Reactive System?**

   a) To ensure all services are tightly coupled and always available.

   b) To enable synchronous, real-time communication between components.

   c) To establish a boundary that ensures loose coupling, isolation, and location transparency.

   d) To perform distributed transactions across multiple services.

2. **How does a Bounded Context from DDD contribute to the Assert Autonomy principle of Reactive Systems?**

   a) It centralizes all business logic into a single, monolithic service.

   b) It defines a logical boundary for a service, allowing it to own its data and logic independently.

   c) It forces all services to share a single, unified domain model.

   d) It requires all services to communicate via direct, synchronous API calls.

3. **Which NATS feature is most crucial for ensuring a system remains Resilient by handling consumer outages?**

   a) Core NATS's "fire-and-forget" Pub/Sub model.

   b) The JetStream persistence engine.

   c) The ephemeral nature of NATS messages.

   d) The Request/Reply pattern.

4. **In the context of the in-depth example, why does the Kitchen Service use a pull consumer instead of a push consumer?**

   a) To simplify its codebase, as pull consumers are easier to implement.

   b) To force the publishing service to wait for a response before continuing.

   c) To manage back-pressure and consume messages at its own pace, preventing overload.

   d) To enable the at-most-once delivery guarantee.

5. **What is the main benefit of using the NATS KV store's watch functionality in a Reactive System?**

   a) It provides a simple polling mechanism to check for configuration changes.

   b) It allows services to react to changes in state or configuration in real-time without polling.

   c) It enables distributed transactions across multiple services.

   d) It is primarily used for storing large binary files.

CHAPTER 14

A Working System

14.1 Introduction

The journey we've made through the architecture of distributed systems has progressed from the basic principles of communication to the intricate details of internal service design using Domain-Driven Design (DDD) and Hexagonal Architecture, and finally, how to connect everything to make asynchronous reactive systems. This chapter now guides you through the transformation of the original restaurant system from Chapter 4, "Working System," into a resilient **Reactive System**, as defined by the principles of the Reactive Manifesto.

The initial "working system" introduced in Chapter 4, "Working System," while effective for illustrating basic Publish/Subscribe and Request/Reply messaging, was intentionally designed with a "very minimalistic" internal structure. This simplicity served to highlight the practical challenges inherent in rudimentary implementations, such as hardcoded data and tightly coupled, fire-and-forget communication, thereby underscoring the necessity for a more sophisticated approach. In contrast, Chapter 8, "Sample Service," detailed a significant re-architecture of the Order Processor, thoroughly applying DDD and Hexagonal Architecture to enhance its maintainability and alignment with core business objectives. This progression—from a simple functional system to a rigorously designed individual service—lays the groundwork for the system-level design and orchestration of multiple such services.

This chapter directly addresses the concept introduced in Chapter 9, "A Whole System vs. a Bunch of Services." The primary objective is to transform the foundational restaurant system into a truly **responsive and resilient** application by re-implementing the core workflow from Chapter 4, "Working System," using a modern, reactive architecture. This involves a seamless integration of advanced architectural patterns and technologies, including:

- **Reactive Principles:** Applying the principles of the Reactive Manifesto, where the system is primarily message-driven and designed to embrace failure.

- **Extended NATS Features:** Leveraging the full power of the NATS ecosystem, including NATS Jetstream for reliable event streaming, the NATS Key-Value (KV) store for dynamic configuration and menu data, and the NATS Object Store for large binary assets like menu item images.

- **Cloud-Native Orchestration:** Using Kubernetes (specifically Minikube) for container orchestration and automating the development and deployment lifecycle with GitHub Actions.

The final architecture presented here is a complete blueprint that embodies the principles of a reactive ecosystem. The flow mirrors that of Chapter 4, "Working System," but each interaction is now handled by a purpose-built service that is independently scalable, fault-tolerant, and designed for actual production readiness.

We will not get into the details of authorization or tests in here, as we assume tests and their importance are already clear to you, and we consider the system not to be open to the web but only to in-shop devices.

We present here the list of services and components for the system and an example of a single service folder structure. If you were to pack the whole system's code and infrastructure code in a project folder in your system, it will be like:

api-gateway: The single entry point for all client requests.

delivery-service: Manages the delivery of completed orders.

kitchen-service: Handles the preparation of food orders.

menu-service: Stores and retrieves menu data and images.

notification-service: Sends real-time updates to in-shop devices.

order-processor: The core service that processes and orchestrates the order workflow.

infrastructure: Contains shared configuration and deployment files for foundational components like NATS and the PostgreSQL database.

Each service, such as the order processor, follows a consistent structure to ensure maintainability and scalability. This pattern, which is based on the **Go cmd pattern** and **Domain-Driven Design (DDD)**, isolates the service's core logic from its external dependencies.

Example order-processor folder structure:

```
order-processor
├── .github/workflows
├── cmd
│   └── main.go
├── internal
│   ├── application
│   │   └── order_processor_service.go
│   ├── domain
│   │   ├── order.go
│   │   └── order_repository.go
│   └── infrastructure
│       ├── nats
│       └── persistence
│           └── postgres_order_repository.go
├── dockerfile
└── kubernetes
```

- The **cmd** directory contains the entry point for the service's executable (main.go). This keeps the build command and startup logic simple and consistent across all services.

- The **internal** directory encapsulates the service's entire codebase, making it clear that this code is not meant to be imported by other services. It is further divided into three key layers, reflecting the **Hexagonal Architecture**:

    - **Application**: Contains the use cases and application services that orchestrate the domain logic.

    - **Domain**: The core of the service, containing the business entities (order.go) and business rules (order_repository.go interface). This layer is completely independent of technology choices.

- **Infrastructure**: This layer contains the implementations for external systems. It connects the core business logic to things like the NATS messaging system or the PostgreSQL database.
- The **dockerfile** and **kubernetes** directories contain the necessary files for containerization and orchestration, respectively, enabling automated, independent deployments via the **.github/workflows** CI/CD pipelines.

Each service follows the **cmd** pattern, where a folder called cmd includes the main package and script, and the rest is organized following a business-aware DDD structure.

We also have Dockerfiles, Kubernetes YAML files, and GitHub Actions folders. Bear in mind that we will not give the whole code here, as it would be too long, but we will focus on the most important parts, referring you to the GitHub repository for the complete system.

14.2 Minikube Skeleton

We will refresh here what Minikube is and why we suggest you use it here. In essence, for local development and testing, Minikube provides a lightweight yet representative Kubernetes cluster, which is extremely useful for deploying and interacting with our distributed restaurant system in a way that mimics what you would have on a cloud provider or Kubernetes managed service.

Minikube allows developers to run a single-node Kubernetes cluster locally, simulating a production environment on a personal machine. This is useful for testing deployments and understanding Kubernetes concepts without the overhead of a full-scale cloud setup. It provides the necessary environment to deploy and interact with our distributed restaurant system components.

Helm charts, a standard packaging tool for Kubernetes, simplify the deployment and management of complex applications, allowing for versioned and repeatable deployments. We will use Helm to deploy our NATS messaging system with the necessary configurations for a production-ready setup. You can create a Helm chart for your application, here the restaurant ordering system, and this can be installed on any Kubernetes distribution, including, obviously, Minikube.

Before deploying our services, we'll set up a dedicated namespace for our restaurant system to ensure logical isolation within the Kubernetes cluster.

We provide you with a YAML file that you can use to create a namespace in a Kubernetes installation, including Minikube. Let's call the file **namespace.yaml**

```yaml
apiVersion: v1
kind: Namespace
metadata:
  name: restaurant-system
```

We assume that you have Minikube installed in your environment, so to apply the previous YAML file, run: **kubectl apply -f namespace.yaml**

This command creates a namespace that will be used to add all your services.

14.3 GitHub Actions

In order to have your services running on Kubernetes, you need to have them in a format that Kubernetes supports. We will use Docker images built via GitHub actions as an example. You could use other systems, like manually creating the images via Docker, or you could use CircleCI or any other tool. For simplicity, as GitHub is still the most used repository management system, and it offers its own CI tool, we will use that. Still, you could use anything else you wish.

Inside your repositories, in this case, each service, including the API Gateway, you can create a folder called **.github** and inside that one more called **workflows**. This is where you will put all your GitHub action files, which in this case will be just one per service repository. We assume that you will call this file **docker_image.yml**, but you can call it as you please.

We provide you with a simple YAML file that you can use for any repository, although you should customize it for your different needs:

```yaml
name: Docker Image CI
on:
  push:
    branches: [ "*" ]
    # Publish semver tags as releases.
    tags: [ '*.*.*' ]
```

CHAPTER 14　A WORKING SYSTEM

```
env:
  # Use docker.io for Docker Hub if empty
  REGISTRY: ghcr.io
  # github.repository as <account>/<repo>
  IMAGE_NAME: ${{ github.repository }}

jobs:

  build:

    runs-on: ubuntu-latest
    permissions:
      contents: read
      packages: write

    steps:
    - name: Checkout repository
      uses: actions/checkout@v3

    - name: Log in to the Container registry
      uses: docker/login-action@v2
      with:
        registry: ${{ env.REGISTRY }}
        username: ${{ github.actor }}
        password: ${{ secrets.GITHUB_TOKEN }}

    - name: Extract metadata (tags, labels) for Docker
      id: meta
      uses: docker/metadata-action@v4.1.1
      with:
        images: ${{ env.REGISTRY }}/${{ env.IMAGE_NAME }}:${GITHUB_REF##*/}

    - name: Build and Push image
      run: |
        echo ghcr.io/${{ github.repository_owner }}
        echo $IMAGE_NAME
        echo ${GITHUB_REF##*/}
        IMAGE_ID=ghcr.io/$IMAGE_NAME
```

```
        # Change all uppercase to lowercase
        IMAGE_ID=$(echo $IMAGE_ID | tr '[A-Z]' '[a-z]')
        # Strip git ref prefix from version
        VERSION=$(echo "${{ github.ref }}" | sed -e 's,.*/\(.*\),\1,')
        # Strip "v" prefix from tag name
        [[ "${{ github.ref }}" == "refs/tags/"* ]] && VERSION=$(echo
        $VERSION | sed -e 's/^v//')
        # Use Docker `latest` tag convention
        # [ "$VERSION" == "master" ] && VERSION=latest
        echo IMAGE_ID=$IMAGE_ID
        echo VERSION=$VERSION
        echo NAME=$IMAGE_NAME
        docker build . -f infra/docker/Dockerfile --tag $IMAGE_ID:$VERSION
        docker push $IMAGE_ID:$VERSION
```

This file is pretty general, it uses variables like:
```
registry: ${{ env.REGISTRY }}
 username: ${{ github.actor }}
 password: ${{ secrets.GITHUB_TOKEN }}
```
From GitHub, and creates image IDs like:
```
IMAGE_NAME: ${{ github.repository }}
IMAGE_ID=$(echo $IMAGE_ID | tr '[A-Z]' '[a-z]')
```
Inferring the name from the repository name. If you have a repository with a Docker file following this path structure:
```
docker build . -f infra/docker/Dockerfile --tag $IMAGE_ID:$VERSION
```

The command above will make sure that the image is created and is the command that you can also run locally to build your images manually.

14.4 Dockerfile

We have seen how to create a GitHub Action, but not how to create the Dockerfile used inside the action or any other CI/CD tool. We provide here a basic template for a service written in Go:

```
FROM golang:1.21.6-bookworm AS build
WORKDIR /app
```

```
RUN ls
COPY go.mod ./
COPY go.sum ./
RUN go mod download

COPY . ./
RUN pwd
RUN ls

RUN go build -o order-processor ./cmd/main.go
##
## Deploy
##
FROM gcr.io/distroless/base-debian12

WORKDIR /

COPY --from=build /app/order-processor /order-processor
USER nonroot:nonroot

ENTRYPOINT ["/order-processor"]
```

You can change the lines where you see **order-processor** to whatever you need, using the name of your service. We stress again that this is a basic template, and you should customize it and improve it for your needs; however, if you have a standard Go repository, this should work.

14.5 NATS Deployment and Initialization

At this point, you must have Minikube running with our namespace created. We will deploy now a NATS SuperCluster with Jetstream enabled using its official Helm chart, which, as we said, is the official package manager for Kubernetes. This **nats-values.yaml** file configures a resilient, production-grade NATS cluster.

```
nats:
  jetstream:
    enabled: true
  cluster:
```

```yaml
  enabled: true
  replicas: 3 # A replica count of 3 is recommended for production to tolerate a single server loss
  affinity:
    podAntiAffinity:
      requiredDuringSchedulingIgnoredDuringExecution:
        - labelSelector:
          matchExpressions:
        - key: app.kubernetes.io/name
          operator: In
          values:
        - nats
          topologyKey: "kubernetes.io/hostname" # Ensures pods are spread across nodes
podDisruptionBudget:
  enabled: true
persistence:
  enabled: true
  size: 50Gi # Allocate sufficient disk space for Jetstream file storage
  storageClassName: "standard" # Or your preferred high-performance storage class
container:
  resources:
    requests:
      cpu: 100m
      memory: 256Mi
    limits:
      cpu: 500m
      memory: 512Mi
```

To deploy NATS using Helm, go to your command line and run:

```
$ helm repo add nats https://nats-io.github.io/k8s/helm/charts/
$ helm upgrade --install nats nats/nats -f nats-values.yaml --namespace restaurant-system
```

CHAPTER 14   A WORKING SYSTEM

At this point, you should have the NATS supercluster installed. In order to check that, you can use:

```
helm list -n restaurant-system
```

And you should see something like:

NAME	NAMESPACE	REVISION	UPDATED	STATUS	CHART	APP VERSION
nats	myns	1	...	deployed	nats-x.x.x	x.x.x

which means it is installed, and then you can check for the pods with:

```
kubectl get pods -n restaurant-system
```

This command searches for all pods in the specified namespace, and you should see three NATS instances.

14.6 Menu Service: NATS KV and Object Store for Menu Data

We will start our journey through this ordering system by looking at how the MenuService demonstrates how to use the NATS KV Store to manage dynamic, real-time configuration data and the NATS Object Store to handle menu item images. We will see later the full flow of the application, which essentially is what you've seen in Chapter 13, "Reactive Systems," already. For now, we focus on this specific service. It receives messages from the **Order Processor** to validate an order against the menu. After validation, it either republishes the order message to a different subject or sends a status update if the validation fails. In order to dynamically change the menu, it will also accept some synchronous messages to add, modify, and delete menu items. For the requested Req/Rep functionality, it uses the micro package to expose a simple API for manual menu updates. It also includes a push consumer that validates orders coming from the **Order Processor**. This service is a perfect example of a hybrid design that integrates both synchronous and asynchronous communication patterns.

We will start by showing a sample **cmd/main.go** file, but we will not repeat this for the other services, unless necessary:

```
package main
```

```go
import (
    "context"
    "log"
    "os"
    "strings"
    "time"

    "github.com/nats-io/nats.go"
    "github.com/nats-io/nats.go/jetstream"
    natsadapter "your-repo/menu-service/internal/infrastructure/nats_adapter"
    natsinfra "your-repo/menu-service/internal/infrastructure/nats"
    "your-repo/menu-service/internal/application"
    "your-repo/menu-service/internal/infrastructure/persistence"
)

func main() {
    // Infrastructure: Connect to NATS.
    url := os.Getenv("NATS_URL")
    if url == "" {
        url = nats.DefaultURL
    } else {
        url = strings.TrimSpace(url)
    }

    nc, err := nats.Connect(url)
    if err!= nil {
        log.Fatalf("Failed to connect to NATS: %v", err)
    }
    defer nc.Close()
    defer nc.Drain()

    js, err := jetstream.New(nc)
    if err!= nil {
        log.Fatalf("Failed to create JetStream context: %v", err)
    }

    ctx, cancel := context.WithTimeout(context.Background(), 5*time.Second)
    defer cancel()
```

```
    // Infrastructure Persistence: Initialize the NATS KV repository.
    menuRepo, err := persistence.NewNatsKVRepository(ctx, js)
    if err!= nil {
        log.Fatalf("Failed to initialize menu repository: %v", err)
    }

    // Infrastructure NATS Client: Initialize a client for outbound
       communication.
    natsClient := natsinfra.NewNatsClient(nc, js)

    // Application Layer: Create the service, injecting its dependencies.
    menuService := application.NewMenuService(menuRepo, natsClient)

    // Messaging Adapter Layer: Create the new NATS Adapter and inject the
       application service.
    natsAdapter := natsadapter.NewNatsAdapter(nc, js, menuService)

    // Start the NATS microservice handlers and JetStream consumer via the
       adapter.
    natsAdapter.StartMicroservice()

    if err := natsAdapter.StartOrderValidationConsumer(ctx); err!= nil {
        log.Fatalf("Failed to start order validation consumer: %v", err)
    }

    log.Printf("Menu Service is ready to serve and validate orders.")
    select {}
}
```

This service uses the NATS KV store for menu items infrastructure/NATS, as we can see from:

```
// Infrastructure Persistence: Initialise the NATS KV repository for the
   menu domain.
    menuRepo, err := persistence.NewNatsKVRepository(ctx, js)
    if err!= nil {
        log.Fatalf("Failed to initialize menu repository: %v", err)
    }
```

The **menuRepo** is a variable that holds an instance of the **NATSKVRepository** that lies in the persistence layer of the project's repo.

This file acts as the program's entry point. It sets up all the necessary structs and prevents the program from exiting by using a **select{}** statement. We've used this pattern in several places in this book, often alongside infinite **for{}** loops.

Following DDD, we define the menu repository in the file **menu-service/internal/domain/menu_repository.go**

```go
package domain

import (
    "context"
    "fmt"
)

// MenuRepository is the repository interface.
// It defines the contract for our persistence layer.
// This is the "port" in Hexagonal Architecture.
type MenuRepository interface {
    Save(ctx context.Context, item *MenuItem) error
    Get(ctx context.Context, itemName string) (*MenuItem, error)
    Delete(ctx context.Context, itemName string) error
    GetAll(ctx context.Context) (*MenuItem, error)
}
```

And this should be implemented inside the infrastructure layer:

```go
package persistence

import (
    "context"
    "encoding/json"
    "fmt"
    "log"
    "time"

    "github.com/nats-io/nats.go/jetstream"
    "your-repo/menu-service/internal/domain"
)
```

CHAPTER 14   A WORKING SYSTEM

```go
// NatsKVRepository is the persistence adapter for the Menu domain.
// It implements the domain.MenuRepository interface. This is the "adapter"
// in Hexagonal Architecture.
type NatsKVRepository struct {
    kv jetstream.KeyValue
}

// NewNatsKVRepository initializes and returns a new repository.
func NewNatsKVRepository(ctx context.Context, js jetstream.JetStream)
(*NatsKVRepository, error) {
    kv, err := js.CreateOrUpdateKeyValue(ctx, jetstream.KeyValueConfig{
        Bucket: "menu_items",
        Description: "Current menu items and prices",
        Replicas: 3,
    })
    if err!= nil {
        return nil, fmt.Errorf("error creating KV store: %w", err)
    }

    // Seed the data if the bucket is new.
    if err := seedData(ctx, kv); err!= nil {
        log.Printf("Failed to seed menu data: %v", err)
    }

    return &NatsKVRepository{kv: kv}, nil
}

// seedData seeds the KV store with an initial menu item.
func seedData(ctx context.Context, kv jetstream.KeyValue) error {
    // Check if the "pizza" item already exists to avoid duplication.
    if _, err := kv.Get(ctx, "menu.pizza"); err == nil {
        return nil // Data is already seeded
    }
    pizzaItem := &domain.MenuItem{
        Name: "Pizza",
        Price: 15.99,
        Image: "pizza.jpg",
```

```go
    }
    val, err := pizzaItem.ToJSON()
    if err!= nil {
        return err
    }

    _, err = kv.Put(ctx, "menu.pizza", val)
    if err!= nil {
        return fmt.Errorf("failed to put initial menu item: %w", err)
    }
    log.Println("KV store is ready and seeded with initial menu item.")
    return nil
}

// Save implements the domain.MenuRepository interface.
func (r *NatsKVRepository) Save(ctx context.Context, item *domain.MenuItem) error {
    key := fmt.Sprintf("menu.%s", item.Name)
    val, err := item.ToJSON()
    if err!= nil {
        return fmt.Errorf("failed to marshal item: %w", err)
    }
    _, err = r.kv.Put(ctx, key, val)
    return err
}

// Get implements the domain.MenuRepository interface.
func (r *NatsKVRepository) Get(ctx context.Context, itemName string) (*domain.MenuItem, error) {
    key := fmt.Sprintf("menu.%s", itemName)
    entry, err := r.kv.Get(ctx, key)
    if err!= nil {
        return nil, fmt.Errorf("failed to get item '%s': %w",
            itemName, err)
    }
```

```go
        var item domain.MenuItem
        if err := json.Unmarshal(entry.Value(), &item); err!= nil {
            return nil, fmt.Errorf("failed to unmarshal item: %w", err)
        }
        return &item, nil
    }

    // Delete implements the domain.MenuRepository interface.
    func (r *NatsKVRepository) Delete(ctx context.Context, itemName string) error {
        key := fmt.Sprintf("menu.%s", itemName)
        return r.kv.Delete(ctx, key)
    }

    // GetAll implements the domain.MenuRepository interface.
    func (r *NatsKVRepository) GetAll(ctx context.Context) (*domain.MenuItem, error) {
        keys, err := r.kv.Keys(ctx)
        if err!= nil {
            return nil, fmt.Errorf("failed to retrieve menu keys: %w", err)
        }
        var items*domain.MenuItem
        for _, key := range keys {
            entry, err := r.kv.Get(ctx, key)
            if err!= nil {
            log.Printf("Error getting value for key '%s': %v", key, err)
            continue
            }
            var item domain.MenuItem
            if err := json.Unmarshal(entry.Value(), &item); err!= nil {
                log.Printf("Error unmarshalling value for key '%s': %v", key, err)
                continue
            }
            items = append(items, &item)
        }
        return items, nil
    }
```

CHAPTER 14   A WORKING SYSTEM

This repository offers an agnostic way to interact with the data, independent of the way the messages are received, and that can be substituted at any time with a different database by simply changing its implementation.

The part of the service handling the messages from the Order Processor is

```
// ValidateOrder handles the business logic for validating an order.
func (s *MenuService) ValidateOrder(ctx context.Context, req *domain.
OrderRequest) error {
    log.Printf("Menu Service: Validating order %s.", req.OrderID)

    // Use the domain repository to check each item's existence.
    for _, item := range req.Items {
        if _, err := s.menuRepo.Get(ctx, item.ItemName); err!= nil {
            log.Printf("Menu Service: Item '%s' not found for order %s.
            Publishing failure.", item.ItemName, req.OrderID)
            statusUpdate := domain.OrderStatusUpdateDTO{OrderID: req.
            OrderID, Status: "Rejected", Reason: "Item not on menu"}
            s.natsClient.PublishStatusUpdate(ctx, statusUpdate)
            return err
        }
    }
    log.Printf("Menu Service: All items for order %s are valid. Forwarding
    to Kitchen.", req.OrderID)

    // Publish the validated order to the next stage.
    s.natsClient.PublishValidatedOrder(ctx, req)
    return nil
}
```

In order to interact with the menu, an adapter is used, implemented in the infra layer, which will have these entry points:

```
root := srv.AddGroup("menu")
root.AddEndpoint("add_item", micro.HandlerFunc(a.handleAddItem))
root.AddEndpoint("remove_item", micro.HandlerFunc(a.handleRemoveItem))
root.AddEndpoint("get_items", micro.HandlerFunc(a.handleGetItems))
```

CHAPTER 14   A WORKING SYSTEM

The entry points are defined using the micro package of NATS. We will not give the full application service here. The microservice repository will also have other files in the domain defining the MenuItem struct, the NATS client, etc.

You can look back at the Dockerfile provided earlier and the GitHub action file. We will now, however, give a YAML file for the deployment of the Menu Service microservice:

```yaml
apiVersion: apps/v1
kind: Deployment
metadata:
  name: menu-service
  namespace: restaurant-system
spec:
  replicas: 1
  selector:
    matchLabels:
      app: menu-service
  template:
    metadata:
      labels:
        app: menu-service
    spec:
      containers:
        - name: menu-service-app
          image: ghcr.io/youraccount/menu-service:main
          imagePullPolicy: IfNotPresent
          env:
        - name: NATS_URL
          value: "nats://nats.restaurant-system.svc.cluster.local:4222"
```

This YAML file requires DockerFile to be present that the GitHub action has been run, and the image is available as **ghcr.io/youraccount/menu-service** with branch main. In the YAML file, **youraccount** is obviously your GitHub account or your organization account.

```
// handleOrderValidation is the application-level handler for validating
an order.
```

CHAPTER 14 A WORKING SYSTEM

```go
func (s *MenuService) handleOrderValidation(m jetstream.Msg) {
    var req domain.OrderRequest
    if err := json.Unmarshal(m.Data(), &req); err!= nil {
        log.Printf("Menu Service: Error unmarshalling order request: %v", err)
        m.Nak()
        return
    }

    log.Printf("Menu Service: Validating order %s.", req.OrderID)

    // Use the domain repository to check each item's existence.
    for _, item := range req.Items {
        if _, err := s.menuRepo.Get(m.Context(), item.ItemName); err!= nil {
            log.Printf("Menu Service: Item '%s' not found for order %s. Publishing failure.", item.ItemName, req.OrderID)
            statusUpdate := domain.OrderStatusUpdateDTO{OrderID: req.OrderID, Status: "Rejected", Reason: "Item not on menu"}
            s.natsClient.PublishStatusUpdate(m.Context(), statusUpdate)
            m.Ack()
            return
        }
    }
    log.Printf("Menu Service: All items for order %s are valid. Forwarding to Kitchen.", req.OrderID)

    // Publish the validated order to the next stage.
    s.natsClient.PublishValidatedOrder(m.Context(), m.Data())
    m.Ack()
}
```

With this, we conclude our exploration of the Menu Service.

CHAPTER 14   A WORKING SYSTEM

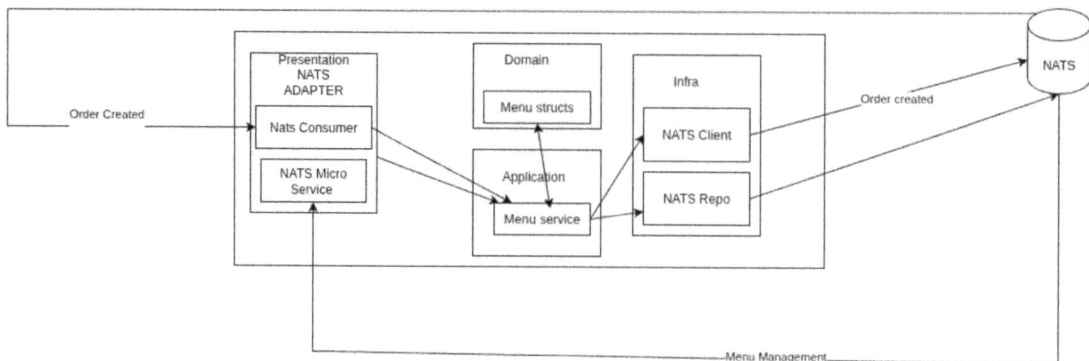

Figure 14-1. Menu service

In order to have a full view of the service, Figure 14-1 provides a diagram of the components of the service, with the adapters clearly visible and the reactive nature of the service easy to notice.

14.7 Order Processor

The Order Processor service is the core of the system's Order Management Bounded Context. It receives new order requests asynchronously, stores them in its own PostgreSQL database, and then publishes an asynchronous validation request to the Menu Service. It also receives updates on the status of an order and stores them. This service is contacted by the API Gateway for new orders, then by the menu service in case something goes wrong, then by the kitchen service, and finally by the delivery service. In reality, these other services know nothing about the order processor but simply publish messages to subjects the order processor subscribed to. This service's code now demonstrates a command chain model.

We start with the domain, which is much more complex than that of the Menu Service:

```
package domain

import (
        "errors"
)
// OrderItem represents a single item in an order.
```

```go
type OrderItem struct {
        ItemName string `json:"item_name"`
        Quantity int    `json:"quantity"`
}

// Order is the aggregate root that contains the business state and rules.
// It is completely free of infrastructure concerns.
type Order struct {
        ID     string
        Items  OrderItem
        Status string
}

// OrderRequest represents the incoming request payload from the API Gateway.
type OrderRequest struct {
        Items OrderItem `json:"items"`
}

// OrderStatusUpdateDTO represents the data structure for an order status update.
type OrderStatusUpdateDTO struct {
        OrderID string `json:"order_id"`
        Status  string `json:"status"`
}

// ValidationRequest is a DTO for publishing validation requests.
type ValidationRequest struct {
        OrderID string    `json:"order_id"`
        Items   OrderItem `json:"items"`
}

// NewOrder is a factory function to create a new Order aggregate.
func NewOrder(id string, itemsOrderItem) (*Order, error) {
        if id == "" |

| items == nil |
| len(items) == 0 {
```

```go
            return nil, errors.New("invalid order data")
        }
        return &Order{
                ID:     id,
                Items:  items,
                Status: "Pending",
        }, nil
}
```

The code above represents all the structs related to an order that have business logic relevance, plus a method to create a new order. We also need to interact with our data source, so we define a repository in the domain too:

```go
package domain

// OrderRepository is the repository interface.
// It defines the contract for our persistence layer.
// This is the "port" in Hexagonal Architecture.
type OrderRepository interface {
    Save(order *Order) error
    FindByID(id string) (*Order, error)
    }
```

The order processor also needs an application service that handles incoming order requests and incoming order status updates. This will use different adapters: the NATS publisher and the NATS consumer. In terms of Hexagonal Architecture, the publisher and the consumer are adapters, and the consumer belongs to the presentation layer and is implemented in the same layer, while the publisher interface, the port, is defined in the application layer and implemented in the infrastructure.

The presentation code is

```go
package presentation

import (
    "log"
    "your-repo/order-processor/internal/application"
    "github.com/nats-io/nats.go"
)
```

```go
// MessageConsumer is a driving port that defines the contract for a
message consumer.
// It is technology-agnostic and allows the application to be driven by any
messaging system.
type MessageConsumer interface {
    StartListening(service *application.OrderProcessorService) error
}

// NatsConsumer is the driving adapter for NATS.
// It implements the presentation.MessageConsumer port.
type NatsConsumer struct {
    nc *nats.Conn
}

func NewNatsConsumer(nc *nats.Conn) *NatsConsumer {
    return &NatsConsumer{
        nc: nc,
    }
}

// StartListening sets up the NATS subscriptions to drive the application.
func (c *NatsConsumer) StartListening(service *application.
OrderProcessorService) error {
    // Subscribe to a Queue Group for new orders
    _, err := c.nc.QueueSubscribe("orders.new", "order-processor-group",
    service.HandleNewOrder)
    if err!= nil {
        return err
    }

    // Subscribe to all status update messages from the other services.
    _, err = c.nc.QueueSubscribe("orders.status.>", "order-status-updates-
    group", service.HandleStatusUpdate)
    if err!= nil {
        return err
    }
    return nil
}
```

We will not digress further with the code, but we present a diagram in Figure 14-2.

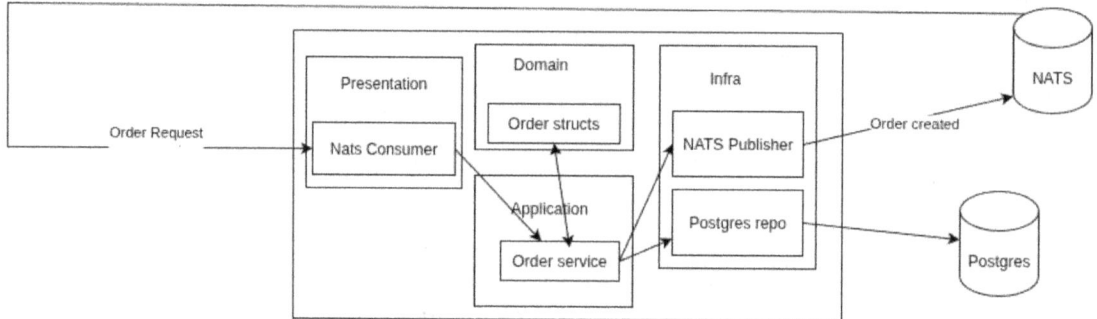

Figure 14-2. *Order processor*

14.8 Full System Overview and Remaining Services

We will get an overview of the whole system, including all the services and their interactions. A request gets sent to the API Gateway, which will send it asynchronously for processing. The Order Processor will capture the message and create an order in the database and send a message with the order details. Figure 14-3 shows the whole flow, although we omitted NATS, which actually sends the messages.

The Menu Service then validates the order. If validation fails, it sends a failure message intercepted by the Notification and Order services. If validation succeeds, the Kitchen Service starts preparing the order. After completion, the kitchen sends a message that the order is ready for delivery, and the delivery service picks it up and completes the process.

The Notification Service receives messages throughout this flow and forwards them to the API Gateway. In a simpler setup, the Gateway could handle this directly, but we keep the Notification Service to show how it can also notify clients via mobile or email.

We stress that although Figure 14-3 shows a workflow that appears sequential, in reality, no service directly calls another. Even the Order Processor does not explicitly ask the Menu Service to validate an order, but it simply creates an order and publishes an event. When the kitchen service receives the order, it starts preparing it. This service does not need to store any information in a database, but it could remove items from the menu in cases where some ingredients finish. We will consider, in this instance, that ingredients are continuously checked by some other service and provided on time, but we leave you the challenge of extending the system so that either the menu will have amounts for every item or another service will take care of this, like an inventory service, and contact the menu item as needed.

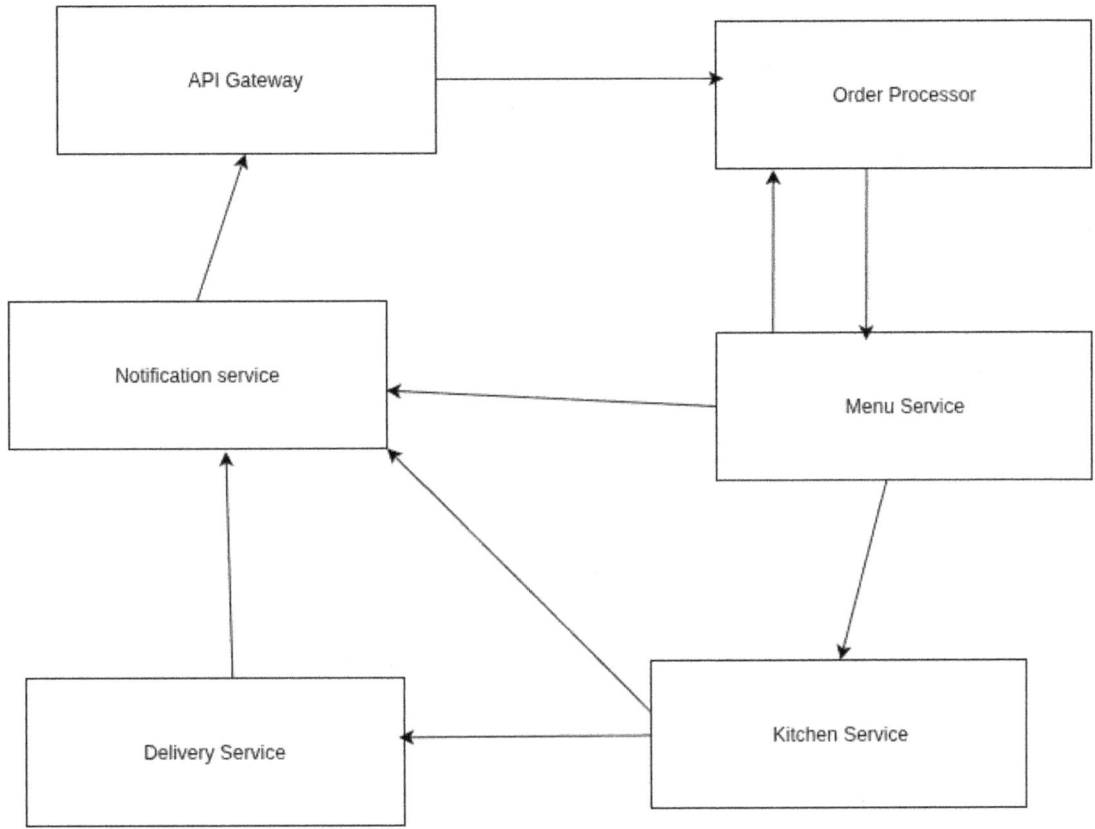

Figure 14-3. *Full system*

Bear always in mind that even when ingredients or items finish, you should keep reactivity in mind and loose coupling. Suppose the kitchen service reduces items from the menu, and these items will finish. In that case, the next order won't pass the menu validation, so it will never reach the kitchen service, which means the kitchen service does not need to store any data about the presence or absence of menu items. Now the delivery and kitchen service will still be very similar, with a structure that can be generically associated with what you see in Figure 14-4, where both driving and driven adapters are NATS clients and publishers.

CHAPTER 14   A WORKING SYSTEM

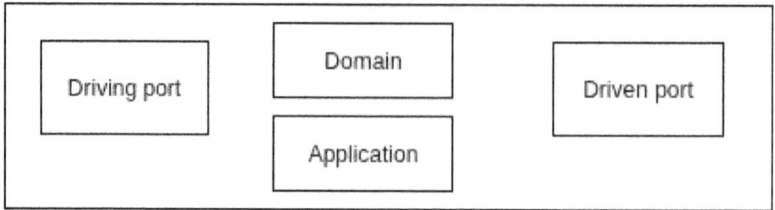

Figure 14-4. *Kitchen, delivery, and notification service*

With this, we have completed all the internal services, and only the API Gateway remains to be analyzed.

The API Gateway will receive order requests and publish server events containing what the notification service will send.

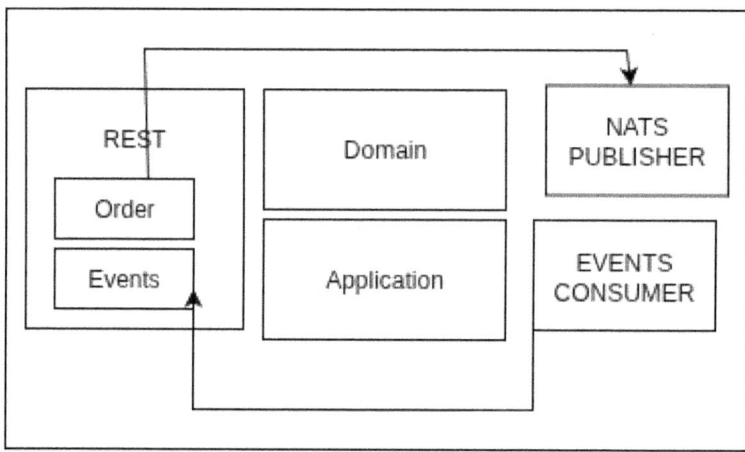

Figure 14-5. *API gateway*

Once an order request is sent, the API Gateway will also subscribe to all events coming from the Notification service and return them via an endpoint used by a REST client as server events, which means an HTTP connection that is not closed and waits for data to continuously come. All this is visible in Figure 14-5, which shows the generic internal parts of the API Gateway.

We will see now how the order requests are received:

```
// PlaceOrder handles the HTTP POST request to place an order.
func (h *RequestHandler) PlaceOrder(c *gin.Context) {
    var req domain.OrderRequest
    if err := c.ShouldBindJSON(&req); err!= nil {
```

```
        c.JSON(http.StatusBadRequest, gin.H{"error": "Invalid request
        payload"})
        return
    }

    // Publish the order request to the Order Processor asynchronously.
    // The API Gateway publishes the message and returns, not waiting for a
        response.
    orderData, _ := json.Marshal(req)
    err := h.nc.Publish("orders.new", orderData)
    if err!= nil {
        log.Printf("Failed to publish order message: %v", err)
        c.JSON(http.StatusInternalServerError, gin.H{"error": "Internal
        server error: failed to place order"})
        return
    }

    log.Printf("API Gateway: Order accepted for asynchronous processing.")
    c.JSON(http.StatusAccepted, gin.H{"message": "Order accepted for
    asynchronous processing."})
}
```

The code above simply uses the Gin framework, but of course, you can use any simple HTTP handler or any other framework. The server events are handled with the following code:

```
// Notifications handles the HTTP GET request for Server-Sent Events (SSE).
func (h *RequestHandler) Notifications(c *gin.Context) {
    c.Header("Content-Type", "text/event-stream")
    c.Header("Cache-Control", "no-cache")
    c.Header("Connection", "keep-alive")
    c.Header("Access-Control-Allow-Origin", "*")

    log.Println("New SSE client connected to notifications stream.")
    clientChan := make(chan domain.NotificationEvent)

    // Subscribe to the NATS notifications stream.
```

```go
    sub, err := h.nc.Subscribe("notifications.events", func(msg
*nats.Msg) {
        var notification domain.NotificationEvent
        if err := json.Unmarshal(msg.Data, &notification); err!= nil {
            log.Printf("SSE Handler: Error unmarshalling
            notification: %v", err)
            return
        }
        clientChan <- notification
    })
    if err!= nil {
        log.Printf("Error subscribing to messages: %v", err)
        c.AbortWithError(http.StatusInternalServerError, err)
        return
    }
    defer sub.Unsubscribe()

    // Keep the connection open and send events.
    c.Stream(func(w http.ResponseWriter) bool {
        select {
        case event := <-clientChan:
            eventJSON, _ := json.Marshal(event)
            c.SSEvent("message", string(eventJSON))
            return true // Continue streaming
        case <-c.Request.Context().Done():
            log.Println("SSE client disconnected from notifications
            stream.")
            return false // Stop streaming
        case <-time.After(30 * time.Second):
            // Send a ping to keep the connection alive
            c.SSEvent("ping", "keep-alive")
            return true
        }, again using Gin.
    })
```

which essentially means that we create a subscriber inside the function, and as soon as a message arrives from NATS, we stream it.

The reason for creating a new consumer every time there is a new client is to have an independent consumer linked to the request. You can decide to use a single consumer if you want, but if your goal is to have events targeting a specific client, with only events for that client, you should use a consumer per request, with properly defined subjects. You could ask only for events for particular orders, then a new consumer is necessary for each request.

14.9 Database

A fundamental principle in microservices architecture, which is mutated by DDD, is that each Bounded Context typically owns and manages its own data. This approach minimizes data-layer coupling, a key aspect of the reactive principle of Decouple Space. For our system, NATS KV and Object stores handle specific, transient data, while a traditional database provides persistent storage for our Order Management context.

This section provides the Kubernetes YAML files for deploying a PostgreSQL database, which will serve as the persistent storage for our Order Management Context.

We will start with the secrets, which include the password:

postgres-secrets.yaml

```
apiVersion: v1
kind: Secret
metadata:
  name: postgres-secret-config
  namespace: restaurant-system
type: Opaque
data:
  password: eW91cl9zdHJvbmdfcGFzc3dvcmQK # Base64 encoded password for
  'postgres' user
```

We then need to define a persistent volume, which is where PostgreSQL actually stores the data:

postgres-pv.yaml

```
apiVersion: v1
kind: PersistentVolume
metadata:
  name: postgres-pv-volume
  labels:
    type: local
spec:
  storageClassName: manual
  capacity:
    storage: 5Gi
  accessModes:
    - ReadWriteOnce
  hostPath:
    path: "/mnt/data/postgres"
```

But to create the volume, Kubernetes (Minikube) also needs a persistent volume claim:

postgres-pvc.yam

```
apiVersion: v1
kind: PersistentVolumeClaim
metadata:
  name: postgres-pv-claim
  namespace: restaurant-system
spec:
  storageClassName: manual
  accessModes:
    - ReadWriteOnce
  resources:
    requests:
      storage: 5Gi
```

Finally, we can use this volume in our deployment:

postgres-deployment.yaml

```yaml
apiVersion: apps/v1
kind: Deployment
metadata:
  name: postgres
  namespace: restaurant-system
spec:
  replicas: 1
  selector:
    matchLabels:
      app: postgres
  template:
    metadata:
      labels:
        app: postgres
    spec:
      volumes:
        - name: postgres-pv-storage
          persistentVolumeClaim:
            claimName: postgres-pv-claim
      containers:
        - name: postgres
          image: postgres:13
          imagePullPolicy: IfNotPresent
          ports:
            - containerPort: 5432
          env:
            - name: POSTGRES_DB
              value: restaurant_db
            - name: POSTGRES_USER
              value: postgres
            - name: POSTGRES_PASSWORD
              valueFrom:
                secretKeyRef:
```

CHAPTER 14   A WORKING SYSTEM

```
                   name: postgres-secret-config
                   key: password
            - name: PGDATA
              value: /var/lib/postgresql/data/pgdata
        volumeMounts:
            - mountPath: /var/lib/postgresql/data/pgdata
              name: postgres-pv-storage
```

Once we have the database running, what we will see is simply one pod, without replication. We will not show you here how to create a PostgreSQL cluster, but pods are by nature prone to going down, even for simple restarts after upgrades, so their names will change over time. In order to have an address a microservice can connect to, we use services. Here is a service definition for PostgreSQL that connects the pods of the previous deployment.

postgres-service.yaml

```
apiVersion: v1
kind: Service
metadata:
  name: postgres-service
  namespace: restaurant-system
  labels:
    app: postgres
spec:
  type: ClusterIP
  ports:
    - port: 5432
      targetPort: 5432
      protocol: TCP
      name: postgres
  selector:
    app: postgres
```

To apply these, run on your command line terminal:

```
kubectl apply -f postgres-secrets.yaml -n restaurant-system
kubectl apply -f postgres-pv.yaml -n restaurant-system
```

```
kubectl apply -f postgres-pvc.yaml -n restaurant-system
kubectl apply -f postgres-deployment.yaml -n restaurant-system
kubectl apply -f postgres-service.yaml -n restaurant-system.
```

The PostgreSQL instance just created can be used by any microservice, but each microservice needs a different database inside it to keep contexts separated. In our example, only the Order Processor will need a Database Engine; the rest of them use nothing or NATS KV and Object Store, but other systems, even an extension of this one, might need other services to connect to a database; they will all use this PostgreSQL instance, but different databases inside it.

14.10 Conclusion

With this chapter, we've given a full example of how a distributed system that uses DDD, Hexagonal Architecture and reactivity can be built for resilience and scalability. As you have seen how much code we provided for the Order Processor in Chapter 8, "Sample Service," you shall understand that providing the complete code for all the services plus all the infrastructure would take so much space that it would be a book on its own. Also, as much as the code can be self-explanatory, it still needs comments, and that would take too much space even in a technical book, and would be difficult to read. We leave you to the repository connected to this book or, even better, we challenge you to follow the directions of this chapter and implement the system on your own.

Consider that each service can be scaled as you please, as they are all independent, and that you could play with different notification systems for your users. The possibilities are endless, as long as good practices are kept in place.

We hope you enjoyed this journey and found it helpful.

Conclusion

This book has explored in depth how to build distributed systems from several different angles. We started with the basics of what a distributed system is and focused on the communication between components. We analyzed different topologies and used a low-level library to go in-depth into the subject and create several more complex topologies. We then introduced NATS as a higher-level tool for achieving the same topologies, and we reimplemented them with it.

We then created a full system, making use of our new knowledge. This gave us all the instruments for creating something that works in harmony under a distributed setup but is not necessarily maintainable and scalable. In order to get to a properly robust, resilient and scalable distributed system, we needed to get into the depths of how to build a single component properly. That's why we decided to introduce you to DDD and hexagonal architecture.

These techniques are much more than coding frameworks; they are real engineering approaches to building a product that works across the whole organization. We strongly believe that coding itself, whatever the techniques used, is not enough to build a great product, be it distributed or not. We've shown how, by leveraging DDD, we can create products that are scalable, maintainable, and above all, facilitate collaboration between all people involved in the creation of the product, be they business, technical, sales, or creative. Through hexagonal architecture, we extended the benefits of DDD, and we've learned how to build a great application that can be a component for a larger system. Having reached this point, we achieved a good amount of knowledge spanning from building components to making them communicate.

Unfortunately, that is still not enough, so we had to dive into the aspects of how to actually create a full system made of DDD and hexagonal components, communicating via the different topologies that we've learned, but also making sure that we were choosing the correct topology for the proper scope. We so analyzed what components a distributed system must have, the authorization functionalities needed, and how to build synchronous and asynchronous services and systems. We analyzed the advantages and disadvantages of each approach and finally concluded by analyzing reactivity and reactive systems.

CONCLUSION

You must have understood that building a distributed system is a complex process and encompasses a wide range of aspects. Infrastructure, although intrinsically more scalable than for monolithic applications, also becomes more difficult to manage. While in monolithic applications, there is no need to consider latency during inter-component communication; in distributed systems, that is totally different. Furthermore, while scaling distributed applications, we would expect that each component can be scaled independently, and only some components might need scaling. Although this seems obvious, in reality, this needs great consideration, because the way components communicate with each other might add coupling, which in turn means two coupled components need to be scaled at the same time.

With our exploration, we've tried to provide the most comprehensive possible view on the topic, using our chosen tools. Many parts of this book, however, are still valuable if you need to use different programming languages or streaming services. Our examples have used NATS and Go, but you could use Java and Kafka, and the principles should still be valid, although Java code would be clearly different, and the implementations of different topologies with Kafka would be different.

After reading this book, you should have a pretty good understanding of distributed systems and what is involved in building one. There are still, however, many other techniques and patterns that can be useful, such as CQRS or different authorization approaches. We couldn't fully explore every aspect because this is neither a DDD manual nor a book focused on every possible distributed microservices pattern.

What we've given you here is a complete vertical view of distributed systems, which should give you enough knowledge to build robust and scalable systems while also leaving room for you to engage more with the topic. A few possible next steps could include exploring advanced patterns like event sourcing, experimenting with different message brokers, or implementing domain-specific optimizations. Still, you also understand the reasons behind them, and you should find it easy, if you want to, to dig even more into the topic and expand your architected systems with more techniques and patterns.

We've tried to give you a blend of theory and practice so that you've seen enough examples. Still, you also understand the reasons behind them, and that you should find it easy, if you want to, to dig even more into the topic and expand your architected systems with more techniques and patterns.

At last, we thank you for having followed us on this journey through distributed systems from the ground up, and we hope your new knowledge will help you in your current or future career.

Answers to the Questions

Chapter 1

1. **What is the primary objective of a distributed system?**

    c) To improve efficiency, reliability, fault tolerance, and scalability

2. **What differentiates distributed computing from distributed systems?**

    b) Distributed systems encompass the infrastructure and resources, while distributed computing focuses on methodology and algorithms.

3. **Which architectural style is best for applications requiring high customizability and extensibility through plug-ins?**

    c) Kernel-based (Microkernel) architecture

4. **Why is asynchronous communication preferred in large-scale distributed systems?**

    c) It decouples sender and receiver, improving scalability and robustness.

5. **What is one major drawback of the monolithic architectural style?**

    c) It poses significant maintainability and scalability issues as the system grows.

6. **Define reactive systems in the context of distributed systems.**

    b) Systems designed to be responsive, resilient, and message-driven.

ANSWERS TO THE QUESTIONS

7. **Which component in a distributed system is critical for managing asynchronous communication?**

   c) Message queues and brokers

Chapter 2

1. **What is the primary purpose of the Req/Rep topology?**

   c) To send a message and wait for a response before sending another.

2. **Which transport protocol is recommended for components running as separate processes on the same machine?**

   d) IPC

3. **In a Pub/Sub topology, what feature allows subscribers to receive only certain messages?**

   c) Topic subscription

4. **Why might one use the Push/Pull pattern instead of Req/Rep?**

   a) For lightweight, asynchronous message sending without expecting a response

5. **What benefit does combining multiple topologies (composed topologies) offer?**

   a) Increases scalability and adaptability of system architecture

Chapter 3

1. **What is the role of subjects in NATS messaging?**

   b) Subjects define the channels through which messages are sent and received.

2. **How can a subscriber ensure that they receive messages in a synchronous manner using the Go SDK for NATS?**

   c) By using the SubscribeSync function

ANSWERS TO THE QUESTIONS

3. **Which NATS pattern would you use to send a request and wait for a single response from a specific service?**

   d) Req/Rep pattern

4. **What mechanism does NATS provide to balance the load among subscribers processing the same messages?**

   b) Queue Groups

5. **How do you implement error handling when sending messages in a NATS network?**

   b) Use headers to encode error information within the message.

6. **Which command-line tool is primarily used to experiment with NATS message flow from the terminal?**

   c) NATS Command-Line Interface

Chapter 6

1. **What is the primary focus of Domain-Driven Design (DDD)?**

   b) Aligning software architecture with core business functions.

2. **Why is the use of Ubiquitous Language critical in Domain-Driven Design?**

   a) It fosters effective communication across teams.

3. **How does DDD propose to connect the engineering team with business objectives?**

   a) By using shared domain languages and engaging experts

4. **What role do services play in the domain-driven approach?**

   c) Services perform domain-specific operations.

5. **What are the main components of the domain layer in DDD?**

   b) Entities, value objects, services, and Ubiquitous Language

ANSWERS TO THE QUESTIONS

6. **How does DDD accommodate different teams with specific domain languages?**

    b) By allowing specific languages to be integrated into Ubiquitous Language

Chapter 7

1. **What is the primary focus of Hexagonal Architecture?**

    b) Decoupling the core business logic from external systems

2. **In Hexagonal Architecture, what roles do ports serve?**

    b) They define interfaces for core application communication.

3. **What advantage does Hexagonal Architecture offer over traditional layered architecture?**

    c) It facilitates flexibility and adaptability when integrating with external systems.

4. **How does Hexagonal Architecture enhance testability in systems?**

    b) Through clear interface definitions that allow independent component testing

5. **What is a potential challenge when implementing Hexagonal Architecture?**

    b) Difficulty in defining appropriate abstraction levels for ports

Chapter 9

1. **What is the primary focus shift in this chapter compared to preceding parts of the book?**

    a) From the internal, granular design of individual services to the macroscopic view of integrating, managing, and optimizing an entire system for production readiness.

ANSWERS TO THE QUESTIONS

2. **What is one of the critical challenges that emerges when deploying multiple instances of services in a production-scale distributed setting?**

    b) Ensuring system coherence, operational efficiency, and consistency of distributed data.

3. **What was a significant drawback of Service-Oriented Architecture (SOA) that led to the concept of a "distributed monolith"?**

    b) Pervasive reliance on a centralized Enterprise Service Bus (ESB), which introduced tight coupling and a single point of failure

4. **How does the "Russian Dolls" metaphor illustrate distributed system design?**

    c) It represents the nested complexity and hierarchical structure where each service is a cohesive, autonomous unit that fits within a larger integrated system.

5. **Which of the following is NOT a key aspect of system-wide infrastructure discussed in the chapter?**

    a) Centralized team communication platforms.

6. **What is the primary goal of Canary Releases as a deployment strategy?**

    b) To minimise risk by gradually rolling out a new version to a small subset of users or servers to detect problems early.

Chapter 10

1. **How does the "Russian Dolls" metaphor relate to DDD in distributed systems?**

    b) It illustrates the nested application of DDD principles at various levels of granularity.

543

ANSWERS TO THE QUESTIONS

2. **Which of the following is a key benefit of applying DDD at the system level in a distributed architecture?**

    c) It fosters a deeper alignment between the entire software landscape and strategic business objectives.

3. **When might a full DDD approach be considered "overkill" for an individual service within a larger distributed system?**

    b) When the service primarily performs simple CRUD operations or acts as a data conduit.

4. **How do message brokers like NATS support DDD principles in a distributed system?**

    c) By enabling loose coupling and event-driven communication between bounded contexts.

Chapter 11

1. **What is the primary purpose of Nginx in a microservices architecture when dealing with synchronous communication?**

    b) To act as a reverse proxy for routing and load balancing requests.

2. **Which of the following is a key benefit of using a service mesh (e.g., Istio, Linkerd) in a synchronous distributed system?**

    c) It provides advanced traffic management, security, and observability for inter-service communication.

3. **How does the NATS micro package simplify building synchronous microservices?**

    b) By offering a declarative way to define services, endpoints, and groups over NATS Req/Rep.

4. **What is the main advantage of space-based architecture (SBA) for synchronous systems?**

    b) It enables extreme scalability and low-latency responses through in-memory data grids.

ANSWERS TO THE QUESTIONS

5. **In the context of an API Gateway, what is the primary function of "request aggregation"?**

    c) To gather data from multiple backend services and combine it into a single response for the client.

Chapter 12

1. **What is the primary benefit of using asynchronous communication in distributed systems, as opposed to synchronous communication?**

    c) Enhanced scalability and resilience.

2. **In core NATS Pub/Sub, what happens to a message if no subscriber is active when it is published?**

    c) The message is lost.

3. **Which NATS JetStream feature allows messages to be stored and replayed, overcoming the temporal coupling of core NATS?**

    c) Streams

4. **When designing an internally asynchronous system, what is the primary role of an API Gateway in relation to NATS?**

    b) To translate synchronous external requests into asynchronous NATS messages.

5. **Which NATS JetStream consumer type provides the application with explicit control over message flow and is recommended for reliable, batch-oriented processing?**

    d) Durable Pull Consumer

6. **What is the main purpose of the NATS Key-Value (KV) store?**

    b) To manage distributed, versioned configuration and shared state.

ANSWERS TO THE QUESTIONS

Chapter 13

1. **What is the primary purpose of asynchronous message-passing in a reactive system?**

    c) To establish a boundary that ensures loose coupling, isolation, and location transparency.

2. **How does a bounded context from DDD contribute to the assert autonomy principle of reactive systems?**

    b) It defines a logical boundary for a service, allowing it to own its data and logic independently.

3. **Which NATS feature is most crucial for ensuring a system remains resilient by handling consumer outages?**

    b) The JetStream persistence engine.

4. **In the context of the in-depth example, why does the Kitchen Service use a pull consumer instead of a push consumer?**

    c) To manage back-pressure and consume messages at its own pace, preventing overload.

5. **What is the main benefit of using the NATS KV store's watch functionality in a reactive system?**

    b) It allows services to react to changes in state or configuration in real-time without polling.

Index

A

ABAC, *see* Attribute-Based Access Control (ABAC)
A/B testing, 399
ACL, *see* Anti-Corruption Layer (ACL)
Actor model, 420
Adapters, 227, 485
Anti-Corruption Layer (ACL), 316
Apache Ignite, 396
API gateway
    authentication, 383
    authorization, 384–387, 389, 390
    deeper level communication, 391, 392, 394
    first-level communication, 390
    pattern, 372–379, 381, 382, 433
AppointmentSlotService, 193
ArangoDB, 199, 200
Asynchronous communication, 5, 21
Asynchronous systems
    decoupling, 403
    example, 405–409
    fire-and-forget, 404, 470
    long-running processes, 432
        pile up, 434
        REST, 433
        scaling, 433
    NATA KV store, 471
    NATS KV store, 458, 459, 461, 463, 464
    NATS object store, 464–470
Attribute-Based Access Control (ABAC), 367
Authentication, 383
Authorization, 365
AxonIQ, 85

B

BC, *see* Bounded Context (BC)
BookAppointment() method, 184, 189, 308
BookingsRepository, 207
Bounded Context (BC), 307, 314
Brute communication patterns, 475
Buckets, 464
Business-first approach, 213, 275

C

Cascading failures, 342
"Cause-and-effect" model, 482
cmd directory, 505
Consume function, 448
Consumer, 442
CreateOrUpdateConsumer, 450
Create, Read, Update, Delete (CRUD) services, 313
CustomerCreator, 375

D

Data replication strategies, 327
Data Transfer Objects (DTOs), 253, 283, 319, 381
DDD, *see* Domain-Driven Design (DDD)
DeliverGroup, 448

INDEX

Distributed communication
    brokered messaging, 28
    low-level approach, 27
    multitransport
        IPC, 71, 72
        memory, 72–78
        memory transport, concurrency, 78
        TCP, 66–71
    product, 30, 32
    socket, 29, 30
    topologies
        Mangos library, 35, 36
        pub/sub, 53–64
        Pub/sub, 80
        push/pull, 45–47, 49–52
        requester/replier, 36–45
        subscriber, 64, 65
    transports, 32–34
    unbrokered system, 28
Distributed computing, 4, 19, 20, 22
Distributed data management, 280, 284, 290–291, 324
Distributed systems
    AI technologies, 22
    asynchronous communication, 21
    banking and healthcare, 3
    building blocks, 6, 7
    DDD, 5
    vs. distributed computing, 19, 20
    hexagonal architecture, 4
    reactive systems, 6
    software system architecture, 8–10
    synchronous communication, 20
    unified entity *vs.* collection of discrete services, 5
Docker, 88, 507
Docker build command, 151
Dockerfile, 506, 509

Domain, 186
Domain-Driven Design (DDD), 5, 163, 169, 231, 235, 287, 480, 503, 505
    app layer, 195–198
    application layer, 213
    bounded context/segregation, 314–316, 318
    business logic, 214
    crafts, 173, 174
    data structures, 182, 183, 185–189
    development process, 171
    domain layer, 309
    infrastructure layer, 213
        database, 199–207
        external services, 208–211
        structs, 199
    infrastructure/orchestration, 320–322, 324, 327, 329
        advanced deployment strategies, 333
        autoscaling types, 331, 332
        data replication strategies, 327, 329
        deployment strategies, 334, 335
        service mesh characteristics, 330, 331
    language, 175, 176
    presentation layer, 211, 212, 214
    product focus, 176–180, 182
    RESTful APIs, 319
    "Russian Dolls" metaphor, 318
    services, 189–191, 193, 194
    system level
        business, 310, 311
        complexity multiplier, 310
        inter-service communication, 309
        layer *vs.* components, 311, 312
    technical design, 172
    traditional approach, 172
    ubiquitous language, 307

INDEX

Domain-first approach, 182
DTOs, *see* Data Transfer Objects (DTOs)

E, F

Enterprise Service Bus (ESB), 281
Entity, 183
ESB, *see* Enterprise Service Bus (ESB)
Event-Driven Autoscaling (KEDA), 299

G

GetAvailableSlots function, 193
GetInfo operation, 465
GitOps, 297
Go cmd pattern, 505
Go struct, 493
GraphQL, 173, 228

H

Hazelcast, 397
Health practice booking system, 182
Hexagonal architecture, 222, 287, 406, 499, 505
    application, 230, 231
    communication, 226-231
    hexagonality, 222-226
    layered communication style, 220-222
    layered systems, 217-219
Hexagonal Architecture, 303, 309, 312, 313, 484, 503
Holistic security posture, 280

I

Identity provider (IdP), 383
IdP, *see* Identity provider (IdP)

Internally asynchronous system
    actor mode, 420-422, 424-426
    API gateway, 410-416, 418-420
    asynchronous services, 426-429, 431, 432
    core processing workflows, 410
Interprocess Communication (IPC), 71
IPC, *see* Interprocess Communication (IPC)
Istio, 351

J

JetStream, 397, 483, 486, 487, 499
    asynchronous services, 452-455, 458
    consumers, 442-445, 447, 448, 450, 452
    persistence engine, 434-438, 486
    retention policy, 439-442
JWT-based system, 373

K

Kafka, 260
KEDA, *see* Event-Driven Autoscaling (KEDA)
Kernel-based architecture
    API, 12
    attributes, 12
    microkernel style, 12
    microservices, 15, 16
    reactive systems, 18, 19
    SOA, 13, 14
    space-based architecture, 16-18
    style, 11
Kernel-Based Architecture, 23
Kubernetes, 90-92, 392, 506, 507

INDEX

L

Lead, Prospect, and Visitor, 180

M

Mangos library, 4, 27, 34, 35, 86, 163
Menu Service, 504, 512–522, 526
Message brokers, 329
Message-driven system, 482
Microservices, 15, 23, 163, 165, 312, 406, 484, 538
Minikube, 5, 90, 122, 123, 149, 151, 153, 155–159, 506
MongoDB, 199, 203, 204, 249, 398
Monolithic applications, 10, 271, 279, 538
Monolithic architecture, 9–11

N

NATS
    alternatives, 85
    brokered *vs.* unbrokered, 86, 87
    client, 83
    cluster, 84
    messaging system, 83
    microservices, 83, 86
    running
        CLI, 92, 93
        command line, 93, 94, 96, 97
        docker, 88, 89
        Go SDK, 97–102
        kubernetes, 90–92
        server, 87, 88
    topologies
        Go SDK, 117
        messaging patterns, 117
        pub/sub, 103, 116
        push/pull, 103–107
        req/rep, 107–115
NATS-CLI, 92
NATS JetStream, 410, 435
NATS Req/Rep approach, 354
NATS-RPLY-22, 109
NATS-test, 92
NATS_URL, 155
NewSocket function, 66
Non-blocking communication, 477
Notification Service, 526

O

OPA, *see* Open Policy Agent (OPA)
OPAL, *see* Open Policy Administration Layer (OPAL)
Open Policy Administration Layer (OPAL), 369
Open Policy Agent (OPA), 368
OrderProcessingService, 244, 245, 248, 249, 252–254
Order Processor, 236, 522
    application layer, 243–247, 249
    database layer, 249–252
    DDD model, 271
    domain layer, 237–243
    flexibility, 236
    infrastructure, 258–260
    maintainability, 235
    microservice, 261, 262, 271
    presentation layer, 253–257
    running, 261–265, 267–270
    testability, 236
OrderRepository, 248
OrderService, 488, 498
OrderStatusPublisher, 248

P

PatientRepository, 200, 207
PaymentProcessor, 489, 494, 498
Ports, 226, 244, 431, 485
Postgresm MtSQL, 199
ProcessNewOrder, 248
Production-ready distributed system, 309
Production-ready enterprise distributed system, 278
"Publish-and-react" model, 482
Publisher, 75
publish method, 113
Publish/subscribe (Pub/Sub) model, 405

Q

queueasync, 107
QueueSubscribe, 105, 153, 426

R

RabbitMQ, 260, 435
RBAC, *see* Role-Based Access Control (RBAC)
Reactive Programming, 478, 479
Reactive systems, 18, 503
    communication patterns, 475
    DDD
        aggregate acts, 483
        bounded context *vs.* autonomous units, 481
        domain events/ubiquitous language, 482, 483
    examples, 488, 489, 491, 493–498
    hexagonal architecture, 484, 485
    microservices, 475
    principles, 476–480
    vs. reactive programming, 478, 479
    tools, 486, 487
Real engineering approaches, 537
ReBAC, *see* Relationship-based access control (ReBAC)
Redis, 397
Relationship-based access control (ReBAC), 369
"Request-response-acknowledgement" pattern, 427
Retention policy, 439
Role-Based Access Control (RBAC), 367

S, T

Sample Service, 535
Scalability protocols, 29
Service
    developer *vs.* engineer, 167, 168
    low-level building blocks, 164, 165
    microservice, 163, 165, 166
Service Bus, 281
Service meshes, 293, 304, 329, 330, 350, 392
Service-oriented architecture (SOA), 13, 14, 23, 166, 167, 281, 303
Socket, 30, 79, 163
Space-based architecture (SBA), 16, 23, 400
    components, 395
    data grid and database, 395
    implementation example, 397, 398
    tools, 396, 397
strconv package, 113
Subscribe function, 408
Subscriber, 75
SybscribeSync function, 100
Synchronous communication, 20, 403
    authorization, 365–369, 371

INDEX

Synchronous communication (*cont.*)
    cascading failures, 342
    microservices package, 343
    NATS services
        direct access, 352–354
        microservices package, 356–364
        REST proxy, 354, 355
    REST/direct service access, 343
        chain failure, 344
        example, 345, 346
        microservice, 343
        Nginx, 346–349
        service mesh, 350, 351
    RESTful APIs, 343

U

Ubiquitous Language, 175, 213, 307, 310
Update method, 468
UpdateOrderStatus, 248

V

ValidateToken function, 389
Vertical Pod Autoscaler (VPA), 299
VPA, *see* Vertical Pod Autoscaler (VPA)

W, X, Y

Well-structured domain model, 182
Whole system *vs.* bunch of services
    architectural patterns and technologies, 503
    database, 531–533, 535
    Dockerfile, 509
    full system, 527, 528, 531
    GitHub actions, 507, 509

    holistic security posture, 280
    infrastructure, 289
        comprehensive obeservability, 292
        configuration management, 294
        distributed data management, 290, 291
        message brokers, 291
        security infrastructure, 292
    infrastructure code, 504
    inter-service communication, 275
    MenuService, 512, 514–522
    microservices, 303, 304
    monolithic applications, 279
    NATS deployment and initialization, 510–512
    one level up, 276, 277, 303
    orchestration, 295
        deployment strategies, 298
        dynamic scaling, 299
        health checks and self-healing capabilities, 301
        resilience patterns, 301
        scaling resources, 300
        service discovery and load balancing, 300
        SRE principles, 302
        strategies, 296, 297
    order processor, 505, 522–526
    responsive and resilient application, 503
    Russian dolls, 284–289
    SOA, 281–284
Workflows, 507
Working system, 235
    command-line application, 121, 122

customer, 137–142, 144–147
delivery tracker, 133–137
NATS, 121, 122
order processors, 128–133, 149
Publish/Subscribe, 503
request/reply messaging, 503
restaurant gateway, 123–127
workQueueStreamName, 448

Z

ZeroMQ, 27, 28, 86

GPSR Compliance

The European Union's (EU) General Product Safety Regulation (GPSR) is a set of rules that requires consumer products to be safe and our obligations to ensure this.

If you have any concerns about our products, you can contact us on

ProductSafety@springernature.com

In case Publisher is established outside the EU, the EU authorized representative is:

Springer Nature Customer Service Center GmbH
Europaplatz 3
69115 Heidelberg, Germany